Sport and the Spirit of Play
in American Fiction

Sport and the Spirit of Play in American Fiction

Hawthorne to Faulkner

Christian K. Messenger

COLUMBIA UNIVERSITY PRESS
New York

Excerpts from *The Sun Also Rises* by Ernest
Hemingway reprinted by permission of Charles
Scribner's Sons. Copyright 1926 by Charles
Scribner's Sons; copyright renewed.

Library of Congress Cataloging in Publication Data

Messenger, Christian K., 1943–
  Sport and the spirit of play in American fiction.

  Includes bibliographical references and index.
  1. American fiction—History and criticism.
2. Sports in literature.   3. Athletes in literature.
4. Play in literature.   5. Sports stories—History
and criticism.   I. Title.
PS374.S76M4   813'.009'355   81-4843
ISBN 0-231-05168-9 (cloth) AACR2
ISBN 0-231-05169-7 (paper)

Columbia University Press
New York   Guildford, Surrey

Clothbound editions of Columbia University Press books are Smyth-sewn
and printed on permanent and durable acid-free paper.

Second cloth and first paperback edition.

For Janet, Carrie, and Lucas

Contents

Preface

AS CONSTANCE ROURKE NOTED in *Roots of American Culture,* the gestation of a native culture is a necessarily long and confusing process that may encompass several generations: "it would seem obvious that our art, if we are to have one, must spring from the center rather than from the periphery of our social pattern."[1] From 1820 to 1900, the sports hero in American fiction was best described in sketches and fragments and not clearly perceived in any fictional tradition. In modern America, however, authors such as Ring Lardner, F. Scott Fitzgerald, Ernest Hemingway, and William Faulkner made clear that sport and play are at the center of our social pattern. Through every indicator we possess, sport and play are at present seen to consume our time and energies. The representative sports action in fiction flows from the author's confidence in his subject and in his certainty that sport is where millions of Americans seek and gain knowledge of their own physical natures. Americans also gain insight into their own emotional and spiritual natures through expression of a varied play spirit that cannot always be bound by sport itself. From the early accounts of Puritans in Boston or backwoods characters in contests on the frontier to the narratives of pitchers who experience moments of triumph or frustration in baseball stadiums is a long leap indeed. What follows is an attempt to chart lines of fictional development that give resonance to play and continuity to the American sporting experience from the earliest accounts up through Faulkner and Hemingway.

Part I surveys what play and sport meant in classic American literature before the beginning of organized American sport and suggests links to modern sports heroes in fiction. Hawthorne (chapter 1) was drawn repeatedly, if contradictorily, to play imagery while Irving, Cooper, and Thoreau

(chapter 2) began to portray sport in society as a living issue with consequences for Americans. The rest of the book identifies, in broad outline,
three different sports heroes in fiction: the Popular Sports Hero (Part II), the
School Sports Hero (Part III), and the modern Ritual Sports Hero (Part IV).

The Popular Sports Hero began as hunter or frontier roarer in the
mid-nineteenth-century Crockett-Fink almanacs and Southwestern Humor
sketches (chapter 3). This figure evolved into the modern professional athlete first identified by journalists and dime novelists (chapter 4) and best
portrayed by Lardner (chapter 5).

The School Sports Hero had his roots in the English schoolboy tradition, in American Civil War experience, and in the aggressive competition
of the post-Civil War period (chapter 6), and became the hero of the boys'
school sports story, a Frank Merriwell or a Dink Stover (chapter 7). During
the modern era this hero was recast in romantic wonder and irony through
Fitzgerald's Amory Blaine in *This Side of Paradise* and Tom Buchanan in
The Great Gatsby (chapter 8), and as satirical emblem through Hemingway's Robert Cohn in *The Sun Also Rises,* and Faulkner's Labove in *The
Hamlet* (chapter 9).

The Ritual Sports Hero is the solitary sportsman who most often
confronts nature or his own nature in the private ritual of hunting or fishing
or in some similar test of courage or endurance. The ritual drama that
sharply etches sporting experience for the individual was what Hemingway
and Faulkner repeatedly developed. *The Sun Also Rises* is Hemingway's
major statement of ritual sport and its meaning for the sportsman and spectator (chapter 10) while Faulkner's *The Hamlet* portrays both driven competitors and desperate pawns in his most comprehensive use of the play
spirit (chapter 11). Ritual sport that mediates between real time and space
and the sacred is the subject of Hemingway's *The Old Man and the Sea* and
of Faulkner's *Go Down, Moses* (chapter 12).

Briefly, I would like to note what I am doing and not doing in this
book. Although sport is my primary subject, it is impossible not to comment
at length on the fictional use of play and game as well. Many expressions
of exuberant or creative play as well as games of strategy and chicanery are
not assumed to be sports but are crucial to any comprehensive look at sport
in fiction; wherever necessary, precise terminology will be used to differentiate among play, game, and sport. The play spirit is too broad and encompasses too many subjects to ever be truly contained in a discussion of
sport in fiction. A thorough examination of the play spirit in American fiction would encompass philosophical, aesthetic, and critical perspectives and

would be applied to phenomena from the pranks of Tom Sawyer to the marriage transactions in Henry James. Indeed, nineteenth-century writers such as Herman Melville, Mark Twain, James, and Stephen Crane warrant a major study of their visions of play and its presence in their works. In this volume, reference to these authors is brief and only as part of a specific argument about the development of sport in fiction.

I am aware of book-length treatment of authors and works that I necessarily treat briefly in specific context. My position has been kept simple: when sport leads me afield (and off the field), I have followed where the vision of major authors has led. In the cases of Hawthorne and Faulkner, for example, I began by investigating their use of sport but then was obligated to follow their imagery out to a full exploration of their vision of the play spirit. Hawthorne's hearty sport on Boston Common in *The Scarlet Letter* provoked a longer look at play in that novel and ultimately to its consideration in other Hawthorne fiction; Faulkner's football fable in *The Hamlet* initially made me aware of the enormous emphasis on both competition and spontaneous play in Frenchman's Bend and led me to other Yoknapatawpha players and games. In effect, Parts I and IV of my book open sport out to an analysis of the boundaries of the play spirit while Parts II and III concentrate specifically on organized sport and its heroes.

In tracing the use of play, game, and sport in American fiction, I am stressing the ways in which conventional story patterns establish ways of dealing with the sports material.[2] These conventions are then either passed along with no significant alteration in formula or are placed in the hands of innovators such as Lardner or Fitzgerald. At some junctures, I consider examples of scant literary value to highlight a stage in fictional development. I relate the history of American sport only as it is pertinent to place an era in perspective or to account, in part, for a shift in the presentation of fiction about sport. Similarly, nonfiction about sport is cited in the same spirit: only as it comes to bear on the fiction, develops a popular philosophy of sport that is bequeathed to authors, or contributes to the growth of narrative techniques appropriated by authors. Whenever possible, I have cited biographical information about authors to show their immersion in sports culture from youth onwards.

I make repeated studies of standard fictional works to place scenes of play and sport in specific context and thereby to investigate further a larger thematic pattern which the play or sports frame throws into bold relief. In the best use of play and sport in fiction, such scenes and thematic patterns appear most often as an organic unit in narrative. For example,

Zenobia's final denunciations of Miles Coverdale and Hollingsworth as defective players in differing roles defines their failure in *The Blithedale Romance*. The astonishment of Nick Carraway when Gatsby blithely points out Meyer Wolfsheim as the man who fixed the World Series in 1919 is a vivid emblem of Gatsby's immorality and Nick's credulity. Authors such as Lardner and Faulkner write of social games and intricate swaps and swindles that are fundamental parts of their characters' lives. In conclusion, no fiction here is pruned to fit a formal critical garden. The identification of play and sports frames is meant to open new lines of inquiry into the cultural materials that our authors have used for more than a century.

The range of fiction examined shows how few well-drawn female characters are part of the world of play and sport, and, alternately, how women in play and sport are not fully characterized. Hester and Pearl play in isolation and are little understood by their society in *The Scarlet Letter*. Women are physical victims in Southwestern Humor tales; dimpled, helpless girl heroines in schoolboy stories; hearty, masculine mate-women in Frank Norris and Jack London. Hemingway depicts Brett Ashley, the splendid matador pursued by the human bulls in *The Sun Also Rises,* or, worse, Margot Macomber, whose quarry is her husband. Faulkner offers the flashing Drusilla Hawk, playing Civil War roles in *The Unvanquished,* or earthmother Eula Varner in *The Hamlet,* Olympian and inert during the competition for her. Fitzgerald's golfer, Jordan Baker, in *The Great Gatsby,* may be someone Nick Carraway might ''disapprove of from beginning to end,'' but she is nonetheless a fully created sporting character. We know who she is by how she plays: she cheats. Perhaps when American society as a whole accepts the role of women in sports, or women as ''playful'' without immediate sexual connotations, then American writers will create their fictional sisters.[3] Until that time, the representation of play and sport in American fiction remains a distorted masculine preserve where sexual stereotyping is even more prevalent than in American fiction as a whole. This is a subject for another volume.

Portions of this book have appeared in altered form in *Journal of Popular Culture, Journal of American Culture, Illinois Quarterly, Lost Generation Journal, Jack London Newsletter,* and *American Literary Realism.* I am grateful for their permission to reprint. I would like to thank Mrs. C. Grove Smith, Mrs. Laidlaw Williams, the Princeton University Library, Rare Books and Special Collections, for permission to quote from the F.

Scott Fitzgerald Collection and the Jesse Lynch Williams Papers; also Charles Scribner's Sons and Random House for permission to quote from *The Sun Also Rises* and *The Hamlet*, respectively.

    I should like to acknowledge Northwestern University Professors Alfred Appel, Gerald Graff, and Harrison Hayford, who initially sanctioned, encouraged, and helped me to define my subject. Professor Allen Guttmann, Amherst College, and Professor Howard Kerr, University of Illinois at Chicago Circle, have my thanks for criticism and advice at crucial periods of the manuscript's life. A special debt is owed to Professor John Huntington, University of Illinois at Chicago Circle, whose thoughtful questions provoked me to find a valid conceptual structure for the book. I note Professor Kevin Kerrane, University of Delaware and Professor Michael Oriard, Oregon State University, players on the field of sport and literature from whom I have learned a great deal. Lastly, I thank my editors at Columbia University Press, William F. Bernhardt and David Diefendorf, for all manner of assistance and encouragement.

    I received prompt and invaluable help from the staffs of the George Hess Collection, Walter Library, University of Minnesota; William L. Clements Library, University of Michigan; and, again, the staff of Rare Books and Special Collections, Princeton University Library. I am indebted to the Howard Phalin Foundation for a 1974 dissertation grant as well as to the Faculty Research Board, University of Illinois at Chicago Circle for leave time in which to revise the manuscript.

    Finally, lasting thanks to Janet Graveline Messenger, my conscience in the matter of straightforward expression, who repeatedly kept this lengthy book from disappearing beneath layers of obscurantist prose.

C. K. M.

University of Illinois at Chicago Circle

Sport and the Spirit of Play
in American Fiction

Introduction

PLAY, GAME, SPORT

SPORT HAS BEEN a vital part of the American experience for the last 150 years. Its patterns have celebrated and reflected the American panorama, shifting from exuberant free-form play on the frontier to encapsulation in a modern stadium. Americans have had to subdue and civilize a vast continent, confronting nature in the raw and often calling on only their own "raw" physical natures as tools or weapons in an unequal contest. From the outset American society has been close to elemental conflict with nature and expressly reliant on physical strength, endurance, and courage. At the same time, America's religious heritage has engendered a profound mistrust of play and sport. This singular American experience required Americans to bring their physical natures into conjunction with the tenets of the mind and the yearnings of the spirit. Their sport has contributed to and been shaped by that American spirit, which is often most fundamentally itself when "at play."

The sports hero in American fiction has been a special figure, a man apart from mass man: whether Davy Crockett, Natty Bumppo, Frank Merriwell, Jack Keefe, or Pedro Romero. Because of particular skills, he is lionized and given heroic status. What happens to this hero is typically described in a series of encounters between the player and his society. While the focus is consistently on physical sport—from the hunt, eye-gouging matches, and country frolics to championship fights, college football, and professional baseball—the competition described often turns ironic, abstract, and metaphorical. Here the play spirit predominates in metaphors of control and loss, mastery and tragic defeat. These metaphors enable authors such as

Hawthorne, Fitzgerald, and Faulkner to invoke play in order to deal with the full complexity of human relationships both in and out of the arena and to define modes of American conduct.

Sport in American life has always been contradictory. It liberates in play, but it binds its players to the most strenuous work. Such irony leads to even greater ironies: a frontier people becomes the greatest industrial nation in the world, its free-form roarers become heroes in urban stadiums.[1] The real descendants of Davy Crockett and Mike Fink are Babe Ruth and Dizzy Dean. The Edenic New World becomes a country of disciplined Alger boys striving for success, embodied in a schoolboy hero such as Frank Merriwell and most poignantly caught in the figure of a Jay Gatsby, who plays his magic illusions across the face of society. America's puritanical society with its fierce work ethic has nurtured a deep suspicion of play, thus fostering the need to express this play spirit in fully sanctioned activities such as frontier games and school and popular sport. Reuel Denney stated, "In the American culture as a whole, no sharp line exists between work and play."[2] Gregory Stone best expressed these contradictions in modern America when he observed, "sports that were once work [hunting and fishing] are never played, but these engage the 'players'—the amateurs. Sports that were never work [team sports] are always played, and these engage the 'workers'—the professionals."[3] Play and game, sport and work. The terminology is most often fluid and ambiguous in the American experience.

The relations among play, game, and sport are constantly being reinterpreted, but it is important to establish categories at the outset that will be used throughout this study. In its broad definition, play signifies something "simulated" or "not real," any activity whose main end lies outside itself. Johan Huizinga in *Homo Ludens* (1938) characterized play as having freedom, separateness, and regulation. Roger Caillois, who, after Huizinga, has most elaborately classified expressions of the play spirit, retained Huizinga's characteristics of play and added three more: uncertainty, unproductivity, and make-believe. For Huizinga, play could be both a competition for something (*agon*) or a representation of something (*mimesis*).[4] Caillois went further, identifying four categories of play: *agon* (the contest, competition with rules); *alea* (games of chance which render decisions independent of the players); *mimicry* (acting on the part of participants and simulation by the audience); and *ilinx* (the irrational whirling state induced by hypnosis, drugs, or any emotional exaltation).[5] Caillois conceives of the "as if" or improvisatory quality of games that replaces and performs the same function in *mimicry* that rules do in *agon*. He also plots these expressions of play along an axis from *paidia* (the most spontaneous of free play) to *ludus* (the most rule-oriented and organized variant of play).

Caillois was inclined to isolate play from reality in the progression of play-profane-sacred, stating that the sacred and play resemble each other but only to the degree that they are both opposed to the practical life.[6] He was dubious about what has happened to play in the modern world, stating that the modern equivalent of a festival is war in all its destructive potential. Caillois believed that one is freer in play than in life. However, his vision of the sacred was one of rigid captivity by a unity; thus play was for Caillois a movement leading down away from the profane in freedom rather than toward a captive prostration before the sacred. Yet everything we know of the ritual motions by which we approach the sacred suggests that our actions of rule-obeyance, motions of grace, cordoning off of a ritual space, the creating of festal time, begin in play. More helpful, while still incomplete, is a progression of reality-play-sacred conceived by the linguist Emil Benveniste, who suggests that play offers an inverted and broken image of the sacred which he defines as "the consubstantial unity of myth and rite."[7]

The current prevailing play theory, best expressed by Eugen Fink and Jacques Ehrmann, is that play is not an activity which can be contrasted to other phenomena such as "reality," "culture," or "the sacred," but that "play is an essential element of man's ontological makeup" because the "decisive phenomena of human existence are intimately related to each other."[8] Play is "a basic existential phenomenon,"[9] and need not be contrasted or compared to anything except itself. Play has great range; it dictates the form of rules that we determine as expressing "work" or "seriousness" while it controls, amplifies, and derigidifies experience. Play may also move through ritual toward final things and an ultimate expression of reality in the sacred.

Ehrmann, in the strongest critique of Huizinga and Caillois to date, states that their error was to define play in opposition to reality and the sacred. He argues that reality cannot be considered an innocent starting point for defining what play is but rather must be the outcome where "it is dissolved in the manifestations analyzed,"[10] where play has produced spatial and temporal illusions that become the content of the real. Our so-called reality is played for, a product of culture, whereas our so-called sacred is approached through ritual. We play our reality, our work, our religion. We play for control, as a talisman, out of fear, for exuberance, and for creativity. Ehrmann concludes there is no *a priori* "real" or "sacred." Play is not Huizinga's ennobled mimesis or Benveniste's inverted image of the sacred.

The gratuitousness of play is only apparent because it is part of a circuit which reaches beyond spatial and temporal limits; one cannot subtract or depreciate the value of play because its utility is in the relocation and redistribution "in pursuit of *immediate* [italics Ehrmann] satisfaction of needs and desires."[11] Play cannot be defined in isolation because "to define play is *at the same time* and *in the same movement* [italics Ehrmann] to define reality and to define culture."[12]

When the categories of play are applied by theorists constructing an order of games, the task is often perceived as vast. Even the master organizer Caillois writes that "the multitude and infinite variety of games at first causes one to despair of discovering a principle of classification," but he also firmly states "that to a certain degree a civilization and its content may be characterized by its games."[13] A game is a rule-oriented variant of play which does not necessarily need a physical object but which absorbs a player or players and takes place in arbitrary time frames and artificially agreed-upon arenas. The definitions of game are synthesized by John Loy, who writes that games are "any form of playful competition whose outcome is determined by physical skill, strategy, or chance."[14] These categories may encompass the role of the athlete (physical skill), the role of the games player or trickster (strategy), and the dramatic naturalistic element of fate (chance). Loy connects play to sport through game when he adds the elements of competition in games to the features named by Huizinga and Caillois: freedom, separateness, uncertainty, unproductiveness, order, and make-believe.[15]

Huizinga had established the linguistic congruences of "play" and "competition" in his search for the similar roots of play terms throughout the Indo-European language system. He traced the English "play," "to play," from the Anglo-Saxon *plega, plegan,* which derives from roots in Frisian and Old German, the oldest of which meant "to take a risk, to expose oneself to danger for someone or something." The *agon* or basis of competition is always stressed in Huizinga's concepts of play. The object for which we play and compete is first and foremost victory, but victory is associated with all the various ways in which it can be enjoyed. We play for victory as a communal triumph with mass acclaim as in modern sport spectacle; we play for the honor and esteem of society; or we play for intense self-knowledge. The root of the Greek word for "prize" yields "athlete," and Huizinga notes, "here the ideas of contest, struggle, exercise, exertion, endurance and suffering are united." He concludes that in ancient athletics "we are still moving in that sphere of serious competition" labelled "agonizing," "involving as [ancient athletics] do mental and physical hardship." [16]

In general, the competitive element defines sport as a more intense game. Sport is an organized game with a variety of rules possessing internal coherence, and it is an institutionalized game that may be an external expression of the order of society responding to or underscoring a national pattern. Sport in American society dramatically portrays the heroic striving of the individual in the contest where he pursues satisfaction in a wide range of behavior form the most splendid moments of isolated achievement to the mass adulation of the crowd.

Caillois grouped sport with other competitive games in his *agon* category. Huizinga cast a very dubious eye on all modern sport spectacle. Neither scholar focussed on sport but suggested initial directions for further study. Caillois attempted to prove the essential distance that existed between play and the sacred, stating that play is born in human invention while the human worshipper is defenseless and prostrate before the sacred. [17] For this reason, Caillois could not adequately deal with predatory sport that highlighted man-in-nature. The isolated experience of the hunter is in a realm that approaches the sacred through ritual motions, but Caillois denied that play was born in the sacred. In reality, the hunter is a throwback to the primitive sportsman whose sport was an expression of training for warfare skills as well as a religious ceremony. [18]

Huizinga wished to show the surviving play spirit in modern institutions though he did not find that spirit in sport. When Huizinga commented in *Homo Ludens* on the relation of play to modern sport, he was firm in his view that, in modern life, "sport occupies a place alongside and apart from the cultural process." [19] He observed, "the great competitions in archaic cultures had always formed part of the sacred festivals" but "this ritual tie has now been completely severed; sport has become profane." [20] As of now, except for isolated ritual sport of the greatest solemnity, modern play, game, and sport are relentlessly secular, and contemporary play theory no longer countenances a separation of play from reality. This separation was particularly noticeable among pioneering play theorists as well as sociologists and historians of religion whose firm categories excluded play from sport, sport from cultural functions, and play from the sacred. Huizinga, Caillois, and Mircea Elaide, for example, were comparativists in their landmark scholarship. With a commitment to ancient, medieval, and nonwestern cultural models, they sought to identify pure embodiments of play and the sacred set against the "real" or the "profane." [21] All were uncomfortable with what they felt to be a disastrous twentieth century and its diluted expressive forms. They consistently resisted acknowledgement of the ritual qualities surviving in modern secularized mass observances in their comments on "degenerated" or "irreligious" human behavior where the intensity of their subject, they felt, had collapsed into debasement and caricature. However, today, that subject is studied with validity as secular ritual in a large number of variations.

Modern America is a long way from Huizinga's medieval pageant of play and contest or his conception of the initially integrated nature of play and the sacred in ancient cultures. Although Huizinga and Caillois by the force of their rhetoric and the breadth of their scholarship argued against the purity of sport, the fact is that sport has swiftly become an immensely influential secular ceremony, part of the ordinary life of the society at large,[22] and a subject of intense investigation. Since the conceptual work of Huizinga and Caillois in characterizing and classifying play, sport itself has accumulated a welter of meanings, and a summary suggests a multiplicity of associations in many contexts: sport is its own system, an institutionalized game demanding physical prowess; games are dramatic models of our psychological lives; sport is popular art as well as applied art; sport regulates social interaction, ritualizing collective unity and pride; sport weds man to technological civilization while supposedly giving him relief from it; sport acts as a transitional institution between work and play; sport is studied as social imagery and is "a currency of communication on every level of American life"; sport is found to be "the success story of the twentieth century, the modern way up the ladder"; sport is the "rationalization of the Romantic" in the modern world; and, coming full circle to confront the heart of Huizinga's argument, sport is flatly labelled a natural religion.[23]

MODELS OF SPORTS HEROISM

The history of American fiction is, as critics such as Richard Chase, Leslie Fiedler, Daniel Hoffman, and Theodore Gross have pointed out, the history of individual, larger-than-life American heroes. The American hero from Natty Bumppo through Captain Ahab, Huckleberry Finn, Henry Fleming, and Nick Adams has had a conflict "between free will as a function of natural liberty and determinism as a result of surrender to society."[24] American Sports Heroes have had to continually make themselves up or redefine their roles in the absence of a place in a traditional culture.

Huizinga dismissed much of modern sport as "a thing *sui generis,* neither play nor earnest,"[25] stating in *America* (1918) that "if we compare the tense athlete in his competitive harness with the pioneer hunter and Indian fighter, then the loss of true, free personality is obvious."[26] In this comparison are grounds for tracing not so much the decline of the play spirit which is *not* so "obvious," but, more accurately, the metamorphoses of the play spirit. These changes mirror and dictate changes in the fiction about sport as well. That America has always been bewildered about what constitutes work and play suggests a tremendous tension in the society *between* work and play. The modern athlete on a sports team does not resolve this tension but actually embodies this paradox as did Hester Prynne and Pearl in their free play in *The Scarlet Letter,* Rip Van Winkle in "Rip Van Winkle," Natty Bumppo in *The Pioneers,* and Thoreau in the "Higher Laws" chapter of *Walden,* as classic American literature confronted the dilemma in differing ways.

Brian Sutton-Smith states that the "primary paradigm" for play is activity taken up voluntarily, usually by a solitary player. The result of the activity is individual gain "in cognitive or creative organization."[27] This definition best describes the play of characters in classic American literature. However, the play of athletes in the organized competition related in modern fiction more closely resembles Sutton-Smith's "secondary paradigm" in which play organizes collective forms of human commnication and "reflects the enculturative processes of the larger society."[28]

The modern sports hero exemplifies a paradox in American society: his drive for individual excellence and acclaim (in the primary paradigm of play) is confronted by democratic consensus, which is adoring and hostile by turns. His drive upward through the classless society celebrates idealism and individual striving that turns, as the American dream turns, toward acquisition, wealth, and power. The success myth champions accommodation to social norms, the prudence of Benjamin Franklin's maxims, and the ability to be a team player (in the secondary paradigm of play). Whatever talent he is blessed with, most often physical grace, power, and creativity masked by an inability to express himself, the sports hero confronts the established society in the largest metaphor, the team itself. Sports heroes are individually isolated in their performing skills, which set them off from mass society, but it is in the performance itself that their status as isolates is severely tested for the mass audience. Here is where the primary and secondary paradigms of play clash in discordant drama.

To deal with the proliferation of meanings that the sports hero has acquired in differing historical periods, it is necessary to draw some broad outlines of sports heroism. Three specific heroic models will be discussed at length in this study. They are the Ritual Sports Hero, the Popular Sports Hero, and the School Sports Hero. While I see the delineations quite clearly, it is inevitable that there is some overlap and direct influence among the three figures—they are not rigidly separated parallel tracks coursing through the critic's imagination. These three heroic models give shape to more than a century of American play, game, and sport in fiction.

The Ritual Sports Hero antedates both the Popular and School Heroes in his wisdom and probity as well as in his personal, isolated frame of competition. An Adamic figure who seeks self-knowledge, he competes to learn what he is capable of against self or natural adversaries. He has origins in sacred ceremony as well as state ritual. He has specifically American origins in the accounts of wilderness heroes, in ordeal and captivity narratives. His exploits are prefigured in the accounts of the great early naturalists, explorers, and historians such as John James Audubon, Meriweather Lewis, and Francis Parkman as well as in the journals of trappers, scouts, and hunters. He is a figure of both surpassing skill and great dignity and is only incidentally defined by a community or society with which he is most often in conflict. His sport is often formalized as ritual, and then sport becomes a way of knowing in the present and a dance toward the dramatic ordering of ultimate meaning, the sacred, for which he has played and has risked the loss of his secular, temporal selfhood.

The Popular Sports Hero was born in exuberant playfulness on the American frontier in the early nineteenth century. He was deeply democratic, raw, humorous, and unlettered. As a hunter, physical wild man, gambler, or shrewd confidence man, he expressed the strength and vitality of westward expansion and growth. He was physically prodigious and boldly manipulative in an environment that demanded such power and deception for survival. His sport grew out of his work with horse, rifle, and riverboat. Gradually, the Popular Sports Hero was refined and scaled down to fit into the modern arena of industrial society where he played for a team before huge crowds. In this volume, "popular" consistently refers to the *sport* and not to the hero. Obviously, by 1900, School Sports Heroes are just as visible in the culture as Popular Sports Heroes; so can Ritual Sports

Heroes be clearly recognized under certain circumstances. "Popular" sport is here defined as that activity which evolves out of the daily life of the culture which is captivated by it. "Popular" sport first denotes the games and contests of the frontier and later the spectatorial pastimes of an industrial urban society. The determination of popular sport is as an end in itself, a thoroughly secular spectacle.

The School Sports Hero grew from the development of a militant sporting ethic in the Eastern colleges in the post-Civil War period. He was more genteel than the Popular Hero and nurtured through American education, privilege, and the assimilation of war through symbolic sports conflict. The School Sports Hero heralded a shift from transcendental speculation in the universities to preparation for the trials of a driving, materialistic American business society and world leadership. The School Sports Hero not only competed for personal victory but for a larger self-discipline and the approbation of an admiring society which then christened him as potential leader. The figure was a prominent symbol of the American aristocracy's last great involvement in national life and affairs and was the most influential American sporting hero at the beginning of the twentieth century.

The three heroic figures diverge at a number of crucial points. The Ritual Hero plays for self, for his own pride or revelation. The School Hero competes for himself only incidentally. He competes for society's praise to establish his place as leader or spokesman. The Popular Hero competes for immediate extrinsic rewards: money, fame, records. The Ritual Hero plays for the growth of spirit, the School Hero for character and recognition, and the Popular Hero for recognition and reward. For the Ritual Hero, sport is a revelation; for the School Hero, a test; and for the Popular Hero, a contest.

The Ritual Sports Hero renounces all public pressures and rewards. His sporting motions and victories are serious and private. His personal *agon* is with nature or a force representing nature. He exemplifies the individual set apart and he always deals with primary experience. To the degree that all players and sportsmen undergo personal, invididual experience, we can say that they are all Ritual Heroes but that School and Popular Heroes subordinate the primary lessons of mastery and victory for externally offered prizes, subordinate intrinsic rewards that can be enlarged upon for extrinsic rewards eagerly accepted.

The School Sports Hero is at the mid-point between ritual and the spectacle of the Popular Sports Hero. The School Hero is an elite son who has the common touch, an uncommon man of ability and discipline who undergoes the tests of sport to learn not only about himself, as did the Ritual

Hero, but about lessons in courage and discipline that he can apply to life and society outside the arena. The School Hero plays for externalized goals as well as personal gratification but ultimately bends his skill and heroism to society's will and tasks. He is most aware of his place in a society in which he desires a leadership role. He makes a prudent investment in society, its continuity and health. The Popular Sports Hero is not sensitive to his conflicting roles. He dominates the *agon* as he would all his problems while he roars out that he is the best, beats down all competition, and wins at any cost. He is a superhero of folklore who expresses our most expansive optimism while he possesses none of the self-knowledge of the Ritual and School Heroes and none of the School Hero's sense of duty.

For the Ritual Sports Hero, play is often work of the most creative and healing sort. The School Hero plays in preparation for life's work. The frontier Popular Hero at first found his sport growing out of work roles in the natural environment and ultimately worked at his play for spectators who were seeking playful respite from their work. Within their play, these heroes respect or grudgingly submit to certain norms. On the frontier, the hunter or woodsman as Ritual Hero exhibited his "fair play" by acknowledging the sovereignty of powerful nature and the limits of the physical body. The School Hero respected the stated rules of the game because they prepared him for "playing fair" by observing other rules in society. The Popular Hero respected the power of his competitors, duelled the authority of the team, or fought the record book containing the inhuman accomplishments of past heroes.

None of the three figures developed along the same paths. The Ritual Sports Hero cannot be reduced to a formulaic pattern. He is a mythical hero performing large, well-established motions and is timeless, creating his time out of all time. While his American setting has enormously magnified his stature as hunter and naturalist in a pristine wilderness, he has links to primitive sacrificial sports and the sports of antiquity where rites sustained culture. Cooper and Thoreau bequeath to Hemingway and Faulkner ritual heroes who perform acts of pride and humility, perception and mastery. They all wished to show sport as a rule-limited activity with limitless reference in a world with consequences for the player. If the hunt cannot rearrange and irrevocably alter lives outside its rite, it may ontologically celebrate reality that can both be lived with and in, controlling, if briefly, nightmares of personal history, and perhaps establishing, if imperfectly, a link with the sacred.

The School Sports Hero, on the other hand, affords a classic study of how a formulaic pattern in a culture grew into an established popular literary formula: that of the boys' school sports story, and how that convention would be subsumed by the ironic and satiric statements of authors such as Fitzgerald, Hemingway, and Faulkner. The Popular Sports Hero is more a concrete illustration of Rourke's thesis in *American Humor* that the accretion of folk materials, legends, and crude sketches that cohere about a cultural figure lead to his birth in serious fiction.[29] The Popular Hero's development is jagged, long-drawn-out, and must be tracked through several large metamorphoses: the country's shift from frontier to urban culture, from outsized backwoods heroes to scaled-down team members, from southern to northern emphasis, and from pre-Civil War to post-Civil War setting. The birth of the Popular Sports Hero in fiction is expressly connected with the development of American journalism and its interaction with traditions of American humor in reporting and narration.

Before beginning extensive examination of these three sports heroes, it is important to reiterate that their broad outlines do not preclude cross-fertilization. Two sporting heroes may begin in similar fashion—Davy Crockett and Natty Bumppo, for example. But where Natty becomes a Rousseauistic philosopher-hunter, internalizing his sporting lessons while instructing the settlement in the correct use of sport, Crockett's fictional persona is created through carelessly sown tales of giantism. He is a raging public patriotic symbol and a popular consensus hero. Two hunters. Two divergent courses toward idealism and humorous realism. Two very different breeds of sportsmen. Yet they both begin as natural gentlemen obeying wilderness laws and performing adeptly in sporting rites. Natty Bumppo, however, is in part the genesis of the upright college sports hero of 1900 in his living by a rigorous code. Coming full circle, Fitzgerald's Yale All-American Tom Buchanan in *The Great Gatsby* is a School Sports Hero but is also prefigured in the blustering, violent athletes of nineteenth-century backwoods tales which, of course, take their outsized conceptions of roarers from Crockett almanacs, among other sources.

Before the Civil War, the beginnings of a fully national literature presented the sports hero as an individual in contest on the frontier with other men or with nature. There the Ritual Sports Hero expressed the heritage of English play forms in ceremony as well as a new world expression of survival skill and mastery. The Ritual Sports Hero and the Popular Sports Hero survived side-by-side in sober achievement or in comic bluster before the Civil War. After the Civil War, the sports hero was most clearly defined on a team to which he was subordinated—military, industrial, educational, societal. He was the uncommon man now representative of the conflict between the individual and the modern organization. He now could best be seen as the School Sports Hero, the modern gentleman sportsman with a code, and as the Popular Sports Hero, the raucous superman of modern spectacle. The modern Ritual Sports Hero is then part of a reaction against collectivized and regulated sports figures.

Thus, American fiction for more than a century and a half has reported both somberly and hilariously on a nation of players and spectators during a great shift in American sport and leisure from spontaneous work-related sport on the frontier to the sport of modern organized industrial society. Whether an aged hunter, steamboat pilot, school football star, rube pitcher, bullfighter, or boxer, the sports hero in fiction has always been the individual performer in a contest. This contest has been with nature, with a solitary adversary, or within a formalized team rivalry. Most fundamentally, however, the sports hero has most often fought the harsh battle with himself as well as in the arena, the public performance taking on a deeper perspective through the private struggle. American sport in fiction celebrates the nation's youth, innocence, and power while focusing on all the tragic contradictions implied in the obverse themes of death, experience, and impotence. Sport has become a binding myth for an intensely organized, competitive society growing from a brawling adolescence into aggressive adulthood. The text of that myth is recorded in sport's varying presentation in our fiction.

Play, Game, Sport:
Classic American Literature

CHAPTER ONE
Hawthorne:
The Play Spirit

CREATING THE FICTIONAL ARENA

CLASSIC AMERICAN WRITERS found the ways in which America
played to be important. Writers such as Nathaniel Hawthorne, Washington
Irving, James Fenimore Cooper, and Henry David Thoreau had particular
visions of play, game, and sport that proved the vitality of play as literary
subject in America. Hawthorne and Irving were most interested in ritual
forms of play that had survived from English and continental sources. They
used the procedures of traditional ceremony to describe through irony and
fancy the play of colonial America. Cooper and Thoreau crafted New World
rituals out of sport in the settlements and wilderness. They transformed the
motions of the hunt into rites that ideally would instruct the community and
nurture the individual. Thus in both the colonial past and in the more fully
national nineteenth century, ritual that thrived on play and sport was a way
to define American communal and personal responsibility.

These writers did not, of course, conceive of modern, organized
sport with its institutionalized role differentiations and extrinsic rewards.
Allen Guttmann has suggested seven characteristics of modern sport in society that he sees as a microcosmic model of the larger society. They are
Secularism, Equality, Specialization, Rationalism, Bureaucratic Organization, Quantification, and the Quest for Records. For Guttmann, these characteristics are "interdependent, systematically related elements of the ideal
type of a modern society."[1] They refer to the team sport of industrial society and professional spectacle where the rewards are more often those of
money and fame rather than skill, hard-won victory, or self-knowledge.

One cannot now, one hundred fifty years later, expect classic American writers to have used the terms "play," "game," and "sport" with the precision of post-Huizinga play theorists and sport sociologists. Modern sports patterns do not reveal much to us about what is profound in play and sport for Hawthorne, Irving, Cooper, and Thoreau in a period that might be called pre-organized-sport America. Already in the seventeenth century, the plantation culture of the Tidewater region had a well-developed sporting life based on horse racing and gambling. However, sport in the modern sense of team, urban, school, professional, spectator, and *national* sport did not really exist. The forms of play which early American writers identified were necessarily more individual, informal, rural, and diffuse. What these writers called "sport" may be defined as a manifestation of a wide-ranging play spirit most often displayed in ritual: dreams, fancy, spectacle, games, contests, and hunts, but only incidentally in what today might be called modern organized sport.

Therefore, in the use of play by earlier American writers, the characteristics of modern sport were simply not evident or possible. One modern sport element generally lacking in their play was the modern insistence on the *agon* or competition. Their more spontáneously playful or ritualized experience differs sharply from the pervasive secularized and organized experience of modern sport. The emphasis of the classic writers was on representation, the embodiment of an ideal or the "as if" quality of *mimicry*. The rewards of play in Hawthorne, Irving, Cooper, and Thoreau were more intrinsic in the knowledge of self, harmony with surroundings, or personal transformation. Ultimately, they were as concerned with spontaneous play (*paidia*) as with play's progressive formalization (*ludus*).

Classic American writers saw sport in a larger pattern of play and gave it a wide number of connotations. Sport had no consensus definition. For Hawthorne in *The Scarlet Letter,* sports were what "the great honest face of the people" indulged in. Sports were "what the colonists had witnessed and shared in, long ago, at the country fairs and on the village-greens of England." Sports should be kept "alive on this new soil, for the sake of the courage and manliness that were essential in them."[2] In *The Blithedale Romance,* Zenobia accuses Miles Coverdale of toying with her "for [his] sport"[3] while in *The Marble Faun,* the water of the Trevi Fountain is "sporting by itself in the moonshine."[4] Irving was similarly indiscriminate in his use of "sport"; in his lexicon, sports were fights, frights, and frolics. A variety of Christmas and May "sports" are described in *The Sketch Book* and *Bracebridge Hall*. Rip Van Winkle enjoys the "sport" of squirrel-shooting but also assists at children's "sports" such as kite-flying and marble-shooting. Dolph Heyliger, the hearty young Brom Bones of *Bracebridge Hall,* "was the ringleader of all holiday sports."[5] Cooper mistrusted the term "sport." He burlesqued it in a settlement parody of a Walter Scott tournament of knights in *The Pioneers* with the pastime of "shooting the Christmas turkey." During Templeton's pigeon shoot, Cooper surveys the slaughter where "the horses were loaded with the dead" and sardonically comments, "after this first burst of sporting, the shooting of pigeons became a business."[6] Sport is a dubious activity that focuses on Templeton's clash of values with Natty Bumppo as overseer of the natural world. Thoreau praised the sports of hunting and fishing for boys and for men trying to recapture their boyhoods, stating, "I am compelled to doubt if equally valuable sports are ever substituted for these."[7]

Thus, all four writers used sport to buttress a vision of what America had been in the prenational era, to explain what we were in the nineteenth century, or to prophesy what we might become. A key question to be asked for each writer is how play in a larger sense fits into the rituals of social life. By stressing the play elements in games and contests isolated by Huizinga and Caillois—those of freedom, separateness, uncertainty, unproductiveness, order governed by rules, and make-believe—we can more clearly see how play was represented by these authors. For Hawthorne and Irving, play was in the realm of *mimicry-ilinx,* representation by simulation or vertigo induced by sensation, rather than in *agon-alea,* the realms of competition and chance which dominate modern games and sports. Hawthorne saw play in the most varied guises: play was freely outside "ordinary" or "real" life, distinguished most clearly by its separate pretending qualities and the desperate playing of roles in *The Blithedale Romance,* the masques and revels of the tales and of *The Marble Faun,* in the sports and ceremony of Election Day and in the creative embroidery of Hester as well as in the fancies of Pearl in *The Scarlet Letter.* Irving's "pretending qualities" are much narrower in scope than Hawthorne's, but vivid, as Rip Van Winkle and Ichabod Crane are caught in vertiginous experiences where reality is blurred and uncertain: Hendrik Hudson's men solemnly bowl the thunder while Rip's world changes forever, and Brom Bones frightens Ichabod into flight from Sleepy Hollow.

Cooper and Thoreau attempted to portray sport as personal and outside community but with pointed reference to societal conduct. None of the classifications of games—*agon, alea, mimicry, ilinx*—deal particularly well with the solitary man-in-nature who moves beyond a specific role in competition, chance, or make-believe. Cooper and Thoreau's man-in-nature internalizes experience, his primary adversary being nature itself, what he is contained by. The isolated sporting experience in nature is in a spiritual vein and is more dramatic, serious, and private. It is an attempt by the individual to integrate himself with his environment and learn its most basic laws. Cooper and Thoreau sense an appeal through sport to individual peace and order, and their repeated sporting rituals produce a clarity of motives. Natty Bumppo possesses a mystical bond with the land and with other living things. Thoreau attempts to go deep within himself to search his own conduct, and sport is an initial station on that journey. In each case, Cooper and Thoreau correct society's view of sport while elaborating their own.

Of course, authors could as yet discern no true organized forms of American sport. Such forms, born on the Southern frontier and in Northern cities, and the literary conventions to express them, would arise through the Popular Sports Hero's portrayal in almanacs, Southwestern Humor tales, early sports journalism, and dime novels (see chapters 3–4). The School Sports Hero as a figure of aggression and privilege after the Civil War would be best expressed in the convention of the boys' school sports story (see chapters 6–7). Play, game, and sport in classic American literature are circumscribed but intense, no one established convention in any mass pattern but emblems informing larger subjects: repressive Puritanism (Hawthorne); national consciousness (Irving); aggressive capitalism (Cooper); and American mistrust and misreading of leisure (Thoreau). Working with the colonial past, regional lore, settlement imperatives, and transcendental goals, Hawthorne, Irving, Cooper, and Thoreau portray play alternately as what Americans do not have, as a nostalgic dream, as a sober responsibility, and as an ethical passage.

PLAY AND THE DANCE OF DEATH

In Hawthorne's fiction, the power of play is always present but never triumphant. Play is ironically defeated time and again as scenes of masquing, pageantry, and exuberance must yield to the dominant context of sin and death. The pattern is consistent from early tales such as "My Kinsman, Major Molineux" and "The Maypole of Merry Mount" through *The Blithedale Romance* and *The Marble Faun*. The play moments abruptly cease as the fictional world devolves down into a common day fraught with knowledge and mortality.[8] Play is wistful and heartfelt in Hawthorne but not an essential human endeavor, complete within itself. Play momentarily denies the terms of The Fall for Hawthorne's characters but is always terminated in the truth of grief. Play confronts the crimes of history but is only a penultimate dramatic ordering of creative illusion before the final judgments in each narrative. Genteel art is unable to grasp the true meaning of play. Only in *The Scarlet Letter,* through the historicizing of a particularly English and then American vision of play and sport, does Hawthorne sustain the public power of sport while Hester and Pearl privately create their own refuge through triumphs of the imagination that begin in play. In *The Scarlet Letter,* Hawthorne relates the conflict between spontaneous, creative play and the measured aims and profound earnestness of the Puritan theocracy. By doing so, he dramatizes the deep American Puritan hesitancy about play. While he is drawn to play's ordering and shaping power as yet another emblem for art, Hawthorne mistrusts play as essentially death-denying and futile. He illuminates this Puritan dilemma while embodying that very ambivalence in his own created scenes.

In *The Marble Faun,* chapter 9, "The Sylvan Dance," Hawthorne provides his most vivid image of the play of *mimicry-ilinx,* one that he had been standing behind for three decades as an author. Donatello and Miriam are in the Borghese grounds seeking to sustain their mirth and joy when Hawthorne makes the analogy with "the sculptured scene on the front and sides of a sarcophagus, where, as often as any other device, a festive procession mocks the ashes and white bones that are treasured up, within. You might take it for a marriage-pageant; but, after a while, if you look attentively at these merry-makers, following them from end to end of the marble coffin, you doubt whether their gay movement is leading them to a happy close. A youth has suddenly fallen in the dance; a chariot is overturned and broken. . . . Always, some tragic incident is shadowed forth, or thrust sidelong into the spectacle . . . ." (88–89). Once this "incident" comes to consciousness, "you can look no more at the festal portions of the scene, except with reference to this one slightly suggested doom and sorrow" (89). Play becomes an ironic subtext that is terminated when revelation is at hand. Play and display are illusions of order within disorder that open into more somber disorder: the dominance of sexuality and mortality and the pull of history. The iconography of Hawthorne's sarcophagus image is indebted to festive Roman burial scenes, but an alternative iconography, internalized and pervasive, might suggest the late medieval *Danse Macabre* (Dance of Death) with its penitents following the hooded figure of death with his scythe. Hawthorne combines the visual image of the Roman sarcophagus with this darker vision. Both images suggest the circularity of the play image in the face of death: the continuous irony of a play that suggests life itself is a harlequinade, that suggests the grinning, frozen skull is already visible in the faces of the revellers.

Mimicry-ilinx is the mode of play which dominates Hawthorne's two early tales, "My Kinsman, Major Molineux," and "The Maypole of Merry Mount."[9] In each tale, the core drama is resolved through spontaneous play and its abrupt overturning. In "My Kinsman," nascent American history pervades pageantry and the masque. Young Robin's wonder at the festive Boston midnight procession changes to incredulity and horror when he finds at the heart of the ceremony, his "kinsman," a despised and ridiculed figure. The procession and its revelation are almost fused and Robin then becomes potentially a good young patriot. In "The Maypole," Endicott sternly marches the Lord and Lady of the May into the grim world of adult marriage and consequence and into Puritan history. He makes a timely appearance such as a *deus ex machina* might effect in a traditional masque and cuts down the maypole while delivering stern reprobations to Edgar and Edith. Yet he bestows upon them the wreath from the fallen maypole in the hopes that they will take something of the best in playful innocence into experience.[10]

Hawthorne's subtle tale offers no clear victory to play or seriousness but dramatizes the insecurity felt toward ritual play in the colony, a heritage of the May controversies then raging in England. He continues this very sober undertone to May observances traditionally dedicated to divine praise when he writes, "This wedlock was more serious than most affairs of Merry Mount," for the Lord and Lady of the May "were really and truly to be partners for the dance of life." Edgar and Edith as Adam and Eve are marched into the world, "their destinies . . . linked together for good or evil"; they will perhaps survive believing not as did the Merry Mount "elder spirits" that "mirth was but the counterfeit of happiness" but that worldly happiness may contain mirth and play for "in the ties that united them, were intertwined all the purest and best of their early joys."[11]

The narrator's tone in "The Maypole" is brilliantly modulated in several voices: at times he is a stately reader of the masque, a stern Puritan, or a gay spirit, but finally he is a reserved ironist satirizing all viewpoints, as narration itself is playful in "The Maypole." The story begins with an epigraph in which Hawthorne states that he has borrowed from Joseph Strutt's *The Sports and Pastimes of the People of England* (1801) and that the facts of the tale "have wrought themselves, *almost spontaneously* [emphasis mine], into a sort of allegory." Thus does Hawthorne slyly announce the antic play quality of his own narrative "spontaneously" coming into creation. Hawthorne also assumes the voice of Tall Tale expansiveness when he jocularly describes Puritan life in terms of play: "Their festivals were fast days"; the whipping post "might be termed the Puritan Maypole." Also, the Merry Mounters are characterized by play even in their quietest of moments for "when sport itself grew wearisome, they made a game of their own stupidity, and began a yawning match." Yet there is no mistaking the didacticism at the core of the tale.[12] Innocence of the May ceremony is not valid, for the "sworn triflers of a lifetime" have created "systematic gaiety." Play has become a consuming task as "all the hereditary pastimes of old England were transplanted hither." One "pastime" clearly heralds the Dance of Death: "Once, it is said, they were seen following a flower-decked corpse, with merriment and festive music, to his grave. But did the dead man laugh?" This pointed question in effect reverberates through all of Hawthorne's play scenes in fiction. A final sardonic truth beyond the Puritan earnestness and the Merry Mounter's playfulness is that the Merry Mounters work harder at their play than any Puritan force arrayed against them. They are obsessive actors without seriousness engaged nonetheless in serious business in which they cannot triumph over death. The movement of the story is down and away into experience without illusion: life is not to be played at or for.

The maxim that life is not to be played at or for becomes multilevelled in *The Blithedale Romance* which is dominated by a narrative voice that is "playful" in a fundamentally defective sense. Miles Coverdale is a genteel poet whose indiscriminate and shallow sense of play leads him to "play at" his life in Blithedale. But while Hawthorne has Coverdale's limited vision convey Blithedale to the reader, Hawthorne's own lens widens and magnifies the play trope: all characters at Blithedale are simulating new roles in the social experiment as a deeper drama threatens in the central love triangle among Zenobia-Hollingsworth-Priscilla. Play thus takes on twin negative connotations. While Zenobia, Hollingsworth, and Priscilla are acting out their own drama, Miles Coverdale is not serious enough or sensitive enough either fully to live or to render the life he sees. He denies both engagement and humane sympathy until Zenobia's death.

Coverdale repeatedly states his sense of himself and of Blithedale through references to play. All the references are derisive and reductive. He calls the "heroic enterprise" at Blithedale "an illusion, a masquerade, a pastoral, a counterfeit Arcadia, in which we grown-up men and women were making a play-day of the years that were given to us to live in. I tried to analyze this impression, but not with much success" (21). When Hollingsworth asks him, "Have you nothing to do in life that you fancy yourself so ready to leave it?" (43), Coverdale replies, "Nothing, nothing, that I know of, unless to make pretty verses, and play a part with Zenobia and the rest of the amateurs, in our pastoral" (43). Indeed, Coverdale opposes "play" to "seriousness" as would a rigid, unimaginative critic of the play spirit. He is a "blithe cover" who keeps truth hidden or does not acknowledge it.

Zenobia at the other pole is playing for absolutely everything; she projects a fierce persona and ultimately uses "play" in bitter mirth at her own flamboyance and defeat. She knows Coverdale for the trifler he is. Early on she speaks to Priscilla of a post-Blithedale period "when our pastoral shall be quite played out . . ." (78). Coverdale muses, "I could not but suspect, that, if merely at play with Hollingsworth, she was sporting with a power which she did not fully estimate" (79). Zenobia, however, accuses Coverdale rather than Hollingsworth of self-indulgent play: "It is dangerous, sir," she says, "to tamper thus with earnest human passions, out of your own mere idleness, and for your sport" (170). Thus both the most committed player who "plays for" and the most dismayed witness who "plays at" are matched in their antipathy and mutual recognition.

If the entire Blithedale experience is a masquerade, then chapter 24, "The Masqueraders," is the play within play (to alter the term), the familiar Hawthorne scene which depicts a masking as nominally innocent for its duration. Coverdale is returning from Boston where he has finally grasped the elusive truth of the triangle of lovers and, psychologically, he needs to find the Blithedale community as it was before he left it. When he approaches the farm, he hears the laughter and shouts of a celebration, a gay, addled historical pageant. He purports to know all the voices in the forest "better than [his] own" (209), but the characters are jumbled: all eras, moods, and folklores are hopelessly confused and we have play through a cracked lens that focuses on the aimlessness of Blithedale without traditions. A Jim Crow Negro, a Kentucky woodsman, Moll Pitcher, and a Shaker elder cavort with Diana, a Shepherd of Arcadia, and the Bavarian Broom Girl. *The King James Book of Sport* controversy is updated as Puritans and Gay Cavaliers are joined by a New World historical figure (now a character in revelry), the British Revolutionary War officer. The masqueraders mock

Coverdale's outsider's status and literally chase him toward the real climax of the scene where, in deadly earnest, Zenobia, the queen of the pageant, is confronting Hollingsworth and Priscilla beneath the rock of Eliot's Pulpit, all masks dropped and denounced. As always, Coverdale has missed the essential drama. He envisions Zenobia "dethroned," "condemned," and "on trial for her life." She is a Hester Prynne dropped into the denouement of a tragic May scene where Endicott the magistrate has been complicated into Hollingsworth the projector-suitor.

Zenobia sardonically tells Coverdale, "This long while past, you have been following up your game, groping for human emotions in the dark corners of the heart. Had you been here a little sooner, you might have seen them dragged into the daylight" (214). Zenobia is weary of her masquerade: "I am awake, disenchanted, disenthralled"); she labels Hollingsworth a "better masquerader" than she for his had been a self-deception. She stops to comment sharply to Coverdale, "Ah, I perceive what you are about! You are turning this whole affair into a ballad" (223). Before going off to take her life, she concludes, "But I am weary of this place, and sick to death of playing at philanthropy and progress. Of all the varieties of mock life, we have surely blundered into the very emptiest mockery in our effort to establish the one true system" (227). Play, in the sense of *mimicry* to erect a greater seriousness, is deluded projection; "playing" always has consequences and the timid genteel aesthetic that would "play at" depicting this play (Coverdale's narrative) is also damned by her.

In *The Blithedale Romance,* Coverdale first sees play as amusing and trifling. It concludes as desperate and deluding, without the power to infuse art or life. Life lived as a projected role in a drama collapses at the very limits of romance as do Zenobia's queenly pose and Coverdale's genteel mask. "The Masqueraders" chapter expands to include all the characters, all the time, in flight from themselves and each other. All the characters in the novel engage in play, but they all project in a void. Their play has no originating center, no agreed-upon public pageantry, nothing but the stratagems of naked psyches. Their sustained illusion is disastrous for the characters who relentlessly try to simulate a new reality by erasing both family history (that of Zenobia and Priscilla) and all guilt. Their roles must be played in a frightening environment which necessarily denies the past because Blithedale has no real history.

The interior play of the Blithedale narrative is replaced in *The Marble Faun* by a number of overt emblem scenes in which Hawthorne obsessively reworked his entire custom-house of play images. There is no way that Miriam and Donatello can truly retain (and later regain) their innocence, while Hilda and Kenyon cannot fully accept the world of fallen experience. Life and art are both impossible, and the play imagery at Hawthorne's command underscores that fact. The scenes are similar to those from his earlier works, but the play is even more arch and self-conscious.

The Marble Faun has three major sections dominated by play. Each major section takes up concepts that absolutely frustrate the play experience for Hawthorne. The first section is chapters 9–10, "The Faun and Nymph" and "The Sylvan Dance," in which play is helpless before the Fall and before history, its temporal arena. Donatello is worried about Miriam's role as nymph, and he hesitates, "a kind of dim apprehension in his face, as if he dreaded that a moment's pause might break the spell, and snatch away the sportive companion whom he had waited for through so many dreary months" (86). " 'Dance! dance!' cried he joyously. 'If we take breath, we shall be as we were yesterday. There, now, is the music, just beyond this clump of trees. Dance, Miriam, dance!' " (86). The urgency of the dance is reminiscent of the Merry Mount players who wished to defeat time and history. Donatello summons the *ilinx* of the previous day for Miriam and himself, and Hawthorne invokes familiar rhetoric: "Here, as it seemed, had the Golden Age come back again within the precincts of this sunny glade, thawing mankind out of their cold formalities, releasing them from irksome restraint . . ." (88).[13] The scene is glossed immediately by Hawthorne's extended sarcophagus image and followed by the appearance of Miriam's dogged pursuer. Her realization is that "such hours [as the sylvan dance], I believe, do not often repeat themselves in a lifetime" (89).

The consistent Hawthorne triad of play-revelation-relapse into common day is complete when the few "merry-makers" still in the wood have "hidden their racy peculiarities under the garb and aspect of ordinary people, and sheltered themselves in the weary commonplace of daily life" (90). They are similar to Hollingsworth, Priscilla, and Zenobia when Miles Coverdale finds them apart from the masqueraders at Blithedale. Hawthorne has once again removed all costumes and props: their joyful arena, referred to as "Arcadia and the Golden Age" (90),[14] stands revealed as "that old tract of pleasure-ground, close by the people's gate of Rome; a tract where the crimes and calamities of ages, the many battles, blood recklessly poured out, and deaths of myriads, have corrupted all the soil. . ." (90). The introduction of Roman history makes the link overt. Miriam and Donatello themselves have been dancing on a sarcophagus lid. The earth itself is a tomb encompassing all the violence of blood shed in history and the play in innocence is shockingly meager and ephemeral in comparison. Miriam asks for Donatello's pity "because in the midst of my wretchedness I let myself be your playmate for this one wild hour" (91) but they are already characters deluded in a drama in which they cannot triumph. They are actors on the gruesomely named "pleasure ground."

Art and nature are both corrupted by man's sexuality and his inescapable personal history which is given expression in the history of nations. Man's play has only added to the chaos and suffering in history as the second play unit, chapters 15–18 of *The Marble Faun,* stipulates. Hawthorne constructs an artists' tour as a nighttime frolic, a gambol through Roman history from the Trevi Fountain to the Coliseum and the Forum. At each point, the experience is punctuated with a vivid play image. The Fountain is the most positive playful artifact in the novel. Made up of more than twenty "artificial fantasies," it is "as magnificent a piece of work as ever human skill contrived" (144). What fascinates Hawthorne is the way in which the water itself has sported with the statuary: "in a century of this wild play, Nature had adopted the Fountain of Trevi, with all its elaborate devices for her own" (145). Hawthorne has found his perfect emblem for art and nature and fused it in play. The Fountain is a playful triumph. The water is an artistic frolic, following both the artist's course and its own. The water which first falls "from a hundred crevices, on all sides" (144) ultimately runs wild, falling into a basin where "a boat might float, and make voyages from one shore to another in this mimic lake" (145). One message inferred is that vulnerable people in history are not capable of this union of art-play-nature; they imprint their "natures," subjective and repressed, onto such antic perfection. Like Kenyon, they chase the goal of great art or, like Donatello, the primal freedom of nature which does not need but *is* creation.

The Trevi Fountain is not human and has no self-consciousness. Yet even its scene is invaded by Miriam's tormentor, bathing his "brown, bony talons" in the "great drinking-cup of Rome" and compelling Miriam to gaze at his and her reflections in the water. Further along during the "midnight ramble," Hawthorne again invokes the blood of Roman history and does so through sport spectacle. From the Roman "pleasure ground," we move to the Coliseum where by moonlight "youths and maidens were running merry races across the open space and playing at hide-and-seek . . ." (154); indeed, "there was much pastime and gaiety, just then, in the area of the Coliseum, where so many gladiators and wild beasts had fought and died, and where so much blood of Christian martyrs had been lapt up by that fiercest of wild beasts, the Roman populace of yore'' (154). Again Hawthorne sets the frolic of sex play against the backdrop of death and history.[15] The "youths and maidens" somewhat resemble water "sporting with the massive rock of the Trevi Fountain, but they do not cancel out the "great black cross, in the centre of the Coliseum,'' even as they sit singing "with much laughter and merriment,'' for the "black cross marks one of the especial blood-spots of the earth, where, thousands of times over, the Dying Gladiator fell . . .'' (154). Into this spectacle setting comes Miriam's shadowy seducer, disguised as a pilgrim making his way through the small shrines and between the "light-footed girls"—"in Italy, religion jostles along side by side with business and sport, after a fashion of its own. . .'' (155). Hawthorne states that "people are accustomed to kneel down and pray, or see others praying, between two fits of merriment, or between two sins'' (155).

The "fits of merriment" in *The Marble Faun* always herald a sin of pride, of weakness, and, finally, of murder when Donatello kills the seducer. In narrative after narrative Hawthorne repeatedly utilized images of play in just such juxtaposed incongruity to construct his own *Danse Macabre*. After the Coliseum scene, "our company of artists sat on the fallen column, the pagan altar, and the steps of the Christian shrine, enjoying the moonlight and shadow, the present gaiety and the gloomy reminiscences of the scene in almost equal share'' (155). The gaiety and gloom are consistently balanced by Hawthorne who then overturns play toward defeat and death. Play is never more than the ironic underscoring of the Fall, while the sport of history is another text confirming the transitory nature and bloody-mindedness of civilizations. The light play of the youths is drowned in the blood of Roman and Christian ghosts, and when Kenyon imagines all the blood shed by the Romans forming "a mighty subterranean lake of gore, right beneath our feat'' (163) in the Forum, the stage is set for Donatello's avenging act of murder on Miriam's behalf. This "lake of gore'' is history's overriding counterpart to the Trevi Fountain's "mimic lake'' but is real and defeating, an image formed by Kenyon as artist which keeps him from innocent enjoyment of the moonlight scene. Man is the animal whose play is always suspended by his image of primal tragedy and evil, and Donatello acts out this tragedy.

If play is paralyzed in "The Sylvan Dance'' by knowledge of the Fall and paralyzed in chapter 17, "Miriam's Trouble,'' by knowledge of the murderous sins of history, one final scene shows play as an unintegrated cascade of images that cannot inform genteel art. In chapters 47–49, Hawthorne summons a last pageant and procession, a grotesque, festive carnival in which Kenyon searches for Hilda. He is as lost and naive as young Robin in "My Kinsman," as doomed to gentility as Edgar and Edith in "The Maypole," as foolish as Miles Coverdale in *The Blithedale Romance*. Donatello and Miriam don disguises of the "peasant and contadina," but it is too late for them and their roles are artificial. While Kenyon laments, "Ah, Miriam, I cannot respond to you. Imagination and the love of art have both died out of me" (427), Miriam desires "to play round this matter [the whereabouts of Hilda], a little while, and cover it with fanciful thoughts, as we strew a grave with flowers" (428). She is described "with a tricksy, fitful kind of mirth" (429), a "spritelike, fitful characteristic of her manner, and a sort of hysteric gaiety . . . ." (429). Hawthorne's narrator reinforces this "hysteric gaiety" as the dominant mood of the last carnival. Before the carnival begins, he is already wearily heralding a "worn-out festival" in a "worn-out world." The carnival pageant is Hawthorne's most elaborately decadent procession but it is a flat and unmoving one as he goes through his play scenes for the final time with bitter showers of lime, miserable wilted flowers thrown, trampled on, and hurled again in a May bedecking turned rancid.

Kenyon is given no respite from the carnival frolic Hawthorne directs squarely at him. The most pertinent masquer is Hilda's surrogate, "a gigantic female figure, seven feet high, and taking up a third of the street's breadth with the preposterously swelling sphere of her crinoline skirts" (445–46). When Kenyon refuses her bouquet of "sunflowers and nettles," the "rejected Titaness" shoots a mock-pistol full of lime at Kenyon's heart. Other "apparitions" surround Kenyon "after the fashion of a coroner's jury, poking their pasteboard countenances" at him, to be followed by a "notary" to take his last testament and a "surgeon" with a three-foot lance to draw blood. Kenyon plunges deeper into the crowd and then stands his ground against the harlequins while he searches for Hilda. When she appears, she flings a rosebud from the opposite balcony. One should not forget the "cauliflower flung by a young man from a passing carriage" at precisely the same moment, a last grumpy play caveat from Hawthorne himself masqued as the "impious New Englander" who earlier "hit the coachman of the Roman Senator [with a double handful of powdered lime] full in the face and hurt his dignity amazingly" (443).[16]

The Marble Faun thus ends with a crescendo of play imagery that is meant to demonstrate Kenyon's inflexibility and his inability to create illusions of richness, to move past classical art into new forms. He chooses

Hilda's safe alternative; they return to America and art is not served.[17] Hawthorne in his last completed romance turns the play images back upon the artist who does not, who cannot perceive them, turns them back, too, on the lovers Miriam and Donatello who are caught in their sinful act and know no more joy. The artist cannot create while the dancers cannot dance. The only integrated, successful play is the Trevi Fountain's "sport" controlled by art and then by nature's artistry, for the Fountain's play is not subject to human weakness and death. But Hawthorne clearly shows the Fountain vulnerable to American genteel imagination when Kenyon jocularly envisions an American Trevi Fountain where each state would be carved and "pouring a silver stream from a separate can into one vast basin, which should represent the grand reservoir of national prosperity" (145). This is the final travesty of a "mimic lake" beyond the free union of art and nature and the innocent rejoinder to the Roman "lake of gore."

The Marble Faun confirms the curve of Hawthorne's use of play from the early tales onward. Play is always vivid, energetic, and creative but anarchic, abrupt, and preliminary. It has the power only to forestall momentarily time's thrall and the knowledge of mortality. Play is not an end in itself: it cannot overturn history or energize art. It is a magic dimension that must dissolve into the revelation which is uniformly one of realistic defeat.

THE SCARLET LETTER: THE ENGLISH GREEN

In The Scarlet Letter, Hawthorne avoided the excesses and dead-ends of the use of play in his other works. He accomplished this in several ways. Hester and Pearl do not play to stave off history or to deny the Fall. The catastrophe has already occurred. They are fallen and begin to play after Puritan religion and society have done their worst. Furthermore, Hawthorne Anglicized and Americanized the basic imagery of play and sport, giving him firm and immediate historical issues on which to comment, specifically the dramatization of The King James Book of Sport debate in England and its resultant carryover into the lives of the first generation of New England Puritans. Lastly, Hester and Pearl are creative beyond suspicious and timid art for they are not caught in its mentality or pressures. Hawthorne was able to comment fully on the Puritan fascination with and mistrust of play and creativity and thereby illuminate a side of the early American character. Most importantly, Hester and Pearl ironically survive the censure of the community in large part by drawing on what that community fears: a sense of freedom obtained through creative play. Pearl's play in her freedom is a fiercer, more fanciful extension of her mother Hester's beautiful embroidery, "her delicate and imaginative skill" which adds "the richer and more spiritual adornment of human ingenuity. . ." (81–82). Hester and Pearl do not take refuge in a masque which momentarily transforms them before the defeat but rather live their play in life-enhancing fashion. They are the only Hawthorne characters to do so, for in *The Scarlet Letter*, Hawthorne's vision of play was not dominated by its role in the dance of death. Their play functions as a stay against submission to repressive orthodoxy. *The Scarlet Letter* is the one Hawthorne narrative where play strengthens his characters while sport describes their society.

The New England Puritan censure of sport and recreation clashed repeatedly with the freer heritage of Elizabethan masques, revels, morris dances, and elaborate wakes that had traditional ritual and political meanings in the battles between the Stuart monarchy and the forces seeking to preserve the English Reformation. The more homely play of seventeenth-century Massachusetts was reflected in various early ball games such as Old Cat, Stoolball, and Rounders, as well as in the life of the country taverns which dotted the communities as social centers. The public house was used for darts, billiards, and shuffleboard, the sort of establishment in early Boston where young Robin Molineux comes seeking his uncle. A particularly generic Puritan ball game called "Last Couple in Hell" began with a man and woman standing on a base where they tried to capture others and put them in hell, too. Through Pearl's curious gaze Hawthorne describes the Puritan children engaged in what passed for child's play in early Boston: "She saw the children of the settlement, on the grassy margin of the street, or at the domestic thresholds, disporting themselves in such grim fashion as the Puritanic nurture would permit; playing at going to church, perchance; or at scourging Quakers; or taking scalps in a sham-fight with the Indians; or scaring one another with freaks of imitative witchcraft" (94).

Fittingly enough, the earliest written comments on sport in Puritan New England were, for the most part, notices of censure or prohibition. It was in Boston that *The King James Book of Sport* (1618) was publicly burned by the common hangman in protest of its liberalization of sports restrictions on the Sabbath. In "The Maypole of Merry Mount," Hawthorne commented on the single most noteworthy New World clash between an individual colonist and early Puritan authority, the struggle between Thomas Morton and his Puritan antagonists in Plymouth led by Governor William Bradford.[18] On Christmas Day 1621, Governor Bradford took away all "sporting implements" in Plymouth because citizens were "in the streets at play, openly, some pitching the barr and some stoolball, and such-like sports."[19] At one time or another, Massachusetts and Connecticut banned dice, cards, quoits, bowls, and ninepins. A Puritan order of 6 April 1644 banned all maypoles in Massachusetts, following the lead of the Long Parliament in England.[20]

In *The Scarlet Letter,* Hawthorne draws freely on this suggestive sporting material and the historical controversies surrounding it. Chapter 21, "The New England Holiday," is a masterpiece of controlled observation of a rigid society at play as Hawthorne builds toward Arthur Dimmesdale's sermon and revelation. Hawthorne's account of the climactic Election Day festivities is a broadly panoramic account of the Puritan adaptation of the entrenched forms of Elizabethan ritual and political games.

It is fitting that Pearl, the spirit of creative play in the novel, should ask Hester in all innocence, "Why, what is this, mother? Wherefore have all the people left their work to-day? Is it a play-day for the whole world?" (228). It is but ironically it is at the behest of the state for the installation of a new governor. As Hester says, people "come from their workshops and their fields, on purpose to be happy" (229). The games and heartiness are doggedly "on purpose" in order to reinforce the secular symbol of organized state repression against freedom and creativity, and this fact frames the entire celebration. Hawthorne maintains the same bemused tone in which he described the May revelries in "The Maypole," yet now the comedy is on the green, on the pillory itself, in the heart of the Puritan town. The novel of clandestine meetings and awesome sublimation shifts at this point to a leisurely stroll by Hester and Pearl through the sunny marketplace of Boston to reveal improbable and colorful sights as Hawthorne controls the public comedy set against the background of the theocracy's power: "The Puritans compressed whatever mirth and public joy they deemed allowable to human infirmity" to "the space of a single holiday" (230). In a direct reference to the fact that English play days and ceremonies were tied to the rhythms of agricultural societies, Hawthorne wrote, "and so—as has been the custom of mankind ever since a nation was first gathered—they make merry and rejoice; as if a good and golden year were at length to pass over the poor old world!" (229). However, this "good and golden year" is not symbolized by harvests but by stately politics.

Hawthorne accurately describes the civic pageant as representative of a Puritan government which opposed masques and maypoles as both heathen and royalist. With the reign of the Stuarts, court masques in England became ever more private while London ceremony centered on the citizen-inspired Lord Mayor's Shows.[21] The functional usage of play to help install magistrates imparts "a needed dignity to the simple framework of a government. . . ." (231). Yet Hawthorne evidences his familiar nostalgia for what is absent in Boston, the more artful masquing of the Elizabethans: "no rude shows of a theatrical kind; no minstrel with his harp and legendary ballad, nor gleeman, with an ape dancing to his music. . . . All such professors of the several branches of jocularity would have been sternly repressed. . ." (231). Thus, the more richly artistic caste of the court arts is lost to the civil celebration in the New World, even as the English ornamental garden is supplanted in Governor Bellingham's courtyard by cabbages and pumpkin vines, and, more tellingly, by rose bushes and apple trees.

What is retained in Hawthorne's view is a broader, more physical democratic camaraderie on the green where "the great honest face of the people smiled" as "sports . . . such as the colonists had witnessed, and shared in, long ago, at the country fairs and on the village-greens of England" took place. As opposed to the Coliseum atrocities in *The Marble Faun,* the English history of sport is a positive legacy. Hawthorne notes, sounding both like a follower of *The King James Book of Sport* and a forerunner of Theodore Roosevelt, "It was thought well to keep [sports] alive on this new soil, for the sake of the courage and manliness that were essential in them" (231). Sport here is expressed as the more public athletic expression of the people and includes exhibitions of wrestling, buckler, and broadsword. These are only a part of the general ceremony, one that emphasizes heartiness rather than art, the body rather than the delight of the eye and the imagination. Men even playfully duel on the pillory and are stopped by "the town beadle who had no idea of permitting the majesty of the law to be violated by such an abuse of one of its consecrated places" (231–32). These athletes are the last robust Englishmen, "the offspring of sires who had known how to be merry" (232), their defection to the New World being prior to the English Civil War. For once, Hawthorne created a "useable past" for his play images. History does not overwhelm the present but rather explains it.

Sport in *The Scarlet Letter* serves not only as a bond with English tradition but as a prophecy of American western "manliness"—a pattern of athletics that would continue in a new land with need of physical fitness and rigor. Hawthorne continues the expansive imagery as he creates rollicking Spanish pirates who come ashore on the holiday much like sea-going rustic frontiersmen. Hawthorne concludes, in the deadpan tone of a Southwestern Humorist, with a party of Indians in "savage finery" with "countenances of inflexible gravity" to match the Puritan fathers. "To combine mirthful recreation with solemnity" was the goal of the Election Day occasion, fusing community athletic participation in spectacle with the state's spectacle, in effect, to dance around the stiff, spare pole of the magistrate's power. Hawthorne declares that the generation succeeding the generation in the novel wore "the blackest shade of Puritanism," and the play spirit was lost in New England, perhaps permanently. Hawthorne in 1850 both identified an uneasiness toward the play spirit in Puritan culture and suggested it would be a continuing condition in an American society that has traditionally and stubbornly refused to sanction play as an activity with intrinsic value.

Dimmesdale leaves the Election Day procession which "summoned him onward—onward to the festival! . . ." (252). He is claimed in Hawthorne's perennial pattern of play when his manic confession and death occur on the pillory (Dimmesdale's personal sarcophagus) and replace the wrestling and hearty sports of the holiday that had preceded his spectacle in this Puritan "arena." Sports on the pillory resemble the dancers' play on the Roman "pleasure ground" in *The Marble Faun*. In each case, the arena is reclaimed for suffering and death by Hawthorne. The English Green cannot survive the intrusion of sexual guilt and revelation in Puritan New England.

THE SCARLET LETTER:
HESTER AND PEARL IN PLAY AND FREEDOM

Hawthorne is for once direct in championing the spirit of play when he intricately weaves the allegorical threads of Election Day sport with the symbols of Hester and Pearl's free play. The allegory and symbolism are nominally in a pattern conforming to what Charles Feidelson has labelled a "noncommittal parallelism" in Hawthorne's work where the real is set against fancy.[22] However, the communal festivities and individual spontaneity do explicitly converge through Hawthorne's grouping of scenes and similarities in language: "The persons now in the market-place of Boston had not been born to an inheritance of Puritan gloom. They were native Englishmen whose fathers had lived in the sunny richness of the Elizabethan epoch" and "had they followed their hereditary taste, the New England settlers would have illustrated all events of public importance by bonfires, banquets, pageantries, and processions." The key passage occurs when Hawthorne adds, "Nor would it have been impracticable, in the observances of majestic ceremonies, to combine mirthful recreation with solemnity. . . ." Election Day sport is, then, a "grotesque and brilliant embroidery to the great robe of state . . ." (230), standing in relation to Election Day as the festive day stands in relation to the state. This sport embroidery is an exact parallel to Hester's personal creativity in embroidering her gaudy border around the Scarlet Letter, the "specimen of her delicate and imaginative skill." The grotesque embroidery of the "A" is to the "A" as the "A" is to Hester's body. Her creative play personalizes the individual sign of disorder, society's signature, on which she bestows a freedom by her needle. The parallel groupings of Election Day sport / Election Day / State and of embroidery / "A" / Hester's body are public and private related elements of play, symbolic artifact, and host organism. Her needlework is coveted by everyone in the colony of rank and wealth. The decoration is on baby clothes, on burial garments, on everything except bridal dresses! Hester has given birth to Pearl and clothes her in brilliant motley. Her needlework is an infinitely repeatable creative rite.

Hawthorne had prefigured Hester Prynne in "Endicott and the Red Cross" (1838) when he described a young Puritan woman "whose doom it was to wear the letter A": "Sporting with her infamy, [she] had embroidered the fatal token in scarlet cloth." "Sporting with infamy" clearly establishes the playful quality of the embroidery and foreshadows the Trevi Fountain "sporting by itself in the moonshine, and compelling all the elaborate trivialities of art to assume a natural aspect, in accordance with its own powerful simplicity" (*MF*, 145). If Hester's relation to the embroidered "A" was an exact parallel to Election Day's relation to the Puritan state, there is, in her relation to the "untameable water" in the Trevi Fountain, an aesthetic parallel to match the political one. Hester is to the "A" as the water is to the Trevi Fountain. Both the "A" and the artfully arranged rock formation are "artificial fantasies" as ingenious "as human skill had ever contrived" (*MF*, 144). The "A" and the rock are "elaborate devices" (*MF*, 145), the one for punishment, the other for aesthetic pleasure. Yet these artifacts are taken toward the "powerful simplicity" (*MF*, 145) which only the most compelling art produces as Hester stands closest to free-flowing nature in her role as artist.[23] Hester's embroidery is improvisational commentary, the illuminated text both drawing greater attention to the symbol and mastering it through personal signature. Its allusiveness confers freedom while allowing expression conveying the separateness of play itself.

When Hawthorne finds the worn and faded letter in the Salem Custom House, it "gives evidence of a now forgotten art" (31), that of expert needle-work. On Election Day, Hawthorne comments, "the generation next to the earliest emigrants" had "so darkened the national visage" (231) that all sense of Elizabethan play spirit was lost. He concludes, "We have yet to learn again the forgotten art of gayety" (231). The twin "forgotten arts" are a communal ritual that momentarily expresses the usually repressive symbols of society, and Hester's art that staves off the complete authoritarian control of that society.

Even Hester's inscrutable and serene return to her cottage at the conclusion of the novel may be interpreted through the "embroidery" image. Edgar Dryden conceives of Hawthorne's "dialectic of enchantment and disenchantment" (examined in the context of play and sport in this chapter) as replaced by "the metaphor of the web of fiction" in which "narrative or story is the product of will and desire. . . ." This web is a "series of circumferences linked by sensitive strands to a structuring and originating center." This web "does not represent some universal order but has been designed to meet the dark purposes of the creature that has produced it."[24] Viewing this "original ground" to be the center of the web sought by the heroes of Hawthorne's last fragmentary romances, Dryden nonetheless fails to apply his insight to Hester's condition. Surely this web can be seen in Hester's role as she has embroidered a fate around that compelling center of the web, in this case, the Puritan dispensation upon her. The dispensation pulls her back *to* her place in the society as the good martyr where she ministers to the spirit as well as the body. Puritanism is the "structuring and originating center." Hester has spun the web; it has met her purposes but she cannot delimit it. "Embroidery" as art allows her the freedom to move within the web but not to move out of the web. Finally, the cottage is her place of creation, her center; if as Dryden suggests, for Hawthorne, "the possibility of story" is precluded without the web, then Hawthorne had to draw Hester back to New England to conclude her tale for "here had been her sin; here her sorrow; and here was yet to be her penitence" (*SL,* 263). Embroidery as play is not ultimate freedom for Hester because it must connect to a core or be unanchored and meaningless. Her Fall which solidified the core of the web holds her. The play of her needle is a brave gesture which saves her within the circumference of her plight, but that is all.

Pearl is a living symbol of the "A" as is her mother but she is a child of dazzling freedom, not caught in any web or stricture of society until the end of the novel. She is as close to an ahuman sprite as Hawthorne repeatedly tells us she is, and in his mind her play is an almost pure blend of art and nature, enabling him to write of her without reference to the decline and defeat of transitory play. Pearl projects dreams and games in the free play of the child's imagination. She is befuddled by the Puritan children at their comically hateful games; the "little urchins" want to fling mud at Hester and Pearl but Pearl shoos them away. Indeed, "the spell of life went forth from her ever creative spirit, and communicated itself to a thousand objects, as a torch kindles a flame wherever it may be applied" (95); "the unlikeliest materials, a stick, a bunch of rags, a flower were the puppets of Pearl's witchcraft . . ." (95). Her imagination "was like nothing so much as the phantasmagoric play of the Northern lights. . . . the mere exercise of the fancy, . . . and the sportiveness of a growing mind . . ." (95): we see her in the full flower of her "early joys," which are unlike the Maypole revellers' "systematic gaiety." Since she obviously had a "dearth of human playmates," she was "thrown more upon the visionary throng which she created" (95). Her child's play is similar to the play of Hester's needle, a creative response to isolation by the acts of a fearful society.

Pearl is explicitly a child of the masque and the May. At his ornate mansion, ex-Governor Bellingham exclaims over Pearl, "I profess I have never seen the like, since my days of vanity, in old King James's time, when I was wont to esteem it a high favor to be admitted to a court mask!" (109). He remembers, "There used to be a swarm of these small apparitions, in holiday-time; and we called them children of the Lord of Misrule" (109), the master of ceremonies at the Christmas revels in the great English halls. Hawthorne carefully points out that Bellingham no longer countenances his "days of vanity" at the royal holiday festivities. In their latter observances these activities were expressly advanced as a show of Stuart power and consolidation during the reign of James I. The court masques had a welter of associations. They were perceived as the vestiges of heathen rites and Roman Bacchanals extant in Britain before Pope Gregory's missionaries brought Christianity to the islands in 597. The Renaissance masque was a hymn to the power and grace of the Christian king. The English Puritans violently opposed the Christmas and May traditions, which were linked together as celebrations of fertility and rebirth.[25] Hawthorne showed his grasp of the history of Royalist and Puritan conflicts over holiday play when he deftly fused in America the tripartite associations of paganism, Christian authority, and politics in Pearl's encounter with Bellingham: the May child identified with Christmas and the Lord of Misrule by the symbol of the Puritan theocracy.

Pearl's association with May observances is clear and unmistakable. When Hester leaves the prison in June with infant Pearl in her arms, the child is "a baby of some three months old" (52) and was thus conceived in May-June of the preceding year in the forest. While Hester and Dimmesdale watch Pearl at brookside in the forest, Hester exclaims, "But how strangely beautiful she looks, with those wild flowers in her hair! It is as if one of the fairies, whom we left in our dear old England, had decked her out to meet us" (206). Pearl's role is that of Christmas and May child, bedecked by English fairies. She, too, takes pleasure in embroidery, as when, in an expression of pure delight, she wonders at the intricately decorated front of Bellingham's mansion "and imperatively required that the whole breadth of sunshine should be stripped off its front, and given her to play with" (103).[26] Mercurial, inventive Pearl stands immune to the "blackest visage" and has forgotten no arts. She preserves the legacy of her mother's artistic spirit and her independence.

Pearl sees art as a "breadth of sunshine." Her joy is direct and spontaneous and the link between art and nature is forthright and unmediated by human catastrophe. The closest to a natural force among Hawthorne's characters, Pearl is the most perfect human approximation to Hawthorne's most tantalizing play image, the water of the Trevi Fountain. Pearl *is* the "untameable water, sporting by [her]self . . . [in] powerful simplicity" (*MF*, 145). But finally, Pearl plays because there is no choice. She has no human family, no center. She is only born into a family at the center of the web—the pillory and scaffold—when she stands freely with her father and mother as Dimmesdale reveals the truth and expires. Pearl's play, like Hester's, comes about because she is forced beyond the community—outside the continuing scrutiny of the world of the Fall, outside personal history, and outside any restrictions on creativity. To survive, she generates her play until she is recalled to human suffering.

For Hawthorne, play was suggestive, fascinating, and imaginative, but never dominant. He was the first great American writer to firmly sense play as a response to the human need to move out of the tormented self.

However, he limited his perception of play by defining it in opposition to reality and the sacred as Huizinga and Caillois would by isolating play rather than seeing it as a vital circuit of life. Those of his characters who would "play," such as Coverdale, Zenobia, Donatello, and Kenyon, are destroyed or remain wounded and confused. Hawthorne's irony and firm sense of the primacy of the Fall overturned all the play emblems which were powerful, disruptive, but ultimately superseded in the narratives. He did not believe play inherently ordered real life in any lasting sense, except in the long battle for survival of Hester and Pearl. He did not see his characters approaching mysteries of sensuality or sacrality through play but rather desperately staving off the claims of these forces. Play could not drive toward a sacred center for that center was a dark sin. There is, finally, in Hawthorne, a bemused sadness cloaked in manipulative irony that play cannot accomplish more than it does, a view that Hawthorne perhaps extrapolated from his deepest misgivings about art. The "powerful simplicity" of the Trevi Fountain could not survive the gaze of the ironic romancer.

Hawthorne's sense of play's power was strong but his sense of play's limits was profound. What sets him apart from American fiction's other master sportsmen and players, Hemingway and Faulkner, is that while Hemingway placed great trust in the power of competition and Faulkner in the power of play to motivate and sustain their characters, Hawthorne could not finally countenance that power to the same degree. He identified forces that to him were obdurate: the Fall, history (both collective and personal), and conventional art. The dimension of his arena remained the sarcophagus lid. The author/narrator held uneasy dominion there, a most Puritanical player whose repeated scenes of *ilinx-mimicry* were always followed by sober emotional accounting that tallied massively real fates.

CHAPTER TWO
Sport and Society

HAWTHORNE BROODED over the manifestations of the play spirit in art and literature, in religious and civil ceremony, and in ancient as well as in modern history. He measured play's role in the projection of individual personality and in the individual's battle to hold or regain innocence in a fallen world. Yet what he lacked was a real sense of the part play and sport might have in defining a society of the American present and future. Furthermore, his play was solely of the head and heart. Except for sports on the green in *The Scarlet Letter* and assorted anarchic experiences in pageantry, physical activity in play and sport were unknown to his characters. Representation in *mimicry* and the playing of roles in ritual were his clearest visions of play.

While Hawthorne took play imagery to real depth, he wrote no fictional commentary on play, game, and sport in a developing America. While Hawthorne staged delicate performances, Irving, Cooper, and Thoreau produced records of secular society in which play and sport grew out of everyday life and commented on the tenor of that life. They drew on the rituals of hunting and frontier sport and on the power and wonder of nature. They created a living record of sporting pastimes that questioned the goals and means of collective American industry and purpose and highlighted their dilemmas: for Irving, how to preserve the freedom and uncertainty of play within an organized society which does not heed these play elements; for Cooper and Thoreau, how to underscore the integrity of the sportsman and define his stature as idealistic spokesman for conscience and conservation. For these authors, sport was as it would become for later generations of writers—part of a social record of our preferences and cultural contradictions.

IRVING: HAPPY VALLEY

Three distinct forms of play interested Irving. He was captivated by the antiquated English holiday games, by the dreams and fantasy of German superstition tales, and by the pastimes of Dutch burghers in the Hudson River Valley. Play is a recurring understructure to his chronicles of an innocent eighteenth-century society and reiterates the timelessness of both country-house England and old Dutch New York. Irving used many words and phrases almost interchangeably, such as "fight," "frolic," "sports," "playthings," "all kinds of rough wild expeditions," as well as long lists of games to describe an environment in the Valley. He was committed to describing the play and sport of the past but he raised questions about the American present and future through that description.

Irving's concerns with ritual observances, individual and psychological manifestations of the play spirit, and with "manly" sport coincide with Hawthorne's subjects: Irving's May and Christmas games with Hawthorne's May and Election Day play; Irving's haunting of Rip and Ichabod with Hawthorne's power of creative play for Hester and Pearl; and Irving's frontier athletes Brom Bones and Dolph Heyliger with Hawthorne's hearty contestants on Boston Common. But where Hawthorne illuminated Puritan history through play, giving rootedness and complexity to his New England through the ironies surrounding the uneasy acceptance of Elizabethan ceremony, Irving was content to depict the drama of play as an element of social cohesion in a largely vanished and decorative England, or, alternately, as personal disruption among the Dutch burghers in the Hudson River Valley.

Irving's antiquarian narrator of *Bracebridge Hall*, Geoffrey Crayon, relates the revival of holiday customs under the direction of Squire Bracebridge and maintains a popular nineteenth-century stance toward such occasions when he laments their decay and the passing of their true spirit. The lack of vital observation of holidays had been the target of an elegant criticism in the reign of James I through the masques and antimasques of Ben Jonson and the poems of Robert Herrick.[1] Irving depicted the sport and rites of the English squirearchy but did not transfer its forms to the New World as had Hawthorne, who may well have had his interest piqued by Irving's accounts.[2] Irving did not allude to the religious and political issues involved as would Hawthorne. He conveyed the ordered scene in its pleasing gentility and nostalgic picturesqueness. He wrote in the Preface to *The Sketch Book* that he had studied countries "with the sauntering gaze with which humble lovers of the picturesque stroll from the window of one print-shop to another."[3] As his epigraph from Burton's *Anatomy of Melancholy* states, Crayon is "a mere spectator" of men in the eighteenth-century tradition of "Spectator." He watches men "and how they play their parts" "as from a common theatre or scene." The Christmas and May games were a perfect "common theatre" for Geoffrey Crayon, who delighted in recording the actors and actresses "playing their parts."

In "Christmas Eve," Crayon reports that Squire Bracebridge's father "consulted old books for precedent and authority for every 'merrie disport' " but the good squire is finally himself, like Crayon, just a tame revivalist carrying on ceremony that has outlived its vitality. Mourning "the deplorable decay of the [Christmas] games and amusements" (292), he has his servants keep up "the old Yule games of hoodman blind, shoe the wild mare, hot cockles, steal the white loaf, bob apple, and snap-dragon" (267). His main hall is dominated by "an enormous pair of antlers," the branches of which served "as hooks on which to suspend hats, whips, and spurs" while "in the corners of the apartment we're fowling-pieces, fishing rods, and other sporting implements" (269). The Squire's son, who plays the Lord of Misrule on Christmas Day, explains that his "whole stock of erudition" comes from some half-dozen sporting books.[4]

In *Bracebridge Hall*'s May festivities, Irving does little more than stipulate through the Squire his own intent in "surrounding [the Squire] with agreeable associations and making a little world of poetry about him" ("May Day Customs," p. 41). On the appointed day, gymnastic contests are held, country lads engage in a melee on the green, and schoolmaster Slingsby is Lord of Misrule during spirited dancing. The mood is melancholy as the Squire bewails "the total decline of old May Day" (40). Irving concludes whimsically on his own indulgence as "spectator" when he admits, "little is heard of May-day at present, except from the lamentations of authors, who sigh after it" (44). A recorder of fashionably archaic custom, Irving had a clear idea that play was a civilized cultural activity and, when tied to ritual observance, identified and ordered a traditional scene. However, his play contained no terrors or potential traps as Hawthorne would identify in *The Blithedale Romance* through Miles Coverdale, a similarly complacent but more neurotic and troubled narrator than Geoffrey Crayon. Such candid assessment of play did not interest Irving. The more a playful rite or interlude belonged to the safe past, the more idealized it became for him and the more carefully he described it.

Irving could not identify a consistent body of play lore in the America of 1820. Only in his two great tales does he write "as if" his settings had real antiquity, "as if" America had a past,[5] but he does so with pointed reference to his own era as well. There are several strong threads of play woven into the tales. In "Rip" and "Sleepy Hollow," the central dream and nightmare incidents have their sources in the German tales as Irving freely admitted.[6] "Rip" is dominated by a supernatural play of the gods while "Sleepy Hollow" has a simulated prank, a great haunting that disorients Ichabod Crane. These elements from myth and ghost stories are fanciful and more traditional while each tale also has an emphasis on more homely American images of play and sport. Rip is the town idler, the boy who never grew up who lives in perpetual childhood. Brom Bones is the braggart athlete of the taverns and horse races. Rip plays his life away, unmindful of responsibility and change. Brom is a healthy competitor who plays to win; he knows how to project a haunting when the stakes are the Van Tassel daughter and farm. In each tale, an American prototype is born in specific reference to play and sport: the perennial American innocent in flight from domesticity and adulthood and the vital young American frontier "sport."

The play in "Rip" and "Sleepy Hollow" blends early American sporting custom with fanciful and ahistorical occurrence. Irving's Dutch Hudson River Valley was historical fantasy reshaped by the relaxed storyteller. The country comedy of Ichabod Crane, the quilting frolic, and the Van Winkles' domestic strife are all Irving's creation of local color and lore from the Dutch legends he had absorbed since he was seventeen years old in 1800 and first tramped the farms and valleys around Tarrytown. Sport and recreation in the middle colonies were influenced primarily by a combination of the religious restraints and prohibitions of the New England colonies and the freer sporting culture of the plantation South. In the cities of Baltimore, Philadelphia, and New York, prerevolutionary revellers reported varieties of loosely organized city sports such as marbles, swimming, fishing, and running. The agricultural society of the region also heavily influenced amusements as frolics, quilting bees, corn huskings, and barn raisings dominated the social life of the New York and Pennsylvania Dutch. Bowling and nine-pins were the most frequently asserted sporting pastimes in pre-Revolutionary Dutch New York, and Irving gave these sports a mythical significance in "Rip."

In both of Irving's great tales, a stasis deeply related to the homely play is posited against enormous energy and national change. In "Rip," the childlike, innocent idler remains muddled and mystified as the American nation is born. In "Sleepy Hollow," "populations, manners, and customs remain fixed; while the great torrent of migration and improvement . . . sweeps by them unobserved." The abundant Van Tassel farm will continue untouched by time presided over by Brom, the innocent prankster after Ichabod flees toward success in the city. The *ilinx* experience dominates both tales, in the Hendrik Hudson dream and twenty-year sleep as well as in the pursuit by the terrible Headless Hessian. Rip is paralyzed and Ichabod maddened in a reverie, in a whirling and dizzying loss of self. A new reality takes hold of them for the duration of the fantasy, Rip by supernatural play, both stately and comic, and Ichabod by fantasy orchestrated by Brom Bones who simulates a horrifying, uncertain environment in *mimicry*.

"Rip" and "Sleepy Hollow" are written in what has been called "sportive gothic" with their genial, humorous presentation of potential terror and the fantastic.[7] The control of this "sportive gothic" has a source in the repeated play imagery that blends the fanciful and the homely. Rip, the town idler, is just the man to witness the bewildering high ritual play of the bowlers in the mountains. Although Rip had never fit in with the adult life of the town, "the children of the village . . . would shout with joy whenever he approached. He assisted at their sports, made their playthings, taught them to fly kites and shoot marbles, and told them long stories of ghosts, witches, and Indians." Rip "was a foremost man at all country frolics for husking Indian corn." Even so, when he enters his fantasy sojourn with the ghostly bowlers in the mountains, he can make nothing of their rites. The spectral players roll out their balls in "profound silence" in a "hollow like a small amphitheater, surrounded by perpendicular precipices," a natural play arena set apart from the world. Here Rip becomes Irving's "spectator" and watches a mysterious playlet or homely masque in mime. He witnesses rites which may stand for ancient myths of the secrets of nature as described in Norse sagas but which have no meaning for him whatsoever.

The dwarf bowlers are, in Philip Young's terms, aged little boys playing games, who have "grown old but not up,"[8] missing an adult stage as Rip himself has turned it aside. Although Rip is in touch with the play spirit, first in his own childlike existence and then in the mountains, he cannot decipher the meaning. Irving suggests that post-Revolutionary America has little use for Rip's idleness and Rip cannot bring to consciousness what he has seen. Fink remarks that "play is a strange oasis" where we "sense the eternal pulse of the world,"[9] and Rip's play experience underscores this sensation. But his failure to comprehend his experience cancels out the potentially most powerful and primal play ritual in American fiction as Irving's desire for a more pedestrian comic denouement takes precedence.

Homely and fanciful play imagery likewise inform "Sleepy Hollow" from the outset. Diedrich Knickerbocker tells the reader that his first vision of Sleepy Hollow, "one of the quietest places in the whole world," was on his first exploit in squirrel-shooting" (play in nature), while he also exclaims that the Hollow may have been bewitched by a German doctor or an old Indian chief whose "spell over the minds of the people" causes them "to walk in a continual reverie" (supernatural play). Although Ichabod as an industrious Yankee is as diligent and tireless as Rip is indolent, he, too, lives amidst children. As a teacher he is the "companion and playmate of the larger boys." He himself listens to ghost stories of old Dutch wives and then regales them with "anecdotes of witchcraft" much as Rip had told children "long stories" of ghosts and witches. Although Ichabod assimilates these stories of witchcraft, nothing prepares him for his great fright but rather his childlike imagination, buttressed "with large extracts from his invaluable author, Cotton Mather," sets him up for the prank of Brom Bones. Ichabod is a descendant of the Puritan children in *The Scarlet Letter* "scaring one another with freaks of imitative witchcraft" (*The Scarlet Letter*, 94).

Contrasted with the physically grotesque Ichabod Crane, Brom Bones is "a burly, roaring roystering blade," "the hero of the country round" with "a bluff but not unpleasant countenance."[10] He was "famed for great knowledge and skill in horsemanship, being as dexterous on horseback as a Tartar. He was foremost at all races and cockfights" and "always ready for either a fight or a frolic." Verbally dexterous as well, he is a skilled storyteller who relates his tall-tale duel with the Headless Hessian at the Van Tassel quilting frolic. Irving blankets all areas of play and contests in his description of Brom Bones, a man's man in brawls but one who can compete successfully for the hand of rosy-cheeked Katrina and the Van Tassel farm. Brom Bones is a genial bad-good boy, the town swell whose proficiency at games and sports give him his local stature, the first American sports hero to get the girl.[11]

In each tale, the play is the pivot without which there would be no tale. The dreams and pranks are simulated experiences of vertigo in the *mimicry-ilinx* pattern. In "Rip," the supernatural dream of play by the childlike player is wondrous but airy and insubstantial, and it bursts before the reality of the new American town. Rip returns innocent but bewildered. In "Sleepy Hollow," Brom Bones' athleticism and trickster's fantasy drive Ichabod Crane from Happy Valley forever. Brom wins Katrina and the farm and life continues undisturbed. If "Rip" and "Sleepy Hollow" do point to issues of national self-definition and character, as critics have repeatedly suggested, the play spirit dominating the ritual at the core of each tale works to assert the fantastic and timeless that pull America back from development and organization. The childlike player and the hearty athlete achieve the same stasis. As in Hawthorne's fiction, play in Irving's tales is finally not serious enough to effect any lasting change in serious affairs but is posited as an alternative life for Irving's perennial players who are innocent in ways uncomplicated by Hawthorne's irony and postlapsarian fatalism.

COOPER: CORRECT CONDUCT IN NATURE

Hawthorne and Irving in their regional tales of Puritan New England and Dutch New York cast play into the realm of nostalgia for lost traditions and suggested we as a nation no longer had knowledge of playful spontaneity or ritual. Cooper and Thoreau depicted a measured, sober sporting activity that was not instinctive or free but rational and sustaining. They viewed sport as a way to begin to define distinctly American virtue through attitudes toward sport, the use of the land, and the growth of the spirit. Chapters 16–24 in *The Pioneers* are sections centered on settlement sporting activity that thoroughly describe Templeton's values set against Natty's wisdom and opinions about physical prowess and the correctness of its application. Cooper expertly dramatized the debate between individual and collective responsibilities as America settled and developed its lands. In "Higher Laws" in *Walden,* Thoreau saw the solitary pastimes of hunting and fishing as those which begin to educate the whole man and begin his ascent toward the sensibility of the naturalist.

Cooper confronted the question of how competence in the hunt and woodslore could be elevated to principles of correct conduct. These principles were to be harmonious with natural law, which clashed with the man-made laws of civilization. Sporting scenes enabled Cooper to dramatize the conflict between the settlers encroaching upon the continent and the sanctity of open land. Much has been written about Natty Bumppo as the classical western hero—autonomous, unique, and outside his society, yet able to inform society of proper modes of conduct.[12] The Western, based on Cooper's conception, traditionally focused on the debate over land and land resources. This clash is the central concern of *The Pioneers*, but for Cooper in 1823 the issues were not railroads or sheep or cattle, as in later Westerns. Cooper identified the more general problem of productivity and resultant despoliation of resources, and his central sporting scenes in *The Pioneers* dramatized the settlement's attitude toward hunting and the kill.

The hunter was an American prototype already fading into popular lore by the time Cooper came to write his Leatherstocking Tales. The hunter was a necessary figure, the man who, as explorer and colonizer, opened the wilderness for domestic life. But his function was transitional, his role impermanent. Crevecoeur's *Letters from an American Farmer* (1782), recognized as the most incisive definition of a free American husbandryman in the New World, was a catalogue of democratic imperatives and prescient statements about the emerging American character. Crevecoeur foresaw that the "hitherto barbarous country" would be transformed "into a fine, fertile, well-regulated district." However, he also warned that "in all societies there are off-casts; this impure part serves as our precursors or pioneers." Crevecoeur wrote that by constant use of the gun to defend their property, these outcasts became professed hunters and "once hunters, farewell to the plough." Crevecoeur concluded, "the unlimited freedom of the woods" is extremely dangerous and may result in a primitive man of no use to an emerging society, "a mongrel breed, half-civilised and half-savage."[13]

Natty Bumppo, American fiction's first great mythical hunter, proved to be the most stylized rejoinder to Crevecoeur's misgivings. He was certainly intransigent toward the "plough" and "well-regulated districts"; however, at the same time, Natty held virtues that did not take their legitimatization from institutions but from direct intuition. He was a hunter more virtuous than farmers or lawmakers. Cooper's prototype for Natty was Daniel Boone (1734–1820), the first wilderness hero to become a popular national figure. By 1790, Boone's trail-blazing years in the Kentucky-Tennessee territory were over. Portrayed as a middle-aged wanderer unable to hold land, he was nonetheless a fit spokesman and symbol for the frontier, both in his virile prime as Indian fighter and then as aging hunter pushed further along by the developing settlements.[14]

Boone's biographers stressed that Boone had stood above the hunters, "that wretched class of men who are so often the preliminaries of civilization"[15] as Crevecoeur might have ruefully described them. Boone had the best of civilized and wild attributes and abilities: "the man who could see and find and do all that the savage could, and beyond him had the arts and wisdom of the white man" (87). The stock description of Boone in his thirties was of the athletic hero who possessed "strength to his frame" by "exercise and vigorous employment" and was "robust, clean-limbed and athletic, fitted by his habit and temperament, and by his physique for endurance—a bright eye, and a calm determination in his manner" (72). Yet Boone's achievements are carefully separated from any play spirit. He was a serious family man who tramped 300 miles into the wilderness with five other families to settle Boonesboro in August 1775. Even if Boone has all the attributes of the athlete, "it is of little importance to narrate the incidents of the amusement or support he received from the woods" (303). A sport is no endeavor in which to achieve a reputation; the man who founded Kentucky had been engaged in "a better enterprise than the chase" (303). No sport in society can be conceived by Boone's chroniclers for a landscape as empty as the Kentucky wilderness.

Boone is no sportsman but rather a throwback to a more primitive time when physical skills, courage, and judgment were used for subsistence killing or preparation for war, for tribal roles where "play" is in eclipse. Certainly the young Natty Bumppo of *The Deerslayer* (1841) shades very close to the Boone of the wilderness in the 1750s. Only in the last novels of the Leatherstocking cycle did Cooper confront the youthful Adamic hero whom he drove back in time to early manhood.[16] This stark, threatening world of Indian attacks, massacres, imprisonments, and escapes includes no sport or celebration. Natty's physical prowess, endurance, and ability to make quick correct decisions are individual attributes displayed in his fight for survival. Even then, in the harsher, presettlement forest, young Natty's attitudes were forming around correct conduct in the hunt and the kill. He told Hurry Harry March, "I am no trapper, Hurry—I live by the rifle."[17] Natty is a trader but literally has a law for his killing: "I never offer a skin that has not a hole in its head besides them which natur' made to see with or breathe through" (7). Natty has a host of personal codes: he won't scalp; at the outset of the novel he had never taken the life of a "fellow-creatur'" but he said he was "ready to enlist in any enterprise that's not agin a white man's lawful gifts" (75). That "law" is a "gift" from a god watching over nature. Natty tells Judith Hutter that the whole earth is "a temple of the lord to such as have the right mind" (269); "all is contradiction in the settlements, while all is concord in the woods" (269).

In *The Pioneers,* two decades before *The Deerslayer,* Cooper had eloquently dramatized the "contradiction" and "concord" through veteran Natty's sporting example and commentary. Cooper first recreated the historical Boone as the aging woodsman of vast experience and crowned him philosopher instead of progenitor, the most immediately available mythic role for Boone three years after his death at 86. Natty in *The Pioneers* is at intervals noble and calm, but just as often bewildered and angry or foolish in a new world he cannot tolerate. These vacillations could be ascribed to Cooper's notoriously inconsistent narration. However, in essence, what Cooper has done in *The Pioneers* is to continue and to widen in scope Irving's vision at the conclusion of "Rip Van Winkle" of a new American village in a national state. Templeton (Cooperstown), although not precisely in Irving country, is further Northwest, where "beautiful and thriving villages are found interspersed along the margins of the small lakes" with their "neat and comfortable farms" (9). Cooper pointedly contrasts the New York area before the Revolutionary War—"a narrow belt of country, extending for a short distance on either side of the Hudson" (10) plus Manhattan, Nassau and Staten Island, and the banks of the Mohawk "then inhabited by less than two hundred thousand souls"—with a New York now spread and "swelled to a million and a half of inhabitants" (10). Cooper states in chapter 1 that the tale of *The Pioneers* begins in 1793 when Templeton is seven years old. In effect, Cooper will show the new America after the transformation of Irving's Happy Valley. Through Natty's misgivings, he will identify the real dilemmas of the world that Rip Van Winkle returns to: rapid growth, radical change, and constraints upon the individual. The pre-Revolution Rip countered that bustling, growing world with escapist play. Natty Bumppo offers to correct Templeton's conduct through a display of higher sportsmanship.

The Pioneers was Cooper's first Leatherstocking novel and it included the most tense interaction between Natty Bumppo and organized society. Cooper portrays Templeton as ignorant of respectful sport and heedless of natural law. Natty lives at the edge of the Templeton settlement but is most often at odds with its laws and customs. The central dramatic action of *The Pioneers* concerns Natty's clash with Judge Marmaduke Temple over the killing of a deer and Natty's resultant fine, imprisonment, escape, and ultimate commitment to the wilderness in opposition to expanding civilization. The clear right of the hunter to provide for his needs is the heart of the dispute with "deer hunting season" but Cooper's drama has further specific relation to sport.

Chapters 16–24 at the heart of the book define Natty's role as caretaker of the wilderness, Judge Temple's vacillating position between developer and conservator, and Billy Kirby's economic depradations. Cooper shows settlement attitudes toward sport to be deficient, part of deficient perception in a larger sense. As R.W.B. Lewis noted, the most fundamental insights and conflicts in Cooper occur in the margins of his plots and his great gift is his ability "to transmute American experience into story," "the gift for seeing life dramatically as the measurement by conduct of institutions and the measurement by institutions of conduct."[18] The sporting interludes—shooting the Christmas turkey, the pigeon shoot, and the fish kill—are a varied group of scenes that dramatically limn the theme of *The Pioneers* and let the reader see the aging Natty in action as he "measures" settlement "conduct." Marginal to the central plot though they may be, these scenes show Natty interacting with the settlement more than at any other juncture in the novel. They are not integral to the central romance and history but they underpin Cooper's primary subject: developing attitudes toward the land.

Shooting the Christmas turkey, the sporting scene in chapter 17, is prefaced by an inscription from Walter Scott, "I guess by all this quaint array/The burghers hold their sports to-day." Cooper sets this chapter as a light interlude that burlesques a tournament of knights, an Ivanhoe-like competition to win the turkey for the fair Elizabeth Temple. The "burghers" pursue "the ancient amusement of shooting the Christmas turkey" for it "is one of the few sports that the settlers of a new country seldom or never neglect to observe" (173). Cooper revives the "ancient amusements" of Christmas games as did Irving through Squire Bracebridge, but Cooper immediately expands the imaginative framework of the sketch: shooting the Christmas turkey (a suitably American bird) "was connected with the daily practices of a people who often laid aside the axe or the scythe to seize the rifle, as the deer glided through the forest they were felling, or the bear entered their rough meadows to scent the air of a clearing, and to scan with a look of sagacity, the progress of the invader" (173–74). The axe and scythe set against the rifle define Crevecoeur's image of farmer-hunter conflict; but Cooper makes it clear that sport is expressly connected with hard work in the settlements and that the implements for clearing the land may give way to implements that provide meat and hides and may also be used for sport without clash or contradiction.

Yet the scene also shows Natty at his most trivial for he allows himself to be part of Templeton's competition and thereby loses his perspective. Cooper draws him as a faithful yeoman transformed into a comic aging champion who is persuaded by Elizabeth Temple to enter the turkey-shoot contest. She feels concern for the woods trio of Natty, old John Mohegan, and the young disguised Oliver Edwards, portrayed here as sad loiterers, tramps on the periphery of the settlement with only one shot left in Natty's rifle and no money to buy more powder. Elizabeth dubs Natty "Sir Leatherstocking" and gives him the honor of trying her "chance for a bird." Natty "seemed pleased with the frank address of the young and beauteous Elizabeth, who had so singularly interested him with such a commission . . ." (172), but then he grumbles his way through the sport with objections and arguments about rules. He is made to look foolish and, in effect, loses control by his sporting participation. Economics and haggling over the price of birds control the turkey shoot, which is presided over by a wily free Negro. A large crowd of boys and men watches the spectacle, "listening eagerly to the boastful stories of skill that had been exhibited on former occasions" (174).

In a foreshadowing of Natty's battle with Judge Temple over the killing of the deer, Natty complains about payment of one shilling to shoot, but the pompous Richard Jones, newly appointed "High Sheriff," makes Natty play by the settlement's rules. Natty is full of talk about the old days in Dutch settlements when he "won the powder-horn, three bars of lead, and a pound of as good powder as ever flashed in pan" (179); he complains that he cannot find any good Indian flint: "it's ten to one but they will be all covered up with the plough" (181). The burlesque moves to its conclusion. Natty stops being the old comic sourdough long enough to hit the turkey with one shot and, as Sir Leatherstocking, drops the turkey at the feet of Elizabeth Temple to end his role as her agent in her game of amusement that plays off Richard Jones against Oliver Edwards. Cooper scales Natty down into a falsely merry old-timer, part of the "quaint array" where he will never truly belong. The sporting antics of "shooting the Christmas turkey" will yield no sustaining ritual. Such Christmas sport does not show Natty at best advantage, not in skill, experience, or wisdom.

Natty's rival in the Christmas turkey shoot is the Bunyanesque woodchopper, Billy Kirby, whose greatest skill is levelling forests. Over and over again in *The Pioneers*, Cooper has Natty and Billy Kirby square off in debate and competition. In "Sleepy Hollow," Irving created Brom Bones with a "Herculean frame," "great powers of limb," and "a mingled air of fun and arrogance," who was "always ready for either a fight or frolic," and who possessed "more mischief than ill will." But Irving gave him no economic relation to the Hollow while Cooper made Billy Kirby not only a sporting hero but also an aggressive spokesman for economic expansion and rape of the land. As Brom Bones had "great knowledge and skill in horsemanship" and was "foremost at all races and cockfights," Billy Kirby was the "rider of scrub-races, the bully of cock-fights, and not infrequently the hero of such sports as the one in hand" (176). Billy Kirby, however, is a genial ravager of nature. While he blusters that he will turn his "back to no man in the Otsego Hills, for chopping and logging" (208), Judge Temple censures him for making dreadful wounds in the trees to draw out the maple sap for his maple syrup trade. Billy answers in a grimly humorous agrarian maxim, "I call no country much improved, that is pretty well covered with trees" (212). He even sings a lusty ballad about the destruction of trees which Cooper juxtaposes with chapter 20's inscription from Byron.

Thus, Billy Kirby is both comic woodchopper and articulator of Templeton's most extreme opinion about necessary encroachment into the wilderness. During the pigeon shoot, he downs one bird after another and serves as spokesman for the farmers who dislike what the pigeons do to their crops. Yet within this scene in chapter 22, Natty asserts his moral authority in commenting on the slaughter and on correct attitudes toward sport. Cooper's account of Templeton's frenzy during the shoot is one of the graphic written records of the massacre of millions upon millions of the now-extinct passenger pigeons in North America. The so-called civilized spectacle draws Cooper's ire: "Horses were loaded with the dead, and after this first burst of sporting, the shooting of pigeons became a business . . ." (231). Judge Temple vacillates as usual and remarks, "Full one half of those that have fallen are yet alive; and I think it is time to end the sport, if sport it be" (231), whereupon Sheriff Richard Jones exults, "Sport! it is princely sport! There are some thousands of blue-coated boys on the ground, so that every old woman in the village may have pot-pie for the asking!" (231). The success of the sport is determined by its immediate utility for the kettle. Templeton thus either trivializes sport as in "shooting the Christmas turkey" or justifies a delight in sport because of the economic reward.

Natty counters these views and activity as an "uneasy spectator." For the duration of the scene, he conducts a lesson in ritual sporting observance. He is finally moved to comment when the ancient miniature cannon from the Indian Wars, heretofore fired only on the Fourth of July, is impressed back into service during the pigeon "war." Natty ruefully declares, "This comes of settling a country" (227). He "loved to see [pigeons] in the woods" but now he knows "it's only a motion to bring out all the brats in the village" (228). Cooper portrays the whole settlement—men, women, children—with rifles, pistols, and bows and arrows in the harvest of dead and dying birds. Billy Kirby loaded an old musket "and without even looking into the air, was firing and shouting as his victims fell even on his own person" (228). Natty admonishes him, "it's wicked to be shooting into flocks in this wasty manner; and none do it who know how to knock over a single bird" (228). Natty's way is to find one bird "and then I shoot him off the branches without touching the feather of another, though there might be a hundred on the same tree" (228). Then, to validate his statement, he takes Billy's challenge to fire one shot at one bird. Billy misses badly but Natty gets his bird and "the wonderful exploit was noised through the field with great rapidity, and the sportsmen gathered in, to learn the truth of the report" (229). By both word and deed, Natty establishes rules for his ritual and shows a higher sporting ethic, one that aligns skill and conservation through fair play.

This impressive demonstration of a true meaning of sport is further embellished in chapter 24 during the fish kill on Lake Otsego. Once more, led by Richard Jones and Billy Kirby, the men of Templeton gleefully net as many bass as they can on a night foray without relation to need. Again, Judge Temple wavers in his ambiguous sense of their squandering: "This is a fearful expenditure of the choicest gifts of Providence," while he muses on their quality and flavor and how fine they will be "on the meanest table in Templeton . . ." (240). In this scene Natty moves from being spokesman and adept shot to an almost mystical unity with the lake and its surroundings. While the Christmas turkey shoot imprisoned Natty in settlement customs and frivolous byplay, the pigeon shoot brought the settlement closer to Natty's own world and generated a great tension between their plunder and his warning and example in a sort of uncharted boundary arena between village and wilderness.[19] But Lake Otsego, Cooper's beloved "Glimmerglass," is Natty's own territory and on it he is in perfect balance and control, exhibiting both skill and the motions of grace.[20]

Nowhere in *The Pioneers* is Natty more the attending priest than in this sporting ritual. The approach of his canoe from across the lake is majestic and spectral. "A brilliant, though waving flame," it glides "with a motion so graceful and yet so rapid. . . . The water in front of the canoe was hardly ruffled by its passage . . ." (245). Natty is revealed in tableau, erect in the prow with a long fishing spear used as an oar, propelling the vessel not "through, but over, the water" (245). The spell of the ghostly boat is broken when the hapless Richard Jones exclaims, "Ho! Natty, is that you? Paddle in, old boy, and I'll give you a mess of fish . . ." (245).

Natty is appalled by nets full of fish. He tells the men, "I call it sinful and wasty to catch more than can be eat" (246). Reaffirming his practice of fair play, Natty states, "to me, the flesh is sweeter where the creature' has some chance for its life: for that reason, I always use a single ball . . ." (246). Backing his views with his skill, he directs his spear into the waters: "the long, dark streak of the gliding weapon, and the little bubbling vortex which followed its rapid flight, were easily to be seen"; then, "a fish of great size was transfixed by the barbed steel . . ." (250). The ritual motion is complete as one shot is perfection for Natty. The fishermen are irked by his success and blame his torch for scaring fish away from the nets. Billy Kirby once more belligerently intercedes and argues with old Benjamin about right-of-way on the lake. His hasty motions with the net cause Benjamin to plunge into the dark lake. Benjamin cannot swim. Everyone is helpless but Natty who calmly says, "I'll spear the creatur up in half the time, and no risk to anybody" (252). As a fisher of men, Natty is no less adept: the "shining tines" of his spear entwine "dexterously in the hairs of [Benjamin's] queue and the cape of his coat" (252), and Benjamin is saved while Cooper humorously plays on Natty's reputation as part Indian and scalper.

Natty Bumppo has no great personal dignity in *The Pioneers*. At times he is an old dog with a "single tusk of yellow bone" for a tooth. Often he becomes a garrulous, boring veteran with Indian war and hunting stories. He is at his best where his practical skill demonstrates his strong beliefs about correct conduct in nature, where proper sport leads to rite. Even Billy Kirby, who is deputized to bring Natty in after he defied the Judge's ruling, admires Natty's courage and skill. At the climax of the siege of Natty's fortress, Billy cheers him on, "kicking the earth with delight . . ." (404). Billy's "good-natured vanity" stemmed from his pride in "the powers of the physical man, like all who have nothing better to boast of" (308). Cooper gives Natty both the physical prowess and the insight into how it is to be used in nature. Judge Temple attempts to wean Oliver Edwards from the forest life by offering him a job in the settlement since "the unsettled life of these hunters is of vast disadvantage for temporal purposes, and it totally removes one from the influence of more sacred things'' (186).[21] Yet Natty stands up for his beliefs, his conduct, and his world, forcing Judge Temple to grudgingly sniff, "Thou hast a temperance unusual in thy class . . ." (186). Natty is not only a temperate hunter but a perfect sportsman in the rites that he himself designs and then carries out.

In wholly original ways, Cooper dramatized the idealized hunter and practical woodchopper in sporting confrontations which illuminated the central dialogue of *The Pioneers*. For Cooper, then, the real meaning of sport was neither play nor fancy nor even competition but rather ideals represented and attitudes struck and acted upon in daily life. These were serious matters which demanded careful attention in individual and community conduct.

THOREAU: THE HUNTER
AND HIGHER LAWS

If Cooper's hunter instructed the settlement on correct conduct in nature, Thoreau's overriding aim was to instruct himself. Thoreau believed that hunting and fishing in and of themselves were violent and useless without some higher purpose, even as Natty had disgustedly categorized Templeton's attitude toward the wasteful and shameful. When Thoreau scrutinized the figure of the hunter and fisherman in the "Higher Laws" chapter of *Walden*, he acknowledged his own propensity toward the hunt and admitted, "There is unquestionably this instinct in me which belongs to the lower order of creation." In contrast, "Higher Laws" is a chapter about abstention in the deepest sense, refining the mind and bodily appetites to develop a moral appetite. Thoreau recognizes, "we are all sculptors and painters, and our material is our own flesh and blood and bones. Any nobleness begins at once to refine a man's features, any meanness or sensuality to imbrute them." He concludes with a parable of a farmer desiring "to practise some new austerity, to let [his] mind descend into his body and redeem it, and treat himself with ever increasing respect." Thoreau's comments on the ways in which hunting and fishing may be seen as practical stations on a journey toward such self-knowledge strike a new chord in arguments for sport. He explicitly assigns sport a role in a moral education as preparation for other lives and other duties.

Thoreau begins by echoing Hawthorne, observing that New England "men and boys do not play so many games as they do in England" but he does not ascribe this state to vestigial Puritanism, rather to the fact that the New Englander's "hunting and fishing grounds were not limited, like the preserves of an English nobleman, but were more boundless even then those of a savage." "Almost every New England boy among my contemporaries shouldered a fowling piece between the ages of ten and fourteen," writes Thoreau, adding it was "no wonder then, that [the boy] did not oftener stay to play on the common." Thoreau's goal was to find the balance that would teach the boy and restrain what is "savage" in the sports. He saw that sportsmen may be embryo naturalists: "Fishermen, hunters, woodchoppers and others, spending their lives in the fields and woods, in a peculiar sense part of nature themselves are often in a more favorable mood for observing her, in the intervals of their pursuits than philosophers or poets, even, who approach her with expectations"; such a man, "if he has the seeds of a better life in him, he distinguishes his proper objects, as a poet or naturalist, it may be, and leaves the gun and fishpole behind." The heightened state lies in his moving out of primary physical relation to nature as predator and becoming interpreter. It is toward this potential that Thoreau states, "I am compelled to doubt if equally valuable sports are ever substituted for these." In a developing paradox, Thoreau casts sport as activity with a higher utility, a practical value refined from Cooper's premise that sporting conduct embodied attitudes about land and its conservation. For Thoreau, the question is not primarily *how* we practice our sport but *why?*

Thoreau is more amused than censuring when he observes busy Bostonians coming to Walden Pond to fish, walking the treadmill of a schedule. He sees them take their recreation very seriously for "commonly they did not think they were lucky, or well-paid for their time, unless they got a long string of fish, though they had the opportunity of seeing the pond all the while." They have transformed their play into work, for that is the only yardstick by which to measure activity: either in money or in acquisition. "The governor and his council faintly remember the pond, for they went a-fishing there when they were boys; but now they are too old and dignified to go a-fishing, and so they know it no more forever." Thoreau stipulates that sport keeps men forever in touch with their youth. None of the town fishermen knows of "the hook of hooks with which to angle for the pond itself" and Thoreau's sly wish is to take young boys and "*make* them hunters, though sportsmen only at first, if possible, mighty hunters at last, so that they shall not find game large enough." He concludes this plea to let them seek out their true relation to nature by hoping they will become "hunters as well as fishers of men," the larger Christian metaphor reminiscent of Cooper's scene of Natty's rescue of Benjamin by deft spearing on Lake Otsego.

Sport for Thoreau is not a way of life but a way to a deeper, more integrated knowledge of how a man's more primitive instinctual needs and experiences may inform his character and develop discipline.[22] In his brief commentary, he refines the argument for correct conduct in sport to an intimate duty to be performed by the individual on his own behalf. Taken together, Cooper's instruction of society by the sportsman and Thoreau's instruction of self prefigure later generations of American idealized sports heroes who may be identified in their roles as spokesmen and articulators of moral opinion while they play for self-control and maturation. The public and private roles of the sportsman are seen most clearly in the figure of the School Sports Hero after the Civil War. In its purest form, the figure of the solitary sportsman as hero and teacher is best seen in the modern Ritual Sports Heroes of Hemingway as well as in Faulkner's Sam Fathers and Ike McCaslin in *Go Down, Moses.*

PART II
The Popular Sports Hero

CHAPTER THREE
Sport and the Frontier

THE POPULAR SPORTS HERO in fiction began as a frontier roarer in the mid-nineteenth-century Davy Crockett–Mike Fink almanacs and as an athlete, gambler, or trickster in Southwestern Humor sketches. He evolved into the modern professional athlete of organized sport who was first identified in print by journalists and dime novelists. The Popular Sports Hero was finally best portrayed by Ring Lardner who had codified a literary formulaic hero by 1920. As a literary character, the Popular Sports Hero had to be amended from generation to generation to reflect the influences of the frontier, the industrial organization of urban life, and the birth of professional sport.

Daniel Hoffman has written that the American folk hero has no past, no family, that he is an expression of the youthful culture which produced him. The American folk hero is self-confident, often courageous, and immature. He aggressively seeks mastery over nature and himself.[1] Such a general description fits the American Popular Sports Hero as he was reworked by many different writers with different aims. Sport in whatever particular permutation is both a playful celebration and an act of control in mastering nature, an opponent, or self.

From the outset the Popular Sports Hero was a democratic hero arising out of the culture's work roles and resultant folklore. A character often of wide acclaim, this hero could be a physical wild man, a grotesque giant, a sly wagerer, or a misfit gamester. This hero performed in roles of sheer physical dominance or of strategic survival in a threatening environment. In whatever guise the Popular Sports Hero expressed a more fully national sport culture of the common man from Davy Crockett through John L. Sullivan to Babe Ruth. He was an expansive, physically prodigious, often outsized character who gradually shifted from feats in the wilderness to feats in the modern sports arena. There was an intimate relationship between the creation and presentation of the Popular Sports Hero and his portrayal and dissemination in developing journalism, both in sporting papers and in daily reports in urban newspapers. Unprivileged, brawling, often broadly comic, the Popular Sports Hero was most often presented at the center of colorful spectacle, and as a fictional character he became part of a vivid record of American play and sport as the culture simultaneously moved both westward and toward greater urbanization.

AGON AND *ALEA:* COMPETITION AND CHANCE

The emphasis on the play spirit in the work of classic American writers had most often been on *mimicry* and *ilinx,* the representation of attitudes through play or the giving up of self to another reality. Cooper's Natty Bumppo had stood for values through his sporting conduct. Hawthorne and Irving had both conveyed the historical record in the patterns of English pageantry and its ceremonial aspects, while the frenzy of the May celebration in "The Maypole of Merry Mount" or the confusion of Rip Van Winkle and the haunting of Ichabod Crane had been prime vertiginous episodes where play became irrational in celebration or fear. Yet Hawthorne and Irving had also portrayed play as community spectacle in the Election Day festivities or in the country quilting frolics. Hawthorne's jocular aura of frontier openness surrounding the games of Election Day on the Boston green and Irving's comic sports heroes, Brom Bones and Dolph Heyliger, suggested, respectively, broad panoramic sporting scenes and sports prowess as a feature of individual heroism. Their celebratory play events are analogous to the wild activity of the race days, frolics, and camp meetings of Southwestern Humor tales which are secularized, ahistorical equivalents of traditional holiday play. Such events solidified community rather than observed church or state holidays. Sport on the frontier was the forerunner and link to modern secular sports spectacle.

What was most noticeable about the sport of frontier heroes in the almanacs or in Southwestern Humor tales was the relative slighting of *mimicry* and *ilinx,* the embodiment of a role or irrational transcendance of a role in favor of the twin play domains of *agon* and *alea,* the realms of competition and chance. Whole sketches were built around fierce contests with animals or other men while obsessive wagering on most any competition was an absolutely essential component of Southwestern Humor tales. On the frontier, contests and betting of all sorts established a temporary play community with an improvised arena. The common characteristics of such play included much boasting and stock protestations of skill, heavy gaming on the outcome, and a valued prize. On the frontier, sport was extrinsically rewarded. One played for money or for some acquisition of goods or animals whereby victory was decisively awarded. Instead of Natty Bumppo's reverence shown through his sport in *The Pioneers*, the almanacs and Southwestern Humor tales mixed hijinks with irreverence. Victory became important by any means, fair or foul. The only dignity exhibited was in the persona of the Southwestern narrator, a gentleman whose pomp existed ultimately to be abused.

Two strains of contests were prevalent. First, there were the overtly physical pursuits of hunts, races, and fights, where the requisite virtues of athletic prowess—endurance, strength, and courage—determined the battle against great animals or other men. Closely linked to the physical contests were the varied games, pranks, swindles, or wagers that demanded verbal dexterity, deception, illusion, and wits. The interaction of the contests (*agon*) and the elements of chance (*alea*) was intense. Not only could Davy Crockett tame a hyena: "I jist run my forefinger through his nose, making a nateral ring and led him home as docile as a frosted fly,"[2] but he could also outtalk or deceive an opponent or a wild animal. A hotly contested quarter-horse race might highlight the skills of animal, jockey, and breeder while the crowd bet continually on the outcome. In Thomas Kirkman's "Jones' Fight," the narrator has "been told a man won a wager in Philadelphia, on his collecting a crowd by staring, without speaking, at an opposite chimney."[3] Hawthorne recounted the Merry Mounters' "yawning match" when they became bored of more strenuous revels. Mark Twain had the last word on this betting mania, integral to a generation of Southwestern Humor Tales, in "The Celebrated Jumping Frog of Calaveras County" with frogsman Jim Smiley, such a demon wagerer that "if there was two birds setting on a fence, he would bet you which one would fly first."[4]

Two different Popular Sports Heroes represented the realms of *agon* and *alea*. The first hero was the comic superman of the almanac tradition, Davy Crockett or Mike Fink, whose hyperbolic legends centered on their strength and victories in the *agon*. The second hero, who appeared in countless Southwestern sketches, was the trickster, the sly wagerer whose games made him a survivor in a hostile society as he created illusions through ingenuity. Crockett and Fink were the broad national heroes of simple tales as well as heroes of early popular fiction, while the tricksters—who would include Augustus Baldwin Longstreet's Ransy Sniffle, Johnson Jones Hooper's Simon Suggs, and George Washington Harris' Sut Lovingood— were heroes to no one, were, in fact, isolated outcasts albeit protagonists of their tales. Thus, there were two Popular Heroes in frontier accounts: heroes of physical skill and heroes of chicanery. The physical heroes were traditional victors of strength and resultant fame while the trickster heroes duelled society and played their individual games of "confidence" against authority. The physical hero duelled nature in frontier tales, while the trickster hero battled society on the periphery of that spectacle where he created his own game for fulfillment or survival. The physical hero became the modern athletic professional in the full glare of spectacle while the trickster became manager, owner, or obsessed fan.

Whether the early Popular Sports Hero participated in *agonistic* and/or *aleatory* play, his deeds were a literal record of American pastimes on an ever-expanding front of social penetration into the west. As colonial society redefined its boundaries, the frontier, too, was redesignated, always on the edge of civilized territory. In *The Scarlet Letter,* the forest lying just beyond Boston is where Hester lives in semi-exile with Pearl. For Captain John Farrago and his squire, Teague O'Regan, in Hugh Henry Brackenridge's *Modern Chivalry* (1792), the frontier is in the Allegheny Mountain country between Philadelphia and the outposts at Pittsburgh. In Cooper's Leatherstocking novels set in the mid-1700s to 1800, the frontier was just beyond the settlements of upper New York State. By the time Cooper came to write *The Pioneers* in 1823, the fictional frontier was located along the Ohio River of Mike Fink and the keelboatmen, and in the wilderness adventures of Boone and Crockett who pushed westward through Kentucky and Tennessee. From 1830 to 1860, the Southwestern writers located the frontier in isolated communities through Kentucky, Georgia, Alabama, and Arkansas. Wherever the actual frontier existed, it was fundamentally a state of mind where the writer's imagination confronted both limits and the lack of limits: the constraints that society placed on play through organized, rule-governed competition and the exuberance of spontaneous play commensurate with the freedom of a vast wilderness. It was in this fictional region that the Popular Sports Hero was born of strength and gamesmanship as he battled natural obstacles and other men.

SOUTHERN AND BACKWOODS SPORT

Sport was expressed in the greatest variety of informal and organized forms in the southern colonies. A horse culture predominated as the single most important facet of plantation agricultural life and recreation. In the late seventeenth and early eighteenth centuries, the Virginia gentleman spent a disproportionate amount of his time in competitive gaming that included cards and backgammon but primarily centered on the sport of quarter-horse racing. Such racing and wagering displayed the central elements of the Virginia gentry culture: competitiveness, individualism, and materialism. The tense contests involved the personal honor as well as the personal fortune of the great planters and attracted wide interest as a public spectacle. Thus, quarter-racing was the first organized sport in America that combined elements of *agon* and *alea* and focused the concerns of owners, breeders, bettors, and spectators. By 1700 the race days were regularly scheduled in Virginia, primarily on Saturday afternoons.[5] Pre-Revolutionary War English travellers criticized southerners at play for "indolence and dissipation" and gave the impression that southern gentlemen did nothing except "bowl, play cards, fish, ride to hounds, race horses, and gamble."[6]

Before the Revolution, thoroughbred race week in Williamsburg was the major sports event in the New World and the biggest social event in Virginia. Finally, the eighteenth-century popularity of thoroughbred racing in more settled regions along the Atlantic coast drove quarter-racing into the backlands.[7] More raucous and colorful, the quarter-horse meet was always a social event where freemen and common planters, who until the early 1700s had been mostly excluded from quarter-racing because of the size of the wagers,[8] would come hundreds of miles to match the best horses in the territory and bet continuously on the outcome of each heat. After the Revolution, Virginia maintained turf supremacy, and racing enthusiasm between Appalachia and the Mississippi River mounted with each decade. Thirty North-South thoroughbred match races were held between 1823 and 1834.[9] Although intersectional competition had almost ended by 1850, the huge state fairs as well as area and county fairs had mushroomed to include not only important races but also "working sport" competition in Kentucky, Tennessee, and Missouri.[10]

It must be remembered that the horse was essential for labor and transportation in addition to being the focal point for wagering sportsmen at racing meets. Antebellum sport in the southern frontier grew out of a society's close proximity to both agriculture and the hunt. The great naturalist and ornithologist, John James Audubon (1785–1851), contributed factual accounts of frontier sport as he related the pastimes of corn shucking, "driving the nail," "barking off squirrels," and the snuffing of a rifle ball. To the Kentuckian, he concluded, the rifle is not only "the means of procuring them subsistence during all their wild and extensive rambles" but "is the source of their principle sports and pleasure,"[11] an observation repeatedly borne out in the sketches of Crockett and Fink. Sports pastimes included squirrel hunts, wolf drives, ring hunts, shooting matches, "throwing the long bullet," "hurling the tomahawk," wrestling and boxing (with diverse and arcane rules), quilting, husking, and reaping bees, log-rolling, Virginia reels, and country jigs. The dividing line between work and play in rural southern areas was extremely ambiguous; frontier sport had no arenas, tickets, or schedules, no daily papers following chosen athletes, no structure such as that which would evolve later in the century for organized sport.

In the almanacs, the backwoodsman and his harsh life were rendered in a tone most often described as comic-grotesque, much of the laughter at his deeds serving as a stay against the terrible emptiness of the vast continent and the realities of life on a threatening frontier where the frontiersman in comic tales attempts to outyell the awful silence or outbrag his comrades.[12] The raucous personal response to terror on the frontier, specifically in behavior that could be classified as unfeeling or inhuman, was partially due to a lack of community or civilization which could be only temporarily alleviated by mastery of nature or of a great animal. In more civilized areas, racing days and camp meetings produced scenes of settlement and town life that were reported by sharp-eyed social commentators like Longstreet, Hooper, and Harris to be representative of a society that only fitfully came together in social situations. The diverse games at these events often provided the underlying richness of detail and the basis for plotting and characterization in narratives that became records of a society at leisure. These backwoods sketches also helped form the conventions of narration in the reporting of contests that would be carried over into later sports journalism and, ultimately, into sports fiction. In frontier America, the establishing of social community through games and their players and spectators was deeply rooted in the life of the society. A writer who would imaginatively explain frontier life had to work through the forms of that activity.[13]

THE ALMANAC HERO:
CROCKETT AND FINK

An examination of the backwoods Popular Sports Hero must begin with a study of the fragmented legends of Davy Crockett and Mike Fink. The almanac writers pulled a Brom Bones or Natty Bumppo out of the settlement and isolated him as a larger-than-life physical prowess hero or a distorted wild man. Crockett, both a story-teller and the subject of tales, was a contemporary of Irving and Cooper. He became a convenient backwoods representative of the fledgling Whig Party which was organized in the 1820s specifically to oppose the banking policies of the Jackson administration and which needed its own folk hero to counter the Jacksonian image.[14] In a series of almanacs published from 1835 to 1856, Crockett became widely known for his fantastic exploits as well as for his homespun philosophy. His death, supposedly as a hero at the Alamo in 1836, spurred the sale of literature about him which became ever more grotesque and overblown.

Crockett bore all the marks of what would become the modern American sporting hero. His feats were based on his physical skills, he was famous for his endurance, and he had a reputation as a mighty athlete. He was brave yet irresistibly comic in speech and action, and he was sold to an admiring public through popular literature. His feats grew more and more obscured in comic legend as he became the humorous vernacular successor to Boone as a more vital, sensual, and younger hunter and frontiersman. Crockett was a democratic roarer, although his "official" 1834 autobiography was much tamer than the later legends in the almanacs because it was intended to be an 1835 campaign document when he ran for Congress and lost.[15] The Crockett of the autobiographical narrative is a practical man, a wily trader, and a man of keen wits with a strong kinship to the narrators and characters of Southwestern Humor.

A majority of entries in the chapbooks and pamphlets were straight natural history or woodslore with descriptions of hunting wild animals. Many of the Crockett sketches were objective accounts of travel or correct technique that were akin to the most interminable lectures by Natty Bumppo. Yet they depicted actions of physical mastery which, if repeated and codified, became ritual action as in the more pragmatic and instructive sporting scenes of Cooper and Thoreau. These sketches were "sporting epistles," and only intermittently was wilderness fact transmuted into wilderness lore. However, the almanacs also subsumed the historical Crockett in colloquial sketches which developed the Crockett legend through a coarsening giantism. The sketches provided scores of detailed physical encounters in which Crockett contested with alligators, panthers, bears, wolves, Indians, old frontier enemies, cantankerous Congressmen, and Mexicans. This is the Crockett remembered by American folklore: Crockett as conservator or guardian of the natural world; but unlike the classically spare Natty Bumppo who shoots one pigeon or spears one fish in displays of discipline, Crockett would punch a panther or even duel the earth and sun when it pleased him. His hyperbolic deeds in the almanacs were the legacy to Southwestern Humorists, rather than realistically performed rituals.

One year after his death in 1837, the cover of a Nashville Crockett Almanack showed him in full woods garb with the title, "Davy Crockett's Almanack, of Wild Sports in the West, Life in the Backwoods & Sketches of Texas,"[16] in short, something for every reader—sportsman, naturalist, or traveller. The most recurring image of Crockett in the series is of a hand-to-hand fighter of great power and violence striding across the American landscape with a patriotic heart and ready to do battle in the *agon* for food, for amusement, or for his country.

While Crockett's largest role in the almanacs is that of national protector born out of his death at the Alamo, simpler contests stress his physical power and skill in more homely, if outlandish encounters, as in his "converting" a panther to Christian civilization: "I put my tusks into his front parts till his bones creaked, and the way the wind carried the fur about was equal to Samson and the lion."[17] The panther serves a utilitarian purpose as well for his eyes "light me up to bed with the fire of his lookers; he brushes the hearth off every mornin with his tail" (119). Many Crockett fables turned on his control and transformation of wild nature through fantastic physical power and then through practical ingenuity, recapitulating both frontier mastery and positive domestic achievement as a blend of Apollo and Benjamin Franklin.

Not only a tamer and utilizer of wild beasts, Crockett is the bravest, most resourceful fighter of men, usually with cause and justice on his side. Nowhere was the apocryphal frontier "sport" of eye-gouging more publicized than in the Crockett almanacs. Always the antisocial limit of barbaric fighting (along with biting matches) in sketches of frontier bouts, Crockett lauds fingers as "true nat'ral gouging instruments." One sketch, complete with gruesome drawings, related the "great claw" of Ralph Nimrod, the "wildcat gouger": "his nails war a kind of natural spring steel; they stuck out about a feet . . . and their sharp points grinned out at you like a row of sharks teeth in a shoal'' (42). All the bluster about gouging notwithstanding, Crockett is most often shown in combat as the settler of a grudge or as a peacemaker. Walking down "Pennsilvany avenoo," in Washington, D.C., Congressman Crockett sees a squatter who had wronged him years before on the frontier and Crockett has to be restrained from gouging out his eye "like taking up a gooseberry in a spoon" (83). Another time, Crockett comes between two fighting congressmen and threatens "to take you both across my knee, scald all the clothes off of you, and kick you all the way home" (85).

Personal belligerence in the *agon* is always seen to be healthy for Crockett and for a young America. Never strongly identified in the almanacs as a settler or explorer, Crockett is a buoyant, mature fighter, who sometimes uses a rifle but most often literally takes matters (and animals and men) into his own hands, shaking sense into adversaries. His nativist threat to the Mexicans (posthumous, of course) is to "mount my alligator, travel into the middle o' Mexico. . . . [and] teach the natives, red niggers and creoles the true bred Yankee Independence and Republicanism" (158). Crockett's broad feats as a fighter in the almanacs began with his physical strength in great deeds and were extended in baldly patriotic exaggeration into national competitive victories in a flush of chauvinistic sloganeering. He was the greatest physical-prowess hero of the mid-nineteenth century. Like no other American popular figure before him, the Crockett of the almanacs personified raw power and exuberance and displayed great athletic skill, unending combativeness, and continual victory. Crockett's literary persona is a primary example of a popular hero created through dilution, reproduction, and the reworking of stories by emerging media.[18]

The legend of Mike Fink was similarly diffused into the almanacs after Fink's death in 1823. Fink's career as the captain of a keelboat on the Ohio River began in the early 1800s when the boatman joined the Kentucky rifleman as a frontier hero. The keelboatmen were reputedly the best athletes on the frontier; they needed great physical strength to pole along the flat cargo boats. The boatmen had several attributes that combined strenuous work, free play, and imagination. They were free agents on the river yet engaged in the active life of river commerce, and their carousing and wenching when they came ashore at night in various towns was widely reported.[19] Fink could be the "half-horse, half-alligator" of folk fame with his strength and physical cruelty; the Crockett almanacs prove him a great eye-gouger as well, Crockett lauding the way Fink "used to gouge thar eyes and tongues out first, and then punch thar bodies out of thar shells as handsome as a kernel out of a nut."[20] In a typical domestic scene, Fink used his own wife for target practice for a mythical pigtail shooting match because he was furious at the competition of Col. Crockett.[21]

When keelboatmen lost their economic role on the river, writers portrayed Fink as both a sad and dangerous figure. His status as physical prowess hero was meaningless for he now had no outlet for his strength and skill and was no longer a popular hero. His sport became antisocial on a more civilized frontier, and his clownish bragging turned violent and menacing. Fink then resembled no one as much as a veteran athlete cut loose, in this case without a team or game to participate in. No sports culture on the frontier existed to accommodate a Fink, as Southwestern Humor sketches indirectly pointed out.

In Joseph N. Field's "Death of Mike Fink" (1844), Fink joins a fur company "after a term of idleness, frolic and desperate rowdyism" following the demise of the keelboats. He becomes a public nuisance and demands whiskey from the fort.[22] In a sad exhibition of markmanship, he kills his young friend, Carpenter, while trying to shoot a can off his head. The boy had previously creased Mike's scalp on a shot and the whispered accusation is that Mike has taken his angry revenge. Field sympathetically maneuvers Fink into a martyr's death when the boatman is shot at the fort while explaining Carpenter's accidental death to a gunsmith frightened of his approach.

An even less positive description of an aging Fink past his heroism and usefulness is contained in Thomas Bangs Thorpe's "The Disgraced Scalp-Lock" (1842)[23] in which Fink and his boat mates are survivors of a different sort of life. Of these "singularly hearty-looking men," Thorpe writes, "their forms always exhibit a powerful development of muscle and bone"; they are "full of self-reliance; the language strong and forcible . . . the dress studied for comfort, rather than fashion." "The swift-running and wayward waters had to be overcome by physical force alone"; the boatmen were "brave, hardy, and openhanded men; their whole lives were a round of manly excitement; they were hyperbolical in thought and in deed."

Thorpe is self-consciously knowledgeable about the almanac hero whom he can meticulously describe through the conventions of deeds and strength. One purpose, however, in "The Disgraced Scalp-Lock," is to prove Fink not merely an anomaly but a dangerous anachronism. With Fink, the physical-prowess hero is expressly a nostalgic figure for the first time, an initial casting of the athlete with no game in a "limited excellence" that does not carry him beyond the hero's role into more complex relationships. "Wild and uncultivated as Mike appeared, he loved nature" and "was his own master by law." His one remaining pastime is having sport "at the Indians' expense." Mike humiliates a Cherokee called Proud Joe by severing his scalp-lock with a rifle ball and thinks little of it. He and his merry louts consistently "wanted more lasting excitement." Mike exclaims in a contentious, agonistic cry, "I must fight something, or I'll catch the dry rot—burnt brandy won't save me." "These displays of animal spirits generally ended in boxing and wrestling matches, in which falls were received, and blows were struck without being noticed, that would have destroyed common men." At the conclusion of the tale, Fink kills Proud Joe and Thorpe elevates the Indian to the status of dignified victim, while Fink, mechanically skillful and brutal, is not apotheosized. Without the mitigating laughter, the frontier athlete is a cruel bully. Thorpe suggested that the Brobdingnagian wild man and his carousing were threats to the order of the settlements. Thorpe punctures Fink's sentimental lament: "Who ever found wild buffalo, or a brave Indian in a city? Where's the fun, the frolicking, the fighting?" Thorpe realistically gives the brief against Fink through Proud Joe's heroic pursuit and death. Fink has no job and no sport or socially approved game for his energies, and both he and society suffer. In an organically conceived union of work and play on the frontier, when work is terminated, so is its current toward play.

WILLIAM PORTER
AND THE *SPIRIT OF THE TIMES*

By 1840 the popular legends taking shape around frontier heroes were already more influenced by print than by any other factor. Two prominent sporting papers were begun during this period. The first was John Skinner's *American Turf Register* (1829–1845), a publication largely devoted to breeding records and racing results in an effort to collect and systematize American racing facts and traditions. The second was William Porter's *Spirit of the Times* (1831), which for thirty years was the leading sporting newspaper in the United States. The *Spirit* not only reported organized sporting events all up and down the coast but also printed backwoods sketches of frontier life for a wider public than ever before. By 1850, the *Spirit* sometimes contained two columns of agricultural news and the report of a cricket match framing a tall tale from a "correspondent" in Arkansas or Georgia.

The *Spirit*'s breadth of interests reflected no consistent policy of presentation on the part of its editor, William Porter.[24] A New York state native, Porter always identified himself with the land-owning southern gentry, and his real interest in the antebellum South, particularly its racing meets, was continually reflected in his paper. Porter's *Spirit* was aimed at a general sporting public before any differentiation of sport periodicals had taken place. At times the paper resembled little more than a large weekly clipping service, for its articles in the first decade or so of publication were most often culled from the pages of the *St. Louis Reveille* or the *New Orleans Times-Picayune,* or from any number of fashionable English papers, including *Bell's Life* in London, Porter's model for the *Spirit.* Although he was very interested in frontier tales, Porter in 1839 was already speaking from the vantage point of the urban sportsman. That same year he purchased the *American Turf Register* in his desire to centralize all racing publications in New York City,[25] and Porter himself often covered the important match races of the day as well as prominent prize fights.[26]

Porter edited two collections of backwoods writing, including *The Big Bear of Arkansas and Other Stories* (1845) and *A Quarter Race in Kentucky and Other Stories* (1846), the first real displays of the vitality of the Southwestern tradition. By 1848, Porter's anthologies had encouraged many publishers to place his correspondents under separate contract, and the publication of tales rapidly increased.[27] The number of articles written expressly for the *Spirit* had increased tenfold by 1850; a column entitled "Yankee Humor" had begun on March 15, 1845, and in that same year, Hooper's shifty army captain, Simon Suggs, appeared in a story alongside the results of the English racing season.[28]

Indeed, in the mid-1840s, Porter describes his intention to "beat into lint" anything he has ever done before. The issue of March 1, 1845, has a list of "pedestrian races," as track was called at the time, with lists of record times from one hundred yards up to eighteen miles (with a 5:02 mile). On pp. 15–16 are "A Sketch of a Creole Hunter" by "a new correspondent of Louisiana"; Dayton, Ohio, racing results; "Occidental Reminiscences: 'Prairie Leg Book; or, Rough Notes of a Dragoon Campaign to the Pawnee Villages in 1844' by 'an officer of the U.S. Army' "; and an essay, "Life in the State of Iowa." Advertisements had first appeared with some frequency in the *Spirit* in 1842, and this 1845 issue offers cricket supplies and Rodger's Gymnasium, "the most complete one in the United States. Open sunrise to 10 P.M. Fencing and sparring taught by an experienced professor."[29] Other sketches in that month's issues included "Night Attack on Fort Erie" (March 15) and "Daddy Bigg's Scrape at Cockrell's Bend" by Hooper, who has, as Porter reminds us, "keen perception of the ludicrous and comic."[30]

Out of this erratic miscellany of romantic trash, backwoods humor, veterinarians' advice, breeding manuals, social chitchat, bloody boxing reports, and cricket scores comes the picture of a sporting world in America that was wildly heterogeneous and unpredictable in its scope and variety.[31] While New York had a yachting season and cricket clubs, Crockett's heirs were embroiled in eye-gouging contests at camp meetings. While arranged match races in New York City would draw upwards of 20,000 people, spontaneous squirrel hunts, wolf drives, pigeon shoots and quarter races were the pastimes on the frontier. The *Spirit* became the journal where the feats of backwoodsmen in informal sport were narrated alongside the stirrings of an American sporting establishment.

The *Spirit* was so avowedly a sporting paper that it was inevitable its fictional sketches would constantly describe a world of competition and wagering. That sporting world was dominated by racing and fighting with heavy betting as a major plot complication. As early as 1792, Brackenridge opened *Modern Chivalry* with a brief account of a spontaneous backwoods horse race where gentleman Captain Farrago discourses on Greek and medieval sport, horse breeding, and the lineage (breeding) of great leaders to bewildered jockeys who suspect he is hoodwinking them. By the 1830s a whole body of lore had grown up around the racing meet habitués, including the poker-faced breeder and owner, the gamblers, the stake-holders, the outlandish bluffers, and the participants in the frolics engaged in after the races.

Kentucky horse breeder Thomas Kirkman's "A Quarter Race in Kentucky,"[32] published in the *Spirit* in 1836, is one of the earliest successful blends of the sporting sketch, elements of tall-tale humor, and the restrained style of the gentleman essayist.[33] "A Quarter Race" takes place in the world of the sporting tough, an environment into which the gentleman narrator steps unknowingly, believing himself to be dealing with fellow sportsmen. The reality is that he is a spectator at a race where menacing characters refuse to play by the rules and will not pay off on his winning wagers. He is threatened by a gambler who snarls that he won't be pushed for his money; however, Kirkman undercuts the menacing scene: "My respect for Mr. Wash's dirk-knife, together with my perceiving there was nothing else to be had, induced me to express my entire satisfaction with Mr. Wash's dubisary. . . . He proposed that I should let him have five dollars more for a stake, but on my declining, he said, 'Well, there is no harm in mentioning it.' "[34] The judge for this splendid race is right out of tall-tale tradition: "his likeness had been moulded on dog irons to frighten the children from going too near the fire, and his face ached perpetually; but his eyes! his eyes! He was said to have caught a turkey buzzard by the neck, the bird being deceived, and thinking he was looking another way; and several of the crowd said he was so cross-eyed he could *look at his own head!*" Nature has designed him to be a racing judge, for "he could station one eye to watch when the foremost horse's toe struck the score, and could note the track of the horse that followed at the same moment with the other eye." Kirkman's sketch proved the quarter races contained raw material for the fictional transformation of many elements that best characterized backwoods sporting life, including physical humor, intense gambling, and outrageous boasting.

If the racing meet is one successful environment for a sporting sketch in the *Spirit,* the tiny backwoods hamlet is another. Kirkman's "Jones' Fight," published in the *Spirit* in 1840, has several sports frames.[35] The town's leading citizen, the pompous Col. Dick Jones,[36] is a gentleman sportsman who becomes the butt of a larger game that the village of Summerville wages with a village "over the mountains." Ultimately, Col. Jones, the Summerville champion, must meet the man who has insulted him in a knock-down, drag-out brawl while all of Summerville bets on the outcome.

Col, Jones is a proud, condescending lawyer, "vice president of the jockey club," whose "manners were the most popular" in the village. As he rides off to court over the mountain, "the young store boys of the village . . . conjectured how the fight would go" and "the whole town was alive to the consequences of this trip." The narrator confesses, "I watched the road from Louisville two days, to hear of Grey Eagle beating Wagner, on which I had one hundred dollars staked," in one of the great match races in 1840. The aleatory instincts of the hamlet are aroused and life stops. Their drooping champion, Col. Jones, limps home, defeated in the *agon,* with "a pair of dark green specks on, his right hand in a sling, with brown paper bound round his wrist. . . . His face was clawed all over. . . . His general swelled appearance would induce a belief he had led the forlorn hope in the storming of a beehive." Jones tries to talk his way out of a humiliating defeat. His compensatory story of his great heroism becomes the final verbal game while he constantly tries to back his way through the quizzical crowd and into a friendly tavern. He exaggerates his own eye-gouging, chewing, and teeth-extracting heroics. The gentleman is once more the butt while the exuberant wagering of the townsmen gives life to the tale.

SOUTHWESTERN HUMOR
AND FRONTIER SPORT

Kirkman was only one of a score of early commentators who contributed different styles of reportage on frontier contests and sporting life, including Field, Sol Smith, Alexander McNutt ("The Turkey Runner"), Charles F.M. Noland ("Pete Whetstone," "N,"), and Henry Clay Lewis.[37] Thorpe and Longstreet were journalists and authors in the tradition of Brackenridge who wrestled with the problem of the new mass democracy and changing political and social realities of the Southern rural and town society.[38] Thorpe perfected variations on the mask of the gentleman narrator who reported on his travels through the rural South and Southwest. Longstreet retained the persona of the gentleman while functioning as an angry satirist and social critic. Hooper wrote his sketches of Simon Suggs in the third person while moving his trickster hero closer to the center of the narration. Finally, Harris turned his sketches over to his boy narrator, Sut Lovingood. The gentleman narrator remained only to listen to Sut's tales and to transcribe his experience. The Southwesterners did not concentrate on a particular fantastic comic hero like the almanac writers but instead, in a commitment to realism, portrayed an entire society of players, wagerers, and spectators. The verbalization of play by backwoods heroes was yet another game narrated in boastful zest. The extempore fight is exaggerated into an event of great importance with meaning for the entire town. Kirkman deftly builds a minor incident into a legitimate sport spectacle.,

Contemporary with the Southwestern Humorists were writers who skirted the boundary between the naturalist essay and the fictional sketch and who further spread the popularity of sporting narrative. Among the most important were Henry William Herbert ["Frank Forester"] (1807–1858) and William Elliott (1788–1863). Herbert, an English gentleman-in-exile, was Porter's resident naturalist in the *Spirit*. He affected the pose of a New

Jersey country squire in the 1840s and 1850s with a manor house on the banks of the Passaic River. He aimed to elevate the title of "Sportsman" by shifting the focus of tales from racing meets and card tables to Natty Bumppo's more pristine world of the naturalist or to the excitement and adventure of the hunt.[39] He became the *Spirit's* most popular nature writer in his "My Shooting Box" column begun in 1845. His most encyclopedic studies were *Field Sports of the United States and British Provinces of North America* (1848) and *Horse and Horsemanship in the United States of America* (1857). Herbert, like Porter, possessed a wide knowledge of field sports and games while his prose shaded closer to that of the sentimental romance than towards backwoods realism. For years, "Frank Forester" appeared in the *Spirit* alongside more homely reporters of frontier customs and manners.

Elliott was a prominent South Carolina journalist, politician, and landowner who was also an innovative agriculturalist and sportsman.[40] His *Carolina Sports By Land and Water* (1846) was a collection of sporting essays written for Skinner's *American Turf Register* and for various Southern newspapers in the 1830s under the titles of "Piscator" and "Venator." His grasp of the intense pleasures of the hunt and the chase was related with style and a keen sense of atmosphere. Elliott and his gentleman friends pursued "devil fish," bucks, and small game on the Carolina coast through forests, bogs, swamps, and out into the Atlantic Ocean itself. Elliott was a graceful, sophisticated occasional writer. He saw a fundamental link between sport and writing and stated, *"Celerity of movement* [italics Elliott] is the play—whether in the field or in the narrative."[41] Elliott's essays touched on the mystical power of great animals, the conservation of game, and the resultant need for hunting laws, and he left a full rather than a fanciful record of Southern sport.

The Southwestern Humorists constructed a more sophisticated literary frame for the conveyance of these sporting characters and scenes than either the almanac writers or the naturalists and essayists. In "The Legend of Sleepy Hollow," Irving's whimsical gentleman narrator surrounded the tale in several frame layers. The story is a found manuscript written by Diedrich Knickerbocker who had the story related to him by an old Manhattan resident. This ploy further established the American tall-tale genre as one couched in layers of distancing between gentleman author and subject, between formal and colloquial language, and between incipient civilized forms and a freer frontier culture. By the late 1830s, the Southwestern Humorists had begun to transform the almanac superman into a more multifaceted comic hero. The Southwestern gentleman narrator detached himself from the characters he was describing as would modern sports writers assigned to teams and their heroes. The Southwestern reporter's tone was laudatory and somewhat apologetic, both out of pride in frontier vitality and dismay at the democratic chaos.

Thomas Bangs Thorpe (1815–1878) described the political and cultural life of the frontier through a series of narrative convolutions. He had an eye for the realistic description of frontier life although he was pulled toward romanticizing it by pressures of popular taste. He had a checkered career as a newspaper editor and publisher in the 1840s and finally in 1853 migrated back to New York where for a time he edited a version of the *Spirit* after the death of Porter in 1858.[42] His most famous sketch, "The Big Bear of Arkansas," which appeared in the *Spirit* on March 27, 1841, was the title story in the early anthology of backwoods writing that Porter published in May 1845. Kenneth Lynn has written that the ideal Southwestern humorist was a professional man, a lawyer or newspaper editor, a well-educated Whig who was aghast at Jacksonian democracy.[43] Thorpe, an educated Southerner, was less virulent a polemicist, however, than Longstreet or Harris, and he often clearly took the side of the backwoods character. Sporting morés were often the basis for his satire. In "A Hoosier in Search of Justice," a country gentleman who is also a lawyer can tell an inquiring flatboatman nothing whatsoever regarding cock-fighting laws in Louisiana. Thus, the frontiersman's awe in the presence of such a gentleman gradually turns to "a broad grin of supreme contempt." The implicit lesson is that laws on the frontier are worthy of little respect if they cannot be applied to the rules of sport. The order of the lawyer's society does not reach to the arena of fighting cocks and the rows of law books which define the country lawyer's role wither before the vitality of the boatman and the ferocity of his bloody birds.

As critics of society, the Southwestern writers wrote of social pretensions as a new sort of American competition, a game eagerly engaged in by members of a presumably "classless" society. In Thorpe's "A Piano in Arkansas," (*Spirit,* 30 October 1841), the uncultured residents are mystified when they hear of a strange object called a "piano" among the personal belongings of a Northern family just moved into the area. The "piano" is confidently pointed out through the window by Mo Mercer, a young swell who has "visited the capital." However, what Mercer thinks is a "piano" turns out to be a handcrank washing machine.

The western sportsman in Thorpe is not inflated to heroic proportions but is more often a deceptively shrewd observer and the vessel of good sense and competence in woods lore. This is the case for Jim Doggett, the gamecock narrator of "The Big Bear," a character in the tradition of expansive first-person narrators and an elegiast for the vanishing backwoods life.[44] Thorpe's Mike Fink in "The Disgraced Scalp-Lock" is another elegiast. Thorpe continually stresses the physical skills of the woodsmen, whom he saw as our true national heroes. He is consistently impressed with their practical accomplishments as well: "among this backwoods fraternity, have flourished men of genius, in their way, who have died unwept and unnoticed, while the heroes of the turf and of the chase have been lauded to the skies for every trivial superiority they may have displayed in their respective pursuits." In conclusion, Thorpe reminds his readers how "unsatisfactory" it is that Tom Owen, the Bee Hunter, remains unknown while Davy Crockett has become a familiar figure.[45] Thorpe sought to answer the question of Cooper: how is backwoods competence to be elevated to principles of conduct? For Thorpe, the answer is that the bee hunter is both woodsman and productive capitalist. Tom Owen, the Bee Hunter, is a convenient symbol of practicality, industry, and sport, the new American frontier figure, less rapacious than Billy Kirby in *The Pioneers*. Owen is rather a counterpart of Cooper's bee hunter, Ben Boden, in *The Oak Openings* (1847).[46] Thorpe's *Far West Letters* (1846) showed him capable of deftly satirizing the tall-tale tradition he had in "The Big Bear." They included not only realistic descriptions of life on the trail but also burlesques of outlandish yarns which he sent to Porter along with fake travel notes of a Rocky Mountain expedition.

Thorpe influenced Southwestern Humor toward something more than the recasting of violent and crude braggart tales from the almanacs. His humor seldom turned on grotesque physical characteristics. Thorpe took the literary mask of the rather stuffy gentleman for his primary narrator, a position that produced delicate comedy between the gentleman and his amused subject such as wily Jim Doggett in "The Big Bear." Thorpe did not fear backwoods vulgarians nor was he moved to deflate them by a gentleman's scorn. Of all the Southwestern writers, Thorpe was the least outraged social critic, the most self-conscious craftsman, and the most balanced objective reporter. That balance is clearly seen in his utilitarian view of sporting skills and bemused views of social games.

An influential Southwestern writer who never appeared in the *Spirit* was Augustus Baldwin Longstreet (1790–1870), who published *Georgia Scenes* in 1835.[47] Longstreet's jaundiced ironic first-person observer embodied a narrative style assumed by many reporters of backwoods life, and his astringent tone leads to the modern sports section and its literary masters such as Heywood Broun, Damon Runyon, and Ring Lardner. His repeated subject matter was that of *agon-alea,* the combative narcotic of competition in rural towns and the variety of betting on the outcome. Longstreet's sketches were written consistently in a sardonic, restrained tone as he reported scenes of not only tomfoolery but also of real brutality as well. Now amused, now scathingly satiric in his treatment of both polite society and the uneducated poor whites, his narrators had a wounding, critical view of small-town life.

Longstreet had a true interest in American social gatherings for, as his narrator says in ''The Turf,'' ''I visit it to acquire a knowledge of the human character as it exhibits itself in various scenes of life.''[48] Men, women, and children are all depicted as continuously betting with each other during the heats. An indignant owner, furious that his jockey is not following orders, says, ''Don't you see that I can't make Bob do anything I tell him? I'll learn him how to take a *bribe* in future'' (158). The narrator is all over the grounds, now talking to the grooms, now visiting with the ladies amongst the carriages.

The art of horse-trading is itself a competitive game. In ''The Horse Swap,'' two men trade lies about their animals before reaching tentative agreement. The tale is a classic of deadpan bragging to put one over on the opponent: ''Well, fetch up your nag, my old cock; you're jist the lark I wanted to get hold of. I am perhaps a *leetle,* jist a *leetle* of the best man at a horse-swap that ever stole *crackling* out of his mammy's fat gourd. Where's your *hoss?''* (''The Horse Swap,'' p. 24). One horse is blind; the other has an enormous festering sore on its back.

In ''The Fight,'' Longstreet creates Ransy Sniffle, a small-town boy who receives vicarious enjoyment from watching violence. ''The Fight'' is unequalled in its rendering of a populace just waiting for Sniffle to foment disorder, never far from the surface in Longstreet's work. The narrator is fascinated by society's pretensions of civility which are swamped by ugly violence. Sniffle promotes a fight between two heavyweight friends by stirring up rumors about one's insults to the other's wife. The battle engages the blood-lust interest of the whole town and the contestants' battered faces become unrecognizable. Perhaps the most intriguing description is in Ransy Sniffle as a disturbed vision of the modern fan: ''There was nothing on this earth which delighted Ransy so much as a fight. He never seemed fairly alive except when he was witnessing, fomenting or talking about a fight. Then, indeed, his deep-sunken gray eyes assumed something of a living fire, and his tongue acquired a volubility that bordered upon eloquence''

("The Fight," p. 55). His love for blood is all that brings his body alive out of its sluglike torpor.

Longstreet's humor was not as generous as Thorpe's. Indeed, he was angry all the time: in "The Fight" he finally enters the tale to say that only barbarians would act in such a fashion; in a sarcastic piece, "The Mother and Her Child" he destroys the harmless practice of baby talk; or in "The Debating Society" the group's task is to produce a debate topic that has absolutely no substance and then to watch hypocrites wrestle with this language game in earnest. Other pieces in *Georgia Scenes* that dealt more directly with sport included "Georgia Theatrics" where a young man practices eye-gouging with "the prints of his two thumbs plunged up to the balls in the mellow earth, about the distance of a man's eyes apart" ("Georgia Theatrics," p. 11); "The Gander Pulling," an account of a little-remembered sport practiced on horseback; "The Fox Hunt," in which the narrator mocks the intensity of his fellow fox chasers; and "The Shooting Match," which relates details of rules, scoring, and gamesmanship. No Southwestern writer illuminated more corners of a fledgling culture of games and sports than did Longstreet.

While Thorpe and Longstreet's gentleman narrators were above the action, two other Southwestern writers, Hooper (1815–1862) and Harris (1814–1869), created backwoods characters who not only observed but also participated in the fun, chicanery, and energy of rural life. Hooper's Simon Suggs and Harris' Sut Lovingood were not physical prowess heroes. They lived by their wits and cunning in a society where the stratagems for success might range from subtle persuasion in conversation to broad farce in practical joking. Suggs' milieu was that of *alea;* he wagered on anything and made his way in a sporting world through his deception and role-playing. Sut Lovingood's great talent was in initiating pranks in which he simulated *ilinx* that catapulted playful social occasions into a chaos of physical comedy. Both Suggs and Sut were master illusionists in *mimicry* with words as Suggs' weapons and physical mayhem as Sut's specialty. They both played to survive. The confidence man and the prankster, well represented in backwoods humor, have given the modern sporting world its most richly colorful characters from King Kelly to Dizzy Dean to scores of gamblers, promoters, owners, and simple hangers-on.

While Hooper retained the device of the gentleman narrator, Simon Suggs was the first of the Southwestern characters to be at the center of a continuing series of adventures. He represented a consistent conception of a sporting trickster in an identifiable society. One facet of the move toward realism in Southwestern writing was to bring the frontiersman from the role of physical wild man into a more normal relationship with his society and fellow men.[49] The role of the player or trickster could then be examined by the participant himself while not excluding his description of the social environment in which he is acting. Hooper's character appeared in a series of adventures published in the 1840s, many of the sections appearing in the *Spirit,* for Porter was one of Hooper's earliest champions.[50] The dialogue portions of the sketches were in the vernacular while description was in the control of the gentleman narrator, making the Suggs canon a transition between Longstreet's lofty survey of lowlife activities and Harris' Sut Lovingood tales, where Sut's rich dialect is most often the only narrative voice.

The Suggs character was portrayed briefly as a youngster, but the majority of the sketches show him as a middle-aged trickster in Alabama in the 1830s. All his dealings turn on his capacity for deception, for assuming false roles in social gatherings, at poker tables, or in camp meetings. Suggs' famous motto was "It's good to be shifty in a new country," and he faithfully followed that maxim throughout his adventures. Young Simon was an active gamester from the beginning:

> He stole his mother's roosters to fight them at Bob Smith's grocer, and his father's plough horses to enter them in "quarter" matches at the same place. He pitched dollars with Bob Smith himself and could "beat him into doll rags" when it came to a measurement. To crown his accomplishment, Simon was tip-top at the game of "Old Sledge," which was the fashionable game of that era; and was early initiated into the mysteries of "stocking the papers."[51]

He pointedly tells his father, "I'm gwine to play cards as long as I live. When I go off to myself, I'm gwine make my livin' by it. So what's the use of beatin' me about it?"(17). One of his first card-playing triumphs was to convince his fundamentalist father to cut a deck of cards for the old family horse. If he won, Simon promised to leave and refrain from plaguing his father with what old Jedediah Suggs terms "wild sporting notions." Simon cheats, wins, and rides away exclaiming, "I'm off old stud: remember the Jack-a-hearts"(26). As a parting gesture, he lards his mother's pipe with gunpowder.

In 1833, he is to be found settled on the Tallapoosa River in Alabama, from which he sallies forth to earn daily bread for his family. Many of Hooper's sketches turned on a single theme of Simon being mistaken for a man of means and his playing on that fact. The gullibility and greed of his opponents who let him establish unlimited credit or advance him considerable amounts of money are other recurring elements. In "Simon Fights the 'Tiger,' '' he poses as a wealthy hog-driver at a high-stakes faro game and builds on his name for credit on drinks, dinner, promissory notes, and large cash advances as Hooper exposes a wagering mania in the small community. A twist on this theme occurs in "Simon Suggs Attends a Camp Meeting" where Hooper not only describes that often *ilinx*-like atmosphere of redemption, dollars, and sex, but also has Simon neatly adapt his line to fit the occasion, for the old trickster views with admiration the whole affair as a "grand deception" and as "a sort of 'opposition line' running against his own" (115). Simon's consistent judgment is "mother-wit kin beat book-larnin, at *any* game!"(49).

In homage to Hooper, Simon Suggs, Jr. was created by Joseph G. Baldwin, whose *The Flush Times of Alabama and Mississippi* (1853) was another fine portrayal of frontier society from the vantage point of the refined gentleman. Simon, Jr. becomes a lawyer, his career culminating in his incredible job as a lobbyist for an Indian tribe. In Washington, D.C., he cheats both the government and the Indians in true Suggsian fashion. His early years had been spent around the grocery store where "it was the general rendezvous of the fast young gentlemen for ten miles around; and horse-racing, shooting-matches, quoit-pitching, cock-fighting, and card-playing filled up the vacant hours between drinks."[52]

Harris was an early master of the grotesque style of the Crockett almanacs which was expressed through his adolescent narrator, Sut Lovingood. Harris' career began in the *Spirit* in February 1843 when he sent the first of his "Sporting Epistles" to Porter. The very first one announced that in East Tennessee, "the sporting men in this quarter have to amuse themselves with the cheaper sports: such as Quarter racing, Cock-fighting, Deer-driving, Fox, Coon and 'Possum-hunting, Turkey-shooting, and Partridge-netting."[53] In the next decade he perfected a dialect humor of great skill and a major character who enabled him to present a picture of backwoods life solely through the eyes of one of its most disreputable citizens. Sut was a hero to no one; he had no physical skills, no money, no gift for swindling. What he possessed can best be described as keen wit and a painful knowledge of society's norms, for which he exhibits profound distaste both out of a strange idealism and considerable disorder in his own personality. He then uses his prodigious talent for disruption to turn the world of frolics and races upside down. Sut has a vivid sense of being outside that social community at play, a community whose spontaneous sporting life is examined by a resident vulgarian with the sensual longings of a fan excluded from participation. It is as if Longstreet's Ransy Sniffle had assumed permanent control of the narrative.

Through sketches such as "Sicily Burns's Wedding," "Mrs. Yardley's Quilting," and "The Knob Dance—A Tennessee Frolic," Sut reveals what he believes to be the congenial moral climate of such social gatherings: "Es I swung my eyes over the crowd, George, I thought quiltins, managed in a morril an' sensibil way, truly am good things—good fur free drinkin . . . good fur free fitin, an' goodest ove all fur poperlating a country fas'."[54] Sut is a fully sexual being, an antidote to sentimentalized child heroes. He represents a frankness about the uppermost concerns of hot-blooded young people at camp meetings, quiltings, and dances. Yet he keenly feels his exclusion which causes him to let loose a bee-stung cow in "Sicily Burns's Wedding" (to repay her for her prank of disguising an emetic as an aphrodisiac in "Blown up with Soda") or to engineer the destruction of a quilting party by means of a frantic horse in "Mrs. Yardley's Quilting."

Sut has no conception of the gentleman sport; he can describe a racing day, as in "Bill Ainsworth's Quarter Race,"[55] but he does so from the vantage point of a scornful spectator, not truly a participant. Harris is more at home in a comic tale such as "A Snake Bit Irishman" in which a hunter is made to believe he is being bitten by a poisonous snake to the great glee of the assemblage around the campfire. In "Mrs. Yardley's Quilting," a young swain gets a frying pan banged so hard on his skull that it breaks and the metal circle left hanging around his neck has to be broken off with a cold chisel. In his lustiness combined with a quick temper and considerable self-hatred, Sut knows of many games besides racing and hunting. He concludes,

> "Men were made a-purpus jis' tu eat, drink, an' fur stayin awake in the yearly part ove the nites: an' wimen wer made tu cook the vittils, mix the spirits, an' help the man du the staying awake. That's all, an' nuthin more, onless hits fur the wimen tu raise the devil atwix meals, an' knit socks atwix drams, an' the men to play short kerds, swap hosses wif fools, an' fite fur exercise, at odd spells."[56]

Sut's definition of the backwoods male is of an active, dominant reveler who is richly physical, free, and indolent, and who must be consumed by play. Not allowed to be a traditional hero, Sut's spreading the chaos of vertigo is his countergame to play in the community.

Informal games and sport on the pre-Civil War frontier gave the backwoods writer a choice subject for his humorous realism. Competition and wagering were the activities that excited the rural populace. Kirkman's narrator in "Jones' Fight" described "the whole town alive to the consequences" of the grudge fight and "nothing was to be attended to until they were satisfied about the fight." The diverse manifestations of the play spirit were "attended to": simulation, vertigo, contest, and chance became foci for a country continuing to create itself anew within a developing social fabric in a threatening landscape.

In conclusion, the separate conceptions, Thorpe's realistic assessment of the heroic backwoodsman, influenced by Cooper's idealized hunter, and Longstreet's, Hooper's, and Harris' comic deflation of the competitor and trickster are strands that have continued in the reporting of the modern athletic hero who may be as powerful and outsized as Crockett or as wily as Sut. By the 1920s, the backwoods vulgarian has become Lardner's Jack Keefe in *You Know Me Al* while the gentleman traveller has become the sportswriter travelling with the team. The gamester or athlete may be invested with solid virtues or blurred in grotesque hyperbolic description. The roles are at the root of the Popular Sports Hero whose birth on the frontier was an initial step toward his transformation into an urban team hero by 1900. Confined in ball parks, prize rings, and race tracks, the early American exuberant sporting hero of the frontier would continue to be represented. The irreverent descendants of Crockett, Fink, Ransy Sniffle, Simon Suggs, and Sut Lovingood would fill the urban stadiums as players, wagerers, and fans, and would fill the pages of twentieth-century sports fiction as well.

CHAPTER FOUR

Organized Sport
and Its Reporters

TRANSFORMATION OF SPORT
IN INDUSTRIAL AMERICA

IN *THE MACHINE IN THE GARDEN,* Leo Marx wrote, "Within the lifetime of a single generation, a rustic and in large part wild landscape was
transformed into the site of the world's most productive industrial
machine." This "contradiction between rural myth and technological fact"[1]
also gave birth to a new American definition of sport. During the first half
of the nineteenth century, physical prowess heroes, gamesters, and their
spectators were increasingly the creations of print media: the almanacs, the
Spirit of the Times, and the anthologies of Southwestern writing. After the
Civil War, sports heroes were created primarily in the cities by a mixture of
media, capital, and advertising, and these heroes had a broader, more artificial national audience. As sports shifted from rural to urban areas, the
outlines of the Popular Sports Hero shifted, too, quickly forsaking the initial
identification and glorification of Boone, Crockett, Fink, the idealization of
the hunter, and the comic deflation of the backwoodsman. The decades between 1850 and 1890 produced perhaps the most far-reaching changes in
American sport, moving from the days of little organization, scant codifying
of rules, and a limited communication and transportation network to the
time when boxing, baseball, and college football became American popular
obsessions as spectatorial pastimes.

After 1861, the *Spirit* printed few sporting sketches from Louisiana
and Georgia. The Southwestern Humorists had left the war-torn region,

gone into embittered silence, or died. As the sporting establishment moved northward, their old themes clustered around the hunt, field sports, and backwoods frolics were no longer emblematic of a changing society.[2] The flow of southern correspondence in the *Spirit* was also sealed off by changes at the *Spirit* itself. When editor Porter died in 1858, the *Spirit* passed to the editorship of George Wilkes, an ardent pro-Union man during the Civil War whose stance effectively cut off Southwestern contributors.

Wilkes' subhead for the *Spirit* proclaimed it "The American Gentleman's Magazine, Sole and Official Turf Organ of the American Jockey Club and the National Trotting Association," and the *Spirit* of 23 September 1859 listed turf records and meets in no fewer than eleven states. The *Spirit* functioned as a lively purveyor of northern track news mixed with New York theater gossip. The front-page masthead throughout the 1860s showed something for every sportsman. Its ornate logo included a rifle, a horseshoe, a bust of a horse, a cricket bat and ball, an antelope head, and a string of fish. The few fictional sketches that appeared were as likely to be about foreign sportsmen as in an 1872–73 *Spirit* serial, "Dick Diminy, or, The Life and Adventures of a Jockey," which followed the hero to continental races including the English Derby and St. Leger. Wilkes' *Spirit* lasted until 1873 and returned to the role of *The American Turf Register*, functioning primarily as a sports information paper without contributing to the growth of sports literature.

Other sports besides racing began to be reported with some frequency. By the mid-1850s there would be an occasional notice of club team baseball in the *Spirit*.[3] As early as 1855 in "Song of Myself," Walt Whitman had referred to himself "afoot with [his] vision," "upon the race course, or enjoying picnics or jigs or a good/game of baseball."[4] Urban sport then evolved out of the transformation of associations of club teams into formal competitive leagues. On 25 February 1857, the *Spirit* reported that delegates from fifteen baseball clubs in New York drew up 34 playing rules. The rise of administrative bodies in clubs of different sorts and varying social classes led to standardization of playing rules and equipment up through the 1870s. Athletic clubs, often founded by European immigrant groups in the cities, became a fixture of urban life.[5] Their emphasis on gymnastic prowess and physical fitness brought a new dimension to participant sport in a country chided for years because of its population's lack of exercise and poor physical condition.[6]

On economic fronts, railroad transportation facilitated the travel of both athletic teams and their fans. Travelling professional baseball teams exploited and formalized urban rivalries while every form of horse racing became dependent upon an improved transportation system. In 1870, the Cincinnati Red Stockings travelled almost 12,000 miles by rail and boat, even reaching the Pacific Coast. Telegraph lines laid down in the 1840s faithfully tapped out team scores for publication in the morning papers. Commercial profit grew most readily from fledgling industries allied with the popularity of sport, including sporting goods, vacation resorts, bicycle manufacturing, fishing and hunting supplies, and boat building.[7]

The line dividing the frontier physical prowess hero from the sports hero of industrial society is difficult to draw because the characters flow into one another in suggestive ways. Herman Melville in *Moby-Dick* (1851) managed to suggest a bridge from the individual frontier hero to the team-oriented, truncated prowess hero who still can be recognized as our modern athlete. Melville wrote of an all-male society apart from domestic life, a society of superb athletes, each with a specialized physical function, whose talents were wedded to industrial production for huge profit. *Moby-Dick* has frequently been called the greatest American hunting story, but Melville develops the epic tale by showing how physical prowess had an industrial function in an era immediately preceding the time in which sport became a function of or a response to the industrialism controlling its growth.

The *Pequod*'s crew is a marvellous and varied collection of physical giants and specialists. Ahab possesses a magic-welded harpoon; Queequeg hurls his harpoon for Peleg and Bildad in the whaling equivalent of a team tryout. The "Knights and Squires" sections (chapters 26–27), which provide the exotic backgrounds of Daggoo, Tashtego, and Queequeg along with biographical sketches of Starbuck, Stubb, and Flask, read somewhat like composite descriptions in a modern team yearbook, complete with essentials of personal history, personality, and particular skills. Stubb drives the men in his boat with great Tall Tale fervor.[8] The Pequod's "roster," which chronicles the essential American industrial system of organization, with the Blacks and Indians subservient to the mates who direct the boats—"The native American liberally provides the brains, the rest of the world as generously supplying the muscles" (108)—is also a detailed forerunner of the American sports team profile.

Ahab drives his men to production. Conditioned by a society that demands both "accumulation" and competitive performance,"[9] Ahab bends the great skill and strength of the *Pequod*'s crew toward the accumulation of capital, turning the boat itself into a whale oil factory. Yet Ahab must duel Moby Dick. Caught by the imperatives that recast the industrial slave as a metaphysical prisoner, he has no choice but to duel his Leviathan. Melville points to a great hero waging a monumental physical battle with adept mates against the tremendous adversary in an uncharted arena. Ahab drives his team under the terms of a "contract" with owners Bildad and Peleg, but he is driven by his own goal, to kill Moby Dick, god or devil.

The sports dimension to the *Pequod*'s crew can be inferred through their great physical skills, but their contest is one extended *agon* more closely resembling warfare. *Moby-Dick* is more epic romance than novel and the crew's performance is more martially primitive than sporting. Their athletic skills have been sharpened for real battle against a giant foe. Mark Twain in "Old Times on the Mississippi" also portrayed a functioning team of men on a boat on the threatening water. Like the *Pequod,* his steamboats have expressly economic functions yet they are also centers of popular sport spectacle in a recognizable society.

While Melville described a closely working industrial team of flamboyant and individual physical heroes, Twain studied individual heroism in the river mastery of the steamboat pilot as well as the popular spectacle of steamboat racing. He caught the craft of steamboating at its highest moment, turned its deepest secrets into a metaphor of artistic control, and transformed the power of both river and pilot to images of majesty and mastery. Play roles continued to grow out of work roles but were now identified with men at their machines. Twain invested the steamboat pilot with skill and popular acclaim but sadly concluded with the pilot's ultimate irrelevance and defeat. A brief discussion of *Life on the Mississippi* suggests directions in which American sport was heading after the Civil War.

Early in "Old Times," Twain recalls the days of keelboatmen that predated his own years on the river. The era of Mike Fink and his athletic mates was dashed by the invention of the steamboat. *Life on the Mississippi* includes a poignant fragment from the yet-to-be-completed *Huckleberry Finn* in which Huck sees the keelboatmen as jolly old drunks, full of frontier yells and blather, yet "they couldn't keep that up very long without getting winded, so by and by they settled round the jug again."[10] The keelboatmen began to disappear during the "flush times" of steamboating that Twain puts between 1811 and 1842. At first they poled down river to return home as deck passengers on a steamboat, ultimately becoming mere deckhands or mates, their bodies aging, their skills irrelevant. Victims of fast change on the river, the keelboatmen were only a memory by the late 1850s when

Twain was a cub pilot in "Old Times." The death of the rollicking boatman had been Thorpe's lament through Mike Fink's rueful nostalgia for the fun of the river, and the telling of "The Big Bear of Arkansas" ominously takes place on the steamboat *Invincible*. The pattern of fast change on the river recurs only a generation later in the late 1850s with the demise of the steamboat pilot which Twain chronicles. The physical strength and freedom of keelboatmen and the feats of memory and control of steamboat pilots both become nonutilitarian heroic achievements in an era when the railroad grew to dominate the Mississippi Valley. Whole cycles of popular heroism turned over in a matter of years and postfrontier America began to look elsewhere for its heroes.

For several decades, Twain suggests, the steamboat pilot was the heroic model for young boys in Hannibal, Missouri. The pilots were "tireless talkers" and "as they talk only about the river they are always interesting," Twain wrote and observed, "his pride in his occupation surpasses the pride of kings" (63). Exactly as a modern athletic hero, the pilot was idolized for his power, authority, glamor, pride, and salary. Not only did a pilot have privileged status on land but the whole crew—firemen, deckhands, and barbers—would be talked about and tendered favors and homage. They were a lionized team of smoothly functioning players, much as early baseball players traveling the urban circuit would be only a few decades later.

Working pilots were accorded the hero's mantle in river society, but also the steamboats themselves became competitors; during the immensely popular steamboat races, the great boats assumed competitive functions alongside economic ones. One particularly fabled steamboat racer was named *Grey Eagle* after the legendary match-racing thoroughbred of the early 1840s. The steamboat races were popular (and dangerous to crew and passengers) from 1830 to about 1850. The steamboat's economic functions aided the rise of organized sport as well by carrying horse-racing and prizefight news up and down the Mississippi Valley before the telegraph network was fully developed in the 1840s. The steamers also transported racing thoroughbreds as well as their patrons to all turf centers.[11]

Twain carefully describes a major steamboat race in chapter 16, "Racing Days," where "citizens crowd the decks of boats that are not to go, in order to see the sight" (142). A race between notoriously fleet steamers was an event of vast importance. The date was set several weeks in advance, and from that time forward a state of excitement pervaded the Mississippi Valley, a network of towns connected by a sporting event as if they were in a league. Twain writes of "people, people everywhere . . .

and you know the borders of the broad Mississippi are going to be fringed with humanity thence northward twelve hundred miles, to welcome these racers'' (144). Twain carefully describes boats that "will never halt a moment between New Orleans and St. Louis'' and lists charts and statistics of the best river runs and fastest times. The chapter is, in itself, a miniature steamboat sporting almanac, complete with essay and records, and it underscores the ease with which steamboating could pass from commercial necessity to sporting artifact. Twain shows the river become the arena for a great clash. An entire population will be vicariously thrilled and satisfied through sport; the machine as the nominal hero is dominated by the smoothly working team of deckhands and mates, all at the command of the pilot.

The river as arena is where the pilot's education takes place as well as the audience's gratification, and Twain's cub pilot is a relentless student under the tutelage of pilot Horace Bixby, portrayed as the master of the great craft. Bixby's feat of navigating past Hat's Island at dusk is a dramatic contest of its own with an admiring audience of other pilots on hand: "We bore steadily down the bend. More looks were exchanged, and nods of surprised admiration—but no words'' (67). Metaphor after metaphor depicts the pilot's role with continual implied comparisons to the conduct of a life and the processes of art. A pilot has to learn the river both coming and going, must know the tricks of shadows, sunlight, moonlight, and fog, must literally sense the shapes of snags, shoals, water changes, and silt, and be ready to adapt to any new information. Above all, he must possess disciplined confidence in himself and his judgment and must never give up the wheel to panic.

All the glory of the pilot—heroic status, self-mastery, an artist's control of his boat—is dashed by Twain's conclusion of the "Old Times'' section of *Life on the Mississippi;* no sooner has the narrator eulogized keelboating as the "now-departed and hardly remembered raft life'' (31) than he begins to speak of the "old departed steamboat days'' (93) and piloting as a thing "of the dead and pathetic past''(139). This abrupt shift from the time of piloting in the 1850s to Twain's return to the river in 1882 has the violent effect of cutting off romantic remembrance. At the conclusion of his apprenticeship, the narrator's fight with a pilot on duty, his subsequent transfer to another boat, the explosion of his first boat, and death of his brother bring his cub piloting memories to a grim and truncated conclusion.[12]

It is important to point out that the steamboat *Pennsylvania* in "Old Times'' is not damaged or destroyed by the great river but by the explosion of its own boilers, a mechanical disaster. Neither the heroic pilot nor his dominant adversary, the river, is at fault. Twain had prepared the reader for the decline in the pilots' autonomy through a careful account of their growing dependence on each other by the formation of pilot associations, the resultant control of owners and captains, and the concomitant loss of freedom. In "Old Times," the pilot's freedom is a personal sense of power and mastery but it falls prey to technological error (the explosion) and technological advance (the growth of railroads) as well as to advancing stratification and organization (the pilots' association). The pilot's work and art as well as his status as popular hero lose their equilibrium; his control is shown to be illusory. Free prowess heroes on the Mississippi River no longer exist in industrial America. Expansion and invention sealed the fate of both the self-reliant Mike Finks and the aspiring heroic cub pilots. Twain suggests an abrupt end to a brief but expressive tradition of work and competition built on the life of the river.

After the Civil War, spectator sports built to the specifications of industrial society and controlled by businessmen would replace the spontaneity of frontier and river sport. The power of the keelboatman or his more complex brother, the steamboat pilot, was nowhere to be found during Twain's 1882 trip down the river to gather enough material to pad the "Old Times" memoir into *Life on the Mississippi*. This return journey yields many discouraging sights for Twain. No longer an anonymous cub pilot but a nationally known author, he is startled to see a steamboat named the *Mark Twain*. He learns that steamboat pilots might have to wear uniforms, that the river is lit up from shore to shore, that government "snag boats" and more sophisticated compasses diminish the skills needed for piloting. His litany of New Orleans sporting life is trivial, consisting of diversions such as cock-fighting and mule-racing.

In terms of Mark Twain's oeuvre, the conclusion of "Old Times" may be seen as a decisive break in his imagination; in extended terms, it symbolizes the end of an integrated sporting life on the frontier. The functionalism of rifle, horse, and keelboat/steamboat could no longer coexist with their use in sport. Spontaneous quarter races or horse swaps, shooting matches, or great steamboat races became fewer and fewer. Post-Civil War America was in the process of evolving a new order of sport and recreation, more organized, more homogenized, more spectatorial, more dominated by popular philosophies of education and patriotism, and more affected by the availability of capital, developments of communication, and a growing transportation network. It would be like nothing witnessed before in American recreation and sporting life. The modern Popular Sports Hero would work and play in the new industrial society. And if Twain did not preside at the birth of the new order of popular team sport, he most surely delivered a eulogy for the destruction of older sporting pastimes in the decline of the balanced roles of work and play depicted in "Old Times on the Mississippi."

Major league baseball epitomized what Twain saw as vigorous industrialization. In 1889, when American ballplayers returned from a round-the-world trip, Twain said he could hardly assimilate the fact that they had played in such remote lands. He expressed his disbelief in the closing speech of a testimonial dinner given April 8, 1889, at Delmonico's Restaurant in New York City. The dinner honored Albert G. Spalding, the intrepid sporting goods entrepreneur and owner of the Chicago White Stockings, and the major league all-star players he had led on the just finished six-month tour. It was on this occasion that National League President Abraham Mills declared that the heady mix of "patriotism and research" had clearly established that baseball originated in America,and bore no taint of borrowing from the British.[13] The climax of this evening of diamond jingoism was a vintage address by Twain. Less historic perhaps than his vision of President Grant as a baby or his own indiscretions in the Whittier birthday dinner speech, this talk ranged expansively over his own memories of the Sandwich Islands. He had visited the Islands in 1867, and he marveled that baseball had been played in "that far-off home of profound repose, and soft indolence, and dreamy solitude." He mused, "And these boys have played base-ball *there!*—baseball, which is the very symbol, the outward and visible expression of the drive and push and rush of the raging, tearing, booming nineteenth century!"[14] His remarks do not appear facetious in any way. When he exclaimed, they "have played baseball there!," "there" may have been a subconscious reference to St. Louis, New Orleans, or Hannibal as well as to the Sandwich Islands. At some level, Twain was setting up the opposition of a "Happy Valley" derived from his Mississippi childhood, with baseball an emblem of intruding industrial organization. Twain was sensitive to the encroachment of the newly created spectacle of American popular sport. He had an eye for burgeoning industries and heroic young capitalists while at the same time he feared such precision and power. At the time of this speech, Twain was in the last full flush of hope for his monumental investment in the Paige type-setting machine into which he would pour hundreds of thousands of dollars between 1880 and 1894.[15]

Baseball in 1889 was, indeed, all Twain conceived it was: growing, acquisitive, and ultimately monopolistic. In short, it was the new American business reality embodied in sport. Twain has his eminently practical and cynical Hank Morgan introduce baseball as a suitable distraction for his restless knights in *A Connecticut Yankee in King Arthur's Court* (1889). It was Hank's project to "replace the tournament with something which might furnish an escape for the extra steam of the chivalry, keep those bucks entertained. . . ."[16] Twain creates images of one team in "chainmail ulsters" while "the other wore plate-armor made of my new Bessemer steel" (367). The baseballs clank off their armor-plate and bound one hundred fifty yards away, as Twain makes vivid the metallic machine imagery of the sport. The knights are romantic iron men before the age of machines. In spoofing the democratic game and its opportunities, Hank states that he chose his teams by "rank, not capacity," and his full lineups include only kings and an emperor. In a pointed reference to Spalding's famous tour, Hank observes, "the first public game would certainly draw fifty thousand people; and for solid fun would be worth going around the world to see" (368).

Albert Spalding's boyhood was not unlike Twain's, albeit fifteen years later. He was the embodiment of a midwest Hank Morgan in his ambition and empire-building.[17] His career in organized sport was the first clear example of the business opportunities that awaited the heroic athlete in industrial America. Spalding was born in 1850 on the Rock River outside Rockford, Illinois. He pitched for amateur baseball teams in Rockford right after the Civil War and in 1867 clerked in a grocery store for three dollars a week. In 1868, he pitched for the Rockford club that beat a team of touring professionals led by Harry Wright and Wright recruited him for his Boston club in 1871. In 1876 he jumped to the Chicago White Stockings for more money as pitcher, captain, and manager. One year later he retired at age twenty-six. He had won 240 games in six years with a best record of 56–7 in 1875.

Spalding then became the White Stockings' managing club secretary, where he closely worked with White Stockings owner and National League President John Hurlbert. He also devoted increasing time to his fledgling sporting goods business and within one year had secured the monopoly to manufacture all league baseballs as well as to publish the league's *Official Baseball Guide,* securing as editor America's most famous sportswriter, Henry Chadwick. By 1882, he was the principal owner of the White Stockings, the most successful franchise of the 1880s starring King Kelly and Cap Anson, and he had become the most powerful spokesman in league development and player-club contracts and regulations. By 1885, Spalding published dozens of sporting guides and record books, and the first mass-produced line of sporting pamphlets, and he had established a monopoly on sporting goods from all kinds of equipment down to grandstand cushions and turnstiles. In the space of two decades Spalding rose from boy pitcher to sports millionaire. When Twain gave his address, he was conceiving Hank Morgan and helping to finance the dreams of James W. Paige, but sitting right before him at the head table at Delmonico's was the triumphant Albert Spalding, 38 years old and already in command of the "drive and push and struggle of the raging, tearing, booming nineteenth century."

JOURNALISM AND POPULAR SPORT

Reporters of this new sports establishment were the less refined, democratic inheritors of the spectatorial position of the Southwestern gentleman. The sports beat gave them a true picture of changing American preoccupations in a commercialized culture. The flamboyant style of early organized sport further influenced the development of the writing about it. The almanac and Southwestern traditions had fixed a manner of reporting sport in society in more than a half-century of larger-than-life physical heroes and tricksters in realistic comic narrative. The needs of an expanding medium were crossed with older conventions of reporting sporting life. Daily and weekly journalism had grown apace with the development of organized sport, and the identification of Popular Sports Heroes became a necessity for both industries. A host of boxing and baseball heroes existed in modern sport before 1900. Any young reporter going to work on a sports beat after 1900, including Lardner, Broun, Runyon, and Charles Van Loan, had a vast repository of lore at the ready, reinforced by what he himself saw daily in the ring and on the diamond.

     Before 1890, the reporting of sport was left largely to the weekly sporting journals, the most prominent of which were the surviving *Spirit of the Times,* the *New York Clipper,* and the *National Police Gazette.* On April 16, 1887, baseball's Opening Day, the *Clipper* ran a 100-word fantasy about an umpire with a mortar who turned it on protesting players and fans. The *Clipper* had a baseball notes column called "Short Stops," and on April 30 featured a drawing of "Connie Mack, Baseball Player."[18] A weekly feature, "From the Hub," was not only about Boston area baseball but about the entire National League. The *Clipper* carried about 25 box scores per issue with a paragraph description of each game. The issue of 2 July 1887 carried a sketch about a ballplayer who believed his good luck charm at all the games was a mysterious blond lady who turned out to be the fiancée of a teammate. From 1887 to 1893, the *Clipper* expanded its baseball reporting in both major and minor leagues.

The annual edition of Beadle's *Dime Base Ball Player,* published by dime novel publishers Beadle and Adams, was printed from 1860 to 1881 before Spalding began to publish his baseball guidebooks. Its editor was Henry Chadwick, perhaps the first real American sportswriter, a man whose writing career spanned more than sixty years in sport.[19] Chadwick's sporting values were formed in his native England and he never failed to stress the social virtues of gentleman amateurs in his writings on cricket and baseball. The *Dime Base Ball Player* popularized the game by being the first publication to collect and list players' averages. Its inside covers were full of advertisements for baseball caps, stockings, balls, and bats. Each year, more and more cities reported scores and records to Chadwick.[20] The pages of the manual record the expansion of baseball throughout the South and Midwest. Chadwick did diligent work in recording, teaching, and proselytizing for the game.[21]

Horse racing and boxing were the other principle beneficiaries of the rise of organized sport. Racing grew rapidly in the post-Civil War era, supported by newly rich robber barons as well as socialites. The number of turf clubs increased noticeably in all urban areas. By 1890 New York was the undisputed center of thoroughbred racing as the *Spirit* and the *Clipper* proudly proclaimed. Boxing was widely denounced from society's pulpits but no sport was so eagerly followed by wagering sportsmen. Most reputable magazines and newspapers refused to carry accounts of fights before 1890, yet publications such as the *Clipper* and the *Police Gazette* were there to take up the slack.

The infusion of the Irish into sport in the 1850s produced America's earliest popular sporting heroes, who exhibited many elements of the frontier roarers. Specifically, John L. Sullivan, the first great heavyweight champion, and Michael "King" Kelly, the most popular baseball player of the 1880s, were throwbacks to an earlier strain of American hero. They drank copiously, bragged continuously, outslugged and outwitted their opponents, and constantly stayed in the limelight. They were marketed to an adoring public in all phases of show business; they even tried the vaudeville stage as actors and singers, a tradition going back to Crockett and his stage alter-ego, James Paulding's Nimrod Wildfire.

Until Sullivan won the heavyweight championship from Paddy Ryan in 1822, boxing supremacy had been determined in most of the preceding four decades by fights between British and American fighters with bouts held on both sides of the Atlantic. Boxing was the society and court pastime of Regency England where William Hazlitt in "The Fight" (1882), and the great early boxing writer and the Regency's most popular essayist, Pierce Egan, had made it a literary subject. As the sport declined in respectability in England, American fighters, mostly Irish immigrants, began to achieve more prominence. The period from 1850 to 1880 was a muddle of "farces, non-fights, and intimidations,"[22] with matches being halted in mid-round, backers entering the rings with weapons, and referees being terrorized into decisions by the wagering fans.

It was into such a chaotic sport that Sullivan brought a kind of order, at least in the ring itself. At 5'10½" and 190 pounds of robust muscle, the "Boston Strong Boy" ruled the heavyweight division from 1882 to 1892. Sullivan's great feud throughout his career was with the flamboyant Richard Kyle Fox, the editor and publisher of the revitalized *Police Gazette*—the *Playboy, True Confessions,* and *Sport* of its time—all under one cover. The enmity between Sullivan and Fox sold boxing tickets and papers, a fact of which they were both aware. The weekly *Gazette* provided a panorama of boxing matches, a roundup of the week's atrocities (lynchings, child murders, rapes), prurient stories on theater personalities, and, most of all, a vast information sheet on various kinds of betting events. The *Gazette* was a staple, sold not on newsstands but in those late-nineteenth-century male preserves, the barbership and the saloon, where Fox found an avid audience away from home and family. The fact of a *Gazette* appearance was enough to defeat the respectability of all but the most major sporting event. Fox's most important function outside of his paper was as promoter and stakesholder for various "sports," most of them hardly recognized as such until he championed them. Not forgetting his best outlets, he even gave medals to the champion drink-mixers and hair-cutters.[23]

Fox was a heavy wagerer who wished to get in on some of the heavy weight championship money. When Sullivan snubbed him soon after winning the title, Fox embarked on a years-long search for an opponent to thrash the champion. By 1887, the *Gazette* was pushing hard for a Sullivan fight with Jake Kilrain, but the champion expressed his disdain for the *Gazette* Championship Belt by saying, "I wouldn't put it around the neck of a

Gah-damn dog.''[24] The *Gazette*'s taunts and Sullivan's rejoinders undoubtedly popularized professional boxing. While polite society professed to mor-
ally censure the sport, it lent its financial support. Sullivan ultimately met
Kilrain July 8, 1889, at Richburg, Mississippi. The patrons of the fight
boarded a mysterious train in New Orleans with tickets that read ''To Des-
tination'' because the fight was illegal in both Mississippi and Louisiana.
Kilrain's timekeeper was Bat Masterson, and the fight went 75 rounds before an aging Sullivan, who had sweated out months of dissipation in training, finished off Fox's challenger in that last of the great bare-knuckle
brawls. It was Sullivan's finest hour, as even Fox admitted.[25]

Simple boxing stories that were really biographies of leading contenders also were found on occasion in the later dime novels with the ring
action taking up much of the story. However, for the most part, boxing was
shunned except by subliterature.[26] The press satiated the public's curiosity
with copious, freewheeling accounts of actual bouts. The heavyweight division enjoyed a truly golden decade in the 1890s with many outstanding
contenders besides the famous champions, Sullivan, James Corbett, Bob
Fitzsimmons, and Jim Jeffries. By 1905, Jack London could write *The
Game,* a novel with a boxing hero, while American realist painters Thomas
Eakins and George Bellows would capture the power of the ring in their art
(see chapter 10).

The daily newspaper promoted, reported, and advertised sporting
events as it sustained and gave continuity to the results of a season's play.
Newspaper reporters grafted legendary prowess onto commercial players,
not for a conception of national glory or as a model for youth but for the
creation of color and humor in their sketches. In the era of expanded sports
reporting after the Civil War, it was a simple matter to be a fan or ''krank''
as well as a participant. A hero industry for the masses seized on a frontier
tradition of American heroism that was vocal and full of braggarts and tricksters.

As organized sport grew rapidly, its folk heroes also became more
prominent, especially in professional baseball. During Sullivan's rise to
glory in the ring, another flamboyant Irishman, Michael ''King'' Kelly,
gained fame on the baseball diamond. Kelly's fame was built not only on
his physical skills,[27] but on the legend of his nimble brain which enabled
him to skirt baseball rules and create new ones, even in the middle of a
play. Some of his exploits were at least plausible. On a day when he was

not playing, a foul ball was hit toward the dugout but out of reach of any player on the field, at which time Kelly leaped up, announced, "Kelly now catching for Boston," and caught the foul pop. His catch was legal because in the 1880s a substitute was able to enter the game "on notice" to the umpire. Kelly forced a change in that rule. Other Kelly feats were more in line with backwoods tall tales. It was said that he never tagged third base on his way home, that he went from first to third by way of the pitcher's box, and that his uniform letters stood out an inch from his shirt front. However, the most enduring lore centered on Kelly's slides.[28] The song, "Slide, Kelly, Slide" rivalled the popularity of the poem, "Casey at the Bat," in the early 1890s and phonograph records of it were sold widely.[29]

Kelly was a member of Spalding's White Stocking team which dominated the National Leaague in the 1880s. Led by first baseman-manager Adrian "Cap" Anson, a muscular slugger who played for 27 years until 1893, the White Stockings were baseball's first glamor team boasting a lineup of seven "six-footers" and five pennants in 1880–82 and 1885–86. However, Spalding created a furor in the spring of 1887 when he sold the tempestuous, hard-drinking Kelly to Boston for the then incredible price of $10,000 and followed this trade by peddling his 36-game winner, John Clarkson, to the same team at the same price a year later. Anson was a more traditional, bullying prowess hero, not as colorful as Kelly but utterly indestructible and consistent, a man more acceptable to a commercial magnate's desire for a stable product on the field.

Baseball writing remained in its infancy until the late 1880s. Frank Queen's weekly *New York Clipper*, begun in 1853, had assumed the role of the leading baseball paper. It introduced the box score and, by 1868, offered a gold ball to the championship team. In 1883 Francis C. Richter began editing the *Sporting Life* in Philadelphia. In 1886 came the first issue of *The Sporting News*, which remains today the leading weekly sports information paper. *Outing, Harper's Weekly,* and *Frank Leslie's Illustrated Weekly* also carried frequent articles about baseball.[30] The baseball reporters alternated between creating colorful heroes and acceding to wishes of the baseball establishment to champion seriousness and pure performance.

In Chicago, the White Stockings had become big news. In 1887 a 20-year-old city reporter named Finley Peter Dunne was assigned to travel with the team and prepare reports for the six o'clock edition of the *News*. He soon thereafter became famous for creating Martin Dooley, the Irish saloon keeper-pundit of Chicago's "Archey Road" who for twenty years advised local and national politicians on the errors of their ways. Dunne's

Chicago contemporaries included Charles Seymour on the *Herald* and Leonard Washburn of the *InterOcean,* fellow innovators in reporting sports events.[31] The style affected by these reporters was a loose, colloquial account that delved behind the box scores to make use of current baseball slang and breezy talk. The outlandish metaphor, the lively pace of the action, and the emphasis on crowd and environment were their hallmarks.

Like Ring Lardner twenty years later, Dunne got his first true reporting opportunity on his baseball assignment. He found it a cosmopolitan education to travel the National League circuit in 1887, widening his knowledge of American life and of human nature. A chronicle of Dunne's reports on the White Stockings shows how the Midwest's last dialect humorist was also its first deft baseball reporter. From the outset, he paid much attention to the fans in the stands and the improbable happenings both on and off the field. Dunne was constantly revising his perspective and creating new angles of vision from which to view the action. On April 30, the opening game was rained out but the resourceful Dunne filed a story on the doings of the "kranks," the 1880s term for "fans," whom he shows betting, and talking about new rules.[32] Through the artifice of their conversations, Dunne previewed the strengths and weaknesses of the entire National League.

Dunne's favorite target during the season was Anson, the brusque White Stocking leader. Dunne lampooned Anson in subtle fashion. In reporting a serious interview with Anson, Dunne observed: "At this point Capt. Anson's remarks were choked off because he was pulling a flannel shirt over his head" (6/27/87). Charged by the Pittsburgh manager with refusing to play on a wet field, Anson said, " 'That's all right. You tell Phillips we will be there to play. Maybe he'll win and maybe he won't.' And upon delivering himself of this remark the great first-baseman buried himself in a deep reverie" (8/20/87). Anson's wooden personality was one of Dunne's favorite topics for the entire season, yet, for the most part, he remained respectful of the players' individuality and did not belittle them. He quoted their remarks in standard English and was clearly taken by their lives and thoughts. He wrote about them as if they were ordinary people, not stars or brutes. Dunne reported Kelly's triumphant return to Chicago in a Boston uniform on "Mike Kelly's Jubilee Day" and he listed the names of 37 aldermen and 18 ministers who attended the game (6/24/87). Dunne's observations on other league cities were succinct enough. On July 9 in much-maligned Philadelphia, a player says, "It's a good town—so good that the boys can hardly find chewing gum enough to tide them over until Monday" (7/9/87). The White Stockings were a major disappointment during Dunne's season with the club in 1887; they finished third with a 71-50 record. Without Kelly, Anson was their lone .300 hitter. As the summer wore on, Dunne became as frustrated as some of the players. On August 27 he digressed from a strikeout recorded in his line score to note, "Sunday had just four holes in his bat and Welch hit every one."[33]

Dunne's fame lay ahead of him. In January 1888 he moved to the *Times* as a political writer and covered both national political conventions that year; by 1896 he would be reporting the conventions through the mask of Mr. Dooley for the *Post*. While Mr. Dooley occasionally made whimsical references to football, boxing, or cycling, Dunne's sports reporting days were over; yet as a generous and pungent satirist, he left his mark on the craft.

Another young Chicago newsman was George Ade, who began his *Fables in Slang* in the *Chicago Record* in 1897. Ade was another master of the vernacular, possessing a more sceptical wit than Dunne. His ear was flawless, his grasp of popular language unsurpassed.[34] Ade often wrote about American sporting life, including "The Fable of the Coming Champion Who was Delayed" (boxing) and "The Fable of the Caddy Who Hurt His Head While Thinking," a golfing sketch which prefigured Lardner's "A Caddy's Diary." In "The Fable of the Base Ball Fan Who Took the Only Known Cure," Ade recounted the deathbed scene of a baseball fan:

> His wife wept softly and consoled herself with the Thought that possibly he would have amounted to Something if there had been no National Game. She Forgave Everything and pleaded for one Final Message. His Lips moved. She leaned over and Listened. He wanted to know if there was Anything in the Morning papers about the Condition of Bill Lange's knee.[35]

Chicago was not the only city to produce outstanding sports reporters in the 1890s, but Dunne and Ade were the two newsmen who gained the most lasting prominence in American humorous literature. Many cities claimed fine reporters as their own, including New York, Boston, and Cincinnati. When Joseph Pulitzer bought the New York *World* in 1883, he organized the first sports department on a daily newspaper. In 1887 the United Press and the Associated Press could send wire reports of games to a network of seventy cities. By 1892 virtually all the great papers in large cities had sports editors and staffs, although the sports section itself had not yet appeared. Some of the most prominent names in sports writing before 1900 were O.P. Caylor of Cincinnati and later of the New York *Herald;* Charles Dryden, the "Mark Twain of Baseball," who wrote in both Chicago and New York; Harry Weldon and Ban Johnson, later the first president of the American League, in Cincinnati; and Tim Murnane in Boston. A second generation of writers who entered the field at about the time that professional baseball became a stable multimillion-dollar industry included Joe Vila, Bozeman Bulger, Hugh Fullerton, Irvin S. Cobb, Grantland Rice, Sid Mercer, Van Loan, Broun, Runyon, and Lardner himself.[36]

The daily newspaper was *the* exciting place for a young writer to be during the 1890s. The poor writing habits picked up in the face of restrictive editing, deadlines, and the need for a brand of authoritative shallowness were counteracted by the opportunity to learn about city life. Dunne, Ade, and Lardner were all city room habitués at one time or another, cultivating, as Larzer Ziff has put it, "the twin devices of cynicism and sentimentality."[37] Nowhere has this particular heritage from the daily paper evinced itself more fully than in the popular fiction genre of the sports story where the graduates of the press box evolved a style both humorously hard-boiled and idealistic. The daily newspaper served as a spark of inspiration for young writers while providing them with modern urban subjects. It often debilitated their style and prohibited depth in their portraits of character, but it promoted concision, the sharply drawn image, a swift pace, humor, and pathos.

The language of baseball had begun to enter the American lexicon by the 1880s. The metaphors became more and more florid in describing the action as writers attempted to see just how many ways a single play might be described. There were scattered songs about sport before the 1890s. "Finnegan the Umpire" joined "Slide, Kelly, Slide!" and "Casey at the Bat" as the most popular baseball art of the era; Ernest Thayer's "Casey" first appeared in the San Francisco *Examiner* on June 3, 1888, next to a column by Ambrose Bierce.[38] Charles Hoyt, a popular farceur, wrote *The Runaway Colt* (1895), a baseball play where the hero and umpire were stock comic characters. Anson starred in one version and, while trying to escape an effusive female fan, said to a player, "Don't leave me alone with her, or I'll expel you from the league. Worse, I'll sell you to Louisville." "Take Me Out to the Ball Game" was not written until 1908, but barbershop quartets soon made it a nationally known tune.[39]

Occasionally an early baseball life is recorded that reads like perfect material for fiction. Consider the case of Joseph E. Borden. In 1875 Borden became the first pitcher to throw two no-hit games. On April 22, 1876, he was the winning pitcher in the first official National League game, but then he came down with a sore arm and finished the season as a groundskeeper for Boston. Later he stitched baseballs in a Philadelphia factory and died in the Johnstown flood in 1889.[40] Borden did not have his bard but Charlie "Hoss" Radbourne did. In 1884 Radbourne had appropriated the role of physical superman so often assumed by almanac heroes by winning 62 games for Providence and pitching in 35 of his team's last 37 games. Radbourne had engaged in terrible arguments with his manager and another pitcher named Sweeny who promptly jumped the team. Radbourne then swore he would pitch in every game until the end of the season to show up both of them *if* he could obtain his release in October.[41] The braggadocio and legendary feats of Radbourne probably were the bases for Lardner's story, "Sick 'Em" (*Saturday Evening Post,* 25 July 1914), about two vain, strong-armed pitchers who could be goaded into acceptable performances only by continually insulting each other. Such careers, along with scores of others, provided the raw material for modern tall tales of the Popular Sports Hero.

SPORT IN THE DIME NOVEL

The daily newspaper was not the only outlet for tall tales of prodigious athletes after the Civil War. The rise of organized sport in the 1870s occurred at the same time as the proliferation of popular literature in story papers and dime novels, reflecting changing conditions in American national life. The story paper and dime novel became mass cultural institutions in the period between 1850 and 1880. Perhaps the most important effect of industrialization on popular culture, they constituted the only sustained literary expression of the frontier after the Civil War;[42] in fact, the majority of newly literate Americans absorbed the winning of the West through heroes such as Buffalo Bill and Deadwood Dick, who replaced the roarers of earlier backwoods tales.

The story papers of the 1850s were largely legacies and extensions of the various publications that had been in existence since the 1830s in Boston, New York, and Philadelphia.[43] It was the mercurial Robert Bonner of the New York *Ledger* who put story papers on a profit-making basis. He built a commercial newspaper empire on total mastery of the distribution and marketing process. But Bonner had his competitors; in 1855, two young printers, Francis S. Street and Francis S. Smith, bought the *New York Weekly*'s subscription list and proceeded to launch a publishing house that developed into the leading producer of pulp fiction and mass circulation magazines well into the modern era.

What Robert Bonner was to the story paper, Erastus Beadle was to the dime novel. He and his brother Irwin began as printers and booksellers in Cooperstown and Buffalo, New York before they moved to New York City in 1858. They were interested in all sorts of literary ephemera: chapbooks, song books, pamphlets, anything that would sell. By mixing original tales of the frontier with hoary gothic romances reprinted from the 1840s, Beadle presented a diversified product that was eagerly consumed. The relentless emphasis on output by dime publishers produced a subliterature that simplified most aspects of the human condition.[44] As dime publishers began to mine the potential market in the youth audience, the number of gothic tales diminished while frontier stories for boys rapidly became the staple fare along with the urban counterpart of the frontier scout and hunter, the solitary detective battling city crime.[45] Both the male and the adolescent orientation of the Beadle product eased the introduction of the sports hero into the dime novel.

The western experience in the dimes had brought forth the simplifed Deadwood Dick, Wyoming Will, and Buffalo Bill to replace the Crocketts and Finks, but sport was initially not pervasive enough in the culture to gather a cluster of meanings around central heroic figures.[46] In the dimes of the 1880s, however, a new hero began to appear in considerable numbers. Often he was a schoolboy or college youth, but just as often he was a detective masquerading as someone else and the role he assumed with increasing regularity was that of the athlete. When sport first appeared in the dimes and story papers during the 1880s, a number of conditions had to be met. First, sport had to meet the preexisting formula for the basic dime adventure plots. Most dime novels required a limited number of situations that could be manipulated, for example, the abduction, the robbery, the chase, the trap, the prison scene (whether in a cave, cabin, or warehouse), the onrushing disaster of trains, floods, fires, stampeding buffalo or cattle. In short, the dimes required physical action and continual movement, the more aggressive and violent the better. The unfolding of plot in almost any game situation provided liberal doses of such action.

Sport gave the dimes a narrative framework peculiarly well adapted to a formula literature. It provided a simple structure for the unfolding of a plot, the basic framework of which began and ended with a "big game" or pivotal contest. The hero was established at the outset as an outstanding player; the villain just as often as the leader of the opposition. The plot then branched out into stock dime novel fare with mystery assuming center stage. After the plot creaked on through various complications, it returned to the big game where the villain not only lost the match, but also his ill-gotten gains. The game became a simplistic decision of great validity where life's losers were punished and identified as deficient initially by being losers in sport. In addition, sport gave the hero a public arena in which to excel where an audience could duly recognize him as their hero. Confrontations with villains could be carried out on official turf where public thrashings could be administered. Indeed, the very tools of sport often became weapons in the hands of warrior-athletes. Such a simple structure of contest, victory, and defeat had great appeal for the dime novel plotters. Sport in the dime novel refurbished the basic dime adventure plots. The dime novel itself became a familiar game to its readers, a game in which the heroic player always won.

Baseball was the most popular frame for dime authors in the 1880s because it was the most established of organized sports with the largest share of the audience before 1890. Beadle's twenty-one-year run of the *Dime Base Ball Player* had been a money-maker and no doubt encouraged Erastus and Irwin Beadle to try baseball in a fictional format. George Jenks was a Beadle writer who produced three tales of "Double Curve Dan, the Pitcher Detective," between 1888 and 1890. The first tale in the series has a cover showing a flaxen-haired youth about to pitch to a mustachioed batsman wielding a bottle-shaped bat. The wooden grandstand behind the players is packed with fans. The caption reads, "A roar rose from the audience. The unknown pitcher is a terror.[47] Dan is, indeed, a terror, for he is really Dan Manly, detective of the New York Secret Service. Dan is on the trail of thieves, and baseball is merely a "cover" for his police assignment. Jenks is hardly enamored of the professional player. When Dan is believed dead, the boys back at the detective office remember how he never let baseball interfere with his "work," an index to the popular prejudice against sport as proper employment. Jenks concludes the tale:

> Double Curve Dan still plays ball occasionally, though he is not regularly attached to a club. He has done much valuable work for the Secret Service since he hunted down the murderer of young Hetherington and brought a notorious criminal to justice at the same time. He plays ball as a pastime but feels that the real business of his life lies in sterner channels.[48]

Jenks dispenses with sport as education and can see no connection with any higher laws.

The city is prominent in the Double Curve Dan tales because gambling on sporting events had become a considerable problem for urban authorities as early as the 1870s, particularly in baseball and racing. "The Pitcher Detective's Foil" by Jenks revolves around a fixed game and a crooked umpire. Dan's judgment on a fixer is that "a fellow that would debase the national game by introducing such diabolical methods is too good for hanging."[49] These sentiments reinforce quite early the fact that baseball is the *national* game and that tampering with its moral order and rules is a heinous crime. Yet the constant preoccupation of dime sports fiction with the subject of corruption between 1870 and 1900 shows the tenacity of gambling as an endemic part of American sport from the sketches of Southwestern Humor onward.

The theme of gambling in conjunction with sport goes hand-in-hand with the wary attitude of amateur players and fans toward the professional in the dime novel. The hero is always suspected of being a professional in the early baseball tales. An angry town baseball player addresses a college rival: "You college dudes may be in high feather just now, but what would you amount to without your shortstop, a disguised professional expert, and doubtless a sneaking gambler to boot, coming among you from who knows where?"[50] In the spirit of backwoods chicanery, however, the town has bets of its own to cover in another tale:

> "You see, Mr. Sands, there is a great deal of Bluffton money up on this game, and it is important that we should win. Therefore, believing you to be a professional, we mean to do one of two things!"
>
> "Indeed? That is a rather confident assertion to make without knowing what I might have to say about it. *What* do you propose to do. . . ."
>
> "Why sir!" he said, "we will either buy you or we will *bar* you out of the game!"[51]

The practical solution wins over the purity of sport. The early confusion between amateur and professional athlete in the dime novels was an outgrowth of the continuing debate over amateurism versus professionalism in American society by 1890 and was constantly addressed by Henry Chadwick in Beadle's *Dime Base Ball Player* as well as by college coaches and sportsmen such as Walter Camp and Caspar Whitney in *Outing* and *Harper's Weekly*.

However, the dimes did not really explore the tension between player and team/society. The dime sports tales remained in a fantasy world of detectives disguised as pitchers on amateur teams even as John Montgomery Ward in 1890 was organizing professional baseball players into a rival league to challenge the entire existing framework of organized baseball. When actual major league ballplayers were made the subjects of dime tales, the results were often bewildering and bore little relation to reality. Street & Smith ran a series in 1894 about major league players which included a story on none other than King Kelly himself. In each story the focus was on the youth of the hero and his early days on amateur teams before the tale switched to sensational adventure and then concluded tamely with the hero in the big leagues. Kelly's checkered career was not material for children's books. Yet the story of "King Kelly, the Famous Catcher; or the Life and Adventures of the $10,000 Ball-Player,"[52] portrays him as a model of virtue, a "square, honest, upright ballplayer," who was "gentlemanly and kind" and whose exploits on the Paterson, N.J., amateur team caused an admirer to warn, "You had better look out, Mike, or you will find the League people will be after you."

Kelly's amateur play is decribed in similar fashion to that of Double Curve Dan: "When Mike Kelly was not engaged at his business, he spent all his time in the ball field." The reader never finds out what that business might be because it is never mentioned by name. However, his true vocation off the field is to save his girlfriend and himself from natural disasters and town villains. He rescues Katie Kane before she is trampled by horses: "to think with Mike was to act" and "Mike's baseball playing had given him strength to offset the terrible danger from the maddened horses." Arch-enemy Billy Blake, "a player who had formerly belonged to the Paterson Club, but who had been expelled for crookedness," is engaged by Mike in a battle in a balloon gondola where Mike's physical skill enables him to escape certain death. After Mike survives these tests, the offer from the Chicago White Stockings promises a relief from strenuous activity. Mike is an immediate hero and plays with skill and judgment as he starts a triple play in his first major league game. Much is made of his $10,000 purchase price by Boston in 1887, and Mike muses, "there are worse situations in life than that of a successful ball player." The story ends with Kelly in vaudeville reciting "Casey at the Bat" after which a girl singer launches into "Slide, Kelly, Slide!"

The facts of Kelly's later career and early demise were quite different. Spalding had, in fact, traded him to Boston, judging him to be more trouble than he was worth in Chicago because of his repeated absences and drinking problems. After a few good seasons with Boston, Kelly turned increasingly to the music hall and stage circuit. He opened his own saloon (with "Honest John" Kelly, a former umpire) and finally drifted down to

Allentown, Pa., in the minor leagues where he was booed and hissed. He died at 37 of pneumonia on November 8, 1894.[53] The June 1894 dime tale was a bland heroic portrait which functioned as a silly postscript to a colorful career. The dimes were hardly above exploiting sensational personal facts, but Kelly's real adventures were damning to a hero of youth and, in dime terminology, might have "debased the national game."

Evidence of how rigidly the dime sports plots adhered to sensational adventure situations was the sports hero using sporting implements as weapons. Double Curve Dan fires a straight fast ball from a hotel window to knock the knife from a kidnapper's hand, and in a similar situation, he snatches an apple from a basket and hits a villain in the head just as he is about to steal a horse and wagon.[54] Edward Wheeler, the creator of Deadwood Dick, included an even more violent account in his "High Hat Harry, the Baseball Detective":

> A man dashed into the room, armed with a ball bat knocking the sentinel Sylva flat upon the floor.
> It was High Hat Harry, the Baseball Detective!
> With two slashing blows, he struck right and left, laying out first Garrene, then Smiley, and then the disguised Sylva, as she attempted to rise. . . .
> The birds of evil were in the snare at last.[55]

The assimilation of sport into dime plots at this level is crude but nonetheless an index to the growth of reader interest in a sport such as baseball. Bizarre improbabilities surround the players such as Dan's double curve ball or High Hat Harry's neck which can swivel a full 360 degrees, enabling him to keep the whole ball field in view at all times.[56] Such fantasy in the early tales is very reminiscent of the outlandish physical capabilities ascribed to the frontier roarers in the almanacs and Southwestern Humor, and it was a welcome change of pace in the romantic adventure plots. As to the ability of dime authors to describe a contest with any real accuracy, the evidence is discouraging. Wheeler ignored the diamond clash and Jenks managed to avoid the issue by having Double Curve Dan do more apple-throwing than pitching. None of the early dime writers had much feel for the swirl of the action or the grace of the physical contest.

Tales of crude racial and ethnic stereotyping had become staple dime fare during the 1880s. One of the most popular characters in this vein was Clarence Muldoon, who appeared regularly in Frank Tousey's *Five Cent Wide Awake Library*. The dreary round of dialect gags was often built on the adventures of Muldoon's Baseball Club. His all-Irish team would continually meet up with an all-Jewish or all-Italian team, providing opportunities for the author to fire off a rapid succession of ethnic slurs. The low point of the Muldoon series occurs when his inebriated nine plays a team of cripples. The reader is treated to a series of missing arm and leg jokes before he learns that all missing members are somehow concealed inside the uniform sleeves of the supposed unfortunates.[57] This tale is another reminder that grotesque humor is in a classic American strain of tall tale and draws on traditions of physical cruelty and verbal ragging from Mike Fink to Sut Lovingood to modern bench-jockeying and elaborate locker-room pranks.

Dime authors concentrated on baseball more than on any other sport, but horse-racing was another urban sport that continually provided a format for dime plots. In fact, when adapted to tales of city life, the racing plots resembled the baseball stories, centering on sports action, crime, and heroic detectives.[58] As it had been depicted on the Southern frontier before the Civil War, the race track scene of the dimes was rife with corruption; indeed, it was a place where gambling and skulduggery were norms rather than occasional intrusions onto the field of competition. Crooked trainers, jockeys who used barbed whips, doped horses, gamblers who controlled the track operations, and politicians on the take all made their appearances. The track became a particularly effective backdrop as dime authors portrayed a large contingent of urban lowlife characters in search of illegal dollars.

The word "sport" as applied to both heroes and villains in the dimes was a curious appellation that contained a variety of meanings. "Sport" appears in a number of Beadle titles and does not generally refer to an athlete.[59] It could refer to any person of pluck or courage, be he in a mining camp in Colorado or a bar on Broadway. Yet the "sport" could also be a man whose financial dealings took him to the heart of the athletic world as promoter, gambler, or fan. The "sport" interacted with the athlete in some dime sporting plots as the villainous figure whom the athlete had to defeat to assure order in the game.

A general portrait of an urban "sport" in the dimes from 1885 to 1895 would depict a young man of considerable means, not an aristocrat but rather a type that would more closely approximate a modern playboy, easy with his money and always at the gaming table or at the racing meets. "Sport" often referred to his skill at winning a wager or solving a mystery. The competence of the urban playboy in dangerous situations might qualify him as a "sport." The title did not refer to a man of education or social position. Just as often, the "sport" would be only a thin veneer of sophistication away from the belligerent urban tough, the "b'hoy," an earlier free-spirited product of experience in the New York streets.[60]

In summation, sport appeared in dime novel plots for several reasons. The game was perceived as a more than adequate formula for formula literature itself because it had the action and deterministic properties on which the dimes thrived. The game with a mass audience provided a public backdrop for stories of urban crime and greed. Individual larger-than-life heroes, long a dime novel necessity and an American tradition, fit easily into the sporting theme with its emphasis on winners and losers. The sport subject rose in the conventional literary medium best equipped to translate audience experience. The dime novel was the most comfortable and logical place for its first appearance. That the popular player afforded a number of possibilities for individual heroism, action plotting, and definitive winners and losers was obvious to formula writers. The late nineteenth-century industrial organization of American life channeled the more free-form sporting impulse and interest and transformed larger-than-life free spirits into team members in uniform, men who signed contracts and played for a city or who boxed in a ring in which hundreds of thousands and then millions of dollars were to be won or lost.

The story of that new sporting order in journalism and dime novel sketches provided the material for fiction. By 1900, the modern Popular Sports Hero was already present in broad outline, a comic physical-prowess hero in an urban setting, but with a frontier ancestry. He was exuberantly boyish and always dominant, outlandish in character and outstanding in achievement. Yet his individual status had been severely compromised and his sporting skill placed at the behest of an establishment as rigid and demanding as any other bureaucratic organization. It fell to Ring Lardner to explore this central contradiction in the modern professional athlete.

CHAPTER FIVE
Lardner: The Popular Sports Hero

THE MOST TALENTED sportswriter was Ring Lardner, the innovative chronicler of American games, comic players, and their foibles. He allied himself to popular sport and the realist tradition while irrevocably fixing the stereotype of the professional athlete for modern fiction. Lardner stands at the center of any discussion of popular sport in modern American literature. He knew professional sport and suburban recreation to be the average citizen's obsessions, and he worked out of a rich Chicago tradition of sports writers and humorists. He had none of the energy and rawness of American Naturalism and he knew little about it. Throughout his career he affected a classic antiintellectual pose, a stance traditionally feigned by American humorists to enhance satiric thrusts; in Lardner's case, the pose became permanently identified as a trait of his characters, specifically his baseball players. His defensive posture against the world of ideas and, indeed, the world of art as well, seems in retrospect to have been genuine. He was a fearful man, suspicious of his own best and worst impulses, mistrustful of the franker, more open life of the 1920s, proud of his craft as he saw it yet ultimately less than candid about his motivations, both in life and in literature.

Lardner's early primary subjects were athletes. He found a perfect environment for humorous realism in the physical world of professional sport. The sports beat gave him his first writing experience in a milieu that shaped his early attempts at delineating character and writing vernacular speech. By the time he left Chicago for New York in 1919, he had created the first minor galaxy of fictional Popular Sports Heroes. While most of his short stories about sports heroes were simple exercises in broad humor, he was at times able to probe into irrational behavior with characters such as Midge Kelly, Buster Elliott, and blustering Jack Keefe.

Like the Southwestern Humorists a half-century before, Lardner presented the athlete or gamester and his environment as representative of society. In his own reticent fashion he was as angry a stern moralist as Longstreet, as skillful at creating vernacular speech as Harris; his characters could be as sly as Hooper's Simon Suggs or, in another vein, as full of comic bombast as any western roarer. Lardner's links to the Southwestern tradition can be seen most clearly in the role of the narrator as social commentator. The Southwesterners had lashed the rural citizens for their manners; Lardner dissected the urban mass man in his ignorance and insensitivity. Like the Southwestern Realists, Lardner participated in a profound social upheaval, in his case, the twentieth-century urbanization of life and letters.

A philologist of sorts and a writer committed to the vernacular, he found his first congenial subject on the ball field, where his deadpan, laconic narrators related the tallest of baseball tales as in "Horseshoes" (1914), "Alibi Ike" (1915), and "Hurry Kane" (1927). He was the first writer to assume a role critical of the sportswriter's position; he introduced women into sports fiction; he scaled the professional sports hero down into a realistic subject, investing him with physical prowess while comically divesting him of judgment, maturity, and self-knowledge.

Did Lardner mean to criticize athletes as a group? The evidence overwhelmingly suggests that he did not. By making White Sox pitcher Jack Keefe a simple young man with a shrewish wife, unpaid bills, and an apartment he could not afford, Lardner suggested that the athletic hero was not much of a heroic figure and not a symbol of anything, certainly not of the crassness and boobery of all baseball players. Many other Lardnerian urban and suburban citizens shared Keefe's blustering vanity and unrealistic self-image. Lardner mistrusted not ballplayers but popular heroes with self-inflated egos. Also, as ballplayers recalled, Lardner was perhaps never happier than when travelling with the Cubs and White Sox, losing himself in team camaraderie, jokes, and songs.[1]

Critics of Lardner's work suggest that he was either a misanthrope, who saw no saving graces in his characters and thus created less than human subjects, or a repressed idealist, placing all mature experience against some idyllic standard, finding it wanting, and creating strong satire in reaction.[2] Those who feel that Lardner was a misanthrope fail to countenance his tender regard for family and close friends and his many wise, if brittle and cynical, narrators. The idealists cannot come to grips with his rigid censorship of his most personal feelings in print and the paucity of loving, giving characters in his fiction. As a satirist, Lardner felt little responsibility to suggest alternative and more humanizing worlds.

Lardner's achievement remains difficult to assess. Here was a popular artist who constantly professed his desire to attain nothing more lasting than his newspaper columns and stories yet who, almost despite his mistrust of art, created several modern short classics. In the best Southwestern tradition, he debunked his role as author. His consuming ambition was to write for the Broadway musical comedy stage, and his affinity for popular forms remained unbroken until the end of his life. He would have always chosen fame in Tin Pan Alley over a place in the literary pantheon beside Fitzgerald and Hemingway.

At the center of diffuse modern American life, Lardner found a cluster of social games that revealed what passed for reality in social relations. The tensions in this most uncommunicative of men are shown most strongly in his scores of characters who talk past each other in their attempts at finding a link with other human beings. The shallow surface life of his bragging characters is relieved only occasionally by a wise narrator or by their own unconscious hilarity. His work is replete with ballplayers, fans, newsmen, bridge players, and golf caddies, all filling what seemed to be endless days, isolated in one sort of competition or another.

Lardner had a vision of suburban America at play throughout the 1920s, and he wrote that new social freedoms would dictate a widened scope of "games." He saw that the new age's social disorder could be depicted through its games and game players, the roarer sitting in the big league dugout, the con man sitting at the bridge table at a suburban country club, the competitor as a potential menace to the spirit. Lardner was no apologist for organized sport and competition but then he was no advocate of free play either. He discerned no higher American values or common good to come out of a national obsession; he mistrusted obsessions of any kind, communal or personal.

LARDNER AND BASEBALL

Lardner is best known for his baseball stories, specifically those with a vain, bragging hero. "Alibi Ike," once only the title of a thin story, has passed into the general lexicon. *The Busher's Letters,* the continuing saga of Jack Keefe, appeared regularly in *The Saturday Evening Post* from 1914–19. If the American public at this time had any notion of what the average ballplayer sounded like, what he thought about, what he did off the field, the chances are that Lardner's characters provided the clearest image.

After a desultory semester at a second-rate engineering school in Chicago in 1902, Lardner returned to his family's home in Niles, Michigan with little direction or ambition. He read meters for the Niles Gas Company for a year before landing a reporter's job on the South Bend *Times,* where he covered the police station and the courts in the morning and the Central League baseball team in the afternoon. It was there that he first began emulating the styles of some of Chicago's leading sports writers, including Dryden, Hugh Keogh, and Hugh Fullerton of the *Tribune.* Fullerton helped him get his first Chicago job on the *InterOcean* in the fall of 1907.

Before his father lost a great deal of money in land transactions in 1901, the Lardner estate had a baseball diamond, tennis court, and coach house with a stable of horses. Lardner knew baseball as thoroughly as the traditional country gentleman would have known field sports. In later years, Lardner spoke of having figured baseball statistics in the classroom in Niles. In 1908 he began his first major sporting assignment when he covered the White Sox for the *Tribune,* thus following in the footsteps of Dunne, 21 years before on the *News.* After he assumed the column, "In the Wake of the News," in 1913, Lardner perfected the Keefe persona with startling speed. In a few months, he progressed from a parody of the boys' sports hero with one "Verne Dalton" whose adventures were signed by the "Copy Boy," to an account of the 1913 World Series "By an Athlete," to the narrative voice of the Keefe character.[3] In actuality, the entire series of "Busher" tales that made up *You Know Me Al* (1916), plus the baseball stories "Sick 'Em," "My Roomy," and "Horseshoes," were all written in 1914 when he was turning out seven columns per week for the *Tribune.*

A large, muscular man of 6'2", Lardner fit in well with the players, who knew him as shy and private yet ever willing to get into a card game, to drink with them, or to spend hours making up nonsense rhymes and songs. There was a lot of the amateur folklorist about Lardner, who could never hear enough of the ballplayers' speech or their stories. He wrote poems and songs about them, orchestrated the Cubs' barbershop quartet, allowed them guest appearances in his columns, and altogether encouraged their artistic efforts. In "The Wake," Lardner printed outfielder Frank Schulte's poetry (some of which Lardner had written), ghosted his "answers'' to imaginary literary critics, and suspended Schulte from his column for poor writing, then reported that Schulte demanded to be traded to other *Tribune* columns such as "Breakfast Food" or "Day Dreams."[4] At one point he had acted as scribe for an illiterate White Sox pitcher by writing letters home to the player's wife. In recording the repetitive small details, Lardner learned the very cadences and phrasing that he would later perfect in Jack Keefe's letters, a triumph of epistolary style.

Jack Keefe, Lardner's first baseball protagonist, grew out of Lardner's association with ballplayers, their speech, and their lives. The vernacular that Keefe uses in writing letters home to his old friend, Al, is the speech of Niles and semiliterate America. Lardner made a clean break with the dialect tradition. His characters were always representative of the new middle class, suggesting that the new urban and suburban citizen was bound to his neighbor by immersion in the common milieu of the present rather than the linguistic roots and customs of an ethnic past. Baseball, the great unifying force of American popular sport, was a superb choice for creating a bewildered representative of mass man—at once a hero to thousands yet under financial and emotional stress, a character caught in a commercial system against which he blusters with all the instincts of a frontier roarer.

Standing at the center of popular athletic fame in Lardner's work are isolated, ignorant, and frightened men caught in an unreal world of adulation that they could not assimilate into their personal lives. The tension between an individual American athletic hero and his restriction to a commercial team is highlighted in Keefe, the "busher," a young man lacking self-knowledge, control, and tenderness. The role of Keefe suggests not that ballplayers are all braggarts and louts, but that the modern popular hero is an artificial creation fed by the hero's knowledge of his own heroism in the public eye; however, he is mystified by how to transfer this leverage and notoriety into his personal life, which remains a romantic and financial shambles. Nothing in Jack Keefe's life in Bedford has prepared him for the daily stresses of life in Chicago, performance on a major league team, the advances of designing women, and the frustration of his own appetites. He learns nothing; his teammates, manager, and owner alternately write him off as not worth the trouble in spite of his talent.

The epistolary form is here almost that of a diary, a perfect format for a ballplayer's life that moves slowly, day by day and game by game. Jack reports incidents that fix him in the reader's mind while passing over his own head. His run-on quotations and repetitive word choice add to the dreariness of his accounts. He knows nothing of why the joke is so often on him; fully half the remarks made in the novel are beyond him. His own gaffes are seized on by others in derision, causing him to become belligerent and to withdraw further into the shell of his wounded vanity. The recurrence of Jack's crises and his failure to learn from them are exemplified in the account of a New Year's Eve argument in Chicago with his wife Florrie, her sister Marie, and her husband Allen, a left-hander on the White Sox. Jack, always mindful of his money, suggests that they leave an expensive restaurant before running up an enormous bill:

> Then Marie says Oh, shut up and don't be no quitter. I says You better shut up yourself and not be telling me to shut up, and she says What will you do if I don't shut up? And I says I would bust her in the jaw. But you know Al I would not think of busting no girl. Then Florrie says You better not start nothing because you had to much to drink or you would not be talking about busting girls in the jaw. Then I says I don't care if it is a girl I bust or a lefthander. I did not mean nothing at all Al but Marie says I had insulted Allen and he gets up and slaps my face. Well Al I am not going to stand that from nobody not even if he is my brother-in-law and a lefthander that has not got enough speed to break a pane of glass.[5]

The pitchers fight, and everyone is thrown out of the restaurant. Jack is thoroughly whipped by Allen and does a poor job of concealing the fact in the remainder of the letter. The deadening, repetitive insults, Jack's false chivalry, Florrie's abused femininity, the girls' eagerness to see a fight, and the childish performance of the teammates suggest the endless round of Jack's life, the threats, the bickering, and, finally, the self-serving explanations. His fight with Allen proves in part how utterly Lardner has defused and scaled down the frontier braggart and physical prowess hero. Goaded by their less than attractive wives, the best that these two professional baseball players can do is have a stupid quarrel and get thrown out of the restaurant.

Jack's mouth gets him into trouble, never out of it. He jauntily confronts White Sox owner Charles Comiskey with his threat to jump to the fledgling Federal League if he cannot get his salary increased; Comiskey merely toys with him. Jack acts as if he were a free agent who can come and play with whomever he chooses, yet his boasts are severely circumscribed by the fact that he is a commodity and not worth the aggravation he causes other people. His bragging is hollow; he has no free will; his public performance is controlled by the team; his private life is manipulated by his wife and her relatives. Ostensibly a hero figure, Jack is, in actuality, a little man to whom things happen.[6]

Increasingly after the Civil War, the Popular Sports Hero had to perform in the arena for spectators; he was a diminished figure in relation to the backwoods heroes of the almanacs and Southwestern Humor tales. Natty Bumppo's conflict with Judge Temple had been over substantive issues in American conduct. In contrast, Jack Keefe has no sporting code, no ideals. His only issue is money, and he loses his salary battle with Comiskey, owner of his own "settlement." Jack's only function is to win, and by that criterion alone is he judged. Lardner reinforces the *agon* as the only valid category of play in the modern Popular Sports Hero's experience. There is no higher order of sport than competition.

Lardner loaded Jack's letters with references to actual ballplayers and teams. Their appearances enhanced the realism of Jack's letters and allowed Lardner to rework the consistent theme of Jack's overestimation of his own worth. When the White Sox and Giants are in training for an around-the-world tour, Jack meets Christy Mathewson, then in the last years of a splendid career; Jack writes: "Al this here Mathewson pitched today and honest Al I don't see how he gets by and either the batters in the National League don't know nothing about hitting or else he is such a old man that they feel sorry for him . . . all as he does now is stick the 1st ball right over with 0 on it and pray that they don't hit it out of the park" (196). Jack goes on to make excuses to Mathewson for his poor showing: "Then I says a bout me haveing a sore arm Sunday and he says I wisht I had a sore arm like yourn and a little sence with it and was your age and I would not never loose a game . . ." (196–97). Christy Mathewson was *the* Merriwellian figure in professional baseball in the first two decades of this century and was greatly admired by both Lardner and Heywood Broun.[7] As a Bucknell graduate, the idol of boys and the general public, he can tell Jack the truth about himself with considerable authority. Jack is unaware that Mathewson is one who made the sport as popular as it is, a player who paved the way for clowns like Jack.

Jack himself is not a hero-worshipper because, in his view, no ballplayer can measure up to his own skills, except by luck or trickery. In an inversion of a conventional pulp fiction ending, Jack throws a ball at a batter's head in extra innings with the bases loaded and the score tied because he has a grudge against him. Jack gets his man, loses the game, and earns a fifty-dollar fine from his manager. Jack then writes, "And how could a man go to 1st base and the winning run be forced in if he was dead which he should ought to of been the lucky left-handed stiff . . ." (139). This violent reaction is stronger because it comes from Jack who is usually all

bluster with little real animosity. However, Lardner's most intriguing baseball story, "My Roomy" (1914), ends with Buster Elliott, the disturbed
hero, in an asylum for having attempted to murder his girlfriend and her
new lover with a baseball bat. Elliott writes to his former roommate, the
story's narrator, "Old Roomy: I was at bat twice and made two hits; but I
guess I did not meet 'em square. They tell me they are both alive yet, which
I did not mean them to be."[8]

The similarities between these two passages, written at approximately the same period, show how Lardner could take comic material and
turn it into a personal tragedy. Jack's bragging turns chilling with Elliott's
attempted murder of his girl. The pugnacity always lurking in Jack in response to what he feels is a hostile world is carried through by Elliott, who
relates, "That's my business, busting things." Whereas Jack is a sometime-
success, showing just enough promise to be suffered for years by the White
Sox, Elliott is a thorough outsider, a prodigious slugger who refuses even
to attempt to catch fly balls. Indeed, Elliott is a modern athletic reincarna-
tion of a Bartleby, albeit with some manic energy. Elliott's antics are so
bizarre as to dictate his release by the team because his mockery of procedure digs at unity; there is a submerged terror evinced by the player who
does everything backwards, who sees nothing in conventional threats, who
relies on personal quirks to dictate his actions at any given moment. The
game is mocked by his aberrations. Tension increases between Elliott and
his mates. His loneliness is best described by his sympathetic roommate
who comments, "What could you say to a guy who hated himself like
that?"

The sports frame throws into bold relief every personal peculiarity.
Tales of ballplayers' inability to abide by curfew, meal times, train schedules, and simple field procedures are legion. Elliott's disorientations are
overwhelming and all the more so since they literally take place in the public
eye. He is rejected even by the narrator who is the only player who would
finally consent to room with him. The greatest ballplayer of the time, Ty
Cobb, manifested serious personality disorders both on and off the field;
however, Cobb's performance was of such brilliance that often his frightened teammates put up with his violence and paranoia. During Cobb's career, Lardner had nothing but praise for his brainy play and competitive
drive. It is probable that he was glossing over the facts; as his sportswriter
learns in "Champion," "the people don't want to see him
knocked. . . ."[9]

As a member of the team, the problem of belonging, of performing day after day, defeats Elliott and highlights his isolation. Lardner complicated both a ballplayer's psyche and the question of his fundamental duties and relations. The individual problems of a team member would become a major theme in later sports fiction. The theme chronicled an American social dilemma which far transcended the playing field, but the field served as an excellent microcosm for investigation of American society. What is the cost of personal freedom? What allegiances are owed to the team, the group, the company, the family, or the society?

Lardner raised questions but he did not answer them. A sober insider in the life of the teams he covered as a newspaperman, Lardner was always with them but not of them; he always preserved a solitary core. This could be ascribed to the traditional role of the artist; but since Lardner himself would have rejected that notion, one must say that the distance he kept in all his relations was one of fear of deeper emotions spilling over, of scenes that could not be controlled. Control is what his narrators possess over their feelings and desires, what his rubes and bushers never achieve. A game with rules and rigid logic was most congenial to his need for an external order. So many of his disordered characters are kept at arm's length from the reader, their bizarre or foolish actions filtered through a cool narrator who stands between the reader and their anarchy. However, the narrator of "My Roomy" does stand up for Elliott; Al, we assume, reads, thinks about, and answers his old friend Jack Keefe at some length, trying to help him cope with city life.

Most of Lardner's early baseball fiction is lighter than "My Roomy," but still portrays a variety of characters. In "Horseshoes," an exasperated player-narrator relates the impossible luck of a teammate in staying clear of responsibility for on-the-field blunders; however, the reader perceives that it is the narrator's self-hatred and inferiority complex that keeps him from success. In "Harmony," an older player is credited with scouting a young slugger for his team. In reality, he never saw the youth play but championed him because of his excellent tenor voice; the team was short one member in its barbershop quartet. The "harmony" is extended from a musical term to the well-being of the team in general. "Alibi Ike" as a title is almost self-evident; it refers to the insufferable player with an excuse for every miscue whom the team razzes but ultimately nurtures.[10]

As early as 1921, Lardner was revealing his disenchantment with the emphasis on the slugger in baseball:

> A couple yrs. ago a ball player named Baby Ruth that was a pitcher by birth
> was made into an outfielder on acct. of how he could bust them and he begins

breaking records for long distance hits and etc. and he become á big drawing card and the master minds that controls baseball says to themselfs that if it is home runs that the public wants to see, why leave us give them home runs, so they fixed up a ball that if you don't miss it entirely it will clear the fence, and the result is that ballplayers which use to specialize in hump back liners to the pitcher is now amongst our leading sluggers when by rights they couldn't take a ball in their hands and knock it past the base umpire.[11]

Along with his dislike of what he felt to be a poor caliber of play, Lardner also criticized the audience: "We don't play because (1) we lack imagination, and because (2) we are a nation of hero worshippers. . . . But hero worship is the disease that does the most to keep the grandstands full and the playgrounds empty."[12] The heart of Lardner's quarrel with baseball can be seen in "Hurry Kane" when the ignorant but amazing young pitcher, a 36-game winner as a rookie, consents to fix the World Series to enable him to obtain the money he needs to impress a showgirl. When he learns she is only stringing him along, he reverses form to win the deciding game, a cynical transformation of the conclusion of "Along Came Ruth" (1919). Such tainted reformations had their bitter irony. Jack Keefe was many things but one could hardly imagine him as a fixer. Elmer Kane's "moral" decision to go against the gamblers did not exist in reality. In "The Battle of the Century" (1921), "The Venomous Viper of the Volga" (1927), and "Greek Tragedy" (1934), Lardner satirized the fans at wrestling and boxing matches even more pointedly than the performers, who at least knew what they were doing.[13]

Lardner did change his views about sport in the 1920s to some extent but he did not regret his years of writing about it. His defects as a writer were, if anything, masked by his early work in an environment in which he was most comfortable. His creation of baseball "boobs" was extended by others, who attributed to ballplayers qualities ranging from limited intellect to utter boorishness. No small amount of the public's conception of the professional athlete today springs directly from Lardner's early success at creating humorous sports characters in his fiction. Lardner's triumph made the professional athlete a subject for comedy for decades. Lardner's prototypes remain both on the field and in the literary imagination where writers have appropriated his comic ballplayers for more sophisticated ends. Lardner's continual mastery of popular sport consisted in part in his doing what any innovative popular artist does, in giving back mass experience through art with a heightened awareness of its meaning. He identified the Popular Sports Hero and shaped the conventions of his presentation.

Lardner returned to the Busher in 1918 after three years and sent him off to war with an account of army camp in *Treat 'Em Rough* (1918) and his overseas adventures in *The Real Dope* (1919). Both collections were somewhat thin because Keefe learned little and returned as a pitcher still up against the weakness of his own nature and those of his wife and friends. The last Keefe stories, written in 1919, are strangely prophetic for the future of major league baseball. In "Along Came Ruth" (*Saturday Evening Post*, 26 July 1919), Jack is home from the war and begins a new season in fine form, but he sees red when Florrie takes a male partner in a beauty shop business and sits with him in the stands while Jack is pitching against the Red Sox. Jack blows sky-high and does not last out the first inning, vanquished by an enormous home run hit by none other than Babe Ruth, then in his last year with Boston before the 1920 trade to the New York Yankees. Ruth and Keefe were both left-handed rookie pitchers in 1914: one destined to become the slugger who changed forever the tight, low-scoring percentage baseball that Lardner loved, the other destined to be the model for professional athletes in fiction for more than half a century, including the adaptations of Ruth. Ruth eclipsed both Keefe and Lardner's brand of baseball in the 1920s, but his own projected image as the most rollicking, outsized bumpkin of them all secured and validated Lardner's prototype.

The Keefe tales fade out with Jack on the last place Athletics in 1919, the year of the Black Sox scandal in which eight members of a great White Sox team were barred from baseball for life by the new commissioner, Judge Kenesaw Mountain Landis, for throwing the World Series to the Cincinnati Reds. The White Sox had been the team most favored by literary reporters such as Dunne and Lardner. During the 1919 World Series, Lardner wrote a poem commenting on the White Sox collapse and hinting at scandal. To the tune of "I'm Forever Blowing Bubbles," the poem went in part:

> I'm forever blowing ball games
> Pretty ball games in the air.
> I come from Chi.
> I hardly try,
> Just go to bat and fade and die.[14]

In 1920, the experience of watching the criminal indictment of men whom he knew and had admired was not a pleasant one for Lardner, who had written about all of them at one time or another. His 1919 short stories are full of references to the most prominent fixers, Chick Gandil and Eddie Cicotte, of whom Lardner had written, "They ain't a smarter pitcher in baseball."[15] By public record, these Chicago players were the fictional teammates of Jack Keefe as well, a fact that must have been particularly galling to their creator. However, the mask stayed in place. Not through even one of his narrators did Lardner ever reveal the depth of his feelings about the affair. With his move to New York in the fall of 1919, Lardner's close ties with baseball receded into a past of Niles and Chicago, Pullman cars and clubhouses, and, for the most part, his happiest years.

From 1908, Lardner was experimenting with and adding to his vision of professional baseball. His ballplayers were comic conceptions eagerly embraced by the fans, for in only a few cases were they malicious or destructive. The Keefes and Elliotts were created in a desire to confront an irrationality which was always evident in Lardner's work. Light comedy was as irresistible to Lardner as it had been to Twain and other humorists. However, overriding the conventional Lardnerian ballplayer, the genial boob with some talent and some quirks, was a darker picture of lonely and bewildered men whose sojourn in the public arena exacerbated their difficulties, whose emotional problems were those of every man but whose public lives demanded performance and concealment of the problem.[16]

LARDNER AND SOUTHWESTERN HUMOR TRADITION

No evidence suggests that Lardner was conscious of the Southwestern writers, their realism, experiments in narration, or humorous treatment of sport in society. By 1914, that tradition had been diffused into the work of major authors such as Twain and into dialect tales in subliterature, the repertoires of anecdotal platform humorists, and the work of many early sportswriters with whom Lardner was familiar. However, Lardner drew all the elements together again in a resurrection of the comic realism that had been so effective in portraying sport and games in backwoods society.

Lardner's temperament and aims were, in general outline, similar to those of Longstreet, Thorpe, Hooper, and Harris, while his characters were more akin to the first-generation urban citizens of Dunne and Ade. Lardner's conservatism was evidenced in many ways. He was always slightly out-of-date in the songs he preferred, in the kind of baseball he liked to watch, and in his own writing, in which he eschewed any mention of sex at a time when strictures of presentation were being relaxed. Late in life, he led a quixotic campaign against suggestive lyrics in popular music, a crusade that dismayed both Fitzgerald and Hemingway.

In general, he was capable of real anger at modern society which he saw as shrill and full of braggarts and empty people. He was not alone in this critical stance. However, he spent a career writing of his own distaste without ever posing an alternative world. He knew that the idyllic Niles of the Lardner family childhood could not be overlaid on the brittle new society of urban and suburban wealth and power. He implicitly mourned a passing life by criticizing the new order just as the Southwesterners had criticized backwoods manners and mores to show their distance from that scene. His ballplayers and fans existed in the same social stratum, that of the middle class. Just as surely as Longstreet, Hooper, and Harris, Lardner knew that the social bonds of a community were reported through its games.

One of the ways in which Lardner worked with the elements of comic realism was to highlight the disparity between the almanac physical-prowess hero such as Crockett and Fink and the outcast Southwestern hero such as Ransy Sniffle or Sut Lovingood. The character of Jack Keefe has both a public and private role as he is both Crockett and Sut. He performs feats in the full glare of modern spectacle on the diamond, but in his private life he feels rejected and duped and looks to battle his enemies, real and imagined. Jack is constantly contesting his tormenters off the field. He should have heroic stature because of his public role but he does not.

In "Champion" (1916), Lardner took on an entire society's cherished beliefs about its athletic heroes when he wrote about middleweight champion Midge Kelly. Boxers, managers, fans, sportswriters—no one is spared in this tale in which Lardner created not simply a picture of a brutal fighter but of a character who was nothing more than a thug in love with violence. Midge's personality is well known to all who have the personal misfortune to depend upon or interact with him. Yet the public is force-fed conventional lies by the sportswriters about his upstanding character. The tone is established at the outset: "Midge Kelly scored his first knockout when he was seventeen. The knockee was his brother Connie, three years his junior and a cripple. The purse was a half dollar given to the youngster by a lady whose electric had just missed bumping his soul from his frail little body."[17] This paragraph parodies the line account of a fight by a wire service, giving all essential information as to fighter, opponent, and purse. However, the tone is one of derision and even bemused acceptance of Midge's character. The effect of "frail little body" and "knockee" gives the reader an early gauge to the moral stance of the tale. The narrator already knows the truth about Midge Kelly; the reader learns it brutally at the outset but it takes him longer to realize why the narrator is so cynical.

Two pages before the conclusion, a New York sportswriter is assigned to write a major piece on Midge's life. In his search for facts he runs up against a sickening collection of homilies advanced by Kelly's manager about his fighter's exemplary family life. These "facts" become the core of the sportswriter's story. Even so, Lardner's narrator excuses the reporter's failure to obtain the real facts about Kelly's countless victims during his rise to the top, the managers, wives, and girlfriends he cast aside: "But a story built on their evidence would never have passed the sporting editor. 'Suppose you can prove it,' that gentleman would have said, 'It wouldn't get us anything but abuse to print it. The people don't want to see him knocked. He's champion.' '' (258). Lardner directed the brunt of his message in "Champion" at the sportswriting profession rather than solely at Kelly, whom he never really attempts to make into a believable villain. The cartoon monster Kelly is intentionally as unsatisfactory a portrait as the saccharine family man presented in the Sunday sports section. Lardner very neatly balanced these two polarized descriptions to give the reader a chance to be influenced by his final point about the responsibility of the sporting press. In his view, it was a continuing dilemma, one that still rages between those writers who gloss over the peccadilloes of popular heroes and those reporters who sensationalize the men behind the heroic postures or humanize them, all in the name of selling the heroes for the widest possible commercial consumption.

In "The Fight" Longstreet was completely open in his anger against citizens who had patronized the bloody contest fomented by Hansy Sniffle,[18] but in 1916, Lardner is fighting more insidious enemies than official piety, education, or law enforcement. He is exploring a mentality of collusion between fans and a popular press that feeds back the dreams that the fight public wants to believe. Kelly is as violent as any eye-gouger in Longstreet and more unstable than Sut Lovingood; his combativeness burns at a dull heat at all times.

Lardner's conception of American fandom was to become increasingly pessimistic in the 1920s. The atmosphere of hero-worship is criticized in a number of Lardner tales of athletes, usually by the wise narrator, a teammate, roommate, umpire, or writer, who knows the hero behind the scenes. These figures—the sympathetic teammate of "My Roomy"; Al, by implication in *A Busher's Letters;* the narrators of such tales as "Sick

'Em," "Alibi Ike," "Harmony" (1915), "The Holdout" (1917), "The Battle of the Century," "Hurry Kane," "The Venomous Viper of the Volga," and "Take a Walk" (1933)—give testimony to the fact that Lardner's ballplayers were not all dolts and blusterers. The stories are invariably related by a wise, sane, and often kind member of the athletic fraternity whose balance and good humor enable him to characterize the comic hero. "Harmony" includes a touch of pathos in the sportswriter's story of a veteran ballplayer's search for companionship in the team's barbershop quartet. An umpire in "Take a Walk" sympathetically recounts another umpire's lonely life in rented rooms and his fruitless love for a young girl who prefers a vain young slugging third baseman. The manager of "Holdout" stands up for a raise for his first baseman who is about to become a father. The baby is then named after the manager by the grateful player.

Such reporter-narrators were reminiscent of the Southwestern tradition. Longstreet always wrote from the gentleman's viewpoint, a man above the comic action. Thorpe was often the gentleman participant amused by his fellows, be they rustic hunters or yarn-spinners on steamboats. He also satirized the pomposity of this gentleman. Hooper controlled the Suggs stories from formal narration, allowing Simon to give forth an occasional aphorism after a particularly satisfying swindle. Even Harris' Sut was relating all his adventures to "George," the author/confidant, who transcribed Sut's tales just the way he spoke them as one must believe Al has turned over Jack Keefe's letters for publication. The position of reporter is assumed by an insider in Lardner's athletic tales. He functions as an observer of comic heroes, both those of prowess and of wit; he records their boasts, their deeds, and their essential lack of self-control and self-knowledge. However, his status presupposes an alternative world of order and reason within the team itself, a motive force that enables the unit to withstand the stress put on it by the clown or troublemaker. This character has never been given his due by Lardner's critics. This bemused insider, a rejoinder to the stock conception of Lardner's dumb ballplayers, also appears in Lardner's nonsports narratives, most notably as Finch, the put-upon husband in *The Big Town* (1921).

A variation on this narrator is the insider who reveals concrete details as well as his own moral blankness, the best example being the barber of "Haircut" (1925). Although the story is not about sports, it does have links to the tall tale, pulp fiction, and Southwestern prototypes. Not only is Jim Kendall, the town roarer, a relic of frontier humor, but the locale in which the story takes place is a brilliant stroke inasmuch as the barbershop, saloon, and poolroom were the only male preserves left in town life, otherwise a sea of domesticity. Barbershops had the gaudiest magazines and papers in town; they were the chief outlets for *The Police Gazette,* and the seamy little story underlying the plot of "Haircut" would have been a natural for a writeup in it. The perfect environment for the narration of such a story was chosen by Lardner. The barber gradually reveals his own insensitivity as he tells the facts of a murder he does not even recognize *as* a murder. One of his pals is gone; that is the only truth for him. His deathless last line to the man in the chair, the unseen judge possessing moral sensibility, is "Comb it wet or dry?" Lardner was able here to involve his narrators in the moral uncertainties of the story, a complexity of technique that he seldom undertook and one which no Southwestern realist except Thorpe achieved to any extent.

The role of the reporter, so ingrained in Lardner as a newspaperman, was first utilized in his baseball tales and then transferred to his other fiction. Lardner came to the frame narrator in his own way through his newspaper experience, his temperamental role as an observer, and his critical view of modern life. He needed to appropriate a form that would enhance portraits of comic heroes who could only lose force if made the focal point of the narration, since they did not have the depth, moral sense, or self-irony to criticize themselves.

Likenesses to frontier athletes are found in the physical metaphors that Lardner often used to describe his bumpkins:

> Standing six foot three in what was left of his stockings, he was wearing a suit of Arizona store clothes that would have been a fair fit for Singer's youngest midget and looked like he had pressed it with a tractor that had been parked on a river bottom.
>
> He had used up both the collars that he figured would see him through his first year in the big league. This left you a clear view of his Adam's apple which would make half a dozen pies. You'd have thought from his shoes that he had just managed to grab hold of the rail on the back platform of his train and been dragged from Yuma to Jacksonville. But when you seen his shirt, you wondered if he hadn't rode in the cab and loaned it to the fireman for a washcloth.[19]

The subject of this description, Elmer "Hurry" Kane, is a super player whose prodigious appetites are both more and less than human. Far from being the source of amusement to their teammates, the Keefes, Elliotts, and Kanes are exasperating and are suffered by the team in the hope that their performance will cancel out their personal foibles. The player who drew attention because of his personality or off-the-field affairs might have been the best fictional subject but his performance was the opposite of what Lardner admired, namely smart play and consistency as he carefully explained in a 1915 *American Magazine* series. A definite split existed between the comic athletes of his short stories and the winning players he respected most: those who evinced professionalism in their work.[20]

It is erroneous to see Lardner as a descendant of Twain. His narrators finally lacked the breadth of humanity that characterized so many of Twain's narrators. Whole areas of human pathology which Twain vividly exposed were closed to Lardner, the student of surface manners. In this way, too, Lardner can more truthfully be placed in a direct line from the more provincial Southwestern Humorists. His attitude toward undisciplined ballplayers is analogous to the Southwesterners' jaundiced view of the backwoods athlete and confidence man. Both Lardner and the Southwesterners wrote in a mixture of amusement and dismay at their subjects' vitality and energy. They reproduced with fidelity their speech and habits. Lardner's narrators are the equivalents of the Southwestern gentleman travellers and hunters, raconteurs, collectors of tall tales. He, too, wrote of a society in flux and created the Popular Sports Hero as one of its representative men.

The problem of narration was of great concern to the Southwestern writers who had wished to convey realistically not only the daily life of the society but also their more refined perspective of it. The choice of narration was determined by the perspective from which the author wished to view the life of society. Just as the Southwesterners vacillated from amused gentleman narrator to vernacular comedian, so did Lardner attempt the more objective mask of the gentleman as sportswriter, teammate, and manager, as well as the subjective persona of a Jack Keefe. The general movement in contemporary sports fiction has been for the reporter, player, or player-as-reporter to be the controlling narrator, most often in first person. Lardner's fiction firmly established this convention.

LARDNER AND 1920s POPULAR CULTURE

In the 1920s, Lardner had become the nation's best-known short story writer and had bought a large house on Long Island where he lived with his wife and four sons. By 1925 he seemed condemned to live the life that he satirized so well. The golf dates, the bridge parties, the winter vacations to warm climates—Lardner's fiction made these environments, along with the world of show business, his settings for the first literary investigation of a broad range of suburban life.[21] Virginia Woolf's famous insight into Lardner's subject matter was written in 1925:

> It is no coincidence that the best of Mr. Lardner's stories are about games, for one may guess that Mr. Lardner's interest in games has solved one of the most difficult problems of the American writer; it has given him a clue, a centre, a meeting place for the divers activities of a people whom a vast continent isolates, whom no tradition controls. Games give him what society gives his English brother.[22]

Lardner suggested that the player and the fan were intimately related. The fan was bored, repressed, needing release from the prison of self; the athlete was under the tension created by constant notoriety. In suburbia, these qualities merged in the fans who became players, whose lives fed on the small competitions of their leisure world. These competitions in turn reflected on their larger relations with other people.

The baseball players of Lardner's earlier fiction were replaced in the 1920s by suburbanites who bared their teeth in competition at golf or bridge. The obvious implication of their boorishness and frantic desire to win was that all of the traits brought forth in their leisure-time pursuits were simply the reflections of their daily lives in business or in the family circle. Lardner wrote about the first generation upper middle class with money to spend and no real idea what to buy, whom to meet, or where to go. His fictional vision of the 1920s was of terminal boredom, full of meaningless excursions and empty chatter. Social competition, for Lardner, was most often mean and petty with no redeeming features. In "A Caddy's Diary" (1922), the narrator, generously supplied with advice from a philosophical fellow caddy named Joe, watches poker-faced all summer while bankers, businessmen, and housewives lie, cheat, and urge him to do the same on their behalf for tips. The urge to cheat, to go one up on the competition, is almost a narcotic for the characters. The women are as bad as the men; two of them end up betting on a fifty-dollar dress and using all their wiles to get the caddy to change their "lies," a lovely golfing term that acknowledges their chicanery. Lardner's master stroke was to have Charles Crane, the club champion who never cheated ("That is one of the penaltys [sic] for being a good player, you can't cheat"), flee town with $8,000 he had stolen from the bank in which he worked. In this story, the suburban caddy becomes wiser from experience that matches that of the urban bootblack in the pulp fiction of the late nineteenth century. Human folly and greed pass before him daily.

He believes he is untouched and can freely criticize the morals of his patrons until Joe brings him up short by reminding him of the lies he has changed for a one-dollar tip. The complicity of the caddy turns the morality of the tale back on the narrator who represents the moral point of view as in "Champion" and "My Roomy." Joe pronounces judgment on the cheater's world at the country club placed against the theft of Charles Crane: "the bigger it is the less of a sucker the person is that goes after it."

Lardner's characters had been obsessed with money since Jack Keefe and Midge Kelly. For those who have financial security, other conflicts surface. Lardner was able to capitalize on his years of writing sports by turning the competitions of married life into comic contests. In "The Golden Honeymoon" (1922), the flinty old married couple goes south to Florida where they meet the wife's suitor from fifty years before. The husband-narrator then proceeds to enter the lists to prove to his wife that she made the right choice. He loses to his old rival at cards and horseshoes but whips him at checkers. The games revitalize him and put a snap in his step. In "Contract" (1929), Shelton is reluctantly dragged into a social circle by his wife and then is constantly berated by his partners for his poor bridge playing. One night he retaliates by criticizing their manners and grammar, much to the dismay of his wife. Responding to a random statement from his partner that "The itta girl just overslept herself, that's all," Shelton says: "I have no idea who the itta girl is, but I am interested in your statement that she overslept herself. Would it be possible for her, or any other itta girl to oversleep somebody else? If it were a sleeping contest, I should think 'outsleep' would be preferable, but even so I can't understand how a girl of any size outsleeps herself."[23] Shelton is banished from the table in disgrace, for even these dull characters know when they are being insulted. Lardner satirized the excessive insistence on the rules of the game to turn the play back upon the tormenters by having Shelton play the language game, insisting on verbal precision from the less than articulate group. However, the next week finds Shelton playing at the socially respectable Pardees where his name is mispronounced and he is still being chastised for his poor play. His rebellion has been only momentary for he is caught in the web of social games.

During the 1920s Lardner turned his gaze on his readers and showed them to be players as well, though they achieved no more success than his troubled athletes. What both ballplayers and suburbanites had in common was insecurity, competitiveness, and belligerence instead of humanity and tolerance, acquisitiveness instead of love, and a pervasive hollowness. In his ballplayers, these traits were manifested in an inability to handle successfully the pressures that arose from being popular heroes; for the suburbanites, it was a boredom so deep that it could be attained only through leisure pastimes. His picture of a liberated society at play was always rendered from the caustic point of view of the confirmed bourgeois citizen somberly, hilariously reporting on a frivolity foreign to his nature. None of his characters have the romantic vitality and energy of Fitzgerald's flappers, college men, and intense visionaries. They were all a bit tired and found it hard to adapt to the frenetic style of the 1920s.

Lardner's body of work appeared at the outset of a vast revolution in American popular culture. His career spanned the restructuring of baseball as a game of power rather than speed, the rise of tennis and golf personified in heroes such as Bill Tilden and Bobby Jones, the birth of professional football, and, with the careers of Jack Dempsey and Gene Tunney, an unparalleled excitement in boxing. Lardner also saw the birth of radio and the cinema, as well as the flowering of the Broadway musical stage. His enormous interest in popular forms showed itself in areas outside of sport. After years of attempting to write successful plays for Broadway and musical numbers for reviews, he collaborated in 1929–30 with young George S. Kaufmann on *June Moon,* an adaptation of "Some Like Them Cold," which ultimately ran for 273 performances. Hollywood attempted to woo Lardner on several occasions but failed. Much of his humor fit in perfectly with the then reigning comic talents of the screen.[24] His concise dialogue would have been perfect not only for the silent screen but for talkies as well.[25] He had a flair for stand-up comic routines. They were often part of his early baseball stories, in which one teammate plays straight man to another's clown, as in "Alibi Ike" and "Where Do You Get That Noise?" (1915). In his last years, the poker-faced Lardner bore a startling facial resemblance to Buster Keaton, another consummate master of the deadpan.

Lardner returned near the end of his life to baseball as subject matter. Several of his last stories, which retain the framework of his early baseball pieces with a reporter as narrator, show a softening of his feeling toward the ignorant busher. In *Lose with a Smile,* Lardner's 1932 resurrection of the Keefe format, a young Brooklyn outfielder's letters home to his girl in Illinois and her replies are in a more melancholy, sympathetic tone. Danny Warner has only mediocre ability and appears doomed to a minor league career. He is not the defensive, self-inflated Keefe but is rather a good-humored bumpkin. Oddly enough, his best friend on the team is veteran Casey Stengel, a rookie with Brooklyn in 1912 when Lardner had begun on the sports beat. Here he is portrayed as a bulwark of sanity and steadiness in Danny's young life, rather than the eccentric legend he became in his later years. The pathos of the tale lingers when Danny's dejected letter telling of his demotion to Jersey City crosses with his girl's excited announcement that she has convinced her father that she should come to New York to be with her fiancé. In November 1931 Lardner began a final series of reminiscenses in *The Saturday Evening Post* in which he fondly recalled his early days as a baseball reporter in South Bend and Chicago. They are among the sunniest pieces he ever wrote.

When Lardner died in 1933, Broun showed his strong appreciation of what Lardner had achieved in American fiction by commenting in "Nature the Copycat," which ran in his daily column "It Seems to Me" in the *New York World Telegram:* "When Lardner limned his famous character [Elmer Kane] no such person existed. . . . The miracle is reserved only for the truly creative artist." Broun went on, "Before there was a Dizzy Dean, Ring knew him from head to pitching cleat." He concluded, that with "divine arrogance," Lardner had said, " 'I see it this way. Let Nature catch up with my conception.' "[26] Although it is hard to imagine Lardner as such an Olympian artist, Broun is acknowledging Lardner's originality in creating his sports characters.

Lardner's work was a true triumph of popular writing. He wrote for a middle-class audience eager to read about itself and its pastimes. His initial subject matter sprang from a specifically modern sports culture while his narrative technique was in a vital tradition of spectatorial reporting that had begun in the newspaper sketches of the Southwestern Humorists in the *Spirit of the Times,* even as his own stories had been nurtured in the *Chicago Tribune.* Lardner was another American gentleman commentator who viewed play with dismay. His characters gained no control of their lives through competition, which basically became their imprisonment. No individuals controlled their experience through play for Lardner could not see beyond the collective paradigm of play experience, and this dogged conformist stance doomed him to be a writer of the second rank. As a modern Puritan, he admired order, restraint, and solid achievement through work well done in society. But as a modern humorist, he wrote of disorder, oddly spiritless profligacy, and wasted lives of little or no accomplishment. Given his temperamental preferences, it is ironic that his most lasting creation was the figure of the bumpkin athlete which he perfected with such success that more than a half-century later reporters and authors still see the professional Popular Sports Hero through the amused eyes of Lardnerian narrators and describe that Hero's foibles through Lardnerian language.

PART III
The School Sports Hero

CHAPTER SIX

The Incarnation
of the College Athletic Hero

THE POPULAR SPORTS HERO was a conventional figure born out of raucous play on the frontier and transformed by organized, industrial America into a team hero playing for spectators in a modern arena. Lardner's achievements in sports fiction had climaxed the development of this literary convention. Yet there was another American sports hero, more serious, more clearly defined by his relation to American ideals of class, education, and power. This figure was the School Sports Hero, a young man who played to prepare himself for other roles in American society. If the Popular Sports Hero is a comic figure, expressing in celebration a democratic America, defining what the community is in spontaneous expression of self, the School Sports Hero is a serious figure, expressing in sober battle a more elite America, defining what the community believes through a disciplined self-restraint. The School Sports Hero defines himself through his leadership and teamwork, through his conflicting roles of brilliant individual achievement and subordination to a larger cause. He thereby expresses a central contradiction surrounding ambition and success in a democratic society. The School Sports Hero has roots deep in Puritan concepts of discipline and ceaseless labor and embodies a role in which play can be fully approved as the highest calling: the training for harsh tests. The School Sports Hero is, on the whole, a pious, upright moralist born out of Civil War aggression and American society's need to find continuity in peacetime preparedness for further organized activity. He thus embodies values and goals which America believes crucial to its welfare.

One may begin a search for the definition of the School Sports Hero by noting two speeches presented at Harvard 56 years apart; these two speeches best demonstrate America's changing attitudes toward college training and sport in the nineteenth century. On August 31, 1837, Ralph Waldo Emerson delivered his historic Phi Beta Kappa address, "The American Scholar." In a speech that was to set the tone for a generation's conception of the individual American intellect, Emerson began by saying that the assemblage had not been convened for "games of strength or skill, for the recitation of histories, tragedies, and odes, like the Ancient Greeks," but to conceive of a time when "the sluggard intellect of this continent will look from under its iron lids and fill the postponed expectation of the world with something better than the exertions of mechanical skill."[1] "The American Scholar" was a prophetic call for national self-definition, for an intellectual vitalism that would inform the best of American thought and create a national literature.

Fifty-six years later in an utterly new, post-Civil War America, Francis Walker, the President of the Massachusetts Institute of Technology, presented his address, "College Athletics," before Phi Beta Kappa Society, Alpha of Massachusetts at Harvard on June 29, 1893. One of his strongest themes was the way the new emphasis on physical prowess and health in the colleges redressed the imbalance toward "mind and soul" that had been held by American college men whose "affected notions about intellectuality and spirituality had almost complete control of the popular thought." Contempt for physical prowess, he charged, was "in greater part, due to the transcendentalism and sentimentalism of the last quarter of the eighteenth and the first quarter of the nineteenth century" where "languor and pallor were attractive, delicacy of frame and limb was admired."[2] Walker was no militant incarnation of a modern American college football coach but rather a respected and innovative educator with both high government and military experience. His championing of college athletics at the expense of the transcendental spirit underscored the rapid change in opinion about the value of sport in American colleges and the equally rapid overturning of the New England renaissance as the guiding spirit of thought among educators.[3]

Like Emerson's speech, Walker's is not only a criticism but a prophecy of a new American order. His theme is the perfectibility of man— what the American is capable of if he defines his own authentic power. Walker's utilitarian positivism is in the Emersonian optimistic mode but for different ends. As Emerson would have trained the scholar for higher action by refining his potential energy into purer realms of thought, Walker would train the whole man for action in society on a more pragmatic level. As much the new man of 1893 as Emerson had been in 1837, Walker stood as the best example of the new, thoughtful social engineer as educator, possessing experience and conviction along with the authority to implement his views. Walker listed a number of individual virtues that sports demand but followed by extolling teamwork and "a common end." Sport is useful, he said, in that it prepares one for a given profession where the same sort of problems encountered on the playing field might appear in other guises, at which time habits gained on the playing field of discipline, perseverance, and courage might be applied. Emerson had announced "the world is nothing," but Walker saw the world as a place where "man is not a pilgrim but a citizen." The world was "a place to work in" where "the present generation has witnessed a powerful diminution of spiritual self-consciousness."[4]

In the decades between Emerson's address and the Civil War, attempts were made to strike some sort of balance between the imperative of "spiritual self-consciousness" and a growing awareness of man's potential invigoration in nature through strenuous outdoor exercise and the activities of the naturalist. In "Higher Laws," Thoreau stressed that the "American traveller on the prairie" was naturally a hunter, trapper, and fisherman and that "they mistake who assert that the Yankee has few amusements because he has not so many public holidays, and men and boys do not play so many games as they do in England, for here and the more primitive but solitary amusements of hunting, fishing, and the like have not yet given place to the former." As discussed in chapter 1, Thoreau emphasized the hunter as an embryonic stage of development but a necessary one for the poet or naturalist. However, even at the time of *Walden* (1854), his vision of an initial education for the whole man through the hunt was being integrated with a concept of sport as an activity that could be undertaken on a college green or in a gymnasium as well as on Walden Pond or in the woods.

The physical fitness of American boys and men was extremely poor in New England in the immediate pre-Civil War era according to most accounts. Francis Parkman was the principal patron of a crude Harvard gymnasium in the early 1840s.[5] Henry Adams noted in *The Education of Henry Adams* that "Boston at that time [1850] offered few healthy resources for boys or men," with "rudimentary" ball games. He commented that "sport as a pursuit was unknown."[6] Thomas Wentworth Higginson (Harvard, 1841), an influential and genteel man-of-letters, abolitionist minister, and Emily Dickinson's 24-year poetry correspondent, provided the clearest overview of late Transcendental, pre-Civil War opinion about physical training. He wrote from a double perspective of the amateur naturalist and confirmed athlete and saw very little difference between the two roles.

Higginson stated in the *Atlantic* in 1858 that "there is in the community the impression that physical vigor and spiritual sanctity are incompatible."[7] In a reaction against "saints and their bodies," Higginson keenly felt "this moral and physical anhoemia, this bloodlessness, which separates them more effectually than a cloister, from the strong life of the age" (584). There is a hearty muscularity to Higginson's rhetoric: "Let any man test his physical condition . . . by an hour in the gymnasium or at cricket, and his enfeebled muscular apparatus will groan with rheumatism for a week" (587). At the same time he echoes the Thoreau of "Higher Laws": "As the urchin is undoubtedly physically safer for having learned to turn a somerset and fire a gun . . . so his soul is made healthier, larger, freer, stronger, by hours and days of manly exercise" (588), and he champions "the outdoor study of natural history" (594). Higginson's peroration is a grand mixture of Thoreau, Frank Forester, and a coming athletic revolution: "Go out under pretense of shooting on the marshes or botanizing in the forests . . . go to paint a red male-leaf in autumn, or watch a pickerel line in winter; swim with her, ride with her, run with her" (595). What Higginson concludes with is a utilitarian *via media* between work and play that stresses that such sporting activity must be purposeful: "go out merely to enjoy her [Nature], and it seems a little tame" (595); one must have a "collateral aim" of self-improvement, both physical and spiritual.

For Thoreau in "Higher Laws," the physical life of the hunter is a necessary evolutionary step for the spirit. For Higginson, who was observed kicking a ball on the green at Harvard in 1837 with his classics tutor, Jones Very, and who also wrote nostalgically of class melees in spontaneous 1840s football matches,[8] participation in organized athletics on the cricket ground, in regattas, in football, "the most glorious of all games" (593), was a tapping of the refined energy of Transcendentalism for purposeful play. Play thus had utility, a "higher" utility. The justification for organized athletics grew out of the initial impulse toward self-knowledge and self-improvement for, as Higginson wrote, "the secret charm of all these sports and studies is simply this,—that they bring us into more familiar intercourse with nature" (594), what Cooper's Natty Bumppo also taught in *The Pioneers* as he attempted to show the settlement the correctness of sporting attitudes in nature during the pigeon shoot and the fish kill. Such doctrine could now be expressed by an educated Bostonian well-removed from woodslore and Indians but conceiving of a wholeness of body and spirit on the green and in the gymnasium.

Thus the expression of an American collegiate sporting life did not all of a sudden erupt in the 1890s with advocates such as Francis Walker. Its growth was organic, stemming from pre-organized-sport concepts of man in salutary nature as well as from pre-Civil War school and college rites that were given greater credence, in effect sanctioned by experience in the war itself. Evidence of the early roots of this growth of college sports consciousness and its stimulation by the war can be found in the two-volume *Harvard Memorial Biographies* (1866), edited by Higginson, who wrote 12 of the 95 portraits of the Harvard men killed in battle.[9] The biographies ranged from cursory notes of childhood and college career to full, heart-felt testaments of relatives and college friends, complete with personal letters and accounts by comrades of bravery under fire.

More than one-third of the biographies mention athletics or "manly" sports, especially gymnastics, boating, football, and boxing, to validate their subjects interest in physical culture.[10] The initial Civil War postmortem led the biographers to emphasize the prewar heartiness and physical readiness as a way of putting into perspective the ultimate physical sacrifice of the war. The references to sport vary from stock descriptions of "direct, straightforward manliness" to the fact that Sidney Willard '52 "trained his powers at the gymnasium with the method and success of the Greek athlete" (I, 254). Several letters describe the war through football references. George Wellington Batchelder '59 on patrol reminded his biographer "of the old times when he used to plunge headlong into struggling masses of football players, not to make a show of courage, as was the case with some, but with most uncompromising determination to drive the ball to the goal" (II, 10–11). A grimmer vision was portrayed in the sketch of Goodwin Atkins Stone '62: "Imagine the two or three hundred men that used to gather for our football games lying dead about the Delta, and you have an idea of the scene near the earthwork" (II, 344). Both individual courage and mass carnage were served well by football images.

Of the five slain Harvard men to whom the Soldiers Field at Harvard was dedicated in 1890, three—James Savage '54, Stephen George Perkins '56, and Robert Gould Shaw '60—have the most detailed references to sport in the *Memorial Biographies*.[11] Savage is remembered as a boy with an inexhaustible love of sport whose side would win in football if he could play (I, 328), while Perkins is portrayed as a champion rower with great strength and "superb physique" (I, 374). Shaw's biographical memoir is written simply and with dignity by his mother who lets his own letters speak for him through the years. Shaw was lionized immediately upon his death before the battery at Fort Wagner, South Carolina, in 1863 as Civil War New

England's most noble sacrifice. The symbolic reverberations of his burial in a ditch with his black troops of the Massachusetts 54th Regiment inspired a number of tributes, including Emerson's 1863 poem, "Voluntaries," the great St. Gaudens sculpture dedicated in Boston in 1897 by William James, and Robert Lowell's contemporary poem, "For the Union Dead."

In a letter Shaw wrote as a Harvard freshman in 1856, he describes Bloody Monday, the free-form fall football event between college classes. His language changes from youthful amusement at the scuffle to expressions of military imagery: "At half past six we went to the 'Delta' and in a few minutes the whole Sophomore Class streamed into the field at one end, about as large a class of Freshmen into the other, and stood opposite each other about a hundred yards apart, like two hostile armies" (II, 191–92). As the two masses engaged each other, "it resembled more my idea of the hand-to-hand fighting in the battles of the ancients" (II, 192). Although he spent more time looking for his lost hat than being pummeled or punishing someone else, Shaw jubilantly shared the glory of his fellow freshmen in their victory over the sophomores, an almost unheard-of feat: "A good many of our fellows were more badly hurt because they had pluck enough to go into the thick of it each time" (II, 192). He concluded, "Now we play football every evening, but all the classes mix up and there is little or no fighting" (II, 192).

No doubt, Shaw's mother included this letter as poignant boyish play in light of his heroic death. It is not in the 1890s spirit of football as preparedness for battle as much as it appears to be a wistful reminder of martial play when the stakes were the honor of a school class rather than the honor of the Union. By the middle of the war, Emerson had written of the brave youths "tender from school, college, counting room, with no experience beyond football game or schoolyard quarrel now to leap on a battery or rank of bayonets."[12] Thus, in 1866 football was used to highlight *un*preparedness, to show the incongruity of boys' games and battles, and to point out the disparity between them. In Higginson's 1858 *Atlantic* essay, there had been no rhetoric linking sport to warfare. The stress on teamwork, mass, force, and insistence on duty was simply not conceived. In contrast, by 1900, football was used to highlight preparedness for moral and physical tests. The national perception of college football had changed from Shaw's innocent military analogies to Harvard English Professor Bliss Perry's tough 1904 estimate that "the amateur football game, for all its brutalities, has taught a young scholar a finer lesson than his classroom has taught him, namely to risk his neck for his college."[13] In the immediate aftermath of the Civil War, the loss of young heroes was so great, the destruction so immense, that football as incarnated in the prewar Bloody Monday memoirs took place in a veritable arcadia where action was youthful and timeless. Over the next few decades the rhetoric of college sport was slowly tuned to an intense practical note as preparation for adulthood and harsh experience.

In "Voluntaries," Emerson had cast the Civil War youths as those who "Break sharply off their jolly games" while Herman Melville in "On the Slain Collegians" (1866) stated abruptly, "Each bloomed and died an unabated boy." James Russell Lowell's "Ode Recited at the Harvard Commemoration" (July 21, 1865), published as a preface to the *Memorial Biographies,* contrasts their timelessness: "We feel the orient of their spirit glow/ Part of our life's unalterable good/ They come transfigured back/ Secure from change in their high hearted ways" with their transformation of rhetoric into action: "Where Faith made whole with deed/ Breathes its awakening breath/ Into the lifeless creed." Such straightforward estimates of the usefulness of action would gradually assume control over the wistful images of playful youth and alter the role of college sport in the training of that youth.

On June 10, 1890, Henry Lee Higginson, cousin of T.W. Higginson and one of Boston's leading public-spirited Brahmins, bestowed upon Harvard the Soldier's Field in memory of his Harvard friends and classmates who had died during the war.[14] Higginson's address to students on that occasion romanticized his youthful comrades as the fairest of promising youths cut down before their prime.[15] Two years later he invited the Yale and Harvard football teams to dinner at the University Club in Boston where he invoked his dead classmates and their love of "Bloody Monday," the rite that Shaw had described in his 1856 letter. Higginson's reminiscence mentioned his "mate and dear friend [James Savage] . . . now lying there under the shadow of Cedar Mountain" and a boy on his team whom he had blocked for "who afterwards served in the Southern army and was killed at Antietam."[16] Higginson's emotional speeches brought the subject of football full circle from Robert Shaw viewing the football field as battleground to the consecration of a football field in memory of dead war heroes. Such rhetoric enabled Francis Walker to state in 1893, "Were I superintendent of the Academy at West Point, I should encourage the game of football among the cadets as military exercise of no mean importance."[17]

In the decades following the Civil War before Walker's address, an increased interest developed in the athlete in concert with other players in the crucible of competition. The rise of this sports hero expressed a very real sense that the organization displayed in the great war should not be allowed to dissolve into slackness and aimless individual endeavor. By 1910, the year of William James' essay, "The Moral Equivalent of War," it was a truism that the values of competition created a better, stronger, and more competent American leader. In many respects, college and school sport provided the American educated elite, so endangered as a force in national affairs, with a last vital activity to underscore their participation in modern industrial America. To examine the crosscurrents among college, sport, and society at this time and their expression in fiction is to discover men moving with ease from sport to the colleges to journalism to pulp and serious fiction to the military to politics. The cast of players included football coaches such as Walter Camp, educators such as Walker, Nathaniel S. Shaler, Thorstein Veblen, and George Santayana, and young authors such as Stephen Crane, Frank Norris, and Richard Harding Davis. It would be safe to say that the interrelationships among college, sport, and society were more closely integrated in the 1890s than they would ever be again as sports action flowed from widely shared precepts with society's sanctions and promises of sure rewards for the heroes.[18]

Postwar commentary proved that the usefulness of the college athletic spirit did not end with the cessation of conflict. In 1858, T.W. Higginson had innocently stated that "we love to encounter in the contests of manhood those whom we first met at football" (589). One of the earliest popular acknowledgments that the fame of the college athlete may give him "opportunities of advancement" through public recognition was in "Sport and Study," an 1873 *Harper's Weekly* editorial: "Now to the men whose names are known, if only by their reputation as cricketers, oarsmen, or athletes, such favorable opportunities are oftener presented than they are to others not in any special manner distinguishable from the mass of their countrymen."[19] In reference to the climate fostered by Thomas Hughes' English schoolboy hero, Tom Brown (see chapter 7), the editorial suggested that the college athlete is a fine example of the muscular Christian, "beloved erstwhile of novel-writers," who was not merely an athlete of renown but "also a rising . . . clergyman . . . , a medical man . . . a merchant . . ."[20] *Harper's Weekly* described the new athlete as lacking "mainly mental culture, not necessarily capacity for work."

Henry James, seemingly the American author least concerned with college and sport as novelistic subjects, nonetheless drew on the figure of the post-Civil War muscular Christian to inform his portrait of Caspar Goodwood in *The Portrait of a Lady* (1881). James crystallized several of the conventions that would later become the stereotypes for the college athletic hero in popular fiction. As the persistent, positive American suitor who wishes to rescue Isabel Archer from Gilbert Osmond and a life of spiritual bondage, Goodwood is by turns powerful, naive, attractive, and overbearing. He is "good" American "wood" but presumably unvarnished; although he had received "the better part of his education" at Harvard College, "he had gained renown rather as a gymnast and oarsman than as a gleaner of more dispersed knowledge."[21] James, who sniffs at and validates the commercial success of Goodwood as well as his athleticism, jests with the sentiments of the *Harper's Weekly* editorial: "Later on he had learned that the finer intelligence too could vault and pull and strain—might even, breaking the record, treat itself to rare exploits" (105). James emphasizes how accomplished Goodwood is at working his will on people, how, like Civil War veteran Christopher Newman in James' *The American* (1877), he was used to being able to "organize," "contend," and "administer." Through Goodwood's pride in his accomplishments and station runs a streak of the emotional bully who achieves certitude too easily, a prophecy of a figure such as Tom Buchanan in Fitzgerald's *The Great Gatsby*. Goodwood's "jaw was too square and set and his figure too straight and stiff: these things suggested a want of easy consonance with the deeper rhythms of life" (105). Goodwood is alternately a romantic naif and a staunch friend who does not truly understand Isabel's plight but instinctively understands Osmond's evil. James uses an athletic metaphor to describe their competition: "His host had won in the open field a great advantage over him, and Goodwood had too strong a sense of fair play to have been moved to underrate him on that account" (414). Goodwood is James' commercial athletic prince, truly the first of the breed in serious American fiction, both attractive and limited. He is explicitly both a school hero and a tycoon, the one success leading into the other.

University educators such as Walker and Nathaniel S. Shaler of Harvard extended and refined the commitment to athletics with their pragmatic championing of college sport. In "The Athletic Problem in Education" (1889), geologist Shaler presented the classic sober case for football at Harvard. Not surprisingly, as a scientist he gives much weight to the physiological evidence. Like Walker, he alludes to the poor physical condition of students of an earlier generation and to the improvement being wrought by exercise. Football "teaches . . . how to keep a cool head in moments of great activity," he wrote, noting that "those inclined to be good students will do their intellectual work as well as their play, neither harming the other." He concluded, "the world needs rather the swift reaction of man against his surroundings which the athletic habits favor."[22] Thus for Walker and Shaler, a college generation of Caspar Goodwoods would be a positive improvement in their overall fitness and character.[23]

In *The Theory of the Leisure Class* (1899), Thorstein Veblen's anthropology of social evolution commented at length on the athletic spirit of the 1890s. Veblen was hardly interested in the fitness of Goodwoods or the day-to-day curricular problems at Harvard and MIT. He saw the men of the upper classes as exempt from industrial occupations, and he was skeptical of the limited range of their employments, which were rigidly confined to four areas: government, warfare, religious observance, and sports,[24] the matrices for the American college athletic hero in the 1890s. Philosopher George Santayana echoed Veblen's perceptions of the integral nature of college sport to American rites of passage while presenting it in a more positive vein.[25] At the beginning of his teaching career at Harvard in the early 1890s, Santayana published two essays, "A Glimpse of Yale" (1892) and "Philosophy on the Bleachers" (1894) where he saw college athletics as perfectly consistent with what was vital and spontaneous in American life and stated, "A certain analogy to war, a certain semblance of dire struggle, are therefore of the essence of athletics."[26]

Apart from the university educators and their measured support for college sport was the impetus for the movement provided by such men as Walter Camp and Frederick Remington, who not only had the credentials of eastern college gentlemen but who publicized and popularized college football for a wider audience than did sport's academic apologists. Camp's influence was unequaled in pre-1900 college football. He was to football what Albert Spalding was to professional baseball: player, coach, rule-maker, and organization wizard. Richard Harding Davis wrote, "there is one man in New Haven of more importance than Walter Camp and I have forgotten his name. I think he is president of the university."[27] Camp won fame at Yale as a player in the mid-1870s and then became the first head coach at Yale, a position he held until 1911.[28] From 1877 to 1925 he was a member of every national football rules committee and he served on Theodore Roosevelt's commission to investigate the brutality of the sport in 1905. His annual All-America team, appearing in *Collier's* from 1891 to 1924, was widely considered the definitive team, and his reports in *Outing* magazine and *Harper's Weekly* in the 1890s set the tone for a decade's discussion of collegiate fair play and the debate over amateurism versus professionalism. He gave badly needed finesse to the violent power football game of the

1890s, stating characteristically, "Dirty playing is first of all inefficient."[29] During Camp's tenure between 1880 and 1910, Yale had a record of 20-4-3 against Harvard and 20-7-1 against Princeton.

Frederick Remington, the famous painter and illustrator of Western plains life, also exemplified the ideal college hero. He had been a lineman at Yale in 1879 on a varsity football team captained by Camp. His football painting, "A Tackle and Ball Down," appeared on the cover of *Harper's Weekly* on November 23, 1887. His were the earliest popular sketches of football action, although Winslow Homer's drawings of "Bloody Monday" at Harvard had appeared in *Harper's* in 1857. Remington completed two more covers for *Harper's Weekly,* including "A Practice Game at Yale" and "A Collision at the Ropes," and scores of football action sketches as well as a series of cameo drawings for *Outing* on football fundamentals.

Theodore Roosevelt himself frequently spoke of sport as preparation "to do work that counts when the time arises, when the occasion calls."[30] As early as December 1, 1893, he was lauding Francis Walker's "admirable" Harvard address and stating that boys will be taught best by "professors and principals at schools and at colleges . . . who are strong as well as gentle and brave and tender and honest as well as learned."[31] An advocate of the "strenuous life" throughout his public career, a military hero, a sportsman on three continents, a devoted father and popular moralizer ceaselessly preaching duty and service, Roosevelt often outstripped those who wished to describe him in caricature. In May 1898, he resigned as Assistant Secretary of the Navy to organize the First Volunteer Cavalry Regiment in preparation for possible fighting in Cuba. He was flooded with more than 23,000 applications. When one Dudley Dean (Harvard, '91) introduced himself, T.R. smiled and said, "Yes, I know you. You are the man who saved the day for Harvard in the great football game with Yale. You are one of the kind of men we want!"[32]

THE COLLEGE ATHLETIC HERO IN FICTION: CRANE, NORRIS, DAVIS

Young athletes were America's "kind" of men by 1900. The rhetoric of team play after the Civil War has remained the foundation of the American School Sport Hero. The experience of the individual wedded to a unit which is dependent on him has become the team experience for millions upon millions of Americans, preparing them to fit unquestioningly into other teams—industrial, executive, military, family. How this sporting phenomenon was initially examined on varied levels of literary artistry tells much about the creation of an American fiction hero, the college or schoolboy player.

Authors coming of age in the 1890s, such as Stephen Crane, Frank Norris, and Richard Harding Davis, belonged to the first generation of American writers to reach maturity in a country suffused with sporting enthusiasm and increasingly concerned with college athletics. Sport was an early passion with the young writers of the 1890s and shaped their responses to combat. At the same time it perhaps provided some of their first insights into human character under significant stress; this is posed as a hypothesis to be considered in light of the commonality of their athletic experiences. Crane (b. 1871) was an eager baseball and football player at military school and later at Syracuse University. In the fall of 1891 while living with his brother Edward's family in Paterson, N.J., Crane organized the town's first football team and served as both coach and quarterback. In 1896 he wrote two front-page accounts in the *New York Journal* of Harvard's games with Princeton and the Carlisle Indians.[33] Davis (b. 1864) was a halfback in college and on November 12, 1883, he scored the first points made by a woeful Lehigh football team that season. As a reporter he covered his first Yale-Princeton football game for the *Philadelphia Record* in 1886. Norris (b. 1870) broke his arm playing football at Belmont Academy in 1885. At Berkeley he busied himself by diagramming plays for the college newspaper and later wrote a regular football column in the *Wave* in 1896.

Allied with their affinity for sport was the collegiate fraternal life with its camaraderie and competition that Crane, Norris, and Davis embraced with varying degrees of enthusiasm.[34] Within fraternity life, the endless rituals of schoolboy socialization were of importance to each of them. At Lafayette in 1890, when Crane greeted hazing sophomores in his nightgown, he was green with fear and held a revolver in his hand; the boys went away and left him alone. Davis turned on his tormentors at Lehigh with the offer to thrash them individually if they so wished. Norris, seemingly at ease with the fraternity system, lived for three years (1891–94) at the Phi Gamma Delta house at Berkeley. There he began writing *McTeague* even as Crane is reputed to have written a first draft of *Maggie: A Girl of the Streets* in the attic of the Delta Upsilon house at Syracuse in 1891.[35]

Popular writers above the level encountered in the dime novel went

to sport for the same material as the hacks; sport provided young protagonists at play in plots that swept forward as surely as the game itself. Love
interests were fostered because the young athletic hero was seen as a most
eligible catch for a romantic young girl. Sport in the 1890s was part of a
social rite for the college youth. This mock-genteel athleticism was scrutinized best by Crane with his grave philosophical conclusions about competition and teamwork so lauded by the post-Civil War proponents of college
sport.[36] He had no players as such but rather cosmic representatives with no
college emblem on their blue uniforms. Henry Fleming was Crane's representative youth, a far cry from a flaxen-haired halfback at Yale, but a boy
to be reckoned with in competition.

In a note to *Book Buyer* in April 1896, Crane responded to a review
of *The Red Badge of Courage* that had expressed both enthusiasm and surprise at his youthful knowledge of battle and its emotions. He wrote, ''I
have never been in a battle of course, and I believe that I got my sense of
the rage of conflict on the football field. The psychology is the same. The
opposing team is an enemy tribe.''[37] John Berryman added that Crane in
1893 ''read football articles with delight, descanting on military
analogies,''[38] perhaps those of Caspar Whitney, later the editor of *Outing,*
whose column, ''Amateur Sports,'' in *Harper's Weekly* had detailed, sentimentalized accounts of football action beginning in 1891, or the sports reports replete with military imagery of Richard Harding Davis himself.
Crane's observation about football and *The Red Badge,* which he repeated
more than once, has been noted by critics who are usually anxious to put
aside the statement before examining the more ''literary'' sources of his
battle knowledge. However, if we take Crane's remark seriously, a correspondence does appear to exist between his renderings of battle scenes and
the shape and texture of a football game in the 1890s.

The game of football that Crane knew was stark, brawling, powerful,
and altogether a battle in itself. Football in the 1890s was dominated by a
close-order, mass momentum attack that stressed brute power, endurance,
and ability to take punishment. From 1888 to 1896, the years Crane was
playing and reporting football, the game was at its roughest and most violent. In 1888, Walter Camp succeeded in persuading the colleges to adopt
a rule that required blockers to keep arms at their sides, drawing all formations closer together and making mass interference quite popular. Other
strategists such as Amos Alonzo Stagg at the University of Chicago, Charles
Woodruff at Pennsylvania, and Lorin Deland at Harvard created the famous
wedge plays used for kick-off returns where nine of the eleven players

would form a V-shaped wedge and pick up a twenty-yard running start to convoy the ball carrier in the center tip of the wedge. Then at a strategic moment, they would attempt to squeeze him through the hole in the wedge. Play became so brutal that the 1893 season ended in an uproar with Army and Navy cancelling their game for the following year.[39] The football game of the 1890s was so rough that no higher praise for soldiers could be imagined in that decade than comparison with the teamwork of a football squad. Crane, Norris, and Davis all served in 1898 as war correspondents in Cuba; in one war dispatch, Davis reported the Rough Riders in battle "each with his mouth tightly shut, with his eyes on the ball, and moving in obedience to the captain's signals," their spirit the same "that once sent these men down a white-washed field against their opponents' rushline."[40] The physical fitness of the 1850s Harvard students that stood them in good stead in the Civil War is validated once again through the performance of another generation of ex-football men at San Juan Hill and in the Philippines.

The climactic battle scenes of *The Red Badge* at times resemble descriptions of football action. Henry Fleming's role is that of participant in chapter 19 and is that of spectator in chapter 22. This split in Henry's consciousness is tentatively resolved in the novel's concluding pages when his final reflection on action brings about balance and insight instead of further self-delusion. By having Henry Fleming experience dangers in realistic battles but continually misread their lessons in sentimental romantic conclusions, Crane recreated the flow of the conventional sporting tale within the battle framework. Football was a perfect romantic delusion for a youth of the 1890s and Crane posed his Civil War hero as a representative figure.

Much of Henry's longing to join the ranks of men is akin to the desire of a lonely schoolboy to become part of the crowd. No schoolboy sports hero in pulp fiction could be as obsessively insecure about his position within the group as Henry Fleming preparing to join the ritual of war. Like countless boys in the maturation plots of school stories, Henry is an "unknown quantity"[41] who cannot join the team in the true sense until after he has performed with skill and courage in the big game. Back with his unit after a charge, Henry becomes vociferous and militant to compensate for his earlier cowardly behavior under fire. Crane writes, in chapter 17, "The awkward bandage was still about his head, and upon it, over his wound, there was a spot of dry blood. His hair was wondrously tousled, and some straggling, moving locks hung over the cloth of the bandage down toward his forehead. His jacket and shirt were open at the throat, and exposed his young bronzed neck" (80). This description not only mimics the dime novels but also recognizes the polarization of the dashing college hero and his alterego, the brute player.

The suggestion of a football scrimmage as a Civil War skirmish is at its strongest in *The Red Badge* in chapter 19. Upon orders to charge, the regiment moves out from its position into a "cleared space," which corresponds to an open field of play. The line becomes a "wedge-shaped mass" (87) resembling the powerful charge of the flying wedge. The opposition is supplied by "bushes, trees, and uneven places on the ground" which split the command and scattered it into detached clusters," much as a football wedge was broken up by opposing players hurling themselves at it to reach the ball carrier. Finally, "the opposing infantry's lines were defined by the gray wall" (87).

In the first charge of chapter 19, Henry appears much like a lineman in the middle of the field. In the chapter's second charge or play, he resembles a back momentarily free in the open field. In the novel's only specific reference to football, Crane wrote:

> The youth ran like a madman to reach the woods before a bullet could discover him. He ducked his head low, like a football player. In his haste his eyes almost closed, and the scene was a wild blur. . . .
> Within him, as he hurled himself forward, was born a love, a despairing fondness for this flag which was near him. It was a creation of beauty and invulnerability. . . . Because no harm could come to it he endowed it with power. (90)

Just as the woods represent the opposition's goal line which the player must reach and break through, the flag becomes the football, the inviolable object, and whoever carries it becomes the center of attention, ennobled yet extremely vulnerable.

In chapter 20, Crane has Henry and another youth fight for possession of the flag when the color sergeant is killed. "They wrenched the flag furiously from the dead man" (91) as they continued their flight toward the woods. A scuffle ensued: " 'Give it t' me!' 'No, let me keep it!' Each felt satisfied with the other's possession of it, but each felt bound to declare, by an offer to carry the emblem, his willingness to further risk himself. The youth roughly pushed his friend away" (91). Competition, fear, and pride in recovering the sacred object mingle here as the scene suggests that of children arguing over possession of toys or balls. One reason for Crane's continual emphasis of the *youth* in the novel's narration is to underscore the adolescent, gamelike quality of much battle experience.

Upon publication of *The Red Badge,* a *New York Press* review commented, "The reader is right down in the midst of it where patriotism is dissolved into its elements and where only a dozen men can be seen."[42] This review grasps the sense that Crane's battlefield resembles a playing field where the movements of 12 men (or 22) could be highlighted during the action. In a "cleared space" that has a "set-apart look," distinct battles are being fought "as if at a matched game" (99). There was "no interference" between the four regiments and "they settled their dispute by themselves" (100). As a battle reporter, Henry sees "wild and desperate rushes of men perpetually backward and forward in riotous surges" (100). The opposing armies are "two long waves that pitched upon each other madly at dictated points" (100). The regiments move back and forth down the field for possession of territory: "Particular pieces of fence for secure positions behind collections of trees were wrangled over. . . . There were desperate lunges at these chosen spots . . ." (101). Although Henry's regiment is ordered back into the fray, he cannot shake his role for "he was deeply absorbed as a spectator" (101). He has all he can do to remember his own danger.

The novel contains few images that are expressly from the world of football; indeed, by 1890 the vocabularies of war and football were already impossible to separate. Crane, a supremely conscious craftsman, must have realized that repeated specific intrusions of football terminology would defuse the stark nature of the life-and-death competition he was describing. He may have known football and been able to apply its strategy and atmosphere to battle scenes, but for a small-town youth like Henry to have known a great deal about football in 1863 would have created an incongruous effect. Yet Crane's one specific mention of football is hardly jarring and futuristic when read in the context of the *Harvard Memorial Biographies*. It is possible that Crane realistically reimagined the playing field as battleground and then ironically deflated that metaphor by relating it to sentimental heroism.[43]

Frank Norris was an early popularizer of the social philosophy of American college sport. He worshipped force and decisiveness while praising "that fine, reckless arrogance, that splendid, brutal, bullying spirit that is the Anglo-Saxon's birthright."[44] Norris first conceived of sport as a test of merit and of courage in a fictional embodiment of Walker's views on the efficacy of college athletics. His two early stories on sport, "Travis Hallett's Halfback" (1894) and "This Animal of a Buldy Jones" (1897), both published before his novels, contain both the realistic and romantic conceptions of the athlete as hero while *Vandover and the Brute* (1914) shows Norris capable of considerably darkening the outlines of the college hero. "Travis

Hallett'' and ''Buldy Jones'' are among the first real expressions of two strains of American sporting heroism that continue to flourish in modern fiction. ''Travis Hallett'' is a sketch of the college football hero and shows how that figure could be drawn as an American heroic stereotype two years before the creation of America's greatest schoolboy sports hero, Frank Merriwell. ''Buldy Jones'' combines the college athletic hero and the outsized comic athlete with links to American frontier roarers and musclemen.

After his year studying writing at Harvard in 1894–95, Norris returned to San Francisco and joined the *Wave* as writer and editor in April 1896. That fall he wrote a detailed column, ''The Week's Football,'' following the fortunes of the Bay Area's four football powers, Berkeley, Stanford University, and the Olympic and the Reliance amateur clubs. His football columns show a strong grasp of game action and present analytical studies of football strategy. The columns were undoubtedly modelled on those initiated by Davis and then by Camp and Caspar Whitney. Indeed, upon his return to California football in 1896, Norris remained quite enamored of the more developed style of play he had seen in the East, reiterating that Californians ''don't know the meaning of hard playing'' and that ''an eastern game'' would be ''a revelation'' to spectators.[45]

Norris similarly was anxious to define the western college man against his more formal counterpart in the East. He portrayed the westerner as a ''true bohemian,'' more expansive with his chums, with the fraternity as the center of his social life where ''he loves his pipe and his glass and is given over to late hours and to riotous home-comings with a great noise of shouting.'' In the fall, the western college man ''comes back from the mountains, or, perhaps, from the desert with his hair long and his chin rough with an incipient beard and the skin burnt off his nose. . . . Then he settles to the grooves of his college life again . . . [and] returns to the serious business of the fall term, which is coaching the football team.''[46] Finally, Norris went so far as to date the birth of the western college man from the date of the first intercollegiate game at Stanford.[47]

Norris' football reports in the *Wave* in 1896 consistently stressed the need for San Francisco area football teams to ''end the squabbling in the lines that infallibly betrays the want of discipline and organization,'' and observed during one game that there was ''none of that lightning rapidity of attack and machine-like accuracy of manoeuvre so completely demoralizing to ill-trained opponents.'' He concluded one essay in a rigid statement of survival rhetoric: ''The strongest team has not the right—literally not the right—to lose the game.''[48]

Such an emphasis on organization, quick, decisive play, and force was realized in "Travis Hallett's Halfback." Travis Hallett, one of Norris' bevy of masculine-named good girls, watches a halfback named Adler play a flawless game as he leads his college to victory. She catches a glimpse of a disheveled, panting Adler on the field at the end of the game, and a week later she sees him on the court at a tennis tournament "where he was the winner": "She could hardly recognize the graceful young man in the white flannels and dainty-coloured sash as the dirty, grasping, canvas-clad savage of the game."[49] The brute could always surface in Norris' outwardly respectable characters. That this primitivism may be resolved by an outlet such as football was a truism for Norris. His view of sports heroism in "Travis Hallett" mirrored the conventional wisdom about the 1890s college hero, a man at home in country clubs and drawing rooms but also capable of becoming a beast in combat.[50]

Adler's football training pays off during his courtship of Travis when he saves her from a burning theater. Hemmed in by a hysterical crowd, he breaks through it as if he were breaking through an opposing line. He drags Travis out with him, scattering people right and left with his charge, keeping the "cool head" of the athlete "in moments of great activity" as Shaler had described it. Norris builds his survival lesson on a knowledge of football force and psychology. He begins by showing the football crowd at Adler's game to be a chaotic, easily-swayed mass: "The crowd behind the sidelines was beyond all control now; they swayed back and forth with every fluctuation of the ball, tense and white with that excitement that hurts and sickens" (149). He contrasts the disorder of the fans with the purposeful drive and bustle on the field: "the sharp, quick tones of the captains calling the signals; the sound of heavy bodies striking together; the quick, laboured breathing; the occasional, brief, hoarse shouts, muffled by the nose guards; and then the dull and jarring crash, as the whirling wedge smashed its way through the line" (149).

Norris manipulated this on-the-field action into an integral part of his theme in the theater-scene climax where he contrasted the undisciplined, fearful theater crowd with the quick-thinking Adler and his decisive physical action: "The crush and lurch of the crowd was but the old scrimmage of gridiron field, and the confused, blind rush that enveloped him was no worse than the trained and disciplined charges of the revolving V or the flying wedge, and for one brief instant Adler thanked his God that he was a Varsity half back and knew how to use his weight and wits" (159). The surface romance of collegiate athletic heroism glosses over the lesson of survival through quick thinking and physical action. Adler successfully bursts through the lobby with Travis. He is a functioning engine of power contrasted with the unharnessed power of the chaotic fire and the confused crowd.[51] Travis's father observes, as a perfect social Darwinist, "I think you will find that the same qualities that make a good football man would make a good soldier; and a good soldier, sir, is a man good enough to be any girl's husband" (160–61).[52] Thus does Mr. Hallett anticipate Roosevelt's response to Harvard's Dudley Dean: "You are one of the kind of men we want."

In 1894, the same year he wrote "Travis Hallett's Halfback," Norris was already working on *Vandover and the Brute,* the story of a Harvard graduate's degeneration through apathy, a pliable nature, and lack of discipline. In *Vandover,* Norris appropriates the crowd descriptions and football material of "Travis Hallett" to deflate the stereotype of the college hero as a man of power and privilege. He offers Vandover an opportunity for heroics by placing him on a steamer that capsizes off the California coast. Like the football and theater mobs in "Travis Hallett," the ship's passengers are hysterical. Vandover tries to help a young woman but the boom of the foremast breaks her back; she drops in a heap, froths at the mouth, and dies at his feet. Inert, almost paralyzed, Vandover uses neither his weight nor wits. Instead he observes the frenzied rescue scene: "There was nothing picturesque about it at all, nothing heroic. . . . It was all sordid, miserable."[53] Vandover has prepared himself for no heroic action, has not "risked his neck for his college," and cannot do so for anyone else. Norris also transforms the college football game of "Travis Hallett's Halfback" into a nightmare of confusion for Vandover. He uses the game to contrast Vandover's strange, degenerative illness with healthy, collegiate heroism at the conclusion of the novel.[54] Stirred by college memories, Vandover considers going to the California-Stanford game, but it rains and he stays in with his assorted misfit drinking companions. That night the victory phalanx of college fraternity men parades down Market Street celebrating the football triumph. But their energy and loud cheers fail to arouse Vandover, who pads about his room on all fours, far from football, college days, or victory.[55]

In his 1897 story, "This Animal of a Buldy Jones," Norris showed that he could lighten the college sports frame of "Travis Hallett" and *Vandover* by wedding the school sports hero to the comic superman of American folklore. In "Novelists of the Future" (1901), Norris envisioned the new muse of American fiction as she who "rough-shoulders her way among men

. . . who finds a healthy pleasure in the jostlings of the mob and a hearty delight in the honest, rough-and-tumble, Anglo-Saxon give-and-take knock-about that for us means life''; the American muse "will lead . . . far from the studios, the velvet jackets and the uncut hair.'' [56] "Buldy Jones" expresses both Norris' praise for Anglo-Saxon rough high-spiritedness and his mistrust of *fin de siècle* aestheticism in art and literature.

Norris drew on his teenage art student experiences in Paris in 1887–89 for this comic tale. Towering Buldy Jones is an aspiring artist in Paris, a native Chicagoan, and a Yale graduate who has also studied law at Columbia. His greatest talent is pitching baseballs; he has been a champion baseball pitcher on the Yale nine. In his studio he keeps a collection of inscribed baseballs that he had pitched in big games; he reverently shows them to his international cohorts who make up a jocular fraternity of their own. After Buldy is insulted by a French student named Camme, he spins the "little frog-like Frenchman" and then kicks him twice in the seat of his pants whereupon Buldy is challenged to a duel. The American art students huddle and decide to ridicule the solemn occasion. Their choice of weapons for the duel? Baseballs at sixty feet, of course. The duel takes place behind the Longchamps race course. Buldy has lovingly selected the ball he used to defeat Harvard. With a majestic wind-up, he delivers an "in-curve" that dislocates Camme's jaw. The hulking Ivy Leaguer has salvaged America's honor through his expertise in the American game.

The story catches the spirit of the era very nicely, for the college baseball pitcher/artist is now acquiring culture on an extended grand tour. The tradition of duelling has passed to America and, as "Horse" Wilson says, "You've no idea what curious ideas these continentals have of the American duel. You can't propose anything so absurd in the duelling line that they won't give it serious thought.'' [57] Norris writes an early tale of the comic athlete, albeit from good stock, who wins in a humor tale that echoes the nonsense battles of American tall-tale tradition. Here he also lampoons the 1900-era best-selling historical romances that featured the duels of European noblemen or American cowboys, whether in George Barr McCutchean's *Graustark* (1901) or Owen Wister's *The Virginian* (1902).

Norris' stories deal very early with what would become the stock characters of American sporting life in fiction, the serious romantic college hero and the free-form, outsized comic folk hero; he virtually predicts the bumpkin pitcher heroes of Lardner such as Jack Keefe and Hurry Kane. Norris identified with the college sporting scene and possessed a strong philosophical interest in physical power and degeneration. These two links to sport, combined with his remarkable talent for giving realistic descriptions of crowds and action, made him the writer best equipped to develop the subject of sporting life, even as he broke down genteel barriers of presentation with his clinical descriptions of the physical and mental decline of McTeague and Trina in *McTeague* (1899) and Vandover in *Vandover and the Brute* (1914). His creations of Adler and Buldy Jones are developed only within shorter narratives; American college sport had not yet acquired enough cultural centrality to be the subject of longer, serious work. Norris' fiction with sporting heroes in the 1890s was a vein in a tradition that was yet to be mined and enriched. Norris was working through his own major concerns and those of America in the 1890s: how to integrate the differing conceptions of hearty romance and decadence, evolution and degeneration, and moral as well as physical force.

Adler, the heroic halfback, and Buldy Jones, the comic socialite, owe much to the fictional heroes of Richard Harding Davis, perhaps the most popular literary figure of the 1890s, both for the stories and novels he wrote and for the personae he constantly exhibited to an adoring middle-class audience. He was the prototype for a whole generation's romantic image of the fearless American war correspondent. It would be safe to say that the popular reader's conception of a college gentleman in the 1890s was gleaned from a blurred portrait of Davis' fictional New York socialite, Harvard's Cortlandt Van Bibber, merged with the image of Davis himself whom Charles Dana Gibson ultimately cast as his image of the "Gibson Man" to go with his famous drawing of Lillian Russell. On college campuses, Davis was a hero for writing of sports and young lovers, revealing to undergraduates "the astonishing fact that literature might conceivably have something to do with them."[58] As early as 1883 his *The Adventures of a Freshman* had run as a serial on campus in the *Lehigh Burr*.

Davis covered major sporting events for the *New York Evening Sun* in 1890–91 and William Randolph Hearst's crack managing editor, Arthur Brisbane, always insisted that Davis' descriptions of football pageantry were the best sports stories in New York City.[59] When he became managing editor of *Harper's Weekly,* Davis initiated Caspar Whitney's "Amateur Sports" column in 1891 and thereafter Davis himself reported only major events in feature articles, such as his account of the November 30, 1893, Yale-Princeton game for *Harper's Weekly,* which concentrated on the social spectacle, the pregame scenes at hotels, in bars, and along Fifth Avenue. Davis prophesied many a modern Thanksgiving Day when he wrote, "the significance of that day which once centered in New England around a grateful family offering thanks for blessings received and a fruitful harvest now centres in Harlem about twenty-two very dirty and very earnest young men who are trying to force a leather ball over a whitewashed line."[60] Davis' real theme is how a city is completely transformed during the excitement of a major college football game: "The streets are empty, for it is a holiday, and the rifle-like cheer of Yale and the hissing sky-rocket yell of Princeton break in on the Sabbath-like quiet of the streets like the advance of an army going forth triumphantly to war." Indeed, in a direct legacy from Civil War identification with aggressive sport, Davis used more overtly military imagery than any other author who wrote about sport. He commented on the victorious Princeton unit: "any one who has seen a defeated team lying on the benches of their dressing room, sobbing like hysterical school girls, can understand how great and how serious is the joy of victory to the men who conquer."

In *Stories for Boys* (1891), almost every one of Davis' tales, even if not directly about sport, provides a detail of sporting life.[61] In "The Reporter Who Made Himself a King," a newspaper reporter becomes American ambassador to a small island kingdom through an absurd series of events. He gives his two English stowaway aides his Yale football jerseys for their official uniforms. To amuse the tribe and keep its mind off cannibalism, the "ambassador" teaches them baseball. "The Midsummer Pirates" features boat-racing hijinks amongst boys on the Manasquan River in New Jersey. In "Richard Carr's Baby," the captain of the Princeton football team runs over a young boy on the sideline who turns out to be his devoted fan. In anticipation of Babe Ruth's seemingly innumerable visits to tykes in hospitals, Carr stays by the boy's bed for days and secures the services of the finest surgeons. The story concludes with Carr running a ranch "out west" (shades of Roosevelt) and the recovered youth enrolling at Princeton himself.

"The Great Tri-Club Tennis Tournament" features one Charles Coleridge Grace, the "collegiate champ" who helps train a small town team to thrash the bullies from the next village. In "The Jump at Corey's Slip," East Side urchins dare each other to dive off a pier into the East River, a dangerous drop because of huge pilings. The boy who is terribly frightened makes a perfect dive to save his friend who has jumped and hit the wooden piling. Van Bibber happens to be steaming by in his yacht and picks up the whole gang, an example of his heroism on behalf of the masses. In "The Van Bibber Base-Ball Club," Van Bibber takes a group of young unfortunates to the circus and they rename their team after him.

However, Davis' contribution to the popular image of the School Sports Hero does not really lie in specific stories, but in the suggestiveness of the persona of the college gentleman. Norris' Dolly Haight in *Vandover and the Brute* and Ross Wilbur in *Moran of the Lady Letty* (1898) are two further examples of heroes in part crafted on the Van Bibber model.[62] Haight is Vandover's virtuous Harvard friend and the innocent victim of the most absurd case of venereal disease in medical or literary history. Wilbur, a skilled Yale oarsman, is shanghaied in San Francisco Bay, and impresses his captors with his rowing techniques, including " 'the Bob Cooke stroke we used in our boat in '95 when we beat Harvard.' "[63] Davis expertly merged his public image with that of his character, Van Bibber, so that the gentleman, sportsman, and correspondent became a single figure. Davis incarnated the final 1890s metamorphosis from 1865, the war hero become the war correspondent, the romantic Civil War captain become the popular romancer.

College sport in the 1890s was a cultural adaptation of the predatory Darwinian spectacle of self-assertion and survival with military, hence societal, sanction. Sport caught the imagination of young writers initially as part of their adolescent lives, and whether they grew into impressionists, naturalists, or romancers, sport was a subject that enabled them to break through a genteel ban on physical scenes in literature. A new emphasis on realistic description of the whole life, a naturalistic fascination with the contest and its winners and losers mirrored the harsh facts of biological evolution, and contributed to the growth of sport as fictional subject.

For Davis and for Norris as well, college sport remained in the province of the upper middle class; it was the romantic, vicariously primitive activity of a pseudogenteel society flexing its muscle behind a facade of decorum. The college hero of Norris and Davis would become, in adolescent and adult persona, the hero of literally hundreds of boys' books on school, sport, and martial spirit in acceptable society. It is not an exaggeration to say that the college experiences of Crane, Norris, and Davis suggested the outlines of Gilbert Patten's Frank Merriwell before Patten ever created his famous character in 1896. Frank Merriwell fighting on the gridiron at Yale was a perfect trivialization of a Rough Rider (or Henry Fleming) in battle. In pulp fiction, games became the assimilable state of war without death, providing a mass audience with scenes of public victories and vicarious thrills.

Emerson's and Walker's warring conceptions of how the individual might define himself in regard to society continued to set the terms of the fictional college sporting hero. Emerson in 1837 had asked to be shown the "sublime in the commonplace," to make the common American into the subject of art. He concluded that colleges have the duty to "set the hearts of their youth on flame."[64] By the 1890s, the hearty "common" subject of sport was setting college hearts "on flame." However, such enthusiasm was in an aggressive, patriotic mode that fit the terms of the new American condition stressed on different planes by Emerson, Thoreau, and T.W. Higginson, and that suggested the School Hero combined the best of self-development with subordination to national (team) goals. Action was no longer with the scholar who, like Walker and Shaler, was the new academic technician. The image of the college athletic hero was then underscored by Camp, Remington, and Roosevelt, and recreated in fiction by Crane, Norris, and Davis. In his 1893 address on "College Athletics" at Harvard, Walker had moved rhetorically within a dozen lines from "self-reliance" to "ability to work with others" to "qualities useful within a profession."[65] It is within such swift surface transformation that visions of the individual were by 1900 wed to an explicit set of assumptions about group athletics: that a young hero could work for himself and for the goals of society at the same time without conflict.

CHAPTER SEVEN
The Boys' School
Sports Story

BETWEEN 1895 AND WORLD WAR I, the boys' school sports story offered a conventional genre of ritualized aggression where the individual submitted himself to assimilation with the team, the school, and, by extension, the values of American society in exchange for honor and influence in that society. The college hero was fixed in a formula tale whereby his heroism was distilled into scores of fictional boys and young men battling foes on and off the field of play. With his great fame, the School Sports Hero became a clearly defined figure in popular literature and the cultural stereotype born initially out of a search for lofty rules of individual conduct and out of the anxiety for preparedness after the Civil War found its popular expression. In the school sports story, the American hero's "fair play" is shown by his respect for the codified rules of team, school, and society as opposed to the frontier "fair play" of Natty Bumppo which stressed the majesty of the wilderness and respect for the life and land there. Indeed, Natty Bumppo's obsession with his own instinctive code and rules for acting in nature stamp him as an early American sportsman, a gentleman whose emphasis on the principles of manliness and sporting conduct could allow him to pass as the unlettered wilderness great-uncle of Theodore Roosevelt's muscular college gentleman who would preach to a whole society by 1900.

In the boys' school sports story, young Natty, Roosevelt, and the ghosts of H.L. Higginson's Harvard classmates were represented by such heroes as Gilbert Patten's Frank Merriwell and Owen Johnson's Dink Stover, who became as popular as Walter Camp's actual All-Americans. The School Sports Hero provided an elite figure who worked extremely hard at his play, becoming both a lionized individual hero and a staunch defender of schoolboy democracy and equality. Whereas the Popular Sports Hero single-mindedly pursued victory in the *agon* for external reward, the School Sports Hero, while perennially dominant in the contest, also represented the goals of the larger society in education and organization. His sought-for mask of discipline and moral order proved *mimicry* to be as strong a play category in the school sports story as the *agon*. He was an uncommon common man who revealed much about how America conceived of its youth and their responsibilities at the beginning of this century. The School Sports Hero is a modern inheritor of a bifurcated doctrine of "Higher Laws." He becomes a sportsman at a station on a longer journey of discipline and control. But in a more pragmatic sense, the School Sports Hero becomes an essentially innocent representative of aggressive Protestant capitalism where the rewarded (the victors at sport) become the elect (school heroes) by virtue of being rewarded. One plays to win so that by winning, one may play for real stakes of power—in university societies, in politics, in war, in business.

Before 1890, the boy hero had already become a staple of popular literature, for American authors conceived of the adolescent experience to be both representative of and apart from larger questions of good and evil. The ultimate consequences of a boy's actions were not featured as much as his ability to see and judge the world around him, a world in which he was more than likely immune to the evil he could nonetheless perceive in others.[1] Although Huck Finn is descended from an old rotter like Pap Finn, he instinctively knows right from wrong. In the mid-nineteenth century a conflict developed between the romantic view of the child as a pure innocent set against the Calvinist notion that the child needed all the marshalled forces of church, school, and family to keep him from the sins of Old Adam. Certainly the history of children's literature in America until just before the Civil War was largely one of dreary tracts, only occasionally disguised as stories, in which children were tortured with admonishments as to the penalties for straying from godly conduct.[2]

In the boys' school stories published from 1880 to World War I, the problem of good and evil was transferred into secular parables of right and wrong. In this rigorously genteel format, boys' contact with social villains (bullies, classmates, and teammates) enabled adolescent readers to read about the tests and tribulations of the peer-group environment. Personal problems were magnified into real crises of character. The terror of damnation held up as punishment for wrong conduct became, in sweetly moralistic terms, the ostracism from the team (being cast out of Eden, for example) or the suspension from school.

After the Civil War, however, genteel children's literature as a whole showed an increased regard for the sensibilities of children and a more sympathetic view of their characters. Much of the feeling for childhood was contained in nostalgia for the village childhood as portrayed by Thomas Bailey Aldrich in *The Story of a Bad Boy* and by Twain in *Tom Sawyer,* a need to return to youth to recreate an innocence for the nation and promote optimism about the individual citizen.

But even pre-Civil War commentary had expressly linked childhood to sport, where some of youth's finest moments might be experienced. Thoreau had evoked the life of "the gun and the fish-pole" and sta ed puckishly that "The governor and his council faintly remember the pond, for they went a-fishing there when they were boys; but now they are too old and dignified to go a-fishing and so they know it no more forever." At whatever age, there is a spontaneous childlike quality to Natty Bumppo, who is for the most part uncontaminated by sexuality or the drive to wealth and authority. He remains an innocent, especially youthful in the last Leatherstocking volume, *The Deerslayer,* where the face of the young hunter has "an expression . . . of guileless truth, sustained by an earnestness of purpose and a sincerity of feeling that rendered it remarkable"(5). T.W. Higginson concluded his hymn to the virtues of naturalist study, exercise, and organized sport by personifying nature as an all-loving maternal figure of care and love with the sportsman as loved child: Ride, run, swim, shoot, tramp with her and "she gladly takes you back once more within the horizon of her magic, and your heart of manhood is born again into more than the fresh happiness of the boy" (595).

The Civil War itself had fostered the sense that almost before maturity a boy might be forced to undergo horrible trials. Indeed, Aldrich devotes a whole chapter to a major snowball fight in which boys named as generals devise military strategy and draw up battle diagrams. There were further literary forays into the past, into the small village or schoolyard, in search of the youth who then might be brought to the city to seek his fortune. Such characters were featured as Horatio Alger's initially ragged overachievers or the boys of "Oliver Optic" (William Adams). The Alger series stressed abstemious conduct, perseverance, and the element of luck to move a boy into a successful career.[3] Perhaps Ragged Dick could then afford to send his son to prep school and thence to Yale. Certainly by 1890, the boy hero, whether in the dime novel, in a respectable children's magazine, or in the Alger series, was no longer a poor ruffian.

The whole subject of children's literature had become too profitable and important to be left entirely to dime publishers Beadle, Street & Smith, Frank Tousey, and the Munro brothers. The best and longest-running children's magazine of the era was *St. Nicholas* (1873–1930) which from its inception elevated the children's story to a genteel plane where Huck Finn was proscribed. Richard Harding Davis was a contributor of boys' sports stories early in his career and his fictional sketch of a Princeton football captain in "Richard Carr's Baby" (1886) was one of the earliest accounts of an impossibly upright college sports hero.[4]

The few *St. Nicholas* stories that centered on sports were of a type that could be called the village sport story. Not a great deal happened in the plot outside the sphere of boys' recreation activities. Parents were generally absent, and the pleasant narratives highlighted an orderly world where dime novel desperadoes failed to appear. A good example would be Edward Eggleston's *The Hoosier Schoolboy* (1883), serialized in *St. Nicholas* and filled with detailed references to children's ball games such as "three old cat," "hat ball," and "bull-pen." School was not emphasized in *St. Nicholas* sport stories; however, the boys did flourish in a military atmosphere where American patriotic values were of utmost importance. In "The Fairport Nine" (1880), perhaps the earliest of all baseball serials,[5] the setting is a sleepy Maine village where the sons of the town's leading citizens take on the sons of poor fishermen in a 4th of July baseball game. The nine go on bivouacs worthy of an infantry platoon and choose up sides to fight mock battles while taking on the names of revolutionary war heroes. The final baseball game features an umpire whose picture stamps him as Abraham Lincoln's twin, a suitable authority figure for the boys. Patriotic speeches on July 4th concentrate on a boy's duty to his team and country, and the mix of baseball, military discipline, and nostalgia is explicit.[6] A later serial is "The Lakerim Athletic Club" (1897–98) in which another small-town boys' sports team is the protagonist.[7] The town boys, who play against area military academies with many gymnasiums and playing fields, eagerly desire a clubhouse of their own. The prose labors to approximate Crane's narrative voice in *The Red Badge of Courage,* and there are mock assaults, retreats, and injuries in yet another great snowball fight. The "Lakerim" series emphasized competition and military values, while the middle-class youth at play was shown as the ideal American boy. The stories become play-by-play reports, signifying little beyond the action itself, and this formula would remain as the simplest outline of a boys' sports story.

THOMAS HUGHES AND TOM BROWN

While the dime novels introduced sports detectives in urban settings and magazines such as *St. Nicholas* published the village sport story, the emerging popular convention of the boys' school sport story owed its original strength to the interest shown in Thomas Hughes' *Tom Brown* series about the school adventures of a young English boy at Rugby School and later at Oxford University. Here was the classic fictional portrayal of youth's initiation into traditions of school life in which athletic skill defined and singled out the leadership boys more than any other activity. It is fair to say that even as Lardner created the Popular Sports Hero, Hughes, in effect, created the School Sports Hero in the outline of the boys' school story with *Tom Brown's School Days* (1857) and *Tom Brown at Oxford* (1861). By making school sport the basis of so much of the narrative action, formation of character, and social setting, Hughes practically insured the place of sport in the school story genre when it became a staple of popular literature in America. Of books published in 1857, only Charles Dickens' *Little Dorrit* sold as many copies in America as *Tom Brown's School Days,* while *Tom Brown at Oxford* was one of the ten best-selling books published in 1861.[8]

Hughes had attended Rugby from 1833 to 1842[9] under the tenure of Dr. Thomas Arnold, father of Matthew Arnold and England's reforming school headmaster. Through an intense spirituality and love of learning, Arnold had brought the socially moribund eighteenth-century educational tradition of the public school into line with Victorian traditions of morality, humanity, discipline, and scholarship.[10] Rugby and Oxford in the 1840s were true centers of sporting activity, unlike American colleges of the same period, where there was only dormant interest in such pursuits. Football, cricket, boxing, and many varieties of boating were the major sports contested between houses at Rugby or between colleges at Oxford. The first Oxford-Cambridge cricket match was in 1827 and the first boat race in 1829. Hughes himself was a splendid all-around athlete; in his first semester at Oxford in 1842, he was picked for the cricket match against Cambridge, and in his second term he rowed second oar in intercollegiate four-oar races.[11] He decided early on at Oxford that he wished to become a barrister; and for roughly thirty years before, during, and after the Tom Brown series that made him famous in both England and America, he was an earnest but rash liberal gadfly, serving several terms in Commons until 1874 as a committed Christian Socialist who constantly championed legislation in favor of the working man and his health, safety, and education.

Tom Brown's School Days contains a strong vein of egalitarianism and cheerful, manly simplicity that remains attractive to readers of all ages in all eras. Tom begins as the fair-minded boy of Squire Brown to whom "it didn't matter a straw whether his son associated with lord's sons or ploughman's sons, provided they were brave and honest."[12] Squire Brown gives all the village boys "the run of a close for a playground, and provided bats and balls and a football for their sports" (78). He sees no rank in their station and hopes that Tom will "only turn out a brave, helpful, truth telling Englishman and a gentleman, and a Christian, that's all I want" (91). Hughes thus established the fundamental environment of the school sport story: a boys' world in which the hero received his true democratic education by meeting different types of boys in a society dominated by the playing field. Hughes established a convention that would allow the School Sports Hero great mobility as he learned how to lead and represent all groups in schoolboy society before assuming a leadership role in the larger society.

Hughes' Rugby is a difficult testing ground where considerable amounts of pluck, endurance, and discipline are necessary for survival. Tom Brown is a boy of high spirits and earnest nature whom Hughes cares about dearly. His Rugby is fully realized from prefects to school masters, with descriptions of the rigors of Latin, the evils of fagging, the socialization of diverse boys, the odious bullying of schoolboy fiction's greatest villain, Harry Flashman, all overseen by Arnold's sure and steady hand. However, it is in school sport where Tom and Rugby School truly come alive. Tom's first day at school is during a great school house football match, and the vision that the contest presents is later brought home to the young boy: "the meaning of his life—that it was no fool's or sluggard's paradise into which he had wandered by chance, but a battlefield ordained from of old, where there are no spectators, but the youngest must take his side, and the stakes are life and death" (166). Here Hughes prefigures all the later authors who would envision school as battleground with sport providing its major clashes.

The novel becomes increasingly serious in tone near its conclusion as Hughes gets emotionally caught up in writing of the death of Arnold in 1842. The last chapter establishes the durable convention of the climactic school sports match with Tom becoming a hero in the sixth-form cricket encounter with Marylebone. Hughes describes, "a strapping figure, nearly six feet high, with ruddy tanned face. . . . He is leaning forward with his elbows resting on his knees, and dandling his favorite bat, with which he has made thirty or forty runs today, in his strong brown hands. It is Tom Brown, grown into a young man nineteen years old, a praeposter and captain of the eleven, spending his last days as a Rugby-boy" (390). In the pose Hughes most admires, Tom muses, "Only the question remains whether I should have got most good by understanding Greek particles or cricket thoroughly. I'm such a thick, I never should have had time for both" (393). Tom at his leave-taking converses with a master on the value of games and is told that cricket "merges the individual in the leaven; he doesn't play that he may win, but that his side may" (394).

Tom, if not a "thick," certainly is cheerfully willing to admit his intellectual limitations as was Hughes, thereby establishing another part of the convention, to wit, that the School Sports Hero is steady, balanced, tolerant, but not brilliant, incisive, or subtle. Both physical and spiritual straightforwardness is the virtue of the School Sports Hero from Tom Brown onward. Hughes' contemporaries labelled this quality "Muscular Christianity,"[13] a term Hughes adopted and then toyed with in *Tom Brown at Oxford*. The muscular Christians have "hold of the old chivalrous and Christian belief, that a man's body is given him to be trained and brought into subjection, and then used for the protection of the weak,"[14] a statement that leads straight to the higher sentiments of muscular preparedness espoused by the Harvard martyrs with a Christian duty at its core combined with a tough discipline. In 1892 Santayana contrasted Yale to Oxford and Cambridge, suggesting the English universities were more refined yet partaking of the character-building ethic that Hughes had been instrumental in fostering as the educational imperative in both England and America. Santayana expressly stated that the American institution of higher education was intended to be "a mother of men rather than a school of doctors."[15] Thus, Dr. Arnold's revolution, slightly tarnished intellectually and spiritually, had nonetheless, through its militant, character-building rhetoric, taken full hold in American eastern private schools and colleges, with Hughes as architect and Tom Brown as representative boy and young man at Rugby and then at Oxford.[16]

Hughes' Oxford is bursting with life, though less realized dramatically than the Rugby of *Tom Brown's School Days*. The narrative has Tom meet young, somewhat jaded aristocrats, driven scholars, and proud middle-class boys; it deals strongly with the morality of class and caste as Tom exuberantly flirts with and discards bits of Malthus and Bentham and the positions of the Chartists. Hughes himself, though the same age as Matthew

Arnold and friends with Arthur Hugh Clough, appears to have taken little part in Oxford intellectual life.[17] *Tom Brown at Oxford* continues the emphasis on athletics. It has been estimated that three-quarters of the Oxford undergraduates of Hughes' era were active in athletics as opposed to the sad state of American collegiate sporting interest at the time. The boat race among Oxford colleges is the sporting high point of *Tom Brown at Oxford* where St. Ambrose, Balliol, Oriel, and Exeter all go at one another and "a dozen other crews were making their way in the same direction and half the undergraduates of Oxford streamed along with them (140): For Tom, "his whole soul was glued to the back of the man before him, his one thought to keep time and get his strength into the stroke" (145).

Hughes gave his undergraduates a sporting life and integrated it with the life of the school. Although he was capable of lapsing into sentimentality, his Christian piety was worn lightly. His energy, optimism, and concentration on detail in his narratives remain his strengths as each chapter punches forward. By creating Tom Brown as direct, honest, unsubtle, not reflective, intuitive rather than analytical, Hughes set the tone for a century of fictional portraits of the muscular school hero and his counterpart, the professional athlete. Also the conception of Tom Brown gave critics the first target to assail as antiintellectual, rigid, and conventional in thought and action, the perennial adolescent in the case of the School Sports Hero and the "boob" or "dumb jock" in the case of the Popular Sports Hero.

For many years Hughes corresponded with James Russell Lowell whose family had lost eight men not yet thirty years old in the Civil War. Hughes wrote a tribute, *Young Heroes of the Civil War,* to show England the "heroism of the men of gentle birth and nurture" in New England. In 1870 during the first of many trips to the United States, Hughes met almost all of New England's literary personages, criticized the lack of adequate sports facilities at Harvard, and visited St. Mark's School where Lowell's brother, Robert Traill Spence Lowell, was headmaster. Hughes was roundly defeated in 1874 when he stood for reelection to Parliament, and he then threw his energies into aiding the Workingmen's Colleges he had helped found. In 1876 a collection of his lectures was published. Entitled *The Manliness of Christ,* it portrayed Jesus as a true fighter, simple and courageous, Tom Brown at his best. Then in 1878 Hughes undertook a bizarre Americanization of the Rugby spirit when he conceived and sponsored an agricultural community to be worked in part by spirited Etonians and Oxford men. The project struggled on for fourteen years and brought Hughes close to insolvency.[18]

Dr. Arnold did not live to see his reforms seduced into "Muscular Christianity"; but in giving Thomas Hughes and other sixth-form boys the moral responsibility for order in the school, he spawned generations of "old boys" on both sides of the Atlantic whose definition of serious endeavor and leadership was impossible to differentiate from their early roles and successes on the playing field. Lytton Strachey has called the "worship of athletes" and the "worship of good form" Arnold's real legacies.[19] The "good form" may be today a buried vestige of gentility but it is interesting to note, in view of the present worship of athletics in American society, that by 1950 all of Thomas Hughes' direct descendants resided in America[20] and so did a vast number of Tom Brown's fictional descendants in the guise of the School Sports Hero.

Hughes' success in catching the public school milieu piqued the interest of all classes in England and his work immediately began to produce imitations of schoolboy heroes in the early British equivalent of the dime novel and story paper, *The Boys' Own Paper,* begun in 1879. Bracebridge Hemyng's Jack Harkaway was the first popular schoolboy hero to succeed Tom Brown, and his adventures appeared during the 1870s in pirated stories in Frank Leslie's *Boys' and Girls' Weekly.* Leslie then lured Hemyng to America to write exclusively for him at a $10,000 annual salary. Harkaway was a vulgarization of Tom Brown with more emphasis on the baiting of masters, pillow fights, and impossible adventures than on the building of character on the playing field, and Hemyng did little to advance a coherent formula for a sporting story. In "Jack Harkaway in New York" (1879), Jack, a bit of an insolent young fellow, comes to America hoping to investigate buffalo in Central Park, but instead he winds up in a sword fight, after which he debates the merits of cricket versus baseball and even tries the national game.[21] A cheerful Harkaway-like hero starred in "Harry's Career at Yale," an interminable series published by *Outing* in 45 monthly chapters from 1889 to 1893. In the same spirit, Owen Wister wrote *Philosophy 4* (1901), a light-hearted college farce of the 1880s featuring two fastidious young Harvard dandies named Bertie and Billy whom Wister dubs "the tennis boys," while Charles Flandreau's *The Diary of a Harvard Freshman* began as a *Saturday Evening Post* serial in 1900.[22]

The dimes and story papers flirted with school story formats all during the 1880s, and as late as 1895, without really striking a popular note. Street & Smith, already immensely successful with the Nick Carter and Diamond Dick series, provided an abortive format for assimilating the sport hero into a narrative by producing a series of poorly written tales about actual professional baseball players such as Amos Rusie and Billy Nash.[23] However, by concentrating solely on the players' adolescence in small towns, these tales simply became another variation of the village sports story. This attempt to reduce big leaguers to adolescents, to reduce all situations of conflict and aggression to schoolboy dimensions, culminated in Theodore Roosevelt's starring role in "Brave Colonel Teddy; or Ranchero, Rough Rider, and Governor" (1898), a story paper serial in which the national hero of San Juan Hill is portrayed as a Long Island teenager pursuing oyster pirates when not captaining the Oyster Bay baseball club.[24]

The cover of "Brave Colonel Teddy" shows four identical masked men pointing rifles at young Teddy who, in a dark blazer, white trousers, white straw boater, and outsized glasses, looks for all the world like Harold Lloyd startled in a country lane. Teddy is shown dominating his team by force of personality and organizational ability. The group is mobilized to the fullest extent; after he brings back the baseball uniforms from New York City, the boys cheer him the moment he steps from the train and then they all troop over to the blacksmith shop, put on their full regalia, and march two-by-two through the village to the tune of "See the Conquering Hero Comes." After two or three circuits of the square, the teenage Teddy, already a drillmaster at heart, says: "Each boy will, when he gets his other clothing, return to his home, taking his uniform with him. He will be held responsible for its care. All meet for practice tomorrow morning at nine o'clock." On their way to a neighboring village for a ball game, Teddy saves their carriage from a train collision; during the game he hits a home run, then suspends play when the village bell rings and all the boys rush back to catch the burglars in the post office. Young Teddy fearlessly leads his team in aggressive exploits, and the adolescent patterning for his larger role in national affairs is explicit.

The increasing concentration on a single heroic character whose values would draw together the enormous popular interest in school, sport, adventure, the military, and qualities of leadership provided the final ingredient to the boys' formula sport story. No longer would the pulp hero be chosen from the ranks of professional athletes or national heroes and reduced to his youthful adventures. The creation of Frank Merriwell, the most popular of all fictional schoolboy athletes, was to fix a stereotype of the School Sports Hero that could hardly be broken.

GILBERT PATTEN AND FRANK MERRIWELL

In December 1895, O.G. Smith, the controlling editor of Street & Smith publications, sent to Gilbert Patten, one of his many fiction hacks, a letter outlining an idea for a series built around a schoolboy hero who would be primarily an athlete but would have adventures off the playing field as well. The letter stated, in part:

> The essential idea of this series is to interest young readers in the career of a young man at a boarding school, preferably a military or a naval academy. The stories should differ from the Jack Harkaways in being American and thoroughly up to date. . . . After the first twelve numbers, the hero is obliged to leave the academy, or takes it upon himself to leave. . . . When the hero is once projected on his travels there is an infinite variety of incident to choose from. . . . After we run through twenty or thirty numbers of this, we would bring the hero back and have him go to college—say Yale University.[25]

Smith could scarcely have realized to what lengths his innocent suggestion would be carried when Patten, under the pseudonym of "Burt L. Standish," began his remarkable seventeen-year run of Frank Merriwell stories on April 18, 1896 in *Tip Top Weekly,* a smaller pulp version of the old story paper complete with colored covers, advice columns, and inspirational essays. The Merriwell series created a character whose name is invoked by today's sportswriters and fans who may never have read a Merriwell tale or know anything about his genesis except that the name of Merriwell has become synonymous with last-second heroics in major athletic contests.

Gilbert Patten (1866–1945) was of the generation of Crane and Davis, but he was subjected to little of the same collegiate-fraternal environment except for an early and abiding love of sport.[26] Patten was a high-school dropout who ran away from home in a Maine village to work in a factory at age fifteen, yet it was he who ironically would become the exhaustive albeit inaccurate chronicler of the prep school and college athlete. Patten had grown up reading dime novels and at sixteen had sold his first story to Beadle and Adams.[27] He was a moderately successful hack for a decade before turning from western and detective tales to the Merriwell project.

Patten spanned the dime-novel and pulp generations in a way that no other writer really did. He began writing imitations of Deadwood Dick in the 1880s and lived to see the fictional detectives of Dashiell Hammett and Raymond Chandler. If Davis' Van Bibber had been an "office boy's idea of a gentleman,'' Patten's Merriwell was a middle-class dream of elite schools, gentility, manliness, athletic proficiency, and financial success served up with a considerable amount of extracurricular adventure in environments other than the academy. To Patten, the pulps were an amusement business in which it was his task to keep abreast of public taste and to write to meet that preference. With no real literary background, he would cheerfully admit to shallowness on most occasions but sometimes became defensive about his chosen level of artistry.[28] His failure to understand any milieu at firsthand was hardly a drawback, for he diligently applied the areas of adolescent life he did comprehend to the prep and college life he could only imagine. What Patten knew best was sport, particularly baseball and football, and Merriwell's world is filled with sporting contests.

When the Merriwell series was reissued in paperback library form, several *Tip Top* numbers were combined into each "novel" which was then published as a separate entity.[29] Thus, "Frank Merriwell's Trip West" may really have as much as half the novel taking place in New York City, so that it is difficult to speak of each novel as a coherent work. However, the characteristic elements of a Merriwell story line may be isolated. The first and most popular backdrop for Frank's activities was the prep school set in a village community and surrounding environs. Patten's Fardale Academy was an isolated boys' military school in a convenient imaginary New England landscape with the requisite number of mountains, forests, and rivers, areas in which boys could have exciting adventures. Pirates and thieves appeared in prodigious numbers in the Fardale vicinity, and there were more hermits and haunted houses than could logically be expected. When Frank matriculates at Yale, the adventures in the Fardale woods are changed to those featuring real adult desperadoes. Excursions are then taken to sinful big cities as well as to the Wild West or a foreign country. These trips enable Patten to draw on a stock of dime-novel adventure plots of the detective and cowboy variety. On Frank's limited funds, Patten moved his troop all over the world as a travelling sports team or even as a theatrical company.

Initial events in any story may establish an enmity between Frank and a schoolmate villain during an initial game whereupon the loser vows vengeance on Frank. The tale continues with the villain making alliances with other Merriwell enemies and conspiring to make Frank look foolish or untrustworthy to friends, sweetheart, or school authorities. The Merriwell stories have few adults and those who do appear are incompetents, either foolish schoolmasters or outright evil-doers ready to harm Frank or some innocent underdog. The world of the stories remains nominally a boys' world where the adolescents are in total control.

In any given situation, no one really has more authority than Frank himself. He speaks in the stilted prose of a dime novel romantic lead. However, as much as the dime novel may have been Patten's immediate source, Frank's language and opinions are most reminiscent of young Natty Bumppo in *The Deerslayer*. Natty as an instinctive gentleman speaks in maxims: "Fair-minded or not, Hurry, you will find me as plain-dealing in deeds as I am in words" (15); Natty believes in a providence arching over the wilderness: "There is a law and a law-maker, that rule across the whole continent. He that flies in the face of either need not call me a friend" (15). He muses about an evil Huron Indian, "Let the miscreant charge and then we'll take it out like men" (109) but then he stops to allow the Indian a fair chance: "Let him have time to load and God will take care of the right" (109).

Frank has the same firm, simple belief in right action and the ability to perceive it. His decisions and judgment are adhered to as rigorously as in any military unit. As with the young Natty Bumppo, Frank is the boy with the greatest physical prowess and he carries the day in any situation, a convention which hardly resembles the real plight of adolescent impotence in a world of authority. Frank is the unchallenged font of wisdom in all matters of decisive action or moral choice. One of the reasons for the popularity of the series was that it allowed young readers to indulge in dreams of adult authority. Frank was a boy but acted on all fronts as the most powerful of adult authority figures, perfectly in keeping with the Rugby system of student governing and responsibility which in escapist fiction became an unreal world stripped of adults.

The school itself and its hierarchy of authority meant very little in the Fardale or Yale world of the Merriwell series. Patten knew only a little about college life or about fictional conventions surrounding a youth's maturation, but he knew much about dime novel and pulp heroics. He threw a full-blown superboy into the elite prep-school milieu but at the same time he created the illusion of an egalitarian boys' world in which all students were equal. Into the democracy of Fardale and Yale, Patten put many boys who were typed for the duration of the series as comics, ethnics, or both. Harry Rattleton perennially committed spoonerisms in conversations. The essential cast of characters included Ephraim Gallup, a drawling Down Easterner; Barney Mulloy, an expansive Irish boy; and Hans Dunnerworst, a comic Dutchman, whose butchery of syntax and pronunciation rendered his lines almost unreadable. Bart Hodge, Jack Diamond, Bruce Browning, and many others all began as Merriwell opponents and wound up as staunch disciples with abilities only slightly less than Frank's own, but with minor character flaws such as Bart's lack of confidence or Bruce's laziness. Thus, the ethnic boys at Fardale were stick figures expressing Patten's relatively benign nativism while only hearty Anglo-Saxon rivals like Hodge, Diamond, and Browning were potential leadership material. In the Merriwell series, school sports careers were *not* open to talent because of Patten's exclusion of a real American melting pot.

Various threads of plot continued for many numbers of *Tip Top*.[30] The basic plots included the search for Frank's missing father and his gold mine which ultimately made Frank a very wealthy young man; his romances with Inza Burrage and Elsie Bellwood, two dimpled village versions of the light and the dark heroine; and the simple fact of time passing whereby Frank moved from Fardale to Yale and later out into the adult world of business, at which point Patten created a long-lost younger half-brother, Dick Merriwell, to begin the cycle all over again.[31]

A typical Merriwell school story is "Frank Merriwell's Sports Afield" where Frank, already at Yale, is a star pitcher with a famous "double shoot" curve ball. He is being challenged by schoolboy villain Roland Ditson. Early in the narrative, Frank slides home with the winning run against Harvard, an act that only increases Ditson's jealousy of him. Frank has a credo centering on personal ability that each boy must prove; he says, "What's the use to talk about what one has done? It's not that which counts here. It is what a man can do. You know as well as I that every man here is sized up for his ability, and not by what he says he has been."[32] Patten continually preached such schoolboy democracy, that boys were to be judged according to their actions, even as Natty Bumppo had believed Injins and whites were both "men of different races and colors, and having different gifts and traditions, but in the main, with the same natur' " (*The Deerslayer,* 46). Yet Cooper equivocated on the mixing of the races just as Patten more simplistically refused to allow any scope to his ethnic boys beyond that of humorous pals.

Nevertheless, part of the continuing popular appeal of the Merriwell series was its rendering of the spirit of fair play. Patten's optimistic claim of schoolboy equality based on ability was a predigested conventional opinion that, while at odds with the facts, made a firm impression on the readership. Frank played fair and expected others to do the same. He refused to swear, smoke, or drink, his one vice being a minor passion for gambling.

As he said about his own conduct, "all my life I have studied to control myself and never let anger get the best of my judgment . . . [sometimes] it is a difficult thing to do, but I succeed fairly well."[33]

Frank had enormous powers of self-discipline and an almost messianic ability to set an errant chum back on the correct path. In a diminished vein, his preaching to individuals in schoolboy society is analogous to the lessons of Natty Bumppo in *The Pioneers* whose quick thinking, great agility, skill at all contests, and instinctive rightness become the attributes of the School Sports Hero as well. As the adept hunter and articulator of the rules by which society must live in the hunt and in the wilderness, Natty is the sportsman whose fair play will become the square deal, the self-reliant physical man who is acknowledged to be a moral force. In the slaughter of the pigeon shoot, Natty ruefully declares that this is what comes of settling a country and he admonishes the villagers to "Use, but don't waste." The schoolboy community at Fardale and Yale is in need of values which Frank articulates as Natty did for the settlement. Just as Templeton in *The Pioneers* resists the rhetoric of Natty Bumppo, so do Fardale and Yale initially resist the morality of Frank Merriwell. But Patten partially saved Frank from being a tedious moralizer by giving him the common touch; he never failed to be part of boys' mischief (an inconceivable role for Natty Bumppo) while he kept his mates essentially in awe of him as he stiffened their characters.[34]

What propelled Frank into a position of leadership at both Fardale and Yale was his total mastery on the athletic field, just as Natty Bumppo knew more than anyone else about technique and mastery of physical skills on the frontier. Countless team victories were achieved because of Frank's perseverance in the face of injury, illness, jealous teammates, kidnappings, and the law of averages, not to mention the laws of credibility and gravity. A classic football game with Harvard was won by Frank in the closing seconds:

> Frank felt himself clutched, but he refused to be dragged down. He felt hands clinging to him, and, with all the fierceness he could summon, he strove to break away and go on. His lips were covered with a bloody foam, and there was a frightful glare in his eyes. He strained and strove to get a little farther, and actually dragged Hollender along the ground til he broke the fellow's hold. Then he reeled across Harvard's line and fell.[35]

Merriwell was thus depicted in a "Merriwell finish," although Patten was restricted in the number of Harvard-Yale games he could realistically present with Frank in the lineup. Since the reader never really saw Frank at work in any other avenue of school life, his position as school leader was based almost exclusively on his athletic prowess, which validated his judgment in many other areas.

Merriwell's philosophy and value system were rigidly conventional, serious, and success-oriented. He was at his most reflective when he said, "Work is the greatest sport in the world, for it is a game at which one plays to win the prize of his life. The winning of all other games are tame in comparison with this. . . . The man who shirks and fears honest work can never succeed in the world. Determined men will push him aside, and he will be with losers at the end of the great game."[36] Not content with being an Horatio Alger character, Frank's declarations were similar to those of Natty Bumppo in *The Deerslayer* ("Let the miscreant charge and then we'll take it out like men") as well as those of Theodore Roosevelt. Frank stated, "I'm asking no man or combination of men to bend the knee to me. . . . I'm asking . . . I'm demanding a square deal. And I'll have it. If this fight is to go on, say so like men. If you realize that you've blundered and you're ready to call a truce and make peace, say so like men."[37] Patten's remarks about Frank's conception of duty came straight from post-Civil War rhetoric: "'Merriwell was a person who believed that it is the duty of a football player to obey orders like a soldier. It was his theory that the men who obeyed unhesitatingly and without seeming to entertain for a single instant the fancy that they knew better than their instructors what was the best thing to do were almost certain to become the best players for the central good of the team."[38]

Although he professed atheism (and the Merriwell series is mercifully free of religious exhortation), Patten's values were always those of a conventional moralizer. The Merriwell stories masked the didacticism inherent in Frank's ceaseless sermons to his cohorts. His message was embodied in stirring triumphs in games for boys. Such victories provided empirical evidence of the truth of the sportsman's training and beliefs. Patten's pictures of Fardale and Yale were the most easily assimilated view of the elite academy for the mass readership. However, any coherent theme of growth through experience in game or school was dwarfed when set against Street & Smith's need to have a weekly climax in under thirty pages, a need which Patten met by having Frank leap from one scrape to another. Frank's victories on the playing field not only were, in the popular philosophical vein of the 1890s, a preparation for life after the academy, but also were triumphs that were his due as a fantasy hero. Patten's need to reward that fantasy hero further blurred any coherent thematic development. The Merriwell tales made success the ultimate value to be achieved, albeit with honor. The school and team gave Merriwell a realistic base from which to operate, and when Patten restricted him to that milieu, the scenes were often delightful, for Patten was a gentle man whose boys engaged in much kindly, good-natured play. However, Patten felt obligated as an old dime fire horse to thrust his boys up and out of Fardale into silly romantic heroics and posturing, although he vehemently protested the opposite.[39]

The Merriwell formula was not strictly a schoolboy sports story because Patten really created an adolescent version of the old dime-novel hero. The presentation of the first School Sports Hero in pulp fiction was governed primarily by the workings of the medium, including conventions of dime-novel heroics, demand for weekly action segments, reader expectation for adventure tales, and a desire to corner the youth market in fiction by Street & Smith. By 1897, Norris was flatly stating, "I would rather hear [the College Man] talk about the chances of his football team with his . . . deadly earnestness than to listen to the blasé youth of the business office drawling about discounts and margins."[40] Thus would Patten's accounts of Merriwell's last-second victories over Harvard prove more stirring to a generation of popular authors and readers than did Horatio Alger's earlier Ragged Dicks and their mastery of the marketing business. The price and accessibility of *Tip Top Weekly* made the Merriwell series the most popular in pulp fiction, selling 500,000 copies per week at the height of its popularity. Boys by the thousands began to envision careers at Yale as later testimonials made clear.[41]

RALPH HENRY BARBOUR, OWEN JOHNSON, JESSE LYNCH WILLIAMS

No other pulp format before Patten's had integrated the vicarious adventure world with the boys' world. By the time Patten had established the convention of the boy athlete in a series story, other pulp publishers came forth with their Merriwell imitations, which were even more simplistic than the real thing. Street & Smith even created another boy athletic hero, Jack Lightfoot, to rival their own star attraction; Frank Tousey started several different series publications with the Merriwell format featuring Dick Daresome, Frank Manley, and Fred Fearnot, but none of these boy wonders really cut into the Merriwell audience.[42] By 1910, the real pulp-magazine era had begun.

The boy athletic hero attracted popular writers who produced stories for children's library series. Perhaps the most important was Ralph Henry Barbour (b. 1870), a New England contemporary of Patten's who left military school at seventeen and became a journalist on several city newspapers before finding his popular subject with *The Halfback* (1899). More than one hundred books flowed from Barbour's pen before his death in 1946, and fourteen different publishers were required to cope with them.[43]

Barbour tried his hand at historical romances along with his sports novels, but his most typical theme involved taking a lonely new boy at prep school or college through a series of maturation scenes to dramatize his acceptance by his teammates and peers. Each Barbour novel followed a rigid structural form.[44] A new boy at school with a character flaw, ostracized by members of an athletic team, came under the wing of an older boy or professor and worked continually to overcome his difficulties. Finally he was accepted in time to help win the big game against a rival school. Barbour's world was harsh but fair. He portrayed poor boys at school who had to scrimp to pay for food or live off-campus in a boarding house. His narratives produced few theatrics and actually overcompensated for the dime heroics of Merriwell. As gentle tracts of self-improvement, they were as didactic as Patten's novels but without the gaudy effects. At Barbour's academies, boys took examinations, agonized over poor grades, and studied diligently to make up deficiencies. Similarly, no athlete ever walked onto Barbour's field as star; in his view, athletes were made through hard work. In *Left End Edwards* (1914) the hero isn't very good at tackling so the reader receives a thorough grounding in tackling fundamentals until Edwards gets the hang of it.

Each Barbour hero has a flaw. He might have to overcome a predilection for making excuses (*Left End Edwards*), false pride (*Weatherby's Inning*, 1903), or snobbery (*Fullback Foster*, 1919). Professors were capable of giving sound advice. Older boys were not sadistic tormentors but rather guides to success in school life. They were not always athletes either, for Barbour went out of his way to introduce different character types to his boy heroes. Anthony Tidball, the student advisor to Jack Weatherby in *Weatherby's Inning*, was the school's champion debater, a position of respect and importance in the novel; Patten would have made him a lisping ninny in Merriwell's platoon.

Barbour's novels were full of practical hints to boys who had to make their own way, but his sporting version of the Alger ethic was written without the oppressive emphasis on luck that so determined the lives of Alger boys. Barbour stressed hard work for middle-class boys while promising no great fortune at the end of the struggle. In *Weatherby's Inning*, Jack Weatherby is a substitute second baseman until the last game of the season. In *Fullback Foster*, Myron Foster has his nose bloodied in practice countless times before finally getting a chance to play.

The school story as developed by Barbour was more likely to follow fixed lines of development where lessons learned on the playing field were immediately applied to a boy's personal relationships, whereas series with the same hero, as exemplified by Patten's Merriwell, pressed the writer into continually creating new areas of conflict outside the school.[45] School became a prop for the sport, whereas in the British school tradition embodied by Tom Brown the school rituals and games had been "sporting," part of an integrated code preparing a boy to be a man. After World War I, the concept of an elite school that trained leaders was lost in the democratic wash of boy heroes whose goal was success itself through popular victory. The young player came closer to the status of a professional who had a job to do for his school.[46]

As opposed to the earnest adventures of Barbour's boys and the satiric reaction to them, Owen Johnson's school stories about Lawrenceville and Yale, and Jesse Lynch Williams' remembrances of Princeton, contained a nostalgic look at the prep school and college sporting world of the 1890s. Johnson (Yale '00) and Williams (Princeton '92) were purer American descendants of Thomas Hughes and reproduced the fully rounded picture of schoolboy life he depicted in the Tom Brown novels. Old boys themselves, Johnson and Williams were writing for other graduates, pitching their fiction not at a democratic adolescent audience but at college men with memories and reveries. As such, their work stands as the only American contribution to the school-story genre in the true spirit of Tom Brown's Rugby and Oxford. Johnson's serious examination of an aggressive, business-oriented Yale was a reaction against the new university spirit which he perceived as opening out into and being seduced by the larger society and its goals. On the other hand, Williams' Princeton was an arena of schoolboy sensitivity, romantic weariness, battles for status, and athletic achievement. His conceptions certainly influenced the young Scott Fitzgerald, whose adventures of Amory Blaine at Princeton in *This Side of Paradise* (1920) contain many echoes of Williams' *Princeton Stories* (1895).

Unlike Patten or Barbour, Johnson was a writer well equipped to render an elite boys' academy with wit and style.[47] *The Lawrenceville Stories* focus on boys who were classmates at the New Jersey academy in the early 1890s.[48] Johnson's boys were impossibly verbal, with endless schemes for hoodwinking their fellow students in financial deals or pulling elaborate jokes on them. While Johnson emphasized the recreational side of school life, he also involved his boys in the total life of the school, in classes, house rivalries, elections, and athletics, with the latter remaining the greatest determining factor in a boy's success or failure. The boys were known exclusively by their intriguing nicknames, such as the Tennessee Shad, the Gutter Pup, the Wallado Bird, and Lovely Mead. They possessed an inbred aplomb in personal relationships and their insouciance carried the day in almost any social situation, while underneath all the gaiety and charm lay a fundamental toughness and concern for position in the hierarchy of school life.

The Tennessee Shad presents two shrewd protagonists in the Shad and Doc MacNooder, who provide students with opportunities to bet on everything from cigarette-smoking contests to house football, from dog fights between mangy mutts passed off as champions to boxing matches between ballyhooed New Jersey pugilists who are really local grocery clerks. Johnson portrayed prep games of the nineties as an essentially carefree endeavor where intramural play was the campus obsession. In an antidote to the big games and intense players of Patten and Barbour, the Kennedy House–Woodhull House football game in *The Tennessee Shad* is a romp for high spirits. Johnson's sense of style and humor are a respite from tales of "work and win" and "pluck and luck." Johnson's most famous character is Dink Stover, a contemporary of the Shad and Doc at Lawrenceville whom Johnson wrote about in *The Varmint* (1910) and carried on to college in *Stover at Yale* (1911), the finest novel about eastern college life at the turn of the century. Dink is a traditional school sport hero, marked for leadership early by both boys and masters. *The Varmint* and *Stover at Yale* relate his physical and moral growth from a pugnacious little fellow on the Lawrenceville football team, proud, afraid of pushing too hard, easily rebuffed, to an All-American end at Yale and member of the Yale senior honor society, Skull and Bones.[49]

Dink's more frivolous companions do not make it to Yale; Johnson pointedly suggests a split between the prep and college world, the former all play and discovery, the latter a continual competitive test. In the fine account of the Yale-Princeton game in Dink's freshman year, Johnson portrays a grimly martial Dink, playing out of position at fullback for the good of a completely outmanned Yale team and holding the unit together. He saves Yale from a humiliating rout and turns the contest into a character-building loss with a courageous performance. Johnson has Dink take the blows and hold the line as fiercely as any doomed Civil War captain:

> He had never known anything like the fierceness of that first practice. It was not play with the zest he loved, it was a struggle of ambitions with all the heartache that lay underneath. He had gone out to play, and suddenly found himself enchained to the discipline of the Caesars, where the test lay in stoicism and the victory was built on the broken hopes of a comrade.
>
> For the first time, a little appalled, he felt the weight of the seriousness, the deadly seriousness of the American spirit, which seizes on everything that is competition and transforms it, with the savage fanaticism of its race for success.[50]

Johnson looks back on two decades of serious athletic competition in the colleges with the eye of the reformer and pronounces it a mirror of the deficiencies of the American commercial spirit. In the sporting scenes in *The Pioneers,* Cooper had criticized the settlement's view of natural resources and its conduct toward the land. Similarly, *Stover at Yale,* which starts out as a story of a boy athletic hero's maturation, turns into an angry critique of the education system at Yale and, by extension, a criticism of the goals of the country. Dink is torn by allegiance to his class and to a quest for popularity and conventional success through the Yale system of societies, teams, and honors. He wishes to learn more about major social issues and to open Yale to a spirit of democratic community which would not be fixed on business values or goals. Hughes criticized Oxford for its rigid, reactionary castes but Johnson confronted the more modern problem at Yale of a changing society's rapacious competition.

Dink must change his thinking to encompass many different opinions and groups, and Johnson is expert at portraying the uneasiness of a young man forced to choose between the social benefits of his inherited position and his instinctive need for a larger sphere of experience. Stover's split personality is itself a telling comment on the insecurity and obsession with status that pervades all school stories where the goal is traditionally one of integration into team life and, by extension, into the larger society as well, but only as one of its leaders. In the end, Johnson lets Dink have it both ways. His independent stand is respected by all groups but not before attention is drawn to the making of a true leader, for Dink is no prodigious thinker but rather the steady, balanced sort of young Anglo-Saxon who comes to see the worth of other men's ideas and who absorbs influences, a

Tom Brown with the same earnestness and sense of fairness. Dink will work and play with all representatives of young America. To make this point, Johnson contrives to have Dink meet young men with backgrounds vastly different from his own, including working-class students who earned their own fees to reach Yale, budding Socialists (like Hughes' Hardy at Oxford), and hearty boys from "out west." Johnson's diversity is in the spirit of real education: each boy has a great deal to offer Dink from his particular experience. In short, Dink is a prototype for the modern executive or politician who leads through input, synthesis, and organization. His tolerance and absorption of different views is the egalitarian counterweight to his privileged status as School Sports Hero, the power of the latter presumed as a lever for affecting change in Yale society.

Brockhurst, Dink's intellectual conscience, pronounces Johnson's final vision of Yale:

> "I'm not satisfied with Yale as a magnificent factory on democratic business lines; I dream of something else, something visionary, a great institution not of boys, clean, lovable, honest, but of men of brains, of courage, of leadership, a great center of thought, to stir the country and bring it back to the understanding of what man creates with his imagination, and dares with his will."[51]

In actuality, Johnson has not written this ringing testament into the novel's action. Dink compromises too often with the social norms articulated by Yale's rich and influential upperclassmen. Johnson's progressivism is greatly tempered by his love of the "old boy" system. Nonetheless, the level of Johnson's rhetoric is far removed from that of a Patten or Barbour tale, and he refuses to settle for Santayana's concept of America really getting the Yale she deserves.

Competition is fully sanctioned for Dink Stover, and Bones is his reward for virtuous struggle even as his All-American status is the reward for physical strength and courage. Johnson moves Dink from, in Richard Hofstadter's apt phrase describing Social Darwinism, the "natural selection of fitter organisms to social selection of fitter men."[52] Johnson turned from the serious college novel in 1911, having satisfied himself that he had set the record straight.[53] Dink Stover remains the School Sports Hero with substance, not as well-loved and accepted by boys as Merriwell but a hero who stands for critical comment on the college system praised by professors, coaches, popular authors, and American presidents between 1890 and 1910.

Jesse Lynch Williams was one of the editors of *Nassau Literary Magazine* at Princeton and, with Booth Tarkington and others, helped found

the Triangle Club which Fitzgerald joined in 1914. At age 24 (the age of
Fitzgerald when he published his own Princeton memoir, *This Side of Paradise*, in 1920) Williams in 1895 published his *Princeton Stories*, a 1912
edition of which was in Fitzgerald's personal library, a copy which he probably obtained as an undergraduate.[54] *Princeton Stories* is a romantic collection of tales loosely interwoven with a continuing cast of Princeton undergraduates: Stehman, the huge earnest football tackle; Stacy, the proud
college grind; Jim Linton, the effortlessly successful college ironist; Dougal
Davis, the class's budding success story; and Lawrence, the weary senior
athletic executive. There are several incidental sporting characters, including
Hill, the farm boy who wins the heavyweight pulling match for the freshman
class; little Wormsey who has one great day as a freshman quarterback; and
Symington, an outstanding prep-school pitcher and wide-eyed recruit on
campus.

The tone present in all eight stories is romantic, sentimental, retrospective to both golden moments and bitter ones, all within a magic aura of
Princeton as a nurturing, wondrous place. The lightness and sheer whiteness
of Princeton days and nights, so continually invoked by Fitzgerald, is also
evident in Williams' work, such as in this description of a Princeton evening:

> It was a beautiful evening. In other words it was spring term and the night
> was clear. There were still groups of fellows seated on the doorsteps or
> stretched out under the trees. The gleam of their flannels could be seen in the
> dark. . . . One of them knocked the ashes from his pipe and Symington saw
> the sparks float down. . . . Up from Witherspoon came the tinkle of mandolin
> music. They were playing to some visiting girls on those broad balconies in
> front.[55]

The last story in the group, "The Man that Led the Class," ends with senior
men Linton, Stehman, and Davis singing "Old Nassau" "with all their
might" as they march off campus.

Williams added to the characters in *Princeton Stories* with Deacon
Young, hero of *The Adventures of a Freshman* (1899). Young is a poor
Illinois farm boy from a public high school who must navigate amongst rich
private-school graduates and upperclassmen in his first year at Princeton.
Princeton Stories was heavily influenced by Richard Harding Davis' short
fiction; and *Adventures*, three years into the more egalitarian Merriwell era,
is much indebted to Gilbert Patten. Deacon Young even has Merriwell's one
vice: a weakness for gambling; and the tone of the novel is lighter, in keeping with Patten's formula with boys' pranks and class rivalry at the center.

In "The Man in the Window" in *The Girl and the Game and Other College Stories* (1908), Williams humorously places Young, one year out of Princeton, a former football hero now down on his luck, in New York where he gets a job exhibiting barbells and his own muscles in a store window. Young is rescued by bemused Princeton club men and offered a job in a Colorado mining company by an old grad who admires his gumption rather than his football record.

Williams' writing was the classic example of nostalgia for college days where schoolboy heroes become larger than life. He could be outraged like Hughes and Johnson at school snobbery and exclusion but still praiseful of the glories of the house system on the whole. He could wink at the affected pose of senior world-weariness but without Fitzgerald's underpinning of romantic poetry. Thus, Williams provided a light, bouyant reworking of college competition and sport. In *Princeton Stories* he focused on the emotional nature of insecure, easily wounded boys and their upperclassmen heroes. His perception of schoolboy obsession with status and vulnerability would become a staple of the genre. Williams did not see all of this, to be sure, but he bequeathed a sentimental vision of Princeton to Fitzgerald in the next generation.[56]

When Johnson concluded his critique of Yale in 1911 and Patten relinquished control of the Merriwell series in 1913, they left Barbour and a host of newcomers to shift the focus of the school sport story to high school and state university environments which reflected the movement of sport in the nation as well. The reign of the elite schoolboy hero was at an end. His poorer relations swarmed onto the field to engulf the genre in a new series of conventions aimed at a mass society's conception and experience of school athletics. At the heart of the school story was sport, a prescribed activity with lessons of character inherent in its structure. Sport provided a way to determine a hierarchy of power and a way to test a boy's courage and, importantly, it did so in a way that authority sanctioned and, in fact, encouraged. The college story of Norris and Davis evolved into the school sports story with college life as the upper limit of plot time.

The school story had varied possibilities for development in its pure form as it described Patten's Merriwellian fantasy world of athletic boys in improbable adventure, or Johnson's and Williams' elite worlds that essentially made democratic Americans uneasy, if not a bit envious, or Barbour's middle-class world where doggedly serious boys could only grow into solid citizens and presumably send their sons on the same athletic journey. Ultimately the School Sports Hero figure in fiction developed with increasing irony and satire directed against its power, privilege, and cultural relevance. By the 1920s, Merriwell and Stover had become Tom Buchanan at Yale or Robert Cohn at Princeton, two negative portraits of Ivy League gentlemen by the most famous writers of the era. By 1960, a prep-school boy in *A Separate Peace* could believe in his own complicity in the death of an athletic classmate, while the American high-school athlete was no longer Clair Bee's Chip Hilton at his soda-jerk post after basketball practice but rather John Updike's moral failure, ex-high-school basketball star Rabbit Angstrom.[57] Yet the formulaic boys' school sports story withstood the assaults of professional sports and technology to remain the most popular genteel tale of American youth's coming-of-age in this century. At the same time, the prep/college sportsman passed into either aristocratic memory, high-school pulp heroism, or satiric reaction. And it is the reaction *against* the convention of the School Sports Hero which forms the basis of the figure's use in modern fiction.

CHAPTER EIGHT
Fitzgerald:
The School Sports Hero

THE SCHOOL SPORTS HERO was born in American optimistic rhetoric about duty, service, and discipline. His image flourished in the public imagination for decades after the Civil War and was reinforced by the overriding popularity of stereotypical athletic heroes drawn from popular fiction. But for Fitzgerald's Tom Buchanan in *The Great Gatsby,* Hemingway's Robert Cohn in *The Sun Also Rises,* and Faulkner's Labove in *The Hamlet*, there is a major breakdown between the nominal heroism of the School Sports Hero and his embodiment of society's values. These authors alter the emphasis in the school sports story from the actual heroism to the life after that heroism. They portray the hero as limited, his victories as hollow. His heroism does not allow him to gain other victories beyond the frame of the sport. Ultimately, the School Sports Heroes of Fitzgerald, Hemingway, and Faulkner are not boys but bewildered men whose aggression is incongruous and futile when applied to life off the gridiron and out of the ring. Far from being leaders in society, they are, in fact, totally isolated, apart from society's center, excluded from the various "fraternities" of characters in the novels. It is appropriate to begin by analyzing Fitzgerald's transformation of the convention because he very much wanted to believe in the efficacy of the School Sports Hero and thus consistently balanced his twin judgments of emotional identification and dispassionate censure.

PRINCETON AND AMORY BLAINE

Frank Merriwell and his friends prospered in *Tip Top Weekly* from 1896 to 1917. F. Scott Fitzgerald was born in 1896 and left Princeton in November 1917 for army officer's training at Fort Leavenworth, Kansas. The parallels are not without significance. Fitzgerald was captivated by the symbol of a college football hero throughout his literary career. He also was never far from the intense memories of college years, which he saw as golden times of bittersweet romance and glory. He was a child of the Merriwell era who went out from Princeton in the year of Frank's demise, and his attitudes toward college football sum up much of the affect that the sport had on his generation. He commented that "at Princeton, as at Yale, football became, back in the nineties, a sort of symbol. . . . It became something at first satisfactory, then essential and beautiful. It became, long before the insatiable millions took it . . . , the most intense and dramatic spectacle since the Olympic games." [1]

Fitzgerald looked at football and the School Sports Hero through the adoring eyes of Basil Duke Lee and Amory Blaine, and from the ironic viewpoint of Nick Carraway. He identified and isolated a range of possibilities for the college hero from romantic warrior to physical brute and moral weakling. The movement in his fiction from his early romantic wonder and sadness at Princeton heroes in *This Side of Paradise* (1920) to his disillusion with Tom Buchanan in *The Great Gatsby* (1925) provides a perspective for analyzing the decline of the School Sports Hero as a national ideal. Fitzgerald's range of roles for the School Sports Hero reveals his great ability to infuse life into a stereotypical figure and provide it with a complex series of associations.

In his early days in St. Paul, Minnesota, Fitzgerald was an avid reader of children's series books and magazines, and the projection of his imagination into heroic and romantic realms was a quality he never lost but rather augmented by his serious reading of romantic literature beginning at Princeton. Furthermore, his interest in such literature was initially matched by a desire for football glory. "Reade, Substitute Right Half " is the title of one of his first prose works published in his school magazine in Minneapolis in 1910. It dealt with a recurring Fitzgerald dream: that of a second-string player who is called upon to save the game with a brilliant effort. [2] Fitzgerald himself, five-foot-seven and 140 pounds at maturity, was an erratic performer at halfback for the Newman School—fast, strong for his size, but not particularly well coordinated. He was continually fantasizing himself into the role of the hero, always chattering on the field and dramatizing his own successes.[3] Much in Fitzgerald's nervous, high-strung football behavior at Newman reminds one of the pre-Yale Dink Stover at Lawrenceville in Owen Johnson's stories, and Fitzgerald cited Johnson's *The Varmint,* a Stover-Lawrenceville novel, as his most significant book at age fourteen.[4] However, whereas Stover matured and became a dedicated All-American and pragmatic college man in *Stover at Yale,* a major part of Fitzgerald's school and college sensibility remained that of a precocious adolescent whose dreams of glory were brighter and more real than any possible victory on the gridiron could have made them, dreams first articulated by freshman Amory Blaine in *This Side of Paradise.*

The novel is full of Amory's reading lists, beginning with his earliest favorites. No American college novel had heretofore been so preoccupied with what students were reading. No fictional American undergraduates had ever talked so much of poetry and fiction as did Amory and his classmates. Fitzgerald surveys Amory's reading background at no less than five junctures in the novel to chart his maturation in terms of literary influences.[5] Amory's early reading is a mixture of romance and football, gothic decadence and gentility. His unconventional early education is more evocative of an Oscar Wilde character than of an Owen Johnson boy. Fitzgerald gives him a romantic sensibility out of step with the manly unimaginative heroes of boys' pulp fiction.

However, by age twelve Amory is worrying "whether McGovern of Minnesota would make the first or second All-American" and "whether Three-Fingered Brown was really a better pitcher than Christie [sic] Mathewson" (16). He reads "For the Honor of the School" (1900), a popular Ralph Henry Barbour novel, as well as *The Police Gazette,* "Little Women," "The Fall of the House of Usher," "Sappho," and "the cheerful murder mysteries of Mary Roberts Rinehart" (17).

Not surprisingly, Amory carries over his active imagination into his sports experience. His football career at St Regis' is spotty but highlighted by one great game in which he can do nothing wrong, analogous to Fitzgerald's most glorious football day at Newman in his sixth form year in 1912.[6] He writes of Amory:

> The game with Groton was played from three of a snappy, exhilarating after-
> noon far into the crisp autumnal twilight, and Amory at quarterback, exhorting
> in wild despair, making impossible tackles, calling signals in a voice that had
> diminished to a hoarse, furious whisper, yet found time to revel in the blood-

stained bandage around his head, and the straining, glorious heroism of plunging, crashing bodies and aching limbs. For those minutes courage flowed like wine out of the November dusk, and he was the eternal hero, one with the sea-rover on the prow of a Norse galley, one with Roland and Horatius, Sir Nigel and Ted Coy, scraped and stripped into trim and then flung by his own will into the breach, beating back the tide, hearing from afar the thunder of cheers . . . finally bruised and weary, but still elusive, circling an end, twisting, changing pace, straight-arming . . . falling behind the Groton goal with two men on his legs, in the only touchdown of the game. (31–32; ellipses Fitzgerald's)

Fitzgerald has deleted all topical references to the immediate environment of an American prep school, for Amory imagines himself as a great and timeless hero. Conventional heroic tropes abound as young men clash in "wild despair" through the "autumnal twilight." Amory's poor voice is hoarse from barking signals and his bandage is in place, the scene a sharp reminder of Henry Fleming's heroic appearance in chapter 17 of *The Red Badge of Courage*.[7] The glorious heroism of an eternal hero is embodied in Amory who is every valiant soldier who ever was "flung by his own will into the breach"; the indiscriminate grouping of Roland, Horatius, Sir Nigel, and Ted Coy, the last-named a Yale All-American fullback of 1908–9, underscores Amory's undifferentiated sense of euphoria. His final victory is not in facing down the guns but in scoring the only touchdown in the Groton game. The situation and its resolution are pure Merriwell, but Amory's visions are unabashedly romantic, pregnant with history, epic, and the All-America lists.

Amory is never a true Merriwell or Stover. Where they were stolid and serious, Amory is imaginative and flighty. Where they were humble, Amory is all innocent arrogance. Yet in searching for the most furiously romantic possibilities for a prep school boy, the richness of Fitzgerald's imagination came up with the literal facts of athletic success. He banked down his heroic visions into football metaphors, for this is what American society offered its adolescents in terms of heroism. All his life he chafed against the mundane terms of American success, striving to invest his young men with impossible goals and conceptions.

Fitzgerald was not without an ironic perspective on this dilemma but it only developed with time. In 1928–29, his series of nine prep-school stories with Basil Duke Lee as the adolescent hero (his Stover-Lawrenceville cycle in a way) enlarge upon the prep-school situations of the first chapters of *This Side of Paradise*. The scores of American preparatory schools that existed in 1910 were encapsulated by Fitzgerald in an imaginary advertising circular in *This Side of Paradise:* ''To impart a Thorough Mental, Moral and Physical Training as a Christian Gentleman, to fit the boy *for meeting the problems of his day and generation''*(27). Fitzgerald despairs, ''We have no Eton to create the self-consciousness of a governing class; we have, instead, clean, flaccid, and innocuous preparatory schools'' (27). He even has Basil go to St. Regis', as had Amory Blaine. Basil can soberly tell prep school misfit Lewis Crum that he would be happier if he played football.[8] In ''The Perfect Life,'' the impetuous Basil decides to turn over a new leaf and become the embodiment of a saintly Merriwell hero. The girl whom Basil had hoped to impress by his change of character becomes disgusted with him when he tells her, ''I never thought I could lead a perfect life until I tried'' (103). She takes up with a young profligate in reaction. Basil then comes out of his reverie, drinks his rival under the table, necks with the girl, and absorbs this new higher self-indulgence into his changing personality.

In ''Basil and Cleopatra,'' Basil loses his love, Erminie Bibble, but not before he realizes she is an unconquerable coquette. Basil has thrashed his rival suitor, Littleboy LeMoyne, on the football field where he is quarterback for the Yale freshmen. Against Princeton he runs around LeMoyne's end again and again, and later at the victory dance he wistfully watches Erminie but also thinks, ''Presently more freshmen would approach him to congratulate him on the game, and he would like it—the words and tribute in their eyes. There was a good chance he would start against Harvard next week.''[9]

If such prep-school preening were all that the football imagery implied for Basil and for Fitzgerald, the sporting symbols of the School Sports Hero in *This Side of Paradise* and the Basil Duke Lee stories would be no real advance at all on the solid critique of college life found in Johnson or the buoyancy in the entertaining tales of Williams. But Fitzgerald's resourcefulness in using the school sports material becomes evident early in *This Side of Paradise* when he extends the romantic scope of the football player and school hero. Allenby and Dick Humbird are important and vivid emblems of heroism to Amory Blaine, and by examining in detail how Fitzgerald used their brief scenes, we can trace the links back to earlier strong traits of the School Sports Hero as well as suggest how the figures of Allenby and Humbird changed and matured in Fitzgerald's later works.

Amory carries his football dreams of glory and fame to Princeton. He, like Fitzgerald, lasts only a few days on the field before retiring semigracefully with a wrenched knee (43). Fitzgerald had always feared the pounding he took on the field and he eagerly rationalized his retirement by saying, as Crane might have, "if you weren't able to function in action you might at least be able to tell about it, because you felt the same intensity— it was a backdoor way out of facing reality." [10] The "intensity" remained and Fitzgerald found several ways to dramatize it in the novel.

The Princeton night transforms the college's tall spires and shaded walkways into magic symbols for Amory. On his first night as a freshman, a night evocative of Jessie Lynch Williams's magic Princeton evening in "College Men," Amory sits out on his boarding house steps at 12 University Place and imagines hearing "a song with more than a hint of sadness, infinitely transient, infinitely regretful" (41). Youth in bloom is dying even as it reaches toward maturity. To personify that bloom, its promise and its wistfulness, Fitzgerald immediately conjures up a group of men seen far down the walk and marching toward Amory. They are a "white-clad phalanx . . . white-shirted, white-trousered . . . with linked arms and heads thrown back" (41). These proud young Anglo-Saxons are singing "Going Back to Nassau Hall," and their words endlessly repeat the idea of "going back," out of time's purgatory in the recreation of a cherished moment so central to Fitzgerald's conception:

> "From all—this—earth–ly—ball
> We'll—clear—the—track—as—we—go—back
> Going—back—to—Nassau—Hall!" (42)

This vision is most antithetical to Williams' positive young senior Princetonians singing "Nassau Hall" as they march off to their futures in "The Man That Led the Class." [11] Amory "remembered that an alumnus of the nineties [Williams?] had told him of one of Booth Tarkington's amusements: standing in midcampus in the small hours and singing tenor songs to the stars . . ." (41). Here, the song of the "phalanx" "soared so high that all dropped out except the tenors, who bore the melody triumphantly past the danger-point and relinquished it to the fantastic chorus" (42). It is as if the ghost of Tarkington, the lone romantic youth, has carried the melody to triumph in battle with the high notes of the tune.

Amory listens with his eyes closed, afraid the scene might be illusory, but as he opens his eyes, "He sighed eagerly. There at the head of the white platoon marched Allenby, the football captain, slim and defiant, as if aware that this year the hopes of the college rested on him, that his hundred-and-sixty pounds were expected to dodge to victory through the heavy blue and crimson lines" (42). This vision of the football captain, the hope of the "white" platoon, the college's golden boy, represents the apotheosis of the School Sports Hero as a figure of romantic dimensions.

The language of the scene sustains the legacy of the military imagery of 1890s school sports fiction, the mixed languages of football and war utilized by Norris and Davis. The platoon has a "captain" who would "dodge to victory through the heavy blue and crimson lines." Fitzgerald appears to have cast Allenby as a dashing Confederate ranger along the lines of a Major John Mosby.[12] The "blue" and "crimson," while overtly Yale and Harvard, are just as suggestively Union blue and soldiers' blood. The "slim and defiant" leader who would "dodge to victory" also evokes a daring, wraith-like soldier ready to take on "heavy," hence more massively powerful "lines." The Civil War orientation of football terminology was quite prevalent before 1900, as has been shown, but the Confederate orientation is Fitzgerald's. It is reinforced by Amory, who tells Monsignor Thayer Darcy that he is "for the Southern Confederacy" and Darcy replies by telling him of other "romantic lost cause[s]." Fitzgerald is historically as well as imaginatively correct in the curve of this image. Princeton had always had a sizeable Southern representation, beginning well before the Civil War, and a disproportionate number of Princetonians served in the Confederate Army.[13] Finally, by reimagining the "Southern" school from New Jersey against the "Northern" bastions of Yale and Harvard, Fitzgerald has associated qualities with each school; as Amory says, "I think of all Harvard men as sissies . . . and all Yale men as wearing big blue sweaters and smoking pipes," and Darcy concludes that "Yale is November, crisp, and energetic." Whereas Amory sees Princeton "as being lazy and good-looking and aristocratic—you know, like a spring day" (25).

Thus does Fitzgerald summarize impressionistically the ambience of the three schools that a score of writers in school and college stories had been evoking for three decades. He also imagines a specific Princeton environment. In a 1927 article, Fitzgerald referred to Jesse Lynch Williams reporting in 1899 that "Princeton wine helped to make the nineties golden,"[14] and Fitzgerald added that American youth who instinctively cannot abide the competitiveness at New Haven want "something quieter, mellower and less exigent"[15] and would find it at Princeton. The "white platoon," then, is a mixture of both gray (Confederate) ghosts and luminous romantic heroism, warrior death and young hopes. But Amory's vision of such heroism is pointedly not that of a smoothly functioning team as in the 1890s as much as it is of a romantic lone captain with all "the hopes of the college rest[ing] on him." Allenby is a momentary, intense emblem for heroism imagined by Amory, the "romantic egotist," but later Fitzgerald heroes such as Dick Diver and Monroe Stahr will carry Allenby's impossible aura, will shoulder great burdens and deal with practical matters. They will be crushed under responsibilities, yet try to sustain their magical ability. They choose their roles and are "captains" of medicine and industry but, like Amory, are illusionists as well. Allenby is a first representative of this Promethean figure, here unassimilated, largely opaque, and split off from Amory, the creative force of the vision.

Fitzgerald's own freshman year at Princeton in 1913–14 coincided with the senior year of Hobart Amory Hare Baker (1892–1918), Princeton football captain, All-American, and World War I flying ace. Besides scoring 180 points as Princeton fullback, a college record not broken until 1964, Baker was also the finest ice hockey player developed in America before the war. He functioned as the very quintessence of the flaxen-haired natural athlete. Baker bore an extremely strong facial resemblance to the young Fitzgerald, whose marked copy of *This Side of Paradise* has "Hobey Baker" written in the margin next to Allenby. A good case could also be made that Amory Blaine was named for Baker.[16] Finally, Baker's death in a fighter plane crash after the Armistice in France undoubtedly contributed to *This Side of Paradise*'s heavy emphasis on World War I Princeton casualties.

Fitzgerald used the romantic, fleeting image of the football captain more persuasively than any other American author. He has Amory's first night at Princeton center on football heroics, and his white vision of Princeton fixes Amory's lasting impression of Princeton just as Tom Brown's sense of Rugby came on his first day there during the great house football match. Stover's feelings about Yale were stamped during his first aggressive football practice day. In each instance, the revelation about the true meaning of school life and struggle comes through the major character's impressionistic vision of sport, and the crucial school sports frame initially defines the school for the boy hero.

Most prosaically, of course, the "hundred-and-sixty" pound Allenby is a Dink Stover with pressing duties, and to Amory, *Stover at Yale* "became somewhat of a textbook" (33). As in Johnson's portrait of a prep school versus college in *Stover at Yale,* Fitzgerald's university life in *This Side of Paradise* is described as a much more serious affair than the gamboling days of Basil and Amory at St. Regis'. As does *Stover at Yale, This Side of Paradise* rapidly moves from football to a full examination of college life. Amory and his friends spend as much time as Stover and his comrades did in discussing the college system and its relation to American society. Amory is moved to denounce "muscular Christianity" in his junior year, deriding "this fad of popular preachers rising on their toes in simulated virility, bellowing that calisthenics will save the world" (128); there is even an argument as to whether blondes are put into leadership positions disproportionate to their numbers in the university. Fundamentally, however, the novels do diverge, for Johnson wants to speak of issues in progressive thought while Fitzgerald is committed to the depiction of the growth of a young artist.

Major Mosby or Hobey Baker or Dink Stover raised to romantic poetry could only survive as a momentary vision, and Fitzgerald modifies the vision very quickly in *This Side of Paradise*. Amory quickly learns the truth of what happens when bright promise confronts the random processes of the real world. Fitzgerald inserts Dick Humbird, "a perfect type of aristocrat" (77) who "possessed infinite courage, an averagely good mind, and a sense of honor with a clear charm and *noblesse oblige* that varied it from righteousness" (77), qualities that are definitely reminiscent of Stover.[17] But nine pages later Humbird is killed in an automobile accident: "The brow was cold but the face not expressionless. He looked at the shoelaces—Dick had tied them that morning. He had tied them—and now he was this heavy white mass. All that remained of the charm and personality of the Dick Humbird he had known—oh, it was all so horrible and unaristocratic and close to the earth" (86-87). Allenby's "white platoon" is reduced to the "heavy, white mass" of Humbird's crushed body. The reality of sudden death alters Amory's romantic vision of perfect heroism that had formed with Allenby. The death of Humbird is also the end of Amory's idealization of the college hero and the beginning of his larger education at Princeton into the mysteries of death and decay.

Humbird's lifeless form haunts Amory for the rest of the novel, becoming his dark vision even as Allenby had been his sophomoric light vision of heroism.[18] Amory says Humbird is "like those pictures in the Illustrated London News of the English officers who have been killed" (78), and Amory completes the image by making Humbird a World War I casualty when he brackets him with his dead classmates in France, Kerry Holiday and Jesse Ferrenby (244). The sudden death of Humbird is one link between the military imagery of the football "platoon" and the fact that by 1916, "war rolled swiftly up the beach and washed the sands where Princeton played. Every night the gymnasium echoed as platoon after platoon swept over the floor and shuffled out the basketball markings" (147).

The novel's concluding "platoon" is Amory's own unit in France which he remembers on his final pilgrimage to Princeton at the end of the novel. Winter "made him think of a wild battle between St Regis' and Groton, ages ago, seven years ago—and of an autumn day in France twelve months before when he had lain in tall grass, his platoon flattened down close around him . . ." (279–80). Thus the football images of the last game at St Regis' and the first night at Princeton, so martial in Amory's boyish evocation, now are merged with war itself in his summation: "He saw the two pictures together with somewhat the same primitive exaltation—two games he had played, differing in quality of acerbity, linked in a way that differed them from Rosalind or the subject of labyrinths which were, after all, the business of life" (280). Football and war are "played" straightforwardly and quake before Amory's commitment to the mysteries of love and sexuality, and to the "labyrinths" of his egotism in relation to other people. As with Stephen Dedalus, Amory will not serve, will harshly judge his own coldness, and will venture into a world stripped of illusions, a believer only in aesthetic contemplation.

Allenby, the School Sports Hero raised to poetry, and Humbird, the prosaic middle-class aristocrat, are skeletally drawn and hastily dispatched from the novel. Allenby will be complicated into Dick Diver and Monroe Stahr, whereas Humbird, with his "humbird" origins, son of "a grocery clerk who made a fortune in Tacoma real estate and came to New York ten years ago" (78), a "perfect type," is, with his violent death included, a forerunner of a self-made Gatsby. Of course, Fitzgerald is only sketching in the suggestive outlines in *This Side of Paradise* to fuel Amory's vivid illusions. Both characters are carried through the novel like ghosts by Amory, as if they remain to march with him through Princeton in a platoon of his own imagination along with Tarkington.[19] Allenby and Humbird prove how relentlessly Fitzgerald could expand the range of the stereotypical schoolboy hero several years before his original creation of Tom Buchanan.

The novel moves toward Amory's final realization of a hostile external world in which "all Gods [are] dead, all wars fought, all faiths in man shaken" (282). To the end, Princeton remains the touchstone to the mystery of his own temperament. Whereas a grim Tom Brown returned to Rugby to pray at the chapel on the death of his hero, Dr. Arnold, and to praise the network of human relationships that teach us about love, Amory merely haunts the midnight Princeton campus. He broods, renouncing the school hero's roles, "I loathed the army. I loathed business. I'm in love with change and I've killed my conscience" (278). The roles of Confederate and

Princeton captain are left behind as Amory's early infatuation with football and college heroes is overturned in the general disillusionment of post-World War I youth with heroic ideals. The schoolboy hero had traditionally striven toward leadership in a recognized community of men but Fitzgerald leaves him an isolated romantic, as would Hemingway and Faulkner.

YALE AND TOM BUCHANAN

Tom Buchanan represents Fitzgerald's inversion of both the light and dark romanticism of the School Sports Hero. He is associated with many themes in *The Great Gatsby,* including the power of American capitalism and the bankruptcy of America's new monied classes. He is the ironic representative of the class to which Jay Gatsby desperately wants admission. Buchanan lives totally in the present, thrashing in the chains of his own boredom and restlessness, a Yale All-American end ostensibly bred for power and responsibility but reduced to the life of a country squire on Long Island with a string of polo ponies.

When Fitzgerald returned to the symbol of the School Sports Hero in *The Great Gatsby,* his creation of Tom Buchanan was a fully realized portrait in the physical and philosophical sense. Buchanan is not a campus idol or martyr but an individual moral disaster, the objectionable product of an American collegiate heroism that had nurtured the fictional Merriwell and Stover and Amory Blaine and had captivated Fitzgerald himself. Buchanan most strongly reinforces Veblen's anatomy of the leisure-class sportsman as a man "slightly gifted with reflection," one whose "life is substantially a life of naive impulsive action." Veblen's fundamental view that addiction to sports is "arrested development of the man's moral nature" is seconded by Fitzgerald in Buchanan's case while Veblen's descriptive terms for the traits associated with the sportsman—"rant," "swagger," "histrionic nature"—are those that deftly characterize Buchanan.[20]

Whereas Allenby and Humbird are sketched in as outlines, Fitzgerald skillfully builds the physical portrait of Buchanan by repeated descriptions of his mannerisms. Tom's "arrogant" eyes dominated his face and "gave him the appearance of always leaning aggressively forward."[21] Under his riding clothes you could sense "the enormous power of that body" (7); "you could see a great pack of muscle shifting when his shoulder moved under his coat. It was a body capable of enormous leverage—a cruel body" (7). With "eyes flashing about recklessly" and a voice conveying a fractious tone, Tom turns Nick around "by one arm" to survey with "a broad flat hand" his front lawn (7–8). Nick relates, "wedging his tense arm imperatively under mine, [he] compelled me from the room as though he were moving a checker to another square" (12). Daisy Buchanan says, "That's what I get for marrying a brute of a man, a great big hulking physical specimen of a ____" (12). In one of the few physical acts that he performs in the novel, Tom breaks the nose of his mistress, Myrtle Wilson, with "a short deft movement . . . with his open hand" (37). He blocks the very air in rooms with his "thick body" (116), and he can cut the romantic heart out of any scene merely by his appearance; for example, early in the novel: "Then there was a boom as Tom Buchanan shut the rear windows and the caught wind died out about the room, and the curtains and the rugs and the two young women ballooned slowly to the floor" (8). Daisy and Jordan Baker had been floating languidly in the room, wafted on summer breezes, until Tom's "boom" brought them back to earth.

Why was Fitzgerald so disillusioned with the All-American hero? In just five years the slim Allenby leading his sturdy men had been reduced to a brute of lurching physicality whose body almost vibrated with repressed violence and power. One theory is that Fitzgerald was recreating in Buchanan both the father and husband of Ginevra King, whom he had courted for three years in 1915–18. Both had been Yale men and were mid-westerners. Each lived on Long Island in the 1920s and kept polo ponies. The vulnerable Fitzgerald had been summarily rebuffed by Charles King when he had asked for Ginevra's hand and had then been spurned by her in favor of William Mitchell.[22] Also, Fitzgerald could more easily darken his view of a football hero because Buchanan was a Yale man, not a Princetonian. From his own prep school days, Fitzgerald had envisioned Princeton men as "slender and keen and romantic, and the Yale men as brawny and brutal and powerful."[23] This predilection was carried over into the novel with Gatsby functioning as a kind of surrogate Princeton hero, at least in the eyes of Fitzgerald through Nick Carraway. This split was firmly in his mind before the conception of the novel through early fantasies and negative reinforcement during his affair with Ginevra King. Also, as early as 1920, Fitzgerald had created a less-than-flattering Yale graduate in Gordon Sterrett, the weak, depressed hero of "May Day."

Ever since Santayana had written of Yale's hearty, optimistic commercial spirit in 1893, the stereotype of Yale as a training ground for the muscular male elite of American life had been accepted in the popular mind. Walter Camp's position as the dean of American college football was always associated with his early years as captain and coach at Yale. Outstanding professors at Yale included the pioneering sociologist William Graham Sumner (whose sister Alice married Walter Camp) with his harsh, conservative emphasis on social evolution, and William Lyon Phelps, a popular professor of English, famed public lecturer for decades, and speaker always ready with a sporting anecdote.[24] They contributed to the university's dynamic image. Merriwell's amazing career there in boys' books did much to advance Yale's popular acclaim. Dink Stover, too, had fought hard for Yale on the gridiron and was, like Buchanan, an All-American end. It is probable that Fitzgerald's earliest views of Yale were formed by boys' literature. His years at Princeton could not help but firm up his anti-Yale spirit, and his romantic failure with Ginevra King sealed the picture for him.[25]

Fitzgerald was not rejecting his earlier romantic portrayal of football captains and games. He carried these with him to the end. However, Tom Buchanan represented a parallel strain in American life which Fitzgerald both feared and detested. Buchanan's social position, overriding will, and lack of poetry and grace all frightened Fitzgerald. He sensed the power that supported such a man for, in the end, Tom does defeat Gatsby in convincing fashion.

Tom is always close to losing his self-control. He nibbles "at the edge of stale ideas as if his sturdy physical egotism no longer nourished his peremptory heart" (21). He espouses half-baked racial superiority theories without understanding what he is talking about, proudly proclaiming himself a citizen of the dominant race. He exclaims, "We've produced all that goes with civilization" (14), but he is hardly civilized. He takes refuge in rhetoric about lost values and discipline in American life, but he is a pious adulterer. His is the cry of a narrow man who had lived an enforced, official role of heroism and who has come out of it an ugly nativist full of bluster about Imperialism and an American's duties. He rails at the nerve of upstarts like Gatsby who feel they can intrude on the life of a Buchanan from Lake Forest, Yale, and East Egg. Tom knows that the country is managed in his interests. His militance and aggressive tension all seems to herald the utter dead end of the "strenuous life" where strong young college heroes would lead a revitalized America into a new century of high moral conduct and reap the benefits of boundless national energy. Tom has the rhetoric of an elect American but the rhetoric is all there is. There is no private man of conscience behind the public militancy. He has neither intellectual substance nor conscience. Nick's last vision of Tom occurs in New York a month after Gatsby's murder: "He was walking ahead of me along Fifth Avenue in his alert, aggressive way, his hands out a little from his body as if to fight off interference, his head moving sharply here and there, adapting itself to his restless eyes" (179). To the end, Fitzgerald reinforces Tom's suspicious, latent violence through the football imagery.

In the character of Tom Buchanan, Fitgerald caught the fundamental outlines of an American type and deeply personalized him into one of his most fully rendered minor characters. The sketch of Buchanan is always controlled from the physical particularities of body, movement, and gesture. The very physical portrait of Buchanan comments most fully on the sort of man he is. Fitzgerald's famous phrase about Tom's "acute limited excellence at twenty-one"(8) underscores Tom's uselessness. The honor and experience of being an All-American end prepared him for nothing. Never had an American author produced such a savage picture of an Ivy League gentleman. Jay Gatsby, the young man from North Dakota with impossible dreams, a bootlegger and possible murderer, is pronounced the superior man.

GATSBY, DAISY AND TED FAY: THE FOOTBALL METAPHOR

Nick describes Gatsby: "He was balancing himself on the dashboard of his car with that resourcefulness of movement that is so peculiarly American— that comes, I suppose, with the absence of lifting work or rigid sitting in youth and even more, with the formless grace of our nervous, sporadic games"(64). The "resourcefulness of movement" is combined with a restlessness like that of Buchanan. Certainly Fitzgerald links them not only as rival suitors but as driven, pursued men. Whereas Buchanan's energy is unfocused, Gatsby draws on all of his energy to achieve his dream of recreating the past; in "The American Scholar," Emerson stated that the final value of action is that it is resource, and Fitzgerald conceives Gatsby's whole life as a resource toward his goal. He is, in one sense, the pure, perennial schoolboy in the process of "becoming" while Buchanan is the nominal 1890s hero at the center of society. One of Gatsby's photographs that so amazes Nick is of Gatsby at Oxford with a cricket bat in his hand

(67). In his Franklinesque schedule in early youth, James Gatz had allotted 4:30–5:00 P.M. for "Baseball and sports" (174), a proportion in suitable moderation for a serious young boy. Indeed, Gatsby himself is as impossible a figure as an old dime novel or pulp hero. He springs from nowhere with his mysterious wealth after an apprenticeship with Dan Cody, the "pioneer debauchee" who brought back east "the savage violence of the frontier brothel and saloon" (101). The clichés Gatsby often uses to create a past for Nick's benefit could be lifted from countless yellow-backed books. His belief in success and its fruits is more intense than that of any Alger hero. He consistently refers to Nick, in particular, as "Old Sport," a jaunty phrase reminiscent of the dime novel with its emphasis on the urban "sport," which Gatsby certainly is. In his own strange innocence, Gatsby can blithely point out Meyer Wolfsheim to Nick as the man who fixed the World Series of 1919. Fitzgerald utilizes one of the truly dramatic American falls from innocence to comment on the morality of Gatsby's world and the credulity of Nick who believes that such an act is almost the worst that one man could perpetrate.

The intrusion of professional sport in one of its more squalid moments is further explored in Fitzgerald's portrayal of Jordan Baker. She is diamond-hard, Daisy's confidante, Nick's tentative lover, a golf champion, and surely the first serious portrait of a female American athlete. Jordan parallels Tom in her carelessness and lack of humanity. She cheats in golf matches (or so Nick has been told). She is mechanically interested in the Tom-Daisy-Gatsby triangle, much as if she were watching pirhana fish in a tank. She is very attractive to Nick but ultimately he places her in the ranks of those people whose actions he cannot approve.

A masculine hardness pervades the portrayal of Jordan even though she dresses in gossamer white along with Daisy. Her competitiveness frightens Nick. He, too, would like to have a golden girl, but he sees her too clearly as a liar and a tainted matchmaker. Neither character has the strength of their illusions about the other person. She is Tom's complement in her languid way and, one senses, a formidable foe if crossed. She is an independent woman and hardly a representative flapper or romantic heroine. Fitzgerald would seem to have disapproved of her, as Nick would say of Gatsby, "from beginning to end" (154).

Tom Buchanan is all physical power while Gatsby's energy is in his spirit, not his physical presence. Gatsby is the romantic promise of heroism; he has the masculine magnetism of the campus hero. He has, of course, no Ivy League pedigree but two weeks at St. Olaf's College in Minnesota before his hasty departure. He springs rather from his "platonic conception of himself" (98), which matches him in his own mind as a rival to Tom. Both Gatsby and Allenby in *This Side of Paradise* are impossible romantic characters, but Allenby is an emblem, a stick figure; Gatsby comes as close to being a tragic hero as we have had in modern American fiction. The harsh, often cruel physical lives of Tom and Jordan stand in contrast to Gatsby's evanescence, his enormous capacity for dreaming and projecting those dreams. Tom and Jordan are also staunch representatives of competition and power, rooted in the athletic life. Gatsby's tenuous creation of himself in romantic wonder is no match for their solidity.

The *Great Gatsby* makes more skillful use of American college athletic traditions than any novel before it. A generation of American rhetoric about the School Sports Hero was reversed in Tom Buchanan, whose power was evident but whose morals and character were cast in sand. Fitzgerald also surrounded Gatsby with the aura of the romantic college hero; Nick wryly comments on Gatsby's elite college "career" that "after the armistice, he tried frantically to get home, but some complication or misunderstanding sent him to Oxford instead" (151).

In the Basil Duke Lee stories, Fitzgerald returned one final time to the football hero. In "The Freshest Boy," Basil watches the actress whom he had just seen play the heroine in a sophisticated Broadway melodrama emerge on the arm of none other than Ted Fay, the Yale football captain and Basil's greatest hero, "who had almost single-handed beaten Harvard and Princeton" (207). In the didactic scene that follows, Basil tracks the couple to a tearoom where he overhears their anguished conversation. The actress is protesting her love for Fay but hinting that she must give in to the advances of her director in the interest of her career. Fay becomes extremely melancholy and threatens to leave Yale, whereupon she says, "No, you're not. You're going to stay and play baseball this spring. Why, you're an ideal to all those boys!" (207). Young Basil decides that if Ted Fay can deal with such pain and complexity in personal relationships, then so can he, for "he had gathered that life for everybody was a struggle, sometimes magnificent from a distance, but always difficult and surprisingly simple and a little sad" (207). Basil returns to St. Regis' resolved to embark on "the conquest of the successive worlds of school, college, and New York" (208). Fitgerald lightly satirizes his own schoolboy sentimentalism as he ascribes all life's burdens to Fay as a resurrected Allenby.

The name "Ted Fay" is an interesting mixture of Fitzgerald's past, both real and imagined. Ted Coy was Yale's All-American fullback mentioned in *This Side of Paradise*. At Coy's death in 1934, Fitzgerald wrote, "Ted Coy was my idol. I worshipped him and put him in some of my stories. He *was* a back!"[26] Daisy Buchanan's maiden name is "Fay" and Fitzgerald's mentor at the Newman School had been Father Sigourney Webster Fay, a trustee of the school who became headmaster during Fitzgerald's sixth-term year in 1912. Fay was the model for Thayer Darcy, who plays a similar role for Amory Baine. Ted Coy/Fay is also a play on "fey," which aptly describes Daisy's behavior as it does the fanciful pictures of football captains seen from afar by Amory and Basil.

One development in the Basil Duke Lee stories and after was that Fitzgerald came to a realization of his primary love of football. In *This Side of Paradise* he had suggested its romantic power but had not really described the satisfactions of the sport itself. In *The Great Gatsby*, Tom Buchanan feels the loss of something fundamental when his football days are over, but again, the sport is not recreated. But in the last chronological Basil Duke Lee story, "Basil and Cleopatra" (*Saturday Evening Post*, 27 April 1929), and in "The Bowl" (*Saturday Evening Post*, 21 January 1928), Fitzgerald stopped manipulating the abstract vision of the sport and its associations and based the larger action on the sport itself, its rhythms and rewards. The results were different from his portrayal of football's force in romantic projection.

In "Basil and Cleopatra," Basil defeats Princeton's Littleboy Le-Moyne on the freshman football field at Yale but does not get the girl. Erminie Bibble spurns him a final time at the victory dance. LeMoyne is a courtly Southern youth from Mobile, Ala.; Fitzgerald pointedly makes his Princeton football player a son of the old Confederacy, "tall and lean" with fierce, undefeated Southern eyes" (166). Even as a rival, Basil finds it hard to dislike LeMoyne but takes out his romantic frustrations in the game, calling plays to repeatedly take advantage of LeMoyne's weariness. Basil makes many mental and physical mistakes in the game but he is the only quarterback left for Yale and he muddles through to victory, ironically because of his anger as much as his skill. After the contest, in a tense meeting, Basil and LeMoyne almost come to blows but LeMoyne says,

> "The young lady kicked me out about a month ago."
> "Kicked you?"
> "Threw me over. Got a little weary of me. She runs through things
> quickly." (181)

The football terminology is very apt as the truth is brought home to Basil that Erminie Bibble will belong to neither of them. At the dance, a dishev-

elled LeMoyne rushes in to entreat Erminie in a "strained, poignant Southern voice," but he is stopped and led away. Basil has victory to sustain him
and give him perspective but LeMoyne has been left with nothing. When
Erminie is embarrassed and disgusted by LeMoyne's behavior, Basil calmly
replies, "He didn't know what he was doing. He played a hard game and
he's all in, that's all" (184). The twin "hard games" of football and romance are over for LeMoyne, and as Basil sadly watches Erminie leave, he
has finally relinquished his hold on her promise. He walks out onto a ver-
anda and the story concludes:

> There was a flurry of premature snow in the air and the stars looked
> cold. Staring up at them he saw that they were his stars as always—symbols
> of ambition, struggle and glory. The wind blew through them, trumpeting that
> high white note for which he listened, and the thin-blown clouds, stripped for
> battle, passed in review. The scene was of an unparalleled magnificence, and
> only the practiced eye of the commander saw that one star was no longer
> there. (185)

Here is one of the most beautiful endings in all of Fitgerald's short
fiction, one very similar to Amory's vision of Allenby and the white platoon. Basil's stars are his own: the egotist still reigns and commands his
aerie legions. The wind itself is the counterpart of Allenby's platoon in
song, "trumpeting that high, white note." The military caste to the *This
Side of Paradise* football passage is evident here in the "thin-blown clouds
stripped for battle" which "passed in review" by Basil even as Allenby's
platoon had marched by a wondrous Amory before turning through the Princeton campus. However, Basil has both won and lost as a participant in the
contest and knows how to tell the difference. The hero and the recording
sensibility are one and the same. There is a world of accomplishment which
lasts beyond infatuation, a state which still nonetheless may be mourned for.
The deft last sentence of "Basil and Cleopatra" combines both the promise
and loss while sustaining the level of lyricism in sad wisdom. All has been
developed from a freshman football game, and from Amory Blaine's reverie
of a decade before.

Ultimately, it appears that the image of the football hero split in two
for Fitzgerald. The romantic image was whiteness and romance, promise
and loss, symbolized by Amory's and Basil's perceptions. Daisy and Gatsby
are representatives of this romanticism as well; it is no accident that Fitzgerald should give first Daisy and then a football captain the same last
name—that of his strongest influence when an adolescent. Buchanan, on the
other hand, stands as the embodiment of force, a degenerating power source
in the corrupt gentility. All this is personified in the physical descriptions of

the hulking ex-athlete. Buchanan is the unattractive dominant male in a brutal game. Fitzgerald initially sought to extract only the delicate essence of fleet runs and winning touchdowns, in short the Merriwell headlines. But Buchanan is an end; his success is built on using his body for leverage even as he uses his social class to sustain that leverage. His "cruel body" thrusts him into human contact, where his wealth makes him a formidable representative of American capitalism, but in every respect the antithesis of the ideal figure conceived by Owen Johnson. Fitzgerald always saw football heroes as idealized images of accomplishment and potential; at the same time he could cut off their glamor of earlier achievement. He was capable of looking at a Buchanan as a new American reality while still keeping his double image of the golden boy intact. In *The Great Gatsby,* this double image is represented by Gatsby's Allenby-like heroic defiance of time and reality and his Humbird-like violent death.

Andrew Turnbull remembers having football in common with Fitzgerald when he met him as a boy of eleven in Baltimore in 1932. Fitzgerald introduced Turnbull to the *Football Annual* and tried to make a passer out of him. From 1927 on, Fitzgerald was again an ardent fan and analyst, even writing to and receiving letters from Princeton coach Fritz Crisler;[27] in 1936, Turnbull went to a game with Fitzgerald and remembered the tears in his eyes at the singing of "Old Nassau," the song of Williams' Princeton graduates in "The Man That Led the Class." Fitzgerald had his fatal heart attack in Hollywood on 20 December 1940 while sitting in an armchair making notes on the next year's football team in a *Princeton Alumni Weekly.*[28]

Hemingway recounted telling Fitzgerald to "cut out this football" after Fitzgerald had said that it had been the ambition of his life to be on the football team at Princeton.[29] But while Fitzgerald probed the limitations and possibilities of the football hero like a surgeon, his love for the sport was always on the increase after *The Great Gatsby.* In "Princeton" (1927), he wrote of his alma mater that "only when you tried to tear part of your past out of your heart, as I once did, were you aware of its power of arousing a deep and imperishable love,"[30] and, one suspects, after working and reworking the football imagery in the novels, he came to terms with his feelings for football in about the same way.

In "The Bowl," Fitzgerald portrayed Dolly Harlan, a reluctant Princeton halfback, competent but not a star, who has intensely disliked the sport, its pressures and responsibilities. He becomes infatuated with the domineering Vienna Thorne, who urges him to quit football. He then inflicts a broken ankle on himself to resolve his terrible ambivalence about playing his senior year but becomes increasingly bored and annoyed with Vienna Thorne and her circle: "It seems to me that no one I know does anything but talk any more"[31] Inspired by the dedication to work of young actress Daisy Cary, Dolly limps back for the Yale game in New Haven, and in pain, with determination, catches a pass for the deciding touchdown. Fitzgerald concludes,

> Dolly turned away, alone with his achievement, taking it for once to his breast. He found suddenly that he would not have it so long intimately; the memory would outlive the triumph and even the triumph would outlive the glow in his heart that was best of all. Tall and straight, an image of victory and pride, he moved across the lobby, oblivious alike to the fate ahead of him or the small chatter behind. (100)

This fine statement, not overwhelmed by the past or the future, is anchored firmly in the sporting present and contains a love of work well done of which even the master sporting artisan Hemingway would have approved.

THE PLAY SPIRIT:
GATSBY AND DICK DIVER

Beyond the codified sport of football in *This Side of Paradise* and *The Great Gatsby* with its cluster of romantic possibilities and cultural associations is Fitzgerald's exceedingly tenacious vision of a play spirit. Gatsby and Dick Diver in *Tender is the Night* (1934) are master "frame" makers[32] who would coerce voluntary behavior from a group of actors. Unfortunately they cannot negotiate amongst them all, for Gatsby and Dick are simultaneously directors and actors and other characters deny the sheer force of their projection. The play of Gatsby and Dick, then, is not finally "a controllable and dialectical dramatization"[33] for while a primary paradigm of play is taken up by them as solitary players, a secondary paradigm of play as organization of collective experience,[34] is beyond their powers.

While Gatsby can be identified as a double for Tom Buchanan, his own "acute, limited excellence" is exhibited in his talent for projecting his strong illusions. Gatsby's spirited play is in the *mimetic* mode. For Fitzgerald, the heroism implicit in the play spirit was in an individual's holding fast to his own illusion. Gatsby commits himself to the power of a realm that is not real and yet is one that he labors to bring to life as he attempts to sustain an alternative world and to make Daisy act in it. It is a blasphemous, godlike task of creation and one firmly rooted in play.

Young James Gatz is unable to control the "universe of ineffable gaudiness" (99) that spun itself out in his brain as "each night he added to the pattern of his fancies" (100). As a boy, he is a pure fantasist; as Fink comments, "the player experiences himself as the lord of the products of his imagination" for "play is finite creativity in the magic of illusion." The dark side of this freedom is that "precisely in the power and glory of our magical creativity we mortal men are 'at stake' in an inscrutably threatening way."[35] Gatsby is "at stake continually because of his "romantic readiness" (2), the "colossal vitality of his illusion" (95). His commitment is as "the gold-hatted, high-bouncing lover" of Fitzgerald's inscription but behind his studied ease and bizarre chivalry, he is a tough, a psychic bully. Gatsby, too, would browbeat Daisy. He is a ruthless illusionist whose allegiance to fancy and dream is as solid as that of any unimaginative materialist, which he *is* in a thoroughly oxymoronic riddle. Play is actuated as spontaneous, free, separate, and uncertain, yet Gatsby contradicts almost all of play's ultimate glory for he covets the genteel life of Tom Buchanan. There is never a hint that he would offer Daisy anything but perhaps a more imprisoning version of her present marriage. He is not a dashing, sensual brigand. He is, in fact, as conventional as Tom in his own way, and his dreams of Daisy include becoming Tom to get her.

In Gatsby's reckless denial of the present, he attempts to create a spatial and temporal illusion that will being back the glory of the moment on the moon-bathed Louisville street when the "incarnation" was complete, when he had first kissed Daisy: "He knew that when he kissed this girl, and forever wed his unutterable visions to her perishable breath, his mind would never romp again like the mind of God" (112). The childlike "romp" in freedom as creator is denied him as it is in the Dutch sailors' final vision of the New World. To ultimately find an image "commensurate with wonder" is the death of wonder, and the resultant enslavement to the real in an effort to make it part of the enchantment is, in reality, a disenchantment that is not recognized. And "so we beat on . . . . ."

Gatsby goes to enormous lengths to project his dream, creating an order of play that is sustained not only during the pageantry of his nocturnal parties but in the glaring sunlight. Fitzgerald shows Gatsby at his playful best in the reunion scene between Gatsby and Daisy when Gatsby, like a sultan before the queen of his harem, throws his shirts in their silken magnificence into a sumptuous pile as Nick and Gatsby watch. The commercial rajah flaunts his treasures, and when Daisy buries her face in them and sobs, "muffled in the thick folds," that "It makes me sad because I've never seen such—such beautiful shirts before" (94), Fitzgerald has constructed an emblem that is lovely, wistful, and absurd by turns. On one level, Daisy's expense of spirit is as deficient a response as is Gatsby's initial gesture (and as Tom Buchanan crying in front of Myrtle Wilson's box of dog biscuits after her murder). Fitzgerald constructs burlesques of the object "commensurate with wonder" for Gatsby, Daisy, and Tom. The communion artifacts of their "incarnations" are appropriately inappropriate.

This display of Gatsby, so right in its tone and commentary on both himself and Daisy, is what Huizinga calls in play representation "the exhibition of something naturally given" [he speaks of male peacocks]: "the essential feature of it lies in the parading of something out of the ordinary and calculated to arouse admiration."[36] This microcosmic moment embodies in both its romance and bathos Gatsby's essential artifice and playfulness. The image can be extended to the entire life he has crafted for himself with the mansion where he wishes to place Daisy at the center. Nick believes that Gatsby has abandoned his dream in the wake of Myrtle's death and the Buchanans' closing ranks, that it is all up with him even before Wilson arrives to deliver the *coup de grace*. In Gatsby's disenchantment, the props of his play world suddenly are unformed: the "unfamiliar sky," "frightening leaves," and "scarcely created grass" (162). Nature is nothing without the imprint of his art, and he will no longer "sport" with it as the flowing water did with the Trevi Fountain in Hawthorne's *The Marble Faun*, a reverse play image of nature "sporting" with art. A "new world [in dispirited lower case letters], material without being real," is where he and Wilson are both "poor ghosts, breathing dreams like air" (162).

Fitzgerald sees Americans, as the Dutch sailors, afflicted through "aesthetic contemplation" with the "presence of this continent," and the requisite awful burden of striving to play its meaning into creation, to wed the objectless dream and the vast reality. Daisy must not be competed for with the School Sports Hero Tom Buchanan as much as she must be recreated by Gatsby in his own universe. Fitzgerald's players hope to live inside the illusions they compulsively foster, and there is no escape from their burden. No American author makes a deeper commitment to creative illusion for his characters than Fitzgerald. An essential contradiction of American play and sport is embodied in Gatsby: the more he plays his dreams, the more he is bound in strenuous labor. His spirit creates dreams that become the content of the real, and thus his greatest imaginative achievements are encapsulated within a materialist nightmare of his own design. It is fitting that in modern America, a master player plays *for* success and utilitarian result, never countenancing his skill for enjoyment or growth, but enslaved by it.

Gatsby and Dick Diver are examples of what Robert Sklar has called Fitzgerald's "genteel romantic hero." Sklar traces this figure back to the post-Civil War era with his "mingled romantic dreams and sentimental feelings." As Sklar conceives him, the genteel romantic hero is a conception which would be broad enough to include the Anglo Saxon athletic hero, the frivolous young gentleman, and the soulful romantic. After *The Beautiful and the Damned* (1922), Fitzgerald's genteel romantic hero "would be a flawed superman, a man who, merely by his belief that the impossible was still possible, that sentiment and romance could still be resolved, placed himself beyond the safety, and beyond the comprehension, of conventional society."[37] Sklar stresses Gatsby and Dick Diver as Fitzgerald's most refined and complex visions of the genteel romantic hero "who by his strong will and clever imagination nicely preserves social stability while he fulfills romantic dreams."[38]

Dick Diver's will and imagination strive to "preserve social stability," at least that of the society he projects at the beach and the Villa Diana, but he too long defers any romantic dreams and thus falls apart as his creative role cannot hold out against Nicole's enormous needs and the recurrence of his youthful sentiment, the schoolboy persona he had never completely worked through (see chapter 9). His illusion is somewhat different from Gatsby's in that he *has* achieved the goal of making Nicole act in the present; now he must sustain the simulation: "Before her he must keep up a perfect front, now and tomorrow, next week and next year."[39] The perfection of the scenes early perceived by Rosemary Hoyt "was part of a desperate bargain with the gods and had been attained through struggles she could not have guessed at" (21). Dick is captive to a performance that demands his grace, "the tensile strength of his balance" (65), and indeed, Fitzgerald's description of him at Yale states that he "had done the flying rings at New Haven" (116). This gymnastic skill perfectly limns Dick as a man whose agility and balance are part of a solo virtuosity wrested from the air and kept aloft by will and skill, never touching the ground, and going through great, graceful contortions.

The flamboyance of Gatsby's role-playing and the exhausting regimen of Dick Diver have, as their goal, the transformation of their illusions into the content of the real.[40] However, the heroes founder when the solidity of the material world impinges in all its prosaic straightforwardness. Dick's last sad moments as hero in Nicole's eyes are presented through a strong athletic image in which Fitzgerald emphasizes Dick's balance and burdens. He is a long way from the flying rings, and his masquerade is cracking. Nicole watches him on the beach where, several years before, tanned and godlike, he had blinded Rosemary with his charm. Now Nicole believes Dick's "heartsickness had lifted a little as he began to play with Rosemary, bringing out his old expertness with people, a tarnished object of art; she guessed that with a drink or so he would have done his stunts on the swinging rings for her, fumbling through stunts he had once done with ease. She noticed that this summer, for the first time, he avoided high diving" (282). Dick suggests that they all go aquaplaning and "remembering that he once could stand on a chair at the end of a board, she indulged him . . ." (282), but Dick insists that he will not perform at all without lifting someone on his shoulders during the ride. Nicole watches as he strains and fails three times; ultimately, "when the weight of his partner was full upon his shoulders he became immovable" (284). His final pursuit of grace cannot be attained with the weight and, exhausted, he fails in stubborn and clumsy attempts.

Just so has Nicole been the acrobatic partner for years in their game of poise and balance but she is now a Warren again, allied with Tommy Barban with her "crook's eyes." Dick can only play encumbered. He has forgotten the freedom of the flying rings. The athletic imagery makes vivid the physiological defeat which is part of his complete emotional defeat. One of the final descriptions of Dick's intent is, "wanting above all to be brave and kind, he had wanted, even more than that, to be loved" (302). In a considerably more complex situation, this is the plaintive cry of the insecure, dutiful schoolboy hero, but Nicole's darkness is more overwhelming than his deficient idealism.[41] Dick might second Zenobia's last rueful perception of the collapse of her dream with Hollingsworth in *The Blithedale Romance:* "I am awake, disenchanted, disenthralled" (*BR,* 218).

FRANK CHANCE'S DIAMOND
VERSUS HOBEY BAKER'S GRIDIRON

Lardner and Fitzgerald's visions of sports heroes were very different, but both writers were bound by intense early experiences in sport: Lardner with baseball and Fitzgerald with school football. While Lardner appears in retrospect never to have been young and Fitzgerald to have been almost perpetually youthful, they both saw that the ways in which a society plays could be of great importance to the American author. After Lardner's death in 1933, Fitzgerald wrote that Lardner's early adult years reporting baseball in Chicago had provided "the text of Ring's schooling during the most formative period of the mind" and that "however deeply Ring might cut into it, his cake had exactly the diameter of Frank Chance's diamond."[42] His remarks were generally critical of the effect such a "text" might have engendered in Lardner, to wit an isolation and fearful immaturity. However, it should be noted that during the same years for which he would censure Lardner (roughly 1910–1918), Fitzgerald's own "texts" were prep school and college, poetic white nights and football captains, dreams of big games and romantic heroines. The "formative period" of his mind, from ages 14 to 22, like Lardner's from ages 22 to 30, was dominated by a specific, isolated milieu and one closely associated with sport.

Fitzgerald wrote in his Lardner eulogy that perhaps baseball was not Lardner's great discovery of subject but in reality his crutch and limitation:

> During those years when most men of promise achieve an adult education, if only in the school of war, Ring moved in the company of a few dozen illiterates playing a boy's game. A boy's game with no more possibilities in it than a boy could master, a game bounded by walls which kept out novelty or danger, change or adventure. (36)

Surely there were no more or fewer "illiterates" on a professional baseball team in 1914 than anywhere else in the general run of American society, except perhaps at colleges such as Fitzgerald's Princeton. What Fitzgerald regretted about Lardner was not that he trafficked with Frank Schulte instead of Edmund Wilson but that Lardner frustrated him by his disinterest in literature, in learning itself. Fitzgerald could mask this impatience by talking about the deficiencies of baseball. Fitzgerald never had an experience in the "school of war" either, having gotten no further east than Long Island by November 1918, but perhaps believed that Lardner needed to have known the "war of school" with its competitions, intense emotions, and insecurities so that he could have conceived of the right sort of culture hero, an Allenby, perhaps, or a Dick Humbird or a Ted Fay. Furthermore, Fitzgerald was by no means secure in his own talent and achievements in October 1933 at 37, the age Lardner had been when they met in 1922. Fitzgerald was plagued by huge debts for the psychiatric care of his wife, Zelda, and was deeply involved in finishing the eight-year project that culminated in the publication of *Tender is the Night* on 12 April 1934. Fiercely proud of the scope and achievement of that work, Fitzgerald's comments about Lardner reflect both his fear of his own decline and stubborn confidence in his own major claims.

Lardner and Fitzgerald had been close drinking companions and neighbors in Great Neck, Long Island during 1922–24, a period according to Turnbull when Lardner was the "supreme influence on Fitzgerald's life."[43] Their homes in Great Neck were separated by the Herbert Bayard Swope estate where Heywood Broun and other New York publishing personalities visited and revelled at night. They even played croquet by the headlights of automobiles and the estate is generally believed to be one of the models for Gatsby's mansion. For Fitzgerald in 1922, Lardner had reached the pinnacle of popular success and by all accounts the friendship was based on mutual respect and mutual love and capacity for alcohol.[44] To speculate on how each writer influenced the other is to come into the realm of educated guesswork. Fitzgerald changed the public perception of Lardner from magazine writer and columnist to author by persuading him to talk with Maxwell Perkins at Scribner's and by urging him to collect his short stories in single volumes, the first of which was *How to Write Short Stories* (1924), Fitzgerald's title,[45] and then *The Big Town* (1925) and *The Love Nest* (1926). Fitzgerald with his passion for organizing and educating other people's reading and writing took on Lardner as a personal project, as he would Hemingway two years later. Although Lardner did write "Haircut," one of his more complex stories, in 1925, almost all his best work had been completed before his association with Fitzgerald and thus the perception of Lardner's work (rather than its conception) was transformed in part through Fitzgerald's intercession.

Lardner's influence on Fitzgerald, especially during the time of the early composition of *The Great Gatsby,* is at least hypothetically intriguing. There are a number of Lardnerian echoes in the novel as well as points that Fitzgerald never again defined in quite the same fashion. At no other time did he ever evince an interest in professional baseball. Yet his famous emblem of Gatsby and Nick Carraway meeting Meyer Wolfsheim, the man who fixed the World Series in 1919, is a pivotal moment in the reader's early perception of both Gatsby and Nick, for it underscores Gatsby's immorality and Nick's morality. The scene relates most closely to an event central to Lardner's past associations with baseball, Jack Keefe's White Sox, the 1919 series which he covered, his supposed trauma over the scandal, and his abstention for the most part from baseball writing for years afterward. Also, the character of Tom Buchanan partakes of many plebeian Lardnerian athletes such as Jack Keefe, Buster Elliott, and Midge Kelly. Although Buchanan is a patrician, his lurching physicality is comic and menacing by turns, a significant departure from Fitzgerald's earlier idealized football hero in *This Side of Paradise*. Buchanan resembles Lardner's stereotyped "boob" athletes transferred from dugouts to polo ponies. When Fitzgerald wrote that Buchanan had come east from Chicago, was a "national figure in a way"(6), and would "drift on forever, seeking, a little wistfully, for the dramatic turbulence of some irrecoverable football game"(6), he may have been describing, albeit unconsciously, Lardner's move to New York, his literary fame, and his being shaped by "Frank Chance's diamond." Finally, Nick Carraway is Fitzgerald's most balanced reticent narrator—wise, sympathetic, laconic, clear-eyed, fearful of life that might move out of control toward the sensual or excessive. Never before or after *The Great Gatsby* did a Fitzgerald narrator exhibit such low-keyed remorseless honesty, understated wit, solid realism, and fear of emotional entanglements. Such a character evinced all the traits that could be called Lardnerian, documented by his son's memoir, by two biographies, and by scores of friends—traits that continually surfaced in Lardner's own work as well.

Nick Carraway's traits include the instinct for privacy and the personal sexual squeamishness that were part of Lardner's own defenses. Nick watches Jordan Baker and Daisy Buchanan early in the novel as they toy with Tom and interpret the phone call from his mistress, Myrtle Wilson. Nick then comments, "To a certain temperament the situation might have seemed intriguing—my own instinct was to telephone immediately for the police"(16). Fitzgerald also further depicts that "certain temperament" by having Nick at Tom's New York apartment wipe off McKee's face "the spot of dried lather that had worried [him] all the afternoon" (37). Nick ultimately scrubs out the obscene word scrawled on the brick of Gatsby's mansion after his murder. Nick is a midwestern gentleman, moral censor, tolerant friend, "too old to lie to [him]self and call it honor" (179); he muses, "Thirty—the promise of a decade of loneliness, a thinning list of single men to know, a thinning briefcase of enthusiasm, thinning hair" (136). Such self-scrutiny by Nick may partake as much from Fitzgerald's impression of the somber Ring Lardner at 37 whom he knew as well as he knew T.S. Eliot's J. Alfred Prufrock—Lardner whose great sad eyes gaze out of all his 1920s photographs as blankly as those of Dr. T.J. Eckleburg. However, since Lardner never made any substantive comments on *The

Great Gatsby or Fitzgerald on Lardner's influence, such speculation exists for amendment or refutation.

Lardner's physiogonomy, personality, and career undoubtedly were part of the model for the brilliant, erratic pianist Abe North in *Tender is the Night*.[46] Fitzgerald makes shrewd and harsh judgments on Abe North as an artist. Abe's "solemn dignity" and "his achievement, framentary, suggestive, and surpassed" (83), are finally glossed most tellingly by Tommy Barban, who states, "I don't believe his first stuff holds up," for "a dozen Americans can do what North did": " 'The only difference is that Abe did it first' " (199). "Why does he drink?" [Nicole asks]. "So many smart men go to pieces nowadays." "And when haven't they" [Dick replies]. "Smart men play close to the line because they have to—some of them can't stand it, so they quit" (99). In Fitzgerald's view, Lardner always knew how close to the line he had to play to survive. The above form part of Fitzgerald's criticism of Lardner in his Lardner eulogy as well, but Fitzgerald's most interesting comment is that Abe "after a brilliant and precocious start had composed nothing for seven years" (34), and here Fitzgerald surely is wincing about his own progress since *The Great Gatsby*. Fitzgerald's depiction of Abe's death—brutally beaten in a Manhattan speakeasy and crawling home to die at the racquet club—expiates any "anxiety of influence" as starkly as possible.[47]

Ultimately whether Lardner's work had the "diameter of Frank Chance's diamond" or Fitzgerald's work had, as one dimension, the length of Hobey Baker's gridiron at Princeton, can only be hypothetical questions. However, it is clear that at the turn of a modern sports explosion, in an era of great popular sports heroes, the marks of baseball and college football were indelibly on the work of Lardner and Fitzgerald respectively. Lardner literally created the prototypical modern professional athlete in his fiction and, with his ear for speech rhythms, constructed a language for his ballplayers and reporters that remains the *lingua franca* in American sports culture and fiction to this day. Fitzgerald inherited the inflated rhetoric of the boys' school sports story and reshaped it through romantic wonder and sadness at the School Sports Hero and through realistic deflation of the figure. Lardner and Fitzgerald were the first major American authors to incorporate the past popular conventions of sport in fiction into new conceptions that would become a legacy to authors approaching the subject after World War II.

CHAPTER NINE

The School Sports Hero
as Satiric Emblem:
Hemingway and Faulkner

THAT TOM BUCHANAN was "a national figure in a way," as Stover and Merriwell had been, reaffirms the School Sports Hero as a popular cultural symbol of accomplishment and status. However, Fitzgerald undercuts Buchanan's claim to heroism by denying him the ability to carry through the responsibilities of his position: the All-American's "higher duties" to self and country, a conception that had become a cliché by 1925. Although Tom Buchanan is a hero of modern sports spectacle, primarily he makes a spectacle of himself. More extreme satiric emblems of the decline of the School Sports Hero are Hemingway's Robert Cohn in *The Sun Also Rises* and Faulkner's Labove in *The Hamlet*. Far from the notoriety of Buchanan, they are unknowns even in the context of their own feats. Jake Barnes says of Robert Cohn, "I never met any one of his class [at Princeton] who remembered him. They did not even remember that he was middleweight boxing champion."[1] Of Labove, the star University of Mississippi halfback, Faulkner writes through the eyes of the rural denizens of Frenchman's Bend, "they did not know what he did on those weekends, except that he was taking work at the University. They did not care."[2] Hemingway and Faulkner join Fitzgerald in using the School Sports Hero in his nominal heroic role in society as a basis for characterization. However, the *absence* of this heroic role in the society in which the School Sports Hero moves shows the failure of the aggressive, overachieving romantic hero and his failure to stand for any values outside himself.

Cohn and Labove have many parallels as characters. Both are School

Sports Heroes in alien environments—Princeton transferred to Pamplona, Spain and Oxford, Mississippi moved to Frenchman's Bend. Both are isolated romantic suitors controlled by women they pursue in a mock-quest. Not natural athletes, they have deliberately acquired athletic skills: Cohn becoming a boxer to counter feelings of inferiority on being Jewish at Princeton, Labove playing football so he can stay at Ole Miss. Both Cohn and Labove are odd-men-out, excluded from fraternity; and although both play desperately hard for success, recognition, and romantic love, they win no victories. In fact, they both are definitive losers in comic fights, which Hemingway and Faulkner successfully use to highlight the School Sports Heroes' sporting prowess and their weaknesses. Finally, their sporting code in tatters, Labove and Cohn are both banished from their respective novels, Horatio Alger characters who have not come near their goal.

Before Fitzgerald created Tom Buchanan, no writer had really taken the School Sports Hero beyond school life. Previously the School Sports Hero had battled to gain acceptance and power at school through his athletic performance, but Buchanan, Cohn, and Labove overturn this convention of the youthful hero coming of age in a maturation tale. Buchanan is thirty; Cohn, thirty-four; and Labove, a very cold and old early twenties. They are past their school glory, past their big games and fights, yet they still crave the hero's acceptance. In their diminished present, they are bewildered and angry, applying physical force to solve more complex emotional problems: Buchanan breaks the nose of his mistress; Cohn, in response to the question of what he would most like to do, says, "I think I'd rather play football again with what I know about handling myself, now" (44) and later uses this knowledge of "handling himself " in disastrous fashion in his climactic fistfight with Pedro Romero; and Labove, during his sixth year as schoolmaster, finally summons the will to attempt the seduction of Eula Varner and moves "as quickly and ruthlessly as if she had been a football or as if he had the ball and she stood between him and the final white line which he hated and must reach" (121). Not only are Buchanan, Cohn, and Labove not leaders, they are not even fully cognizant of the team's (in this case, society's) rules and mores.

Cohn and Labove compete aggressively but represent a romantic futility rather than an ideal. The reward for their rectitude and idealism is derision and defeat; the elect are not rewarded. They have attempted to be School Sports Heroes where such figures are not possible, in societies that are traditional, agricultural, and lacking in associations with teams and school. By placing their aging School Sports Heroes in Spain and 1890s

Mississippi, places which move to deeper, timeless patterns of life and competition, Hemingway and Faulkner ironically underscore the deficiencies and limits of the School Sports Hero convention. Hemingway's portrait of Cohn, the reluctant Ivy League boxing champion, is, with few exceptions, an extremely negative character study. Faulkner's fable of Labove, the school-teacher by Eula Varner possessed, is the most humorous portrayal of a college football hero in American fiction; in it Faulkner rewrote "The Legend of Sleepy Hollow" in a brilliant adaptation with Labove a composite of not only Ichabod Crane and Brom Bones, but of Merriwell and Stover as well.

The Sun Also Rises and *The Hamlet* contain more varied uses of play, game, and sport than any American novels before them, positing the deepest meaning of sport as ritual for Hemingway and the full complexity of the play spirit for Faulkner. These novels will be extensively examined in chapters 10 and 11. Chapter 9 will analyze the traditional School Sports Heroes in the novels, anomalous figures on the periphery of the deepest character relationships in each novel. To ask how and why they occupy this position, it is necessary to deal with Hemingway and Faulkner in turn, relate their earliest experiences with school sport, and suggest how the conceptions of Cohn and Labove were crystallized. In each case, the schoolboy ideal is overturned and defeated, but Hemingway and Faulkner reinvent and multiply the associations of the School Sports Heroes to further illuminate the society in which they live and compete.

ROBERT COHN: PRINCETON TO PAMPLONA

While Fitzgerald was entranced by the romantic symbol of the school and college football hero, no such heroes exist in Hemingway's abundant writing about sport. To understand why, one must take into account the influences of his youth, his temperament, and his personal view of competition.

Hemingway grew up in Oak Park, Illinois at the turn of the century, a prosperous suburb directly west of Chicago. He attended Oak Park High School, which in 1916 sent two-thirds of its graduates on to college, a remarkably high figure for that era.[3] From 1915 to 1917, Hemingway covered sports for the high school newspaper and wrote some Jack Keefe-like sketches he signed as "Ring Lardner, Jr." He played football for Oak Park

High from 1914 to 1916, but he never really enjoyed it. He was a reluctant recruit, who later recalled, "at Oak Park, if you could play football, you had to play it."[4] He did not play well enough to break into the starting lineup until the last two games in 1916 when he played guard and center.[5] Unlike Fitzgerald, Hemingway never saw himself following in the footsteps of fictional Yale and Princeton All-Americans. He never really wanted to go on to Princeton or even to the University of Illinois, and he never aspired to heroic notoriety on the football field. He later explained, "Football I knew too much about and it did not interest me really and I have never written a line about it."[6]

He did use football in his writing but only to throw another sport into relief or to put it in perspective. His unresponsiveness to football and to most American games or team sports stemmed from a mistrust of them, a belief that they were artificial and unfair. In *The Torrents of Spring* Yogi Johnson reflects Hemingway's attitude: "Yogi had played centre at football and war had been much the same thing, intensely unpleasant."[7] Yogi considered football, like war, "stimulating and exciting." Such generalized and pretentious adjectives are in keeping with Hemingway's parodic style in the novel and, by having a simpleton like Yogi draw the analogy, Hemingway makes it clear that, to him, there is no fundamental comparison between war and football that yields much insight.

Crane appears to have been quite serious in 1895–96 when he commented that the psychology of war in *The Red Badge of Courage* had been learned from his experiences in football combat. However, by age eighteen, Hemingway had been to war and had been badly wounded in Italy; by the time he came to write about his war experiences in fiction, he had no inclination to imagine football or any other sport in genteel disguise. In "Another Country," Hemingway's story of an Italian rehabilitation hospital for wounded veterans, an optimistic Italian surgeon makes small talk with Nick Adams while Nick sits with his shattered leg at a physical therapy machine. The doctor asks, "What did you like best to do before the war? Did you practice a sport?"[8] When Nick says he played football, the doctor responds, "Good. You will be able to play football again better than ever." Nick thinks, "My knee did not bend and the leg dropped straight from the knee to the ankle without a calf," but the doctor exhorts, "That will all pass. You are a fortunate young man. You will play football again like a champion." On the next machine sits an Italian major with a maimed hand. The greatest fencer in Italy before the war, he flaps his "stiff fingers" and derisively asks, "And will I play football, captain-doctor?" "Playing football" again is mocked as a childlike dream from another country in another life.

Hemingway returned several more times in his early stories to images of football and college fraternity to underline the gulf between such innocence and war's shock and death. In the opening of ''A Way You'll Never Be,'' Nick Adams passes a group of slaughtered Italian soldiers: ''There were mass prayer books, group postcards showing the machine-gun unit standing in ranked and ruddy cheerfulness as in a football picture for a college annual.''[9] Nick grimly calls them the ''platoon of the class of 1899,'' the year of Hemingway's birth. In ''Soldier's Home,'' the shell-shocked Harold Krebs ''went to the war from a Methodist College in Kansas. There is a picture which shows him among his fraternity brothers, all of them wearing exactly the same height and style collar,''[10] a reversal of the image from ''A Way You'll Never Be.'' Hemingway used football in *Death in the Afternoon* (1931) to contrast the stories of nostalgic Spanish old-timers about bulls and their prodigious qualities with the feelings that Americans might have when they recall the heroic high school football players of their own youth who ''walked on leather-cleated shoes that printed in the earth along beside the sidewalk in the dusk, a long time ago.''[11] Hemingway sought to demythologize the immediate past. He meant to be free of adolescent dreams except in the crucial way they added to the fund of experience in the present.

In ''The Short Happy Life of Frances Macomber'' (1936), Hemingway depicts Macomber in a vein similar to Fitzgerald's description of Tom Buchanan, with ''his hair cropped like an oarsman . . . he was thirty-five years old, kept himself very fit, was good at court games. . . .''[12] He has an ''American face that would stay adolescent until it became middle-aged,'' and he knows ''about motor cars, about duck shooting, about fishing, trout, salmon, and big sea, about sex in books, many books, too many books. . . .'' Macomber also had ''a great tolerance which seemed the nicest thing about him if it was not the most sinister.'' Many Macomber traits resemble traits that Hemingway also gave to Robert Cohn, including his adolescent quality, facility at sport, notions of life from books, and a tolerance that made even the most knowing of characters in the novel feel chagrined. Finally Macomber, like Cohn, is abused and defeated by a woman he cannot defeat. Macomber is another postcollege sportsman thrust into an environment where his defective sporting code gives him no cues on how to act.

In 1950 Hemingway mentioned to Lillian Roth the case of a war writer who ''was apparently thinking of himself as Tolstoy, but who'd be able to play Tolstoy only on the Bryn Mawr field-hockey team. He never hears a shot fired in anger.''[13] Hemingway always insisted on the experience itself, not a vicarious substitute, and his derisive comment to Roth may be considered representative of his usual estimate of college sport and its relation to war for the would-be writer. After he became established as a famous author, Hemingway bristled when he was asked to set forth his theories of writing in any intellectual context. He always took a perverse pleasure in utilizing images from sport, especially baseball and boxing, to describe his aesthetics; and the results were both amusingly clear and sometimes a bit ludicrous, as if such private questions deserved to be answered in such a frame: simple, direct, and semiparodic.

Hemingway associated football with schoolboy athletic heroism and that heroism itself he considered suspect. *The Sun Also Rises* begins with Jake Barnes noting that Robert Cohn had been middleweight boxing champion at Princeton, but then Jake adds, "Do not think that I am very much impressed by that as a boxing title . . .''(3). For Hemingway, Princeton was *not* where one learned to fight. Boxing was not a profession or a trade acquired at school but an art honed in battle in the ring where courage was tested through pain and punishment. The mere idea of being a champion of anything in a cloistered milieu like Princeton is amusing to Jake. Cohn "cared nothing for boxing, in fact he disliked it, but he learned it painfully and thoroughly to counteract the feeling of inferiority and shyness he had felt on being treated as a Jew at Princeton" (3). Cohn was "very shy," a "thoroughly nice boy"; but, made defensive by his situation, he turned to an aggressive sport that allowed him to burn off his anger. A cruel Hemingway touch was that Cohn "got his nose permanently flattened" in the ring, signifying the violence done to his Jewishness and personality by immersion in the Princeton world.

Cohn "thoroughly" disliked boxing and was no natural athlete. Hemingway was probably transferring his own negative feelings about football, where his work at the center position left him most vulnerable to defensive blows after every snap of the ball. In light of his later bizarre, unpredictable behavior in the boxing ring as well as in unscheduled bouts in offices, restaurants, and bars,[14] it is easy to imagine the fiercely individual Hemingway—proud of his massive torso, injury-prone, and acutely sensitive to pain and the sensation of being buried, as in the rubble after his wounding and living burial at Fossalta—loathing the submersion beneath repeated pile-ups at the center of the line. Therefore, Cohn's wish to play football again after being Princeton middleweight champion is a delusion in the novel but may evince some sublimated Hemingway wish in 1925 to alleviate his early frustration, return with boxing prowess, and wreak mayhem on the innocent victims of Oak Park High.

Cohn's "otherness" is a compound of qualities. He is a bad artist, a novelist without a subject, and a man full of sentimentality and nervous energy, dangerous and self-destructive characteristics in Hemingway's view. In addition, he is, like Buchanan, a man capable of violence, his boxer's hands serving as weapons. Although Cohn comes from "one of the richest Jewish families in New York" (4), his odyssey from prep school to Princeton to California to Provincetown, Mass., was one of financial disaster and marital unhappiness. Cohn is a failed romantic living in the 1920s, one who reads florid romantic fiction and takes it as truth. His restlessness and abused sense of heightened promise are evident quite early in the novel. He attempts to persuade Jake to accompany him to South America, the locale for the amorous adventures of the young English gentleman in W.H. Hudson's *The Purple Land,* Cohn's favorite romance.[15] Paris is not exciting enough for him. As Jake Barnes suggests, "He got the first idea out of a book, and I suppose the second came out of a book too" (12).

The School Sports Hero is shown to have as much faith in books, appropriately enough, as in sports. Cohn, the novelist and editor of a fashionable "review of the arts" in Carmel and Provincetown, is also the escapist of *The Purple Land.* But Hemingway says, "for a man to take [*The Purple Land*] at thirty-four as a guidebook to what life holds is about as safe as it would be for a man of the same age to enter Wall Street direct from a French convent, equipped with a complete set of the more practical Alger books"(9). Cohn reads *The Purple Land* as a guide to personal conduct; Tom Buchanan, the last Nordic holding civilization together, read Goddard's *Rise of the Colored Empires* and inserted the racial superiority theories into drawing-room conversation. For the athletes of Princeton and Yale, books are shields, tools for self-defense to supplement their hands and bodies. Another ironic vestige of school is the distorted world of ideas to match the distorted athletic heroism.

Not only is Cohn a romantic worthy of another Princeton son, Fitzgerald's Amory Blaine, but he is also full of false chivalry. He stands ready to risk himself for his lady, Brett Ashley, but she doggedly resists being saved. Jake and Cohn argue over whether Brett has been insulted and Jake says,

> "Oh, go to hell."
> He [Cohn] stood up from the table his face white, and stood there white and angry behind the little plates of hors d'oeuvres.
> "Sit down," I said. "Don't be a fool."

"You've got to take that back."

"Oh, cut out the prep school stuff."

"Take it back."

"Sure. Anything. I never heard of Brett Ashley. How's that?" (39)

The "prep school stuff" as well as the Ivy League pedigree were terms of little more than derision for Hemingway. Jake Barnes deems Cohn's romantic code a mawkish, weak standard of vision that is inadequate to any stress or test.

A caste-ridden and snobbish quality permeates the in-group of Hemingway's true sportsmen in *The Sun Also Rises*. They constitute an aristocracy of values and judgment of form that is as rigid and exclusionary as a club at Cohn's Princeton or a school athletic team. On another level, chapters 1 and 2, 5 and 6 of *The Sun Also Rises* could come from a "Ring Lardner, Jr." Consider the Lardnerian structure of the initial situation and its development: a reporter-narrator (Jake Barnes) depicts the athletic peculiarities of an odd sports hero (Robert Cohn) and translates these quirks into a real evocation of the athlete's character. The excluded player (Cohn), an Alibi Ike or Grimes or Buster Elliott or Jack Keefe, is then baited into making a fool of himself by statement and action while the narrator and teammates (Jake Barnes, Brett Ashley, Harvey Stone, Mike Campbell) are amused by the spectacle. The group implicitly excludes the outcast male from the team, causing greater complications and disorder in that character. However, unlike the resolution of Lardnerian or school sports plots, Cohn is not taken into the society by dint of courage or victory. Instead, he is continually taunted and derided for his statements and action.

Harvey Stone, another wreck of an American writer, derisively responds to Cohn's statement about football and "handling himself" by saying, "I misjudged you. You're not a moron. You're only a case of arrested development"(44), a phrase that echoes Fitzgerald's "acute limited excellence" and repeats Veblen, who had written that the sportsman's "arrested spiritual development . . . furthers the formation of habits of ferocity which may persist in the later life of the growing generation."[16] Cohn is initially described as having "played a very good end on the football team" (4) at military school before Princeton; when he finally does show what he has learned about "handling himself," he accuses Jake Barnes of being a pimp for Brett and knocks him down. Jake, in a half-conscious state, hazily remembers "once coming home from an out-of-town football game" after he "had been kicked in the head early in the game" (192–93). Cohn's wish comes true but he only complicates the emotional issues facing Jake, adding a further irritant.

Hemingway suggests the incompatibility of the college hero in an unsympathetic post-World War I environment where the traditions of romance, aggression, and inbred competition have little relevance, where, in fact, they have become grotesque jokes. Cohn has been educated to an ideal that does not operate in an adult world of changing relationships, a world where survivors of the war have diverse needs, where history has created a displaced class of artists and the rich on two continents, and where the graduates of the Merriwell years, including Jake Barnes, are impotent. Cohn "had a funny sort of undergraduate quality about him" (45). He wore "what used to be called polo shirts at school . . . but he was not professionally youthful"(45).

Hemingway reworks Cohn's lack of spirit and grace throughout the novel. He repeatedly isolates Cohn: Cohn does not fish; he asks if he can bet on the bullfights; he falls asleep in the most beautiful part of the Spanish mountain country. As Brett proudly goes on about her decision not to pursue Pedro Romero, Jake comments, "You'll lose it if you talk about it" (245). Cohn talks incessantly and he does lose everything. Language, books, and romantic conventions are all barriers set up between Cohn and experience. His final explosions, first against Jake and then against Romero, seal his fate as a "sportsman" whose code of honor is literally riddled by the simple courage of the bullfighter.[17]

Jake regains consciousness after being pummeled by Cohn and shakily starts back to his hotel. He imagines that he is carrying a suitcase with his football gear in it, a memory of the earlier school experience. He carries this imaginary suitcase right up to Cohn's room after Bill Gorton tells him that Cohn had been asking for him. Cohn lies face down on his bed in his Princeton polo shirt, sobbing. Both Jake and Cohn have been reduced to college boys again by their failures with Brett and are linked most strongly by memories of football, polo shirts, and college. Their impotence is underscored by their helpless responses, Jake quietly holding in his grief and Cohn awash in a sea of unattractive self-pity.[18]

Later Jake learns from Bill Gorton that Cohn has seriously injured Romero with his fists. Hemingway's final criticism of Cohn comes in a sharply dramatized scene that shows the complete gentleman's romantic sporting value system, so laboriously acquired by Cohn, to be ridiculous in the face of Romero's fundamental courage. When he finds Brett in Romero's room, Gorton says Cohn "massacred the poor, bloody bullfighter" (201). After his attack, Cohn breaks down and wants to shake hands all around in the spirit of schoolboy "fair play," but Romero will have none of it. He keeps getting up, only to be knocked down. His instincts are to keep after the bull as long as he can draw breath. Cohn becomes nervous, embarrassed. Romero rushes at him but can muster no strength and crumples to the floor again. Cohn, in the spirit of the humble Merriwellian victor, leans down to help him up and offers to shake hands, but Romero warns him away, saying that if Cohn helps him, he will kill him.

Romero's instincts are strong and sure. The halfway measures of Cohn's sportsmanship are demeaning and humiliating to Romero whose courage turns Cohn's rage, and then his apologies, into empty spectacles. Romero is badly beaten but Cohn, unmarked, is a worse loser. He slinks out of Pamplona and out of the novel. Cohn is steeped in romance, shaped by Princeton, boxing, and a code of manliness that does not stand the test of reality. He has administered a sound schoolboy thrashing to no purpose. He is as wounded and angry as Buchanan in a world that had little practical use for these unhappy college warriors with their painfully constructed personalities and values.

In *Death in the Afternoon* Hemingway compares what he calls Anglo-Saxon sport and the bullfight. The primary difference, he suggests, is that American and English sport avoid the element of death:

> I am afraid however due to the danger of death it involves it [bullfighting] would never have much success among the amateur sportsmen of America and England who play games. We, in games, are not fascinated by death, its nearness and its avoidance. We are fascinated by victory and we replace the avoidance of death by the avoidance of defeat. It is a very nice symbolism but it takes more cojones to be a sportsman when death is a closer party to the game. (22).

"Games" construct an artifice of victory and defeat as emblems for life and death. A "nice symbolism" to Hemingway is one without real emotional depth. He does not go out of his way to criticize the Anglo-Saxon sport but merely points up the difference in cultures:

> The English live for this world too and death is not a thing to think of, to consider, to mention, to seek, or to risk except in the service of the country, or for sport, or for adequate reward. Otherwise it is an unpleasant subject to be avoided, or, at best, moralized on, but never to be studied. Never discuss casualties, they say, and I have heard them say it very well. (265)

The emphasis on games is a cultural choice, a kind of courage in restraint, a holding back of one's true feelings. Hemingway has "heard them say it very well"; it is part of his heritage also. He would combine tremendous restraint of the emotions with unswerving fixation on death to create a tension that found primary expression in his many sports narratives on bull-fighting, hunting, and fishing.

FRANK MERRIWELL IN FRENCHMAN'S BEND

Although Hemingway is the modern American author most often associated with aggressive sport both in his life and in his fiction, although most readers could identify Lardner with baseball heroes and Fitzgerald with romantic college heroes, Faulkner could not be identified with any single sport. Rather he dealt with all the conventions of play in fiction: children's games, schoolboy heroism, popular heroism and spectacle, intricate wagering, perverse chicanery, outlandish physical contests, war games, symbolic duels, and high ritual. He possessed as sure a grasp of the grotesquely comic as of the majestically sacramental in play.

The Hamlet (1940) is dominated by images of pursuit, images that sometimes take on a desperate cast within the great scenes of verbal and physical comedy. The men of Frenchman's Bend chase dreams of power, freedom, and feminine bounty while all the time Flem Snopes, a fiercer competitor, is acquiring the roots of commercial empire. Ab Snopes and Pat Stamper, Mink Snopes and Jack Houston, Ike Snopes and the cow, Henry Armstid and Flem, and Labove and Eula Varner interact in grim or Rabelaisian scenes of pursuit and payment due. Possession and dignity become paired precious commodities, one the absolute prerequisite for the other.

The contrast between work and play was Faulkner's great triumph in *The Hamlet,* nowhere more clearly limned than in the Labove tale of the dirt farmer turned star halfback, the schoolteacher whose discipline and achievements are insignificant before the somnolent sensuality of Eula Varner. Labove is the football hero who most emphatically does not get the girl. He is both a dogged worker and achiever as well as a possessed romantic swain pursuing his goal. Not only did Faulkner place this tale in the 1890s, putting Labove squarely in the tradition of Frank Merriwell and his descendants, but he then completely overturned the conventional role of the college sports hero.

Like Fitzgerald, and unlike Hemingway, Faulkner was always interested in football, both as player and spectator. He grew up in a year-round warm climate, and he and his three brothers (two of whom, Johncy and

Dean, were splendid all-around athletes) were eager baseball, football, and tennis players. Faulkner enjoyed golf and tennis in his adult years.[19] In 1915 when Fitzgerald was at Princeton admiring All-American Hobey Baker and living the life of Amory Blaine in *This Side of Paradise,* when Hemingway was a center on the Oak Park scrub team, Faulkner began his junior year at Oxford (Mississippi) High School as the starting quarterback. "I hung around school just to play baseball and football," said the well-built 5'5" Faulkner, sounding like a tough young Stephen Crane. Faulkner's quarterbacking career ended abruptly, however, in the first game of the year on September 24, 1915. Faulkner broke his nose tackling his own teammate, who was running the wrong way with an intercepted pass, thus capping off his one great gridiron day in a tall-tale absurdity.[20]

Faulkner was to experience in a haphazard fashion many scenes of college life over the next several years. In April 1918 he went to New Haven and spent two months with Phil Stone at Yale before reporting to RAF Cadet training in Toronto. In 1919 his father, Murray Falkner, became secretary of the University of Mississippi in Oxford, and later that year moved his family to a university house on campus. At age 22 Faulkner entered the university as a special student, and in the fall of 1919 he even became a fraternity man at Sigma Alpha Epsilon. Faulkner began contributing prose, poetry, and Aubrey Beardsley-like drawings to *The Mississippian* and remained a frequent contributor for four years even though he officially withdrew from the university on November 5, 1920, after little more than a year. He was named acting postmaster for the university in December 1921; the one semiconstant in his environment from 1919 to 1924 was University, Miss., college life, and college ambience.[21] Thus, Faulkner was no stranger to football or to college life and he drew on his knowledge of both for his tale of Labove.

During the summer of 1925 Faulkner repeatedly told "The Legend of Sleepy Hollow" to Phil Stone's brother Jack's children.[22] Reference to "The Legend" becomes explicit in *The Hamlet* when Labove's passion finally explodes and he pursues Eula Varner across the schoolroom; Eula retorts, "Stop pawing me. You old headless horseman Ichabod Crane" (122). Not only has the slow-witted Eula actually remembered something read to her in the classroom, but her labelling of Labove is very apt. Faulkner has consciously drawn the lines of the story in relation to "Sleepy Hollow," a staple of Southwestern Humorists who recast the story in many guises before the Civil War. Part monk, part schoolteacher in his own disciplined rural mind, Labove is an outsider in Frenchman's Bend as Ichabod

Crane had been in the Hudson River Valley. Eula Varner as unmarried daughter of Will Varner is a Mississippi Katrina Van Tassel with Varner's store the prize and equivalent of Baltus Van Tassel's farm.[23]

Cecil Eby provided the early study of the correspondence between "Sleepy Hollow" and "Eula," but Eby ground down Labove to fit as an emblem of the most negative impression of Ichabod Crane.[24] Faulkner does conceive of Labove in part as an Ichabod, "a man who was not thin so much as actually gaunt . . ." (105). However, Labove is a much more attractive and varied character than a straight parallel would imply. Where Irving saw Ichabod as a grotesque Yankee, intelligent but hypocritical and grasping, Faulkner, portrays Labove as an immensely sober young man with "the face of invincible conviction. . . . A thousand years ago . . . [he] would have turned his uncompromising back upon the world with actual joy . . ." (106). Whereas Ichabod had participated in community social life "in the female circle of a rural neighborhood," Labove is totally isolated, though dreadfully drawn to Eula as all-powerful female unity. Labove is not traumatized by a prank of a Brom Bones figure but by his own insubstantial corporeality; *he* is, indeed, a wraith of a "headless horseman." His realization that Eula had not told her brother Jody of the attempted seduction because "she doesn't even know anything happened that was worth mentioning" (127) causes him to nail the schoolhouse key to the wall and vanish as completely as Ichabod Crane had from Sleepy Hollow after his great fright. However, unlike Ichabod, Labove has shown discipline, dignity, and great accomplishment, at least in the classroom and on the football field.[25]

Faulkner actually combined the Ichabod Crane and Brom Bones figure in Labove as a single, more positive conception. Hoake McCarron, Eula's eventual conqueror, is more of a traditional Brom Bones, the lusty local swell, "precocious, well-coordinated and quick to learn whatever he saw to his benefit" (136); however, he does not affect the Labove-Eula tale in any way.[26] Labove is a reluctant physical-prowess hero and Faulkner relies heavily on the reader's knowledge of that *modern* stereotype from the athletic field rather than on the tale of a boisterous colonial Hudson River tavern boy.[27]

Faulkner, however, intentionally stresses Labove's anonymity as opposed to fame and his own and others' mystification about his heroic role. Labove is far from campus heroism; rather than being carried off the field on the shoulders of his teammates and appreciative spectators, each week he retreats from the field on the back of Will Varner's horse and returns to his obsession with Eula in the schoolhouse. The first football game at the University of Mississippi was not played until 1893, the exact time of the peak of college football heroism in the North during the era of Walter Camp of Yale. Faulkner imaginatively recreates the bizarre status in the South of this new football heroism, a product, ironically enough, of the rhetoric of team play and competition in the North after victory in the Civil War.[28] Football is completely irrelevant at the Bend and Faulkner underscores the disparity between rural and school sports traditions, between heroes in contests that grew out of the soil and stock work with rifle and horse (as in Southwestern Humor) and heroes in artificially created sports with rules and uniforms as in the school sports story.[29]

Labove's first job at the university is "grading and building a football field. He didn't know then what a football field was and he did not care. To him it was merely an opportunity to earn so much additional money . . ." (108). The coach, who taunts him into trying out for the team, offers Labove the rural 1890s recruiting package, pre-NCAA: "Your tuition will be paid. You can sleep in my attic and you can feed my horse and cow and milk and build the fires" (108). He urges, "Will you try it and see? Will you stay here and do it until somebody comes to you and asks you for money?" (108). The dubious Labove only asks, "Will I be free to go when they do?" (108). As he begins to learn about football, Labove is totally straightforward and innocent: "But how can I carry the ball to that line if I let them catch me and pull me down?" (109). The reluctant rural Merriwell becomes a great success on the gridiron each Saturday, for "despite his contempt, his ingrained conviction, his hard and spartan heritage, he lived fiercely free—the spurning earth, the shocks, the hard breathing and the grasping hands, the speed . . ." (109).

Even more humorous than Labove's mock-valorous conduct on the playing field is the effect of his gridiron heroics on his entire family. On a visit to the farm looking for young Labove, Will Varner spies "sitting beside the cold hearth and sucking a foul little clay pipe, an incredibly old woman wearing a pair of stout-looking man's shoes" (103); his next vision is that of "a girl about ten, in a tattered though quite clean gingham dress and a pair of shoes exactly like those of the old lady—if anything even a little larger." Labove's father later explains to the baffled Varner that the distinctive family shoes are football shoes: "It's a game. They play it at the university" (103). All the shoes come from young Labove: "In January the son came home. He told them about the game. He had been playing all that fall. They let him stay at the University for the entire fall term for playing it. The shoes were provided them free of charge to play it in" (104) Faulk-

ner's simplistic cadences here are apt: to Labove, such cause and effect
remain a mystery, a wondrous arrangement that he does not eagerly accept
as much as suspiciously, grudgingly assume while waiting for it to end. At
the same time, Labove accepts football as a means to an end, one of Faulkner's Puritans who patiently assumes rigor as a prerequisite for achieving a
goal.

Besides the backwoods family in matching cleats, Faulkner gives us
his great comic vision of great-grandmother Labove in the Ole Miss letter
sweater, "a fine heavy warm dark blue sweater with a big red M on the
front of it," a hybrid weave of Yale blue and Harvard crimson.[30] "The
great-grandmother had taken that too, though it was much too big for her.
She would wear it on Sundays, winter and summer, sitting beside him on
the seat of the churchwood wagon on the bright days, the crimson accolade
of the color of courage and fortitude gallant in the sun . . ." (104–5). By
all conventions of the school sports hero, this sweater should belong to Eula
Varner (or Merriwell's dimpled sweetheart, Inza Burrage) as a token of
love, and the mock valiant "crimson," "courage," and "fortitude" are
undercut by great-grandmother Labove's "sunken chest and stomach; she is
an anti-Eula enduring past gender where she on "bad days" "sucked the
dead little pipe" (105).

Faulkner continues to parody the football frame when Labove perceives the football as "a trivial contemptible obloid" (109). The alien language underscores the ball's strangeness to him. Yet his repressed spirit
does flare freely for these flashing moments of action. Labove tearing down
the field is close to the freedom, if only momentarily, of the spotted ponies
after their escape from the horse lot. Faulkner's physical description of Labove has usually been compared to Irving's description of Ichabod Crane.
However, Irving consistently burlesques Ichabod with his small flat head,
large green glassy eyes, and long snipe nose whereas Faulkner's Labove,
with his "straight black hair coarse as a horse's tail," "long nose of
thought," and "slightly curved nostrils of pride," has parallels faintly
equine but nonetheless grand and potentially heroic (105–6). Faulkner's recurring image for the receding years at Ole Miss becomes "the spurned,
cleat-blurred white lines" (113) as time is transformed into space, "the six
fall weeks when each Saturday afternoon the spurned white line fled beneath
him and the hysteric air screamed and roared and he for those fleet seconds
and despite himself did live fierce, concentrated, even though still not quite
believing it" (116–17). All Labove's college actions are carried out in the
same furious manner against the urgency of time and the resistance of space,

from chopping firewood for the faculty fireplaces to the act of reading it-self.[31]

Labove is adept in all areas, an outstanding scholar as well as athletic hero. Tom Buchanan cited *The Rise of the Colored Empires* while Robert Cohn believed fervently in *The Purple Land*. Faulkner took care to characterize the college hero by his books. Labove, whom the Frenchman's Bend scholars mockingly called "professor," owned "a Coke, a Blackstone, a volume of Mississippi Reports, an original Horace and a Thucydides . . ." (112).[32] Labove's library deftly illustrates his stature. He is striving for a law degree and possesses the works of two of the great authorities on the English Common Law. Horace and Thucydides represent cultural heights in their respective civilizations and are regarded as both master stylists and intense moralists. Labove's library, traditional, ordered, dignified, and moral, clashes with his role as baffled modern hero. Labove graduates with two degrees, a master of arts and a bachelor of laws, a reminder of Ichabod Crane who had taught school and studied law at the same time in his years after Sleepy Hollow.

Labove is Snopes-like in different senses; seemingly as passionless yet determined as Flem Snopes, he is, behind the awesome repression of his lust for Eula, as lyrically romantic as the idiot Ike Snopes. Labove's struggle to free himself from Eula by possession/destruction of her is carried out in the spirit of concentrated ferocity. He feels Eula's power more deeply than anyone in *The Hamlet,* including Ratliff. Labove cannot relinquish his desire to be near Eula Varner, whose inert but incredibly fertile, seductive body is in itself a tall-tale grotesque physical artifact like that of Harris' Sicily Burns. Before Ratliff can articulate Eula's fate with Flem Snopes, it is Labove who thinks, "He could almost see the husband which she would some-day have. He would be a dwarf, a gnome, without glands or desire . . ." (119). Labove has become a satyr, "his teeth clenched in his scholar's face and his legs haired over like those of a faun" (119). He desires neither a wife nor lover but "wanted her one time as a man with a gangrened hand or foot thirsts after the axe-stroke which will leave him comparatively whole again" (119).

When Labove finally moves toward Eula, the football images cohere and are repeated in the comic seduction: "He moved as quickly and ruthlessly as if she had been a football or as if he had the ball and she stood between him and the final white line which he hated and must reach" (121). The either/or doubleness of the image is central to Faulkner's meaning, for Labove both desires Eula (the ball) and desires to be free of her (over the line). He wishes not really possession but the cessation of being possessed which may be reached only *through* possession. The unexpressed (but suggested) football image is for Labove to carry her across the goal and thus be free of her. However, Eula in her vast tranquil strength is more than a physical match for Labove. He calls on all his acquired football ferocity but she, unmoved, "almost eye to eye with him in height" (121), puts up with his scuffling until she knocks him head over heels, a wild spotted pony throwing a man in the horse lot. This Katrina Van Tassel from rural Mississippi fights her own battles with no assists from backwoods suitors. This Ichabod Crane as football hero vanishes, his desires unconsummated. Eula's pulse-beat does not quicken until she drives off the suitors assaulting Hoake McCarron, who then receives her favors despite his amazement and his broken arm.

Faulkner's version of "The Legend of Sleepy Hollow" is haunted by both Labove's quest and Eula's power. The 1890s backwoods dirt farmer as School Sports Hero was an anomaly that Faulkner added to animate *his* legend and to underscore again the provincial isolation of Frenchman's Bend. Labove is one of Faulkner's single-minded, stubborn ascetics with tremendous determination to drive through difficulties as through tacklers, but his one great victory eludes him. Sport is not a focal point in Labove's life but rather another obstacle to overcome in his outrage. As a serious advocate of unceasing labor and application, he comes up against the twin obstacles of school sport and romantic obsession.

THE SCHOOL SPORTS HERO IN ECLIPSE

Fitzgerald showed Buchanan with no role to play in post-World War I American society. The convention of schoolboy preparation for maturity is proven false. Buchanan escapes with Daisy into money and privilege but has been judged deficient in every test of character. For Hemingway, Cohn is irrelevant, irritating, and embarrassing to the group of stoic revellers who seek an emotional balance beyond Cohn's naive romanticism. While Buchanan and Cohn in the 1920s represent the modern failure of privilege and power as they might have been defined by an 1890s gentleman, Faulkner reverses the movement of the School Sports Hero, placing Labove in Mississippi in the 1890s as an alien note of modernity thrust into an uncomprehending society. Labove is the sportsman of the present overlayed onto the unchanging rural society dominated by competition and desire. Flem Snopes and his clan embody a more devastating and dead modern spirit that will alter Jefferson and the Bend forever. For all three original emblems of the School Sports Hero, the modern message is clear: American society cannot be bullied, preached to, or understood by its officially sanctioned School Sports Heroes. Problems of human relationships knit in their complexity beyond the grasp of Buchanan, Cohn, and Labove. As nominal heroes at the height of a cultural crisis of belief in traditional forms of heroism, without an ironic perspective on their roles, they bear the mark of bewildered defeat.

Even the controlled and polished Dick Diver in *Tender is the Night* reverts to confused schoolboy longing and desire "with the fatuousness of one of [Booth] Tarkington's adolescents. . . ." (91),[33] as he rushes to Rosemary Hoyt's movie studio after being titillated through tales of sexual indiscretion by Yale fraternity boy Collis Clay. Dick is Labove-like in his passion: "Dignified in his fine clothes, with their fine accessories, he was yet swayed and driven as an animal. Dignity could only come with an overthrowing of his past, of the effort of the last six years [to sustain Nicole]" (91). Dick moves back in time to a past "unforgotten, unshriven, unexpurgated," born of Yale and his freedom and promise as Lucky Dick, rather than as emotional caretaker. Yet the scene ends in phallic comedy with Dick's desire unsatisfied, his "gold-headed stick held at a swordlike angle" (94). Other chivalric school heroes found wanting in grotesque and comic sexual denouements include Tom Buchanan sobbing over dog biscuits, Cohn sobbing in his polo shirt, and Labove-Ichabod lying dazed beneath a school bench.

In *The Great Gatsby, The Sun Also Rises,* and *The Hamlet,* Fitzgerald, Hemingway, and Faulkner have provided a similar structure for the School Sports Hero, placing him in a larger network of romantic and competitive relationships. Each novel depicts the School Sports Hero in competition for an object of desire, who may be designated the Golden Girl. The School Sports Hero is opposed by a more Competitive Hero who has great reserves of determination and will. Finally, each novel has an overseer, an Exemplary Witness, who functions as commentator on the action and pronounces judgment on all the players—Golden Girl, School Sports Hero, and Competitive Hero. The relationships may be presented this way:

	Golden Girl	School Sports Hero	Competitive Hero	Exemplary Witness
The Great Gatsby	Daisy Buchanan	Tom Buchanan	Jay Gatsby	Nick Carraway
The Sun Also Rises	Brett Ashley	Robert Cohn	Pedro Romero	Jake Barnes
The Hamlet	Eula Varner	Labove	Flem Snopes	V.K. Ratliff

Each novel contains a woman of sensual power. Daisy Buchanan is romantic promise with her thrilling voice and evanescent beauty. Brett Ashley is the magnetic center of *The Sun Also Rises,* the matador around whom all the bulls and steers battle. Eula Varner maddens all the suitors in Frenchman's Bend in her drowsy, idol-like stature. In each novel, a female unity is strong and absolute and draws the men toward it. The School Sports Hero competes for the Golden Girl and loses; only in *The Great Gatsby* are the roles reversed: Gatsby, the Competitive Hero, loses Daisy to Tom Buchanan who bludgeons his way to victory and remains a loser in the moral sense. Cohn's quest for Brett pales before the emotional control and sports skill of Pedro Romero. Labove, though not affected directly in the narrative by Flem Snopes, is eclipsed by the dogged store clerk, as are all the men who would possess Eula. Gatsby, Romero, and Flem are competitors playing for huge prizes, projecting whole personalities like Gatsby, ritualistically facing death like Romero, or ravaging a community like Flem. Finally, the novels are overseen by narrators Nick Carraway, Jake Barnes, V.K. Ratliff, powerless sages with good intentions. They chronicle the unfolding tales but do not play for stakes because of temperament, wounds, or perception of the cost and waste. As Nick ruefully tells Jordan Baker, "I'm thirty, I'm five years too old to lie to myself and call it honor" (179). Jake's last tender, bitter remark to Brett is "Isn't it pretty to think so" (247). As Ratliff watches the buggy taking Flem and Eula out of Jefferson on the wedding trip, he is whimsically but pessimistically humane as he imagines the future generations of human comedy. He *is* Labove and contains Labove and all the suitors as Flem carries off Eula. It is Ratliff who feels a twinge of helplessness akin to that of Labove as he prepares to buy the old Frenchman's place which contains the salted gold mine and asks Flem, "That fellow, that teacher you had three-four years ago. Labove. Did anybody ever hear what became of him?" (361).

In the conventional school sports story, the School Sports Hero had not only aggressive and competitive instincts, but he also had courage, determination, and a wisdom born of the struggle for victory. He was both immensely energetic and humanely tolerant, a leader with the common touch in school and, it was implied, beyond school. In *The Great Gatsby, The Sun Also Rises,* and *The Hamlet,* the School Sports Hero had been designated as, in fact, a third male lead below the Competitive Hero and the Exemplary Witness. The School Sports Hero has neither true courage nor real humanity. The fact is that his traditional virtues are split between the Competitive Hero and the Exemplary Witness. Gatsby, Romero, and Flem Snopes have superior determination and will, and Gatsby also has his own intense creativity and Romero his physical courage. Nick, Jake, and Ratliff have tolerance, pity, and hard-won wisdom but are powerless to act. The School Sports Hero who combined these sets of attributes was a repository of all these values and more during the Merriwell-Stover era; but in these three novels, he is not effectively strong, not humane, and not wise.

Thus, by diminishing the School Sports Hero and bifurcating his virtues into competitors without reflection and witnesses who do not compete, Fitzgerald, Hemingway, and Faulkner have written novels where no hero truly wins any lasting victories as victory itself becomes suspect. The extreme modernist pessimism toward conventional heroism is most evident here. Gatsby, Romero, and Flem represent fierce competition beyond rules into obsession (with the past, with death, with wealth) where no prescribed game or sport can follow. They compete fundamentally and personally in line with their own vision, not dependent on society's definitions of conduct. Nick, Jake, and Ratliff represent a humane witnessing which will not or cannot play and will not alter human lives. The School Sports Hero's two roles of aggressive competitor in rule-governed activity and articulator of fair play and opinion are halved and hence eclipsed. The School Sports Hero in these novels finishes a poor third to these more powerful or humane characters who themselves are flawed. The imperative of correct conduct guided by "Higher Laws" had been the heritage of the School Sports Hero since the Civil War and had its origin as far back as Natty Bumppo's instruction of Templeton during the pigeon shoot and fish kill. Yet no such roles are available to Buchanan, Cohn, and Labove. Only a few decades after the School Sports Hero's entrenchment as a popular stereotype, America's great modernists turned sharply away from the genteel, youthful, confident American hero but found ways to use that figure to underscore limits and failure in more intense and complex worlds that run on levels beyond the grasp of the School Sports Hero.

Yet in describing the roles of Cohn and Labove, one does not learn what Hemingway and Faulkner most valued in play and sport. If the school sports convention was largely antithetical to them, what were their convictions about sports and games for the human spirit? What moments in the realm of play caught their deepest allegiances and how were these moments rendered in fiction? Both authors went to great lengths to stand outside the conventions of popular team and school sport, the dominant American modern sports experiences. They developed their own coherent patterns of play, game, and sport for individual characters in book after book, and what remains is to chart the outlines of Hemingway's and Faulkner's vision of play in turn.

PART IV
The Modern Ritual Sports Hero

CHAPTER TEN

Hemingway: Exemplary Heroism and Heroic Witnessing

PLAYING THE REAL AND THE SACRED

THE RITUAL that suddenly brings experience into a sharply defined realm was what Hemingway and Faulkner depicted again and again. For the Ritual Sports Hero, sport is not recognition, power, or extrinsic reward; rather it means man coming to understand himself and what he is capable of. Play and sport are ways of knowing in altered time and space and are the most direct revelations we can receive. Since Cooper and Thoreau had written of individual sporting conduct in settlement and wilderness, the depiction of American sport had been appropriated by authors who saw it as a vehicle for expressing great shifts in American society's view of collective action.[1] The Popular Sports Hero brought to full birth in Lardner's stories was an athlete totally at the behest of industrial urban society, playing on its teams for financial reward and personal fame. The School Sports Hero moved in another concerted team expression of sport in which his role paralleled that of a soldier in a military unit who received an education through repeated tests. Professional and college sport were microcosms of organization, subordination, and secularization in the larger society.

It cannot be emphasized strongly enough how Hemingway and Faulkner ignored both the realistic comic Popular Sports Hero and the sober upright School Sports Hero except to censure or to satirize the figures. They expressly denied that organized American sporting activity could truly be emblematic of American virtues. At the same time they treated the solitary competitor with dignity even in the most deterministic or comic of scenes.

The most telling fact about the players and sportsmen of Hemingway and Faulkner is precisely their solitariness. They are individual participants and witnesses searching for space where they can be whole.

If Hemingway has direct ancestors in sporting attitudes, they are Cooper and Thoreau. He was intensely concerned with the rules of sport and its technical form, as interested in teaching correctness in his sporting scenes as Cooper was through Natty Bumppo. Hemingway could apotheosize man-in-nature with a clarity and precision not seen in American letters since Thoreau. The isolated, individual experience in sport that had first been spiritualized by Cooper and Thoreau became Hemingway's touchstone to intimate truths about a man's character. As Natty Bumppo had been at his best when demonstrating his practical sporting skills to Templeton's citizens, so, too, do Hemingway's sportsmen not only perform but also instruct in both technique and spirit as heroes and witnesses. He wrote of rule-dominated sport, of formal competition that depended upon strict *ludic* principles. Sport was very serious for Hemingway as it had been for Cooper and Thoreau, involving physical motions and personal attitudes, labor done in everyday life. If Cooper was essentially concerned with *how* we practice our sport and Thoreau with *why*, Hemingway united these concerns and made them crucial to the development of characters who construct solid defenses through mastery of sports technique which becomes its own rule. Ritual sport for Hemingway was a defense against life that could not be confronted in other ways.

If Faulkner has forebears in writing of sport, they are Hawthorne, Cooper, and Irving as well as the Southwestern Humorists. Faulkner was concerned not only with public ritual ceremony and spontaneous play but also with gaming and great competition. Reminiscent of Hawthorne in his Election Day sport and May rites, Faulkner portrayed ritual in a communal spectacle best seen in horse sales in *The Hamlet* and the annual hunt in *Go Down, Moses*. He imparted the most sacramental value to the hunt and its effect on master hunters. He also saw play as a free and separate realm that had potentially life-enhancing power and psychological value for his players. Faulkner drew on Irving's "The Legend of Sleepy Hollow" in its magic, illusory aspects and he described fanciful play in both arrested motion and furious power that caught and bewildered his players and pawns. His tricksters and intense competitors were brilliantly realized, their hyperbolic and grotesque characterization a triumph of modern Southwestern Humor at the same time that Faulkner's created world had a personal *agon* and humanity never approached by the Southwesterners.

Hemingway and Faulkner moved scores of characters through their play experiences and portrayed the clash of individuals with discordant modern society through the play forms that often suggested a strong kinship with more primitive sporting life. Huizinga's "ritual tie" of play to modern sport was not seen as severed so much as hidden by an accretion of forms. The range of Hemingway and Faulkner's use of sport and play is formidable and moves well beyond the conventional categories of modern sport. Guttmann writes, "the preference for play is part and parcel of a Romantic rejection of the basic characteristics of modern society," and suggests that sports are our modern rationalization of the Romantic.[2] Hemingway and Faulkner may be seen as working *against* the rationalization of sport and play and toward a primitive-classical expression of sport in Hemingway and toward a tragicomic vision of play in Faulkner.[3]

Both Hemingway and Faulkner go firmly against the grain of modern American team sports expression. But working through the secularism of spectacle, they posit ritual invested with heightened significance. Far from the equality of team members and leagues, they propose a direct revelation for competitors who are "chosen," who may become part of a priestly class or elect. As opposed to players who perform specialized team functions in organized sport, men such as Pedro Romero, Santiago, and Ike McCaslin are adept and self-sufficient in all the tasks associated with their rites. Beyond rational respect for or fear of an opponent, there is an appeal to a mystical bond with the adversary in which the ritual participant becomes one with his opponent in a giving up of self to another reality: Romero and the bulls; Santiago and the Gulf Stream; Faulkner's yeomen and the horses in *The Hamlet;* and Ike McCaslin and Old Ben. The Ritual Sports Hero shuns the "settlement" organization in favor of charting his own course. Finally, no one in Hemingway and Faulkner hunts marlins or bears, or buys (and chases) horses in any quest for records or quantified achievement but, rather they encounter the "biggest" animal or fish or the most seductive pony. Furthermore, they experience the quality of the pursuit, which cannot be measured in terms of a score or a victory.[4] In narrative after narrative, Hemingway and Faulkner belied the statistical truths of modern sport and its streamlined face by playing the real and the sacred.

As realists Hemingway and Faulkner depicted the profane world that only occasionally approached the heightened realm of the sacred through forms of play and sport. With a commitment to depicting the ordeal of personal heroic survival, they reinvented the modern arena in dimensions of power and authenticity. Again and again, the climactic moments of self-realization, physical mastery, or agonizing defeat in Hemingway and Faulkner occur through scenes of secular ritual or deadly sport. There is emphatically no separation into play versus reality or play versus the sacred. Play occurs in a performance which transforms the individual and shapes his knowledge.

Play drives the ritual in which the hero performs in work roles or on the periphery of the sacred. The concept of ritual that guides this section on the Ritual Sports Hero is best formulated by Sally F. Moore and Barbara G. Myerhoff in *Secular Ritual* (1977). Moore and Myerhoff begin with the supposition that social life can be located "somewhere between the imaginary extremes of absolute order, and absolute conflict and anarchic improvisation."[5] "Absolute order" connotes sacred or religious unity while its opposite is an unmediated spontaneous flux. Rather than assign all forms of ritual and ceremony to the religious as Emile Durkheim did in *The Elementary Forms of the Religious Life* (1915), Moore and Myerhoff attempt to define ceremony in more secular contexts. They state that, while terminology is still fluid, the "secular ritual" and "ceremony" are concepts for investigation in and of themselves.[6] Myerhoff comes close to a formal elaboration of the secular-religious spectrum of ritual when she writes that "rituals are not either sacred or secular, rather in high rituals, they are closer to the sacred end of the continuum, entirely extraordinary, communicating the *mysterium tremendum* and are often associated with supernatural or spiritual beings. Or, they are closer to the mundane end of the continuum, perfunctory genuflections to form . . . eliminating potential disruption, unpredictability and accident."[7] All ritual sport discussed in Part IV is, in effect, *secular* ritual sport which instructs or exalts in a wide range of activity.

When a hero plays the real and the sacred, the ritual is of the greatest significance. It has the power to move work out of itself through play or to play toward the sacred. Huizinga states that participants in archaic sacred ritual were convinced that "action actualizes" and "brings about an order of things higher than that in which they customarily live."[8] Langer contrasted the expressive acts of compulsion in primitive sacred ritual, during which specific dramatic experiences were represented, with the ritual acts of a more sophisticated culture. These acts become not signs of emotions but rather symbols that denote feeling: ritual has reference rather than representation.[9] Ritual then helps us to comprehend a unity of being that we approach through repetition of the ritual reference. Ritual then begins in play; as Langer notes, "long before men perform rites which enact the phases of life, they have learned such acting in play."[10] According to rules, one mimes human attitudes through gesturing that structures a heightened experience. Moore and Myerhoff see ritual as a form which may accommodate almost any aspect of social life or behavior.[11] At its basic performative level, ritual is Nick Adams' individualized behavior in "Big Two-Hearted River," quelling a trauma by the opening of a can; Harold Krebs watching his sister play softball in "Soldier's Home"; or Jake Barnes packing his trout in ferns in *The Sun Also Rises*. At the most intense level, which approaches revelation, the ritual experience may be Ike McCaslin entering the wilderness without gun, watch, and compass in *The Bear*.

Mircea Eliade grudgingly admits that for nonreligious modern man, "who rejects the sacrality of the world," "even the most desacralized existence still preserves traces of a religious valorization of the world."[12] While what Eliade calls "profane experience" maintains "relativity of space," in which no aspects of existence stand out from any others, modern man does find "privileged places," "holy places" of a private universe "as if it were in such spots that he had received the revelation of a reality other than that in which he participates through his ordinary daily life."[13] It is at Templeton's boundary on Lake Otsego that Natty Bumppo not only learns but attempts to teach. Walden Pond takes on the status of privileged arena for Thoreau's growth. Such spots from childhood are fondly recalled: improvised play spaces for marbles, war games, or pursuit games; or the backyard ballpark with bushes, trees, and clothesline as natural obstacles. Such extempore play spaces are the vestiges of sacred space and they defeat the relativity of space which play puts under temporary measurement by becoming arenas. In *The Hamlet*, for example, the desire of the yeomen in Frenchman's Bend is to identify with the spotted ponies, to take on momentarily their power and sensual freedom. The prosaic horse lot itself, site of the ritual sale of the ponies, is transformed into an arena, as is the night countryside after the escape of horses and men. The play spaces are in scenes of grotesque and profane desacralization. But the spaces also orient the individual to another plane of reality. Foremost is the extrareal drive of characters who want to achieve momentary ritual mastery. The acts of sport and play that consume characters in Hemingway and Faulkner are preeminently those that may shade the ritual toward the sacred but that always express the ritual hope to heighten or control reality.[14]

Rituals have the power to break profane *temporal* reality as well as spatial reality. Eliade refers to festivals taking place in "primordial" time in the sense that they recreate a cosmogony and make it endlessly recoverable through present ceremony.[15] Yet play itself is seen as primary phenomenon by Fink and just as primordial ("the essence of unyielding reality") as the sacred is for Eliade.[16] The duration of play or contest, while not explicitly referential to the sacred, is a rupture or respite from profane time. Moments in Faulkner's fiction have the freedom and uncertainty of play; however, these play frames are as often combined in games and sports as they are separate. Game time may be elevated to festal time, when sport is included in a ritual series of observances.

In the most complex and wide-ranging use of ritual, sport assumes a number of contexts. In *The Sun Also Rises,* the bullfight is a well-organized modern sport, a scheduled spectacle with role-differentiation, but also it is existentially uncertain as well as a ritual governed by rules. It is a secular drama recreating a mastery of fear and death but also part of the religious celebration of San Fermin. It is ultimately a highly stylized, competitive battle with ritual framing. While Hemingway suggests several simultaneous meanings of the bullfight, Faulkner consistently modulates ritual games into free play, free play into desperate contest. The dominant modes of *The Hamlet* are the games of *agon-alea.* The horse-lot sale is a competitive game framed as secular ceremony before it breaks into pure play with the pursuit of the ponies. The consequences of the chase are extreme, especially for men such as Tull and Armstid. The bullfight and the horse sale take place in arenas where competition is paramount and playing the reality yields its deeper value.

The hunt for Old Ben in *Go Down, Moses* is an annual occurrence that becomes a festive occasion for Jefferson and all of Yoknaatawpha County. The hunt takes place in festal time, the same two weeks set aside each November.[17] Whereas, as Eliade points out, sacred time takes no part in the temporal duration that precedes and follows it,[18] the two strongest examples in Hemingway and Faulkner are Santiago's battle with the marlin and Ike's moments in the true wilderness. These ritual competitors move out beyond all societal arenas and time frames to become part of an ordered, natural drama. At that point, sport has moved up to approach a divine realm in man's relation to his creator, and sport dissolves in the timeless vision that it has aided in bringing into creation. Play is an omnipresent form that is part of the ritual, illuminating the everyday at one pole and the sacred at the other. If ritual partially domesticates the sacred[19] and makes it retrievable as ritual, one may add that play just as often heightens the real and makes it retrievable as illusion. Moore and Myerhoff sum up: "the referential scope of secular ceremonies can be compared with that of religious rituals with respect to their explanatory content."[20]

Play takes us out of our determined work and societal roles toward an arbitrary, indeterminate freedom. However, if that play is formalized into ritual sport, the ritual may become a mediating element as man approaches mysteries of his own perception and experience where he seeks to shed the arbitrary nature of his existence, to barter freedom for spiritual rest. Play, which always begins as pure possibility, may by performative repetition and symbolic association in ritual sport proceed toward absolute embodiment.[21] The Ritual Sports Hero is an American primitive, desiring to "front essential facts" as Thoreau wrote, wanting to know, as do Jake Barnes and Nick Adams, "how to live in it," hoping to perceive "the good place." The Ritual Sports Hero begins through cleansing or illuminating rites. Whatever measure of control an individual can muster over his environment is, first of all, a physical victory that affects the emotions. For Hemingway, ritual is never vicarious, off-duty play but work which must be done in strict patterns to salvage the individual. Ritual for Faulkner is framed by a comic or tragic inevitability according to which a man performs his nature and does the best he can.

HEMINGWAY: THE SOLITARY SPORTSMAN

Hemingway measured a man's character through his ritual performance in the contest with nature or his performance during a great trauma, where he most often fought a harsh battle with himself. His competitors were stoical, his sporting motions sacramental. Hemingway's obsessive concern with work well done was thoroughly Calvinistic, and he showed that work through sport in many guises.[22] In his comments about authors and writing, Hemingway showed that he admired any task carried out with fidelity to the action, with classical restraint and grace; and he bequeathed the best of such qualities to his positive sporting characters.[23] He possessed a most delicate and well-developed sense of physical action and motion. His lucid, spare style imparted a limpid presentness to any sporting action he described while his discriminating eye always pierced the facade of the sportsman who exhibited false courage, bravado, or deficient form.[24] He wrote scrupulously about all sport that actively engaged him and criticized roundly that sport which he felt to be less than true.

Hemingway consistently returned to the individual in ritualistic sport. However, his use of sport was paradoxical in the extreme. He understood *ludus* and, indeed, gave new dimensions to the value of rules in dictating conduct. Yet the free play of *paidia* and all games of chance were deeply mistrusted by him as intrusions from the chaotic and threatening realms of Dionysus and Atropos. His characters fought to stay clear of irrational *ilinx* and *alea* in the form of fate. In the long run, he had both fear of and contempt for "game." He could not abide the lack of elemental physical danger nor the competitor's inability to control all rules of technique and degree of risk. He limited his competitive sphere to what he could dominate.

Hemingway loathed the rules he grudgingly had to accept as part of the structure of team sport. His description of football in *The Torrents of Spring* made explicit his distaste. As a center, "while your hands were on the ball the opposing centre stood in front of you, and when you passed the ball he brought his hand up smash into your face. . . . He had all the advantage. It was not what you would call fun. When you had the ball he had all the advantage" (71). The football center had no rational defense. He performed his work and within the rules was blasted on every offensive play. Thus for Hemingway, football incorporated a terrifying aspect of rules and games: the rules were always set in his opponent's favor. The man opposite him could strike a blow before Hemingway could set himself and without a defense, Hemingway's sportsman felt foolish and stripped of weapons—a quintessential victim. Hemingway's sustained metaphor of "taking it," so central to so much of his fiction, was logically explained in his view of the football center's vulnerability.

Of the play categories of Huizinga and Caillois—freedom, separateness, regulation, uncertainty, unproductivity, make-believe—the last three were anathema to Hemingway. His sportsmen work to eliminate uncertainty; they produce something of real substance, and they indulge in no illusions. What Hemingway's sportsmen do stress and actually live by are separateness and regulation. They express their skill as solitaries and are bound by technique and aesthetics. Freedom, Huizinga and Caillois' first play category, is contradictory in Hemingway's work for it is achieved only within sharply defined strictures and through high achievement.

The sports action in Hemingway's fiction most closely follows Huizinga's view that the roots of the Anglo-Saxon "play" yield "risk" and "exposure," that the root of the Greek word for "prize" yields "athlete" where (according to Huizinga) the ideas most centrally grouped are those of contest, struggle, exercise, exertion, endurance, and suffering (see Introduction). In scene after created scene, Hemingway seconds Huizinga's description of the qualities exhibited in ancient athletics. The cluster of qualities that Huizinga portrays as surrounding the *agon* form the loci for struggle in Hemingway's sporting heroes. The *agon* in Hemingway is always expressed through ritual that becomes intense labor. Victor Turner has pointed to the Greek roots of "liturgy" as "people" and "work" and has stated that ritual in tribal societies is "embedded in the total round of activities, and is part of the work of the people. . . ."[25] Pedro Romero is courageous and an artist but states simply, "I like it very much that you like my work" (174). Here is Hemingway's instinctive bow to the unity of the contest and "liturgy" in the total life of a society that can appreciate a culture hero such as Romero through his sport.

In Hemingway's sport, a competitor stands alone, physically exposed to the natural world or to danger in the enclosed arena. To combat the elemental threats, Hemingway posits courage and the fruits of its triumph: Romero on the afternoon following his fight with Robert Cohn, knowing that "each thing that he did with this bull wiped that out a little cleaner"; Jack Brennan "holding himself in down there"; Macomber growing in momentary victory; Santiago crooning to his lacerated hands. Hemingway, the author and teacher, made the reader see the competent and sure competitor at work, for work is surely what it was. The ritual observance of sport in Hemingway's fiction suggested that present mastery is not only the best that heroes and witnesses can take from the rite, but perhaps all they can take.[26] As Jake Barnes phrased it, "I did not care what it was all about. All I wanted to know was how to live in it" (148).

What set Hemingway apart from other American authors who have used sport were the sports he valued and the locales he wrote about, as well as his implicit disavowal of our collectivized sports pattern. Fishing, hunting, and bullfighting on the Gulf Stream, in Kenya, and in Spain replaced any American team sports and arenas. To Hemingway sport was vital in more universal metaphors that were not specifically American at all. As discussed in chapter 9, Hemingway had little use for the "amateur sportsmen of America and England who play games" and have a "nice symbolism." Hemingway sensed that in taking to our games in groups, the elemental experience is lost in only simulated conflict and danger. Cooper had written jocularly of a Walter Scott tournament of sporting skills in *The Pioneers*. Thoreau had stated in "Higher Laws" that English sport was not ours because New England boys have the space and wilderness to become hunters. They do not need games on the green. It was this spirit, both denial of gentility and commitment to the elemental arena as the only true testing place, that defined Hemingway's attitude toward sport. Deadly serious in his approach to sport, Hemingway thus belonged to an American tradition of the isolated sportsman as recorder and teacher of values. Since 1900, American popular and team sport has brought forth one school or team sport hero after another, but Hemingway stood largely apart from that sports culture. He infused the idea of competition with a lasting sense of the individual's struggle as a Ritual Sports Hero. Hemingway's protagonist was always warily conscious of being in a dangerous contest where he most often fought the hard battle with himself. His tools were meticulous technique and impressive courage.

THE SUN ALSO RISES: VARIETIES OF SPORTS EXPERIENCE

The Sun Also Rises was Hemingway's lesson in ritualistic sport. It is the one work in his canon where sport and ritual are most fully differentiated and it also portrays the kinds of sport he thoroughly disliked. Chapter 9 dealt in part with the negative characterization of Robert Cohn as School Sports Hero but other emblems of sport in the novel further define Hemingway's disapproval of empty spectacle. Cohn's painfully learned style of boxing as a Princeton "gentleman" and his futile pummeling of Romero at Pamplona are put in a comic perspective by Bill Gorton's anecdote of a black American fighter's misadventures in Vienna. Bill bemusedly speaks of a "big sporting evening": "Injustice everywhere. Promoter claimed nigger promised let local boy stay. Claimed nigger violated contract. Can't knock out Vienna boy in Vienna. 'My God, Mister Gorton,' said nigger, 'I didn't do nothing in there for forty minutes but try and let him stay. That white boy musta ruptured himself swinging at me. I never did hit him' " (71). Providing a comic twist on his own story of Jack Brennan's fix in "Fifty Grand," Hemingway creates a riotous scene with no meaning at all for the Austrian fans and simply a frustrated pay day for the black fighter who is more than willing to throw the fight.

Hemingway matched the emblem of boxing as a deficient public spectacle with another well publicized continental sport of the 1920s, the cross-country bicycle race. Hemingway observes that the racers Jake sees at San Sebastian "did not take the race seriously except among themselves. They had raced among themselves so often that it did not make much difference who won. Expecially in a foreign country. The money could be arranged" (236). The team manager "of one of the big bicycle manuracturers" (236) has coffee with Jake, and through Jake's subsequent summary of the smug entrepreneur's views, Hemingway damns him and his racers: "It was a rich country and more *sportif* every year. It would be the most *sportif* country in the world. It was bicycle road-racing did it. That and football. He knew France. La France Sportive. He knew road-racing" (236–37). The racers, like the black American fighter, are performers in another country, and Hemingway uses them to show the shallowness of sport not linked to culture amongst participants or fans.

It was not that Hemingway categorically denied a valid public response to sport spectacle but that he wished to express a form that would frame the spectacle in ritual meaning, that would swing the sport toward somber revelation about the character of participant and spectator and yet retain the realistic cultural base. In effect, he had to describe sport through ritual to care about it at all. He found his sport and format in the bullfight during the festival of San Fermin at Pamplona.

Festivals are formalized annual celebrations of some intimate and enormous cultural event or belief, and they touch dramatically on both the exaltation and the pain of creation. They are formidable reenactments of the cosmogony and may act as a symbolic staving off of death.[27] Although they may be touching on sacred themes and yearnings, their time frame is initially merely altered; all activity is thus reinvented according to the dictates of the festival, which may become a phenomenon of great magnitude and violence where a populace is thrust into an *ilinx*-like *mimetic* recreation of a new reality on a spontaneous plane. Acts that may have been prohibited are now performed by ritual practices.[28] Reality is thus played throughout the festival in altered festal time which is one of celebrations and spectacles.[29]

The festival's explosion creates a new experience based on the sustained illusion of altered time and space. Actions may degenerate into license or debauchery[30] during ritual time and the ritual drama may result in real consequences. A continuing element of the festival is spontaneous quarreling and combat; the participants are separated and the dance goes on. Couples have assignations and return to the main body of celebrants.[31] As an expression of free play in its compulsive disorder, Hemingway's festival of San Fermin is sensual and disruptive. Characters are wary of its anarchy. No rules prevail and there is a revelation of everyone's nature.

Yet within the celebration, the bullfight itself is an island of rule-oriented sport and a pageant of symbolic control which focuses and shapes the conduct of all the festal participants in the novel.[32] At the heart of *The Sun Also Rises* is the festival and its heart is the bullfight. The bullfight represses into heroic-spectatorial form the license of the festival and becomes its epicenter.

Hemingway's remarks about the symbolism of the sport were best expressed in *Death in the Afternoon* (1931), a long, arch, bombastic, but still fascinating, sporting encyclopedia. Through an analysis of the bullfight, he further clarified his view of the split between the value systems of blood sport and British or American sports and games. His vision of the interlocking functions the bullfight performed in the Spanish culture is apparent in the title of the first published excerpt, "Bullfighting, Sport and Industry" (*Fortune,* March 1930). That Hemingway saw the elements of the bullfight together, its primitive cultural roots and modern commercial imperatives, makes his vision of the bullfight a fine example of what Turner has called a *"liminoid* genre" of ceremony. Turner differentiates between *liminal* and *liminoid* phenomena. *Liminal* genres will be discussed in chapter 12 as they pertain to more primal and integrated ritual action in nature and society. *Liminoid* phenomena are collective rituals ("carnivals, spectacles, major sports events . . ."), both fragmentary and pluralistic and characteristically produced and consumed by known and named individuals. The bullfight is thus *liminal* in its calendrical, cyclical observance in festival but is also generated by modern sports promoters and managers for a mass audience. The bullfight contains the tribal-*liminal* response of a whole society deeply involved in the processes of industrial-*liminoid* culture.[33]

Hemingway's descriptions of the bullfight phenomenon in *Death in the Afternoon,* more detailed and hard-headed than in the festal ornamentation of the bullfight in *The Sun Also Rises,* shed light on the total picture of bullfighting in his novel, both the ritual drama of the *liminal* and the popular spectacle of the *liminoid.* The formal bullfight is "not a sport in the Anglo-Saxon sense of the word, that is not an equal contest or an attempt at an equal contest between a bull and a man. Rather it is a tragedy; the death of the bull, which is played, more or less well, by the bull and the man involved . . ." (16). At the same time, "the formal bullfight is a commercial spectacle built on the planned and ordered death of the bull and that is its end'' (373). Thus, the fight has both actual drama and artificial stimulation but is largely a performative ritual, what Hemingway called "an impermanent art" (99), an art "in which the degree of brilliance . . . is left to the fighter's honor" (91). The "brilliance" in large part consisted of the fighter's ability to work the bull: "he should . . . increase this danger, *within the rules provided for his protection* [italics Hemingway's]" (21). But these rules, as Hemingway labels them, are not so much fixed *ludic* categories of a sport's regulations as they are the accretions of technique established and embellished by brilliant individual matadors over generations. That technique successfully established becomes "rule" shows how crucial ritual motions were for Hemingway in sport as in art; the fighter's style was that of an action painter signing vividly in air. Hemingway believed that technique was passed on to generations of bullfighters, as changes in art or literature are effected by innovators building on tradition. These attributes were all that an athlete possessed to control and enhance his performance.

Hemingway was well aware of the popular sports element to the bullfight and the publicity and economics involved. He wrote that formal fights in Madrid and Barcelona are run on a professional basis and are tied to no ritual observances. Such "seasons" are closely scrutinized in *Death in the Afternoon*. They have all the modern sports apparatus of promoters, critics, sporting papers, and huge galleries. Hemingway acknowledged, "so many people derive their lives from the many ramifications of raising, shipping, fighting, feeding and butchering of fighting cattle . . ." (268). Although critics have stressed the primitivist fascination with the bullfight in Hemingway,[34] the fact remains that Hemingway's scenes succeed so well because he never loses sight of the fact that the ritual sport (a *liminoid* genre) occurs in a modern, secularized culture and is beset by financial and spectatorial pressures. In the strictest sense, the bullfight is popular sport spectacle. However, Hemingway notes that the dates of most formal bullfights coincide with national religious festivals and times of local fairs (37). As such, the professional fights are still subordinated to local, traditional culture.

Hemingway's three coordinates to describe the sport of bullfighting —tragedy, impermanent art, commercial spectacle—are most evident in *The Sun Also Rises*. Chapters 15–18 are the novel's climactic sections in which the competition among Brett Ashley's suitors is exacerbated and finally explodes as the festival of San Fermin begins to order and shape reactions of the ritual participants. Chapter 15 depicts the transformation of Pamplona itself into a festal entity and concludes with Jake's group watching Romero perform for the first time. The group is baptized into the festival itself and moves freely within it, although ultimately they are controlled by the pulse of the crowd. Movement in the mass is to the beat of the festival and the beat intensifies as the bullfight approaches: "There was a close, crowded hum that came every day before the bull-fight . . . This hum went on, and we were in it and a part of it" (161). After the bullfight, the festival resumes, moving to the same beat: "Outside the ring, after the bullfight was over, you could not move in the crowd. . . . The fiesta was going on. The drums pounded and the pipe music was shrill, and everywhere the flow of the crowd was broken by patches of dancers" (164). The chapter concludes, "The next day there was no bull-fight scheduled. But all day and all night the fiesta kept on" (169).

Moore and Myerhoff point out that there may be elements of chaos and spontaneity in prescribed times and places within the order of collective ritual. The festival is deeply upsetting and is a modern variant of what Turner would label a "tribal ritual," "an orchestration of many genres, styles, moods, atmospheres. . . ."[35] Quarrels and love-making are indiscriminately wound throughout the San Fermin festival as disorder becomes its own order. Romero is victorious, explicitly in the bullring, implicitly over Cohn. Brett makes another conquest. Jake is pummeled by Cohn while Cohn as ritual scapegoat is expelled from festival Pamplona as well as from the novel. Everyone is exposed in a dance of desire as within the masquing they become more confused and violent. Only the bullfight at the center of the festival unquestionably orders the passions and accords Romero his magnetism and final victory.

The fiesta's continual frenzy is not an environment where ritual sport can flourish. There is no activity that is "within the rules." Hemingway does show the play of the festival merged with the bullfight in the "running of the bulls," which yields only the chaos of *ilinx* and no meaningful ceremony. As free play, it is out of control and proves only how crucial the structure of the formal bullfight is to its success. In *Death in the Afternoon,* Hemingway distinguished between the formal bullfight, with its predestined killing and artistic heritage, and amateur fights which he sees as group killing, "a very barbarous, messy, though exciting business . . ." (24). The amateur fight is "all chance" and "temper of the populace" (373), in other words, a risky *aleatory* game dictated by the crowds. Even more random than the amateur fight is the running of the bulls.

During the festival in *The Sun Also Rises*, Pamplona itself is altered into an arena for the morning running of the bulls: "Workmen put up the gate-posts that were to shut off the side streets when the bulls were released from the corrals and came running through the streets in the morning on their way to the ring" (149). The crowds become endangered participants in the bulls' random, headlong dash for the arena. One man is fatally gored and trampled as Jake dispassionately watches. Later at a cafe, a waiter dismisses the dead man's bravery as foolishness: "A big horn wound. All for fun. Just for fun. What do you think of that?" (197) Jake asks, "You're not an aficionado?" and the waiter labels bulls as brute animals. Jake takes no position at all on the man's death, but Hemingway goes to lengths to record the dead man's name and to mention, "the day after there was a service in the chapel of San Fermin" (198) where the man appears as a pointless sacrifice to the festival. Without a system of appreciation, the *agon* is meaningless. To punctuate this point, Hemingway concludes by having Jake perfunctorily describe the death of the bull:

> The bull who killed Vicente Girones was named Bocanegra, was number 118 of the bull-breeding establishment of Sanchez Taberno, and was killed by Pedro Romero as the third bull of that same afternoon. His ear was cut by popular acclamation and given to Pedro Romero, who, in turn, gave it to Brett, who wrapped it in a handkerchief belonging to myself, and left both ear and handkerchief, along with a number of Muratti cigarette-stubs, shoved far back in the drawer of the bed-table that stood beside her bed in the Hotel Montoya, in Pamplona. (199)

Romero kills artistically and efficiently as part of the ritual whereas the bull had killed a faceless celebrant at random. Hemingway ends with a mixture of statistics and irony. The "ear cut by popular acclamation" is forgotten as the token of love in a hotel drawer while Vicente Girones' widow and two children accompany his coffin in a train baggage car taking them out of Pamplona toward their farm. There has been no tragedy, no "impermanent art," and no commercial spectacle.

When a professional kills in ceremony, the kill is rewarded; when an amateur performs, he is killed.[36] The crowd claims its own, rolling the music out for Vicente Girones' funeral procession where the marchers include "all the members of the dancing and drinking societies of Pamplona . . ." (198). "For fun" is meaningless to the waiter, to Jake, and to Hemingway. Such courage is a foolish waste and Vicente Girones' death is *alea* at its most fated, not to be dwelled on except as a festival casualty.

EXEMPLARY HEROISM:
PEDRO ROMERO AND JUAN BELMONTE

René Girard comments that ritual sacrifice defeats precisely the elements of death that escape man's control, including the choice of time and place and the selection of the victim.[37] *Mimetic* representation of an ideal of courage and craftsmanship in the face of death are not possible in the running of the bulls. The *agon* cannot be cast in vital terms. The fiesta without the formal bullfight yields no sporting lessons. However, the formal bullfight is a fine example of ritual sacrifice and is clearly set in opposition to the death of Vicente Girones. Hemingway best described the ritual through his metaphors of control and loss of control in Pedro Romero and Juan Belmonte.

The formal bullfight orders some of the randomness and anarchy of the festival and allows for a schedule, rules, and technique while at the same time confronting death in moving fashion. The celebrants swirl into the arena and watch an ordered performance. Pedro Romero is the central figure, a classically dignified athlete subject to risks both physical and spiritual, whose rite elevates himself and the spectators. Hemingway's verbal portrait of Romero dressing for his performance is mindful of American artist Thomas Eakins' paintings of boxers such as *Salutat*. Hemingway wrote,

> There were two beds separated by a monastic partition. The electric light was on. The boy stood very straight and unsmiling in his bull-fighting clothes. His jacket hung over the back of a chair. They were just finishing winding his sash. His black hair shone under the electric light. He wore a white linen shirt and the sword-handler finished his sash and stood up and stepped back. (163)[38]

Romero has blinding purity; he is 19 years old and a hero. As Jake thinks after watching Romero fight, "This was a real one. There had not been a real one for a long time" (164). "Romero never made any contortions, always it was straight and pure and natural in line" (167); "Romero had the old thing, the holding of his purity of line through the maximum of exposure, while he dominated the bull by making him realize he was unattainable, while he prepared him for the killing" (168). The "impermanent art" gave pleasure while increasing the tension before the final tragedy.

Thus Hemingway describes, point by point, the ritual motions of courage and art necessary for exceptional performance, and ideally Romero will live up to them as he concludes the ordered tragedy. However, he first must withstand the temptation of Brett Ashley and the threats of Robert

Cohn. Cohn and Romero stand in considerable contrast to those characters of the cafes for both men believe strongly and will fight: Cohn in romantic, boyish pugnacity, Romero in a kill-or-be-killed response to danger. Romero is shown to least advantage in his unscheduled boxing bout with Cohn in chapter 17, where he has not control of the "purity of the line," where he has, in fact, become the bull. Whereas Romero knows only that he must continue to rise and charge, that the bull must kill or be killed in the arena, Cohn has no arts with which to make the fight a meaningful ritual. His gentleman boxer's system will not sustain him. It breaks down; and when he extends his hand to the loser, the gesture is a gross assault on Romero's absolute courage. This competition is ugly and private. It has no ritual purpose; rather it is a climactic clash of sporting values in the novel.

Cohn and Romero observe different sporting rules. They are hardly on the same field of combat. Cohn knows only the conventions he has been taught; he has no instincts. Whereas Romero, placed in the position of the bull, has only his instincts. His ritual observances cannot control danger; he can only "take it" as do many Hemingway victims from football centers to fishermen who can apply no ritual or technique to the blows that fall on them. In his suffering in the hotel room, Romero is comic, almost a silent movie comedian who keeps bounding up only to be slapped down. He cannot be courageous when the *agon* is out of control. The fight is as absurd as that of the black American boxer in Vienna. Systems of sporting control may be totally meaningless in bad environments and Romero finds himself without defense. As Mike Campbell says after hearing Brett's account of the struggle, "I'm not one of these chaps likes being knocked about. I never play games, even" (191). Campbell has no conception of what has taken place and utters the Hemingway pejoratives "play" and "game," which are as derogatory as "all for fun."

Romero's ability to control the *agon* is shown to be susceptible not only to Cohn, a competitor from outside his sport and culture, but to pressures from within the sport and culture themselves. Hemingway reached into the actual pantheon of bullfighting immortals when he contrasted the confident young Romero with the veteran bullfighting genius, Juan Belmonte, on his reluctant return to the arena in the mid-1920s. Belmonte further comments on the plight of a sportsman who has moved past the framework of techniques and rules. Lardner had surrounded Jack Keefe with actual major league stars: Hemingway would make Joe DiMaggio a touchstone of excellence for Santiago in *The Old Man and the Sea* in 1952. Here, Hemingway portrayed a real champion's return while appropriating a sporting convention, one with roots in the battles of Greek epics and Biblical wars: the veteran champion versus the youthful challenger. In *Death in the Afternoon,* Hemingway notes Belmonte's intricate and dangerous technique: "he did not accept any rules made without testing whether they might be broken, and he was a genius and a great artist" but it had been a "decadent . . . impossible . . . almost depraved style" (69) that had led to great competition with Joselito (another outstanding matador) in a "golden age" (69). Bullfighting was altered as a spectacle to fit the impossible passes of both these champions: "They bred the bulls down in size; they bred down the length of horn; they bred them for suavity in their charges as well as fierceness because Joselito and Belmonte could do finer things with these smaller, easier bulls" (69–70). But with the death of Joselito (16 May 1920) and Belmonte's retirement, bullfighting was left to "a crop of new ones," "decadent, sad, and sickly enough" with "none of the male courage, faculties or genius of Joselito, and none of the beautiful unhealthy mystery of Belmonte" (70).

Pedro Romero is modelled primarily on Cayetano Ordonez who as "Nino de la Palma" had one brilliant year before becoming horn-shy. Hemingway writes, "I saw him in Valencia that year in competition with Juan Belmonte, returned from retirement"; and in *Death in the Afternoon,* he states, flatly, "I tried to describe how he looked and a couple of his fights in a book one time" (89). Indeed he did. Romero's victories are central to the climax of the festival and of the novel. Belmonte's travails in competition are almost as telling as Romero's triumphs and reveal even more about the "impermanent art" and the "commercial spectacle." With passion largely gone and reflexes slightly dulled by retirement, Belmonte returns to the spotlight. The spectators demand that he repeat his dangerous passes but are disappointed "because no real man could work as close to the bulls as Belmonte was supposed to have done, not, of course, even Belmonte" (214). Belmonte had made technique a rule and now could not perform by these rules. Belmonte is portrayed as the solitary, aloof artist, ill and bored. The tragedy is not felt and the sport descends to the worst sort of spectacle. The crowd feels "defrauded and cheated" and Belmonte earns "an afternoon of sneers, shouted insults, and finally a volley of cushions and pieces of bread and vegetables, thrown down at him in the plaza where he had had his greatest triumphs" (214). The crowd excoriates Belmonte as the Vienna boxing crowd had derided the black American fighter.

Yet Belmonte lost much more than the crowd with consequences for his art and his spirit: "He no longer had his greatest moments in the bullring. He was not sure there were any great moments'' (215). He coldly "picked the bulls out for their safety, getting out of a motor and leaning on a fence, looking over at the herd on the ranch of his friend the bull-breeder'' (215). At the conclusion to the climactic day of fighting, Romero is carried out of the arena on the shoulders of the crowd. The reader's last view of him comes in this moment of true public victory. Immediately thereafter, Jake sees Belmonte at the hotel in "a blue-striped shirt and a dark suit'' glumly eating soft-boiled eggs and surrounded by his silent entourage. The veteran star has compromised his great gift and has become simply another commercial athlete. The ritual born of the moment in a codified sport cannot be extended past its organic life. Belmonte is a victim of time's erosion; ritual lost its magic for the veteran star. Uppermost is the loss of passion for one's work which to Hemingway heralded the loss of skill or courage. By juxtaposing Belmonte against Romero, Hemingway offers the most telling comments about the contingencies forced on the Popular Sports Hero, who also has the dimensions of the Ritual Sports Hero. There is a private drama between Belmonte and his spirit, but it is Belmonte's need to strive for the repetition of his heroic performances that marks him as a Popular Sports Hero, compelled to perform before sports fans day by day in spectacle.

Romero's last fight during the festival is perhaps Hemingway's highest expression of sports heroism and it unites the popular spectacle with the "impermanent art'' while the expert kill completes the tragedy. The Ritual Hero triumphs in the popular arena at no cost to himself or his skill and literally pulls up the spectators' spirits along with him. Through Romero's finale, Hemingway depicted the survival of ritual in the organism of popular sport. Belmonte's pain "had been discounted and sold in advance'' but "Pedro Romero had the greatness. He loved bull-fighting, and I think he loved the bulls, and I think he loved Brett.'' During the performance on the afternoon following his battering by Cohn, "Never once did he look up. He made it stronger that way, and did it for himself, too, as well as for her. Because he did not look up to ask if it pleased he did it all for himself inside, and it strengthened him, and yet he did it for her, too. But he did not do it for her at any loss to himself. He gained by it all through the afternoon'' (216). The Ritual Hero performs first of all for his own pride and mastery and enhances the austerity of his performance if he gives no sign of his playing to the crowd. Romero shows his improvisatory skills when he maneuvers a dangerously color-blind bull through intricate passes, using his body intead of the muleta. With each bull, his confidence grows until "when he had finished his work with the muleta and was ready to kill, the crowd made him go on. They did not want the bull killed yet, they did not want it to be over'' (219). The crowd places an intense pressure upon him and, unlike Belmonte, he responds.

The kill is Hemingway's "inevitable tragedy," the ordered death of the bull which Romero handles as surely as he had the other motions. Again, an ear is cut and given to Brett and she reverently holds it in her hand but with this kill, unlike the death of Girones and the bull's ear shoved in a drawer, the ritual has had symmetry and scope and the trophy conveys meaning. The reader's last vision is of Romero in the crowd, not pummeled or diminished but truly heroic:

> They were all around him trying to lift him and put him on their shoulders. He fought and twisted away, and started running, in the midst of them, toward the exit. He did not want to be carried on people's shoulders. But they held him and lifted him. It was uncomfortable and his legs were spraddled and his body was very sore. They were lifting him and all running toward the gate. He had his hand on somebody's shoulder. He looked around at us apologetically. The crowd, running, went out the gate with him. (221)

Here is the real end to festal time and space. Brett and Romero go off together while Mike, Bill, and Jake dispiritedly wait for the festival to end: "the three of us sat at the table and it seemed as though about six people were missing" (224).

Romero finally represents attitudes that purport to show our prostration before mysteries of life and death but more pointedly highlight the will and the heart of the competitor rather than prostration. He is in an *agon* largely predetermined to lead to known conclusions, known to the crowd through repetition of ritual. Romero has climaxed the heightened reality with an expression of tragedy, aesthetics, and spectacle while "increasing the danger within the rules."

The real meaning of sport for Hemingway was not in a metaphor with roots in American culture *or* in Spanish culture but in a code of aesthetics. The sporting scenes and images which engaged him had to possess some fundamental shape and balance, beyond representative symbolism, that could mediate between tremendous natural danger and shock (both that of physical anarchy and random fate) and the ritual moment. Staring down the muleta, the fishing line, or the gun barrel at something enormous and deadly was a transforming experience which had to be carried toward more than it signified. The naturalistic confrontation with death had to be controlled by technique, courage, aesthetics, Guttmann comments that hunting and bullfighting resist rationalization, equality, modernity, and utilitarianism.[39] Just so could they be made to seem timeless and in the realm of performative art. As living rituals, they appeared strange to the American audience of secular spectacle. Hemingway provided Romero with a victory, the stature of which was difficult to recreate in a more frantic American sporting environment. Romero as competitor/artist has fought for human control. Romero has momentarily neutralized the festival's Dionysian spirits and has held off Atropos who hover as always as threats from the worlds of play and fate.

HEROIC WITNESSING: JAKE BARNES

A related issue to the Ritual Sports Hero's performance for Hemingway is the witnessing of his deeds, both individual and collective, for ritual demands that celebrants share in the power and beauty of the performance. What do spectators take from the rite? How do they learn and discriminate among sensations? What does the rite do for their own lives? The evidence suggests that witnesses, as well as Ritual Sports Heroes, seek control and mastery over dangerous experience. Ethical and moral decisions as well as emotional balance cannot be permanently fixed or resolved through sporting heroism,[40] but can be repeated in the manner of dispensations and intimations of control. These intimations are available to the Ritual Sports Hero's witnesses.

Romero provides Jake Barnes with a hero whom Jake can learn from and appreciate by spectatorial comprehension of the sporting rite.[41] Hemingway characters had previously learned much through witnessing. Young suggested that Nick Adams was the true witness born out of trauma.[42] The stories in the Nick Adams cycle were in American fiction's great tradition, that of a boy hero's solitary maturation in an antischool story. Nick is immersed in experience outside domesticity and the academy, as are Huck Finn, Henry Fleming, and Holden Caulfield, rather than in the more genteel and romantic experience of the boys school sports story. What Nick finally performs in the rituals of "Big Two-Hearted River" is done alone, with no wise mentor, no teacher except for the cleansing rite. As witness, Nick records with great clarity each scene as it is played out vividly before him. For Nick, "learning how to live in it" is to gauge exactly what to expect from experience. "He says he's never been crazy, Bugs," remarks Ad Francis in "The Battler," and Bugs' measured reply is "He's got a lot coming to him." Nick Adams is the witness who validates what happened not only "in our time" but in Nick's personal time.

Like Nick Adams, Jake Barnes is a wounded witness, no mere victim, but, like Hemingway, he is also a teacher of considerable discrimination and sensitivity, especially about sport.[43] Jake is not a participant in the ritual in a primary sense although he is the caretaker of Brett's emotional balance. Instead, Cohn and Romero instruct him in the sentimentally romantic and classically heroic modes of approaching experience. The Hemingway hero, for so long equated with the man of action, was also an exemplary witness. Jake is an aficionado who is passionate about not only the bullfight but about his own cruelly damaged life: "Enjoying living was learning to get your money's worth and knowing when you had it. You could get your money's worth. The world was a good place to buy in" (148). Jake's declaration may be contrasted with Belmonte's pain having been "discounted and sold in advance," although it, too, is the voice of prudence and care. In showing how Jake takes the best from even his reading experiences, Hemingway mentions, fittingly enough, Turgenev's beautifully crafted *A Sportsman's Sketches,* a pointed contrast in its conservative traditionalism to *The Purple Land.* Reading becomes yet another ritual that helps Jake hold himself together: "I read the same two pages over several times. . . . I was very drunk and I did not want to shut my eyes because the room would go round and round. If I kept on reading that feeling would pass" (147). In as fine a statement as we possess on the ritual of reading, Jake thinks if he reads Turgenev in "the oversensitized state of mind after too much brandy, I would remember it somewhere, and afterward it would seem as though it had really happened to me. I would always have it" (149). This last statement shows how Jake uses reading to counteract *ilinx.*[44] The bullfight is to the festival as reading Turgenev is to the spinning room, a microcosm of the central problem in a novel so often limned by ritual sport: how to control and discipline the self in the face of chaos.

Ritual may then reactualize any intense moment: to "have it" is mastery. Jake is acutely interested in possessing such moments and he attempts to pass them on as he teaches Brett to appreciate the fine points of the bullfight. Hemingway's phrasing follows Jake through his lesson: "I had her watch how," "She saw how," "She saw why" (167) as the description of Romero's work with the cape moves from instruction through appreciation to knowledge, empirically proving Jake's hypothesis that "Maybe if you found out how to live in it you learned from that what it was all about"

(148). Jake revels in "the absolute purity of line" (169) and by his tutelage literally moves Brett into deep passion for Romero. Witnessing is labor as well. One is *never* off duty. Jake puts final controls on experience, states what it means, and makes witnessing a further extension of the ritual moment. The hero brings his courage and art to the arena and the witness interprets according to rules as well. Eliade describes the initiate as "he who knows,"[45] and Jake is the insider who can differentiate among bullfighters and their styles and courage, as well as between methods of wrapping trout. Seeing "how" is seeing "why": procedure followed in the rite becomes action that can be perceived only by the aficionado.[46]

Hemingway banished the rule of gods, either Christian or naturalistic, renounced historically dimensional relationships for his characters, and sharply ridiculed heroic romantic individualism. He was left with enormous dependence on ritual action, which inevitably called forth its menacing opposite of indeterminacy. Such successive negations of novelistic strategies put great demands on the ritual moment to fill the emotional void of his characters' lives. Even within that moment he winnowed down to strict *ludic* experience to the point of establishing *ludic* categories of appreciation. He denied play and game while he exhibited mistrust of free play, an obsession against collectivization, and a fascination with death. All had to be held at bay. Hemingway was the rule-maker, setting the contest brilliantly and opaquely while measuring risk and victory. This was a doctrinaire sporting religion but, within its limited context, both simple and powerful. Sport became a repeated focal point for participants and spectators. If read out from the efficacy of the rite, a character was cast out of Hemingway's world that was so rigidly attentive to forms. Without the forms of ritual sport, Pedro Romero and Jake Barnes would be diminished in different ways: Romero without expression of his heroic stature, Jake without stays against his impotence.

When Hemingway created Jake Barnes in 1925, he had become the avid aficionado himself, fresh from assimilating the spectacle of the Spanish bullfight as an outsider from another culture. The merging of the Hemingway hero and the code hero in the novels after *Death in the Afternoon* can in part be accounted for through Hemingway's Spanish sporting ritual.[47] In *The Sun Also Rises*, Hemingway was at a rare point of balance in his fiction: Jake Barnes deals courageously with his wound while Hemingway does not yet wholly identify with a code hero. Romero's victory is in a vital sport in a ritual frame. Although Hemingway could tell Fitzgerald to "cut out this football," he himself remarked, "My idea of heaven is a big bull-ring where I have two permanent barrera seats,"[48] and this earthly rapture would dominate his creation of sporting values for the rest of his career. In his writing about sport after *The Sun Also Rises*, Hemingway loses the fine sensibility of the committed witness to the rite and falls away into the quarrelsome aesthetician of *Death in the Afternoon* and *The Green Hills of Africa*. When participation becomes a necessity to the Hemingway hero as it does for Harry Morgan and to essentially nonsportsmen Frederic Henry and Robert Jordan, they labor in the center of an uncertain, uncharted arena and are subject to grave dangers that are more existential in nature and which cannot be controlled through ritual.

BOXING AND HARD TIMES:
HEMINGWAY'S STOIC VETERANS

In his work after *The Sun Also Rises*, Hemingway continued to dramatize his fear of *ilinx* and *alea* through sport. Not until he created Santiago in *The Old Man and the Sea* would he portray another sports hero with sure motions in the *agon*. Fate in its *aleatory* state was a dirty intruder hurled at characters from nowhere and the defense against it was futile. Frederic Henry in *A Farewell to Arms* (1929) clearly demonstrates Hemingway's loathing of the universal "game" that is never revealed. When Catherine dies in childbirth, he denounces the victimizing by Atropos: "That was what you did. You died. You did not know what it was about. You never had time to learn. They threw you in and told you the rules and the first time they caught you off base they killed you."[49] This is the terrifying moment for Hemingway. The blows come down, unexpected; they give no warning and cannot be countered; Frederic Henry mutely walks away into the rain. He had begun the novel by playing "at war" and "in love" but the "biological trap" has ultimately made him aware of a game whose arbiter he does not know. A dubiousness about rules is extended to the "killing game." So many of Hemingway's sporting protagonists must "take it" without defense in precisely this game, one prefigured in the sporting violence of the Nick Adams stories and in the more satiric account of the inequities of football rules in *The Torrents of Spring*.

Hemingway's boxers were isolates who won no classic victories, who plumbed no sacred mysteries,[50] and who were particularly victimized and defenseless. The boxing ring as a theater for resolution was even more deterministic than the baseball stadium or the school playing field and doggedly one-dimensional. Boxing trapped its heroes in a ring and *then* defeated them. The boxing tale, from Jack London through Hemingway, fell into the twin evils of didacticism and sentimentality and highlighted the difficulty of placing the Ritual Sports Hero in the American popular sports arena. London described the bleak naturalistic side of the *agon* at its most simplistic in his boxing tales where his tough heroes and their lonely displays of courage point toward the programmatic Depression veterans of Hemingway, Horace McCoy, Clifford Odets, Faulkner (*Pylon*), James Farrell, and Nelson Algren. Through boxing, London could fully explore his confirmed belief in atavism, for he could portray the primitive responses of the fighter in the ring while he could show him asserting himself within the civilizing framework of the rules and his own strategy.[51] However, he did not believe man in boxing ever really eliminated his savage instincts and, as a result, London's boxers frequently resembled the great dogs and wolves of *The Call of the Wild* and *White Fang,* whose lives at some point demanded a "fight or be destroyed" response to challenge.[52]

London's boxing fiction is not his best work but it incorporated almost all of his major concerns, and the boxing subject proved a versatile one for his imagination as he popularized the *agon* of the Ritual Sports Hero. In "A Piece of Steak" (1909), London portrayed the subject of biological youth dominating the painfully acquired experience of veteran fighter Tom King. He used boxing in *The Game* (1905) as the "game" of existence in which implacable fate claims the young fighter who had been winning the fight of his life.[53] In "The Mexican" (1911), boxing is a contest which proves the discipline of a social revolutionary. In "The Madness of John Harned" (1915), London sharply criticized the bullfight, Hemingway's sporting apotheosis of ritual control, as little more than a slaughter of animals and he did so from the viewpoint of Harned, who contrasts boxing with bullfighting before he himself goes out of control and is slaughtered like a bull. London used boxing as a frame in his novella *The Abysmal Brute* (1913) to write a hymn to a primordial California superhero who marches out of the Sierra mountains to save the corrupt civilized sport in a naive fantasy.

In "A Piece of Steak," London wrote a seminal study of the old pro, of what time takes from his body, and of the knowledge by which he survives, even though Tom King loses the fight, his purse, and money to feed his family, having become "a piece of steak," the training meal he had longed for. Hemingway gave just such rigorous attention to the more subtle lessons gained in losing through Jack Brennan in "Fifty Grand." Both fighters lose their bouts but King's quiet craftsmanship becomes Brennan's desperately improvised defeat on a foul. The "thirty quid" to feed King's family becomes fifty thousand dollars on the line with gamblers attempting to betray the fighters and each other. Jack Brennan is an aging middleweight who believes the fight to be fixed in his opponent's favor. He has coldly bet fifty thousand dollars against himself but is suddenly and brutally double-crossed by his opponent, who fouls him in an effort to lose the bout. Despite the awful pain in his groin, Brennan holds himself together long enough to score his own low blows and lose on a foul. Brennan is furious when the rules are changed on him. His boxing technique is what he clings to during a painful nightmare.

Brennan's agonized final seconds holding on for the money are simply and effectively related by the narrator, Jerry Doyle. Brennan has no love for his sport. As with Robert Cohn, it is a means to an end. He is no competitor: "What the hell's the good in taking chances?" he asks.[54] He is logical: "It ain't crooked. How can I beat him?" His fighting style serves as a metaphor for his life: Doyle thinks, "He's covered everywhere you can hurt him." Jack comes alive only when he knows his money is at stake. His postfight comment is "I'm all busted inside" which tells the truth about his inability to feel passion for his work as well as physical pain; he is an American Juan Belmonte. When Doyle praises him for his quick thinking, Jack replies in the story's last line, "It was nothing." He knows and means it, that his final bravery did not come from individual courage but from anger and need. Brennan has no love of an art or fidelity to a code of conduct; he knows all too well how "busted" he really is when he improvises his response on the turn of the double cross. Emotionally, he is as grim as Ad Francis in "The Battler," as passive and distant as Ole Andreson in "The Killers." Hemingway's boxers simply did not have the measure of dignity that he gave to his Spanish sports heroes and their descendants such as Harry Morgan and Santiago. They are comics (the black fighter in *The Sun Also Rises*), grotesques (Ad Francis), romantics (Robert Cohn), resigned victims (Ole Andreson), or loveless winners (Jack Brennan). Brennan is merely "some boy" with passionless, hence defective courage.[55]

Where London saw a spectacle that civilized and codified violence, Hemingway sensed a public spectacle that perverted the physical pain and underscored the brutality without the ritual surety or heroism. He consistently diminished the stature of each boxing hero he created. The extra-real dimensions to the *agon* were not there. The boxing match was not a scripted tragedy or an aesthetically moving contest. Events were dramatic but not moving, relentlessly secular and too caught up in *aleatory* capriciousness. The individual boxer was vulnerable, either semiconscious, or unconscious.

A grim side of 1930s sport featured the beaten, mauled competitors of Hard Times who resembled the battered veterans of London and Hemingway, whether they were actual boxers such as Curly in John Steinbeck's *Of Mice and Men* (1937), Joe Bonaparte in Odets' play *Golden Boy* (1937), and Bruno Lefty Bicek in Algren's *Never Come Morning* (1942), or Thomas Wolfe's aging outfielder, Nebraska Crane, in *You Can't Go Home Again* (1940), who hopes to hang on for just a few more years in the major leagues because he is a family man plagued by money troubles.[56] There are also the pugnacious, embattled people such as Gloria, the marathon dancer in McCoy's *They Shoot Horses, Don't They?* (1934), neighborhood athletic hero Studs Lonigan in Farrell's Studs Lonigan trilogy, and Hemingway's Harry Morgan and the neurotic, combative World War I veterans of Key West in *To Have and Have Not* (1937).[57]

The 1930s athlete in American fiction was a representative Tough Guy more often than not. He was willing, like Algren's Lefty Bicek or Hemingway's Harry Morgan, to "go bad" for financial reward. The fiction of the 1930s that touched on sport was shrill, despairing, and harshly sentimental.[58] The closer a character came to struggle for biological survival, the more useful the physical struggles in competition became for the writer. Hemingway found the decade a more telling backdrop for his pessimistic rendition of the *agon*. The "over-match" he had so sharply described at the conclusion of *A Farewell to Arms* came to appear a cultural rather than cosmic truth and took on specificity in the American scene. In a decade that denied a man the dignity of work, Hemingway's central concern with a man's work defining the quality of that man became all the more relevant in the figure of Harry Morgan in *To Have and Have Not,* a naturalistic throwback to Norris' and London's tough individualistic heroes.[59] Harry Morgan experiences the extremities of the *agon* while blind chance relentlessly operates to destroy him. He initially believes in technique, then in courage, and neither is enough to save him.

Morgan is not an athlete or a sport fisherman but rather a fishing boat captain, a man who knows intimately the techniques and courage necessary to master the sport: he is also a husband, father, and workman plying his trade in a bad time. When introduced to marlin fishing in April 1932, Hemingway had quickly become a convert, enthusiastically proclaiming it totally satisfying as sport, a living, a spectacle, and physical exercise.[60] His mentor was a middle-aged Cuban commercial fisherman, Carlos Guterriez, both a pragmatic 1930s working man, who refers to a lost marlin as the "bread of my children" in a 1936 Hemingway *Esquire* sketch,[61] and an inventive, adept fisherman "using a handline with baits cunningly lashed at various levels."[62] Guterriez in his work and sporting roles becomes the partial genesis of both Harry Morgan and his purer elder statesman counterpart, Santiago.

In two specific fishing scenes in *To Have and Have Not,* Hemingway deftly criticizes the role of the shallow sportsman and expands the dignity and wisdom of the fishing boat captains, the little men so sorely put upon by the actions and value systems of the sportsmen. Hemingway's attitude toward sport and competition in hard times is first revealed in the dialogues between Harry Morgan, Eddy, his mate, and their client, a Mr. Johnson (a Frances Macomber who learns nothing from his guide Morgan). When Johnson loses Harry Morgan's whole line and rig overboard after hooking and losing a huge marlin, Johnson is not even aware of the disgust Harry feels for his performance. He has lost the line and the fish but, more to the point, his whole concept of sport fishing for "enjoyment" is incomprehensible to Harry and Eddy. His lack of concern for the spectacle he has made of himself further damns him in their eyes. Harry makes his living off these sportsmen, who still have money to charter boats even in the depths of the Depression, but he refuses to countenance their weakness. Johnson's unwillingness to suffer for the fish is extended to cover his unwillingness to see the dilemma of people like Harry Morgan. Johnson avoids unnecessary punishment; he doesn't consider that sport. Harry Morgan knows how to take punishment and sees it as necessary to survival, even as he has a craftsman's respect for the motion of the rite itself. Punishment is part of any satisfactory effort, especially in desperate situations. Harry knows that "a fish like that would kill you"; his respect for the dangerous adversary is a reimagined emblem of the matador and the bull. Johnson runs out on his huge bill, leaving Harry broke and unable to obtain any more charters; thus, it is Johnson's actions that turn Harry toward illegal carrying and personal danger. As with Cohn and Macomber, a deficient sportsman is shown to be a dangerously weak man, one who can affect the lives of other people. As one of the nominal "haves," he is reckless with the well-being of the "have-nots."

The taking of punishment is a central theme throughout the novel. After Harry is shot running liquor to Cuba, he tries to slip his bullet-riddled boat back into Key West. However, he must deal with another "sportsman" on a fishing excursion, a New Deal official on holiday named Frederick Harrison, whose interest in Harry's boat imperils Harry and his calling. Captain Willie Adams, skipper of Harrison's boat and a resolute, working-class have-not, refuses to do the bidding of the powerful visitor from Washington, D.C., proclaimed as "one of the three most important men in the United States today,"[63] Harrison is voracious but not as a sports fisherman; he would rather prey on Harry Morgan. Tracking the wounded man is sport to Harrison, whereas fishing he considers "nonsense": "This is really interesting. I'm glad to see this at first hand. Wounded as he is that man cannot escape," Harrison exults, but he also wants to know, "If you catch a sailfish what do you do with it? You can't eat it" (82). As Willie shouts to Harry lying in a pool of blood in his own boat, "He [Harrison] loves to fish. . . . But the son of a bitch claims you can't eat em" (83). Harrison is just out for the kill; he sees no economic relation between the fish and food. Hemingway turns fishing into a perverted hunt with no resolution. Harry Morgan and Captain Willie Adams pass judgment on Johnson and Harrison as coolly as Jake Barnes on Romero. Harry is a proletarian version of the exemplary witness as well as a man of skill, the natural gentleman secure in his knowledge of techniques. He is as watchful as Natty Bumppo who observes and criticizes the misapplied sport of Richard Jones in *The Pioneers*. Harry begins the novel by obeying all rules of fishing and of society, yet is thrown in, "caught off base," and killed. His skill at what he knows as a working man does not save him from becoming the prey of power. Johnson's criterion of "enjoyment" and Harrison's pursuit of prey are antiritual impulses toward an easy, slack pleasure on the one hand and an artless kill on the other. Harrison is as deficient as Johnson in ethics and courage but his superior power enables him to harm Harry further when he reports Harry's boat and causes it to be confiscated. Harrison's authority may be negated in the arena of the Gulf Steam, but he retains his power on land.

The paying sportsmen intrude on the lives of men who depend on them for survival, even as Richard Gordon (Hemingway's bad novelist, a Key West Robert Cohn) irrelevantly confronts the veterans in Freddy's bar. The veterans are Ad Francis characters, violent and eerily menacing with sickly pride in their defeat.[64] Their eagerness to battle each other is to prove how much they can "take it" for "first it was an art. . . . Then it became a pleasure" (203). When control of danger and pain turns from an earned grace to a masochistic delight, Hemingway sees sport and aggression as perverted, negated violence. They Key West veterans are the final word on mauled competitors in Hard Times, Hemingway's emblem of the last Bonus Marchers as misshapen embodiments of government default. "Taking it" in the 1930s has replaced "having it."

      Hemingway was a master of controlled sportswriting through his clarity in the rendering of action and his creation of the witness to sport as both a student and teacher of values. He remains a challenge to all American writers to perform and witness so clearly and elementally. The straight clean lines of his sporting portraits have been lost in the refractory distortions of modern media and sports hucksterism, which inevitably provided the new material for sports fiction after World War II. Into the carnival-like contemporary arena come Santiago and his great fish skeleton; perhaps they are a pregame novelty act or television happening. We, too, are left with a mere skeleton of skill and surety about sport in nature which Natty Bumppo had respected, which Faulkner's Ike McCaslin would embrace on different terms. We do not believe we can discover the truth of a man's character in competition without the trappings of protective laughter or the comfort of satire. The virtue of our winners is not believed, yet losing remains unacceptable, no matter how honest the effort, no matter how many homilies are advanced about "playing the game." Today's Jack Brennans and Ole Andresons are analyzed and understood all too well while Pedro Romero and Santiago remain as heralds of a more universal sporting order.

      That sporting order was most closely conceived as ritual. Hemingway was fascinated by the risks taken in serious sport, risks rarely taken by anyone in a society of spectators. Ultimately, the ritual crafted out of techniques and courage was created to defend against a world of danger and wounding power. If a character performed the rite, he might control the outcome of his own damaged life, if only momentarily.[65]

      To write of Hemingway and specifically American sport is to come up empty. Sport was an inclusive metaphor for him—part tragedy, part art, part spectacle—but also encased in protective ritual. Whatever sports or games fell outside his rigorous definitions were just not countenanced. Consider that in all his copious writing on sport, there are no American heroes. His two bona fide Ritual Sports Heroes are a youthful Spanish bullfighter and an aged Cuban fisherman. The Americans are defective and damaged competitors or traumatized witnesses: Francis Macomber, Jack Brennan, Ad Francis, Ole Andreson, Nick Adams, Harry Morgan, Thomas Hudson, Robert Cohn, and Jake Barnes. No triumphant American sportsman exists in

Hemingway's work. In his view, American sport could explain nothing positive about the individual because there was nothing positive about the individual American's relation to sport.

Beyond the American consensus figures of the Popular Sports Hero and the School Sports Hero remains the solitary Ritual Sports Hero in Hemingway who battles to combat the anarchy of play or the chance of game through his skill and bravery. Hemingway's great anomaly was his mistrust of illusion, the power of uncertain and creative play. He also was outraged by rules that in their very structure, decreed by sport or by the cosmos, dictated punishment with no defense. However, no American writer has ever so artfully shaped the *ludic* principles by which *his* heroes and witnesses lived, nor showed those principles with such fidelity to the shape of the *agon*. What sport he crafted was performed flawlessly so that we still see it and feel it as did Jake Barnes and Santiago. Yet all sport of any consequence had to be worked up into formal ceremony. If Fitzgerald had complained that Lardner had written of "a boy's game with no more possibilities in it than a boy could master," one might say with more accuracy that Hemingway created an adult's game with no exuberance or joy, its rigid diameters walling off any individual deviation from unswerving competition and emphasis on mortality. Its private geometry housed characters safe "within the rules provided for [their] protection." No play is unexpected or free for Hemingway remains committed to the ritual. Faulkner also felt the compelling power of ritual but he intuited a counterneed on the part of competitors to break into free play and, in effect, his meditations on the attraction-repulsion of ritual and its tantalizing and seductive counterpart of spontaneous play commit him to a wider and deeper universe of forms, which chapter 11 will examine.

CHAPTER ELEVEN
Faulkner: The Play Spirit

IN *HOMO LUDENS,* Huizinga wrote in "Play and Poetry" that "all poetry is born of play: the sacred play of worship, the festive play of courtship, the martial play of the contest, the disputatious play of braggadocio, mockery and invective, the nimble play of wit and readiness."[1] Indeed, so very much of Faulkner's fiction is born of play. Faulkner creates variations and precise approximations of the states of play that Huizinga describes as necessary to culture and to the birth of imaginative writing. The world of *Go Down, Moses* is most exalted when it embodies "the sacred play of worship," turning the hunt into high ritual. *The Hamlet* contains many sketches of the "festive play of courtship": Labove's lust for Eula Varner and Hoake McCarron's amazed conquest of her, Ike Snopes' pursuit of Jack Houston's cow, and the farmers' chase of the spotted ponies across the moonlit landscape. The spirited verbal exchanges, mad dashes behind enemy lines, and improvised battles between boys and men transform the Civil War into the "martial play of the contest" in *The Unvanquished* and *Sartoris* while the serious "game of Sartoris" dominates *Sartoris* and its doomed combatants. The "disputatious play of braggadocio, mockery and invective" is everywhere in Faulkner's fiction. In *The Hamlet,* Buck Hipps' attempts to sell Flem Snopes' ponies, Eck Snopes' taut rejoinders, and the mock trials and lawsuits are all vivid emblems of verbal play. Finally, so many of Faulkner's characters show the "nimble play of wit and readiness." Ratliff interprets sections of *The Hamlet* with great tolerance and whimsical insight. Pat Stamper in *The Hamlet* and John Sartoris and Rosa Millard in *The Unvanquished* talk their way into advantage or out of trouble. In novel after novel, play is expressed in different guises by characters who achieve altered dimensions through temporary rituals.

    Faulkner's use of play and the play spirit has become a subject of increased study; opinion is divided over his estimate of the value of play. Game-playing has been found the least attractive trait of Faulkner's most driven and inhuman characters.[2] Characters such as Flem Snopes, Thomas Sutpen, and Jason Compson toy with other human beings and manipulate them, patiently devising intricate swindles, sometimes waiting years to settle a score or debt. So many of Faulkner's driven characters lose their humanity in an urge to acquire something or somebody. Yet to dwell on the deception and chicanery of Faulkner's characters is to concentrate on a mere corner of the play spirit, and a lower one at that. Such a vision denies the sheer antic exultation of play in Faulkner. Such a vision belies the play, which is most often elevated to a spirited interlude, to an hallucinatory dream of order or mastery, or to sacrament.[3]

Faulkner did not see play standing outside ordinary or real life; he saw it arising organically from conditions of everyday life. He created scenes of play that erupted spontaneously in war, in trade, in the hunt. Faulknerian play is a bursting of restrictive forms in ritual by characters who create in the magic dimension of illusion and modulate *ludus* into *paidia*. In contrast to Hemingway's sport as binding, limiting form within technique and aesthetic capability, Faulkner's rule-governed games and contests metamorphose into fluid play: a horse race turns into a fanciful military attack in *The Unvanquished;* a horse sale becomes an enchanted night chase in *The Hamlet;* a festive hunt reaches up to touch the sacred in *The Bear.* Such shifts in the nature of the play in Faulkner underscore Huizinga's principle that play *is* order and creates order, the order of play, wherever it may be found.[4]

Civil War heroes, horse buyers, pilots, and hunters exist in Faulkner's pantheon but not without witnesses (Bayard Sartoris in *The Unvanquished,* the reporter in *Pylon,* Ratliff in *The Hamlet,* Ike McCaslin in *Go Down, Moses*) who express sympathy and frustration for both the dreamers and the driven: John Sartoris, Ab Snopes, Labove, Henry Armstid, Ike Snopes, the Shumanns, and Boon Hogganbeck. Victory and defeat is never a simple issue for Faulkner, and his characters win no easy victories in contests. Of utmost importance to Faulkner was that a character "did the best he could," as he intoned about Sut Lovingood, a southern boy with an individualist's code.[5] Faulkner also insisted that a character "perform his nature," in effect, play out his yearnings, goals, and propensities and not flinch from consequences, as M.E. Bradford has commented.[6] Faulkner's yeomanlike Armstid and Boon often compete desperately for prizes that are only delusions, whereas other characters ultimately refuse to play. For Bayard Sartoris II, Ratliff, or Ike McCaslin, "performing [their] nature" entails a renunciation and abstention from human affairs born of the knowledge of human limitations and always purchased at a cost. Bayard Sartoris refuses to take the ultimate revenge for his father's murder in *The Unvanquished;* unarmed, he faces Redmond in the rite of the duel but renounces the cycle of violence fostered by the war and the subsequent era of carpet-baggers and instability. In *The Hamlet,* Ratliff avoids major confrontations with Flem Snopes, while Ike McCaslin in *Go Down, Moses* is so appalled at the moral disorder of his ancestors that he refuses his birthright and the chance for descendants. Through these heroes and their abstention from rites, Faulkner makes a major statement on the cost of striving for a goal or competing for a prize. Such characters are struck by the fury of human aspiration and the resultant pain. They come to *represent* something, in Huizinga's terms, rather than to *compete* for something.[7] Hawthorne had tentatively championed the power of play to sustain personality and integrity in *The Scarlet Letter;* Faulkner's characters similarly play to salvage themselves. They strive in states ranging from low physical comedy to exalted witnessing.

While Hemingway sought out sporting environments away from the United States, in Africa, Spain, or the Gulf Stream, Faulkner never moved except into his own mythical terrain. His visions of play were immune to a northern, urban, industrial, educational pattern. He reached back in time for his settings—the Civil War, the 1880s, the 1890s—where he portrayed play as free of modern constraints. In *The Unvanquished,* he deepened our knowledge of the vestiges of the play spirit surviving in warfare. In *The Hamlet,* he humanized the Southwestern Humor tale, showing competitors in the *agon* as vulnerable and pathetic, yet in brave *aleatory* play. The movement of play from *Sartoris* to *The Hamlet* is one in which players begin as driven pawns of the Player-deity in *Sartoris* and end as pawns of Flem Snopes or of a more powerful Deity-player. In *The Hamlet,* players and spectators express an outrage against the distortion of nature by a force that competes and rules blindly in its power. The players demonstrate their spontaneous rebellion in tragicomic striving through play. Their play gives *The Hamlet* its small human triumphs which Faulkner stitches together in tolerance and sympathy.

SARTORIS, THE UNVANQUISHED:
PLAY AND WAR

In his chapter "Play and War" in *Homo Ludens,* Huizinga wrote of the archaic traditions governing war as a contest in which participants regarded each other as equal antagonists. He stated, "Fighting as a cultural function, always presupposes limiting rules, and it requires . . . the recognition of its play-quality." Caillois, however, writing to gain a perspective on modern warfare, sees the collapse of ritual and festival as directly applicable to the rise of destructive war, which rushes in to fill the cultural void.[8] Both points of view are seen in Faulkner's Sartoris chronicles of war. *Sartoris* (1929) shows play turning from insouciance and defense of honor to desperation and repetitive sensation-seeking after World War I, while *The Unvanquished* (1938), written almost 10 years later, is Faulkner's examination of the play spirit surviving in warfare and responding to war's intolerable impositions. Play is mechanical and compulsive in *Sartoris,* for its modern warriors have no meaningful rituals and attempt to recreate the equivalents to the violence of the war, while in *The Unvanquished* play both sustains culture and fosters dangerous illusions.

The Sartorises are Faulkner's most playful family in Yoknapatawpha County. Often foolish and "vainglorious," they have moments of spontaneous creativity coupled with rash, destructive, and wounding behavior in succeeding generations. Their decline as a family from Civil War leadership and gay heroics to World War I death and terminal depression is also the decline of the South's heroic ideal. Whereas John and Bayard Sartoris in the first generation played at war for stakes of honor, John and Bayard Sartoris III in World War I and its aftermath have only the ability to inflict injury on themselves through quixotic empty gestures.

Sartoris, completed as *Flags in the Dust* in 1927 and extensively revised, is now recognized as an expansive clearing house for many themes and characters which Faulkner would clarify in major works during the next decade. The Sartoris family is portrayed at the end of their line after World War I. Yet the Civil War is the scene for vignettes that establish the family's heroic and often foolish past glories and it sets the stage for a fuller examination of war and play in *The Unvanquished* which takes place during the Civil War and its immediate aftermath. In "An Odor of Verbena" in *The Unvanquished,* John Sartoris' brother Bayard receives only one brief mention,[9] but in *Sartoris,* Faulkner made the first Bayard Sartoris into a flashing emblematic figure, full of "frank and high-hearted dullness,"[10] an aide to the fabled Jeb Stuart. Bayard dies early one morning in a daredevil dash into a Union camp in search of a general's anchovies. He is shot in the back by a cook hiding under the mess table. This frivolous farce of a sacrifice sets the tone of play in the Civil War in *Sartoris:* both spirited and essentially trivial, not life-enhancing. A decade before the ebullient play world of *The Unvanquished,* Faulkner was not sanguine about the efficacy of play imagery and presented it suspiciously overlaid by knight-errantry and a predominant doom.

Jeb Stuart in *Sartoris* is one of those knight-errants, nothing less than a courtier from the Renaissance: "Stuart now carried his plumed hat in his hand, and his long tawny locks, tossing to the rhythm of his speed, appeared as gallant flames smoking with the wild and self-consuming splendor of his daring" (28). If Fitzgerald had Allenby, the football captain, as heroic emblem in *This Side of Paradise,* Faulkner offered the real romantic Civil War captain who in *Sartoris* plays hide-and-seek with Yankee pickets in and out of the woods, not as part of an attack or concentrated strategy but just for the mischief of it "and still in a spirit of pure fun" (26). Faulkner's Civil War play is not for the goal of winning the war but is the spontaneity of individual improbable gestures that have no direct utility. This Civil War play is in contrast to the stern reports of the valor of the Harvard martyrs and the organized efficiency of the Union officer class. For the southern daredevils, post-Civil War society was impossible or intolerable while the northern heroes went on to incarnate aggressive competition in the colleges and all through society.

The other side of Sartoris courage and sense of honor in *Sartoris* is a recklessness that is both wasteful and dangerous. In the fourth generation during World War I and its aftermath, Bayard and Johnny do not play as children but *are* children, self-indulgently trampling on their own lives with neither the high nonsense of Bayard I nor the stern leadership of John I. John Sartoris III ("Johnny") is almost successful in recreating the gestures of Bayard I. He goes up in a carnival balloon and lands in a briar thicket before a delighted country crowd. He and his brother Bayard are sent to the University of Virginia where "they shot dice or something to see which one would be expelled" (284) and when Johnny loses, he goes to Princeton! Johnny meets his death as a World War I solo ace, thumbing his nose gaily at his brother as he bails out of his crippled plane with the grand insouciance of the aristocrat choosing to die.[11] Faulkner uses the description of Jeb

Stuart again to describe young Johnny with his "tawny curls," "child's mouth," and "warm radiance something sweet and merry and wild" (284). Johnny thus joins Princeton's (and Fitzgerald's) Hobey Baker as college man and dead flying ace in Faulkner's bow to that popular image. Johnny is the Anglo-Saxon college hero, Confederate branch, with links not to Robert Shaw but to Jeb Stuart.[12]

Bayard III contradictorily uses will and determination to prove himself a free spirit. The flat-out speed of Jeb Stuart's and Bayard I's horses had been functional, enabling them to flee Yankees; Johnny and Bayard III have speed and power in their Sopwith Camel planes. However, after the war Bayard craves only speed and sensation for its own sake, announcing to Aunt Jenny that a horse war is a two-bit war (190); in fact, when Bayard tries to break a wild stallion, the horse unmercifully throws him. Bayard careens around the countryside in his car, "lipless and savage derision in his teeth" (107). Narcisa Benbow pointedly addresses his lack of spirit when she says, "You do things to hurt yourself just to worry people. You don't get any fun out of doing them" (208).[13]

Bayard's desire to get back to his brother Johnny in death defeats the play spirit. He hates his term of survival and wishes to be free of it. When his car veers away over a precipice to avoid a statue of John Sartoris, Bayard kills his grandfather Bayard II. Thus, Bayard II, who had avenged his father by a ritual duel, lives only to die in Bayard III's playless attempt to confront family history and violence. In his story "All the Dead Pilots" (1931), Faulkner had written that the World War I aviators in faded photographs had "a look not exactly human, like that of some dim and threatful apotheosis of the race" and added, "they are dead, all the old pilots, dead on the eleventh of November, 1918";[14] like the heroes of the Civil War, their utility dies with them. Bayard is a warrior whose "limited excellence" places him in the ranks of the irrelevant along with sportsmen Buchanan and Cohn who have no ritual surety. Bayard's death while testing a plane in the alien land of Dayton, Ohio portrays his end as a displaced wanderer outside the South and its history.

By the time of *Pylon* (1935), Faulkner's fliers have lost even any vestigial link to history and are midwesterners wandering through a new South of business executives, politicians, and new airports. The post-Sartoris doomed flying hero is the strangely inert and mechanical Roger Shumann, an enigmatic and soulless competitor akin to Bayard Sartoris III. The Shumanns, Jack Holmes, and Jiggs are perfect Hard Times characters, on the road, broke, and cynical, comprising a disaffiliated, asymmetrical nuclear family with few goals besides survival. Roger Shumann from Ohio dies futilely in New Valois (New Orleans), the mirror opposite of southern hero Bayard Sartoris crashing in flames in Dayton, and his death is even more pointless and spiritless.[15]

Although the subject of air acrobatics should have been congenial to Faulkner with his grand rhetorical style and its interludes of soaring imagery, in *Pylon* he seemed unable to keep his flourishes up, unable to approach the subject in high style. Faulkner at Virginia in 1957 dismissed airshow pilots as a "fantastic, bizarre phenomenon with no place in the culture or the economy"; he called them "frenetic," "almost immoral," and "ephemeral as a butterfly."[16] Like World War I pilots, such heroes were suspect, not tied to tradition or to the South or its land. For Faulkner the subject was ultimately frustrating, perhaps contributing to the dense prose of *Pylon,* the elaborate religious and poetic imagery, and the device of the troubled reporter-narrator.[17]

Sartoris is heavily portentous and very pointed in its *lack* of the play spirit except for the vainglorious aura surrounding the Civil War, an aura that will not come again. The game in *Sartoris* is explicitly, programmatically overseen by the author as the "game of Sartoris" which Faulkner described in the conclusion of the novel. Without the ingenuity and spirit he would ascribe to the Sartoris family in *The Unvanquished,* Faulkner concludes *Sartoris* with an elegy for "pawns shaped too late and to an old dead pattern" (303). Sartoris men as heroes have lived past an heroic age. Bayard III does not compete, nor is he spontaneous or free in his action. He only tempts fate in his *aleatory* obsession with achieving authentic pain. Thomas Carlyle's *Sartor Resartus* (1834) concluded that life was the robe behind which is the divine spirit; Faulkner's *Sartoris* has transformed the image of the robe to that of a game, behind which is the "Player Himself," the godlike novelist. Bayard never perceives this omniscient figure, but he has the last overview in the novel. Faulkner, the self-conscious author-god, offers the concluding observation: the "Player Himself is a little wearied" (303), the pose he affects throughout the lushly romantic anatomy of Sartoris decline. Unfortunately, Bayard as pawn is dragging mechanically, past liberating ritual, looking for the grace of *last* rites. Faulkner's initial attempt at working with concepts of play resulted in the image of a remote, cold providence and his pawns. Sartoris' playful creativity and spirited attention to duty were to be positively rendered in *The Unvanquished* when Faulkner cast them as virtues.

In *The Unvanquished,* play is represented in acts of momentary creative control that wrest dignity and humanity from the chaos of a war-torn culture. Yet the act of fierce *mimetic* representation in a wartime role is also shown to be an imprisoning choice for John Sartoris and Drusilla Hawk. Between these extremes of control and imprisonment, Faulkner examines the contradictions of play in war. The Southern Civil War effort as portrayed by Faulkner is less grimly martial than the Northern effort, more chivalric, and centered on individual bravery and daring rather than submission to a vast team effort. In *The Unvanquished,* play is not for preparedness for war or submission to its aggressive aftermath but is an emotional necessity. The opening of *The Unvanquished* is framed by boys' play and games as well as by boys playing at war and in war. As young Bayard and his black companion, Ringo, play at storming Vicksburg in the dust of the Sartoris yard, Vicksburg's "handful of chips" become vivid and real for "To Ringo and me it lived . . ." (3). The boys' play in the yard is reanimated at various junctures in the novel and culminates in Bayard's duel with his father's murderer in the concluding story, "An Odor of Verbena."

While Colonel John Sartoris is off fighting with his regiment in Tennessee, the boys play at being generals, "the two supreme undefeated like two moths, two feathers riding above a hurricane" (8). Bayard and Ringo play with a huge musket and carry it like a log at each end. They shoot a Yankee soldier's horse out from under him and believe they have killed the soldier. They then hide under grandmother Rosa Millard's skirts while a Union colonel bemusedly interrogates her according to rules of banter. When she insists she has no grandchildren, he remarks, "What a pity in a place like this which two boys would enjoy—sports, fishing, game to shoot at, perhaps the most exciting game of all . . ." (36). Rosa Millard asks if he would care for a glass of milk, but the colonel "just looked at Granny with his hard bright eyes and that hard bright silence full of laughing. 'No, no,' he said. 'I thank you. You are taxing yourself beyond mere politeness and into sheer bravado' " (37). The "sheer bravado" is the "nimble play of wit" that Rosa musters to protect the boys and which the colonel acknowledges as a game. Thus, the boys' play at war turns into Rosa's verbal defense of her kin and home. Her play spirit establishes a sense of equality between Rosa and the colonel. Faulkner further establishes the playfulness of the incident when it becomes clear that the horse the boys had shot was the "best horse in the whole army! The whole regiment betting on him for next Sunday—" (33). Thus, the horse's function is not martial but agonistic and integral to the regiment's sports.

The entire society in *The Unvanquished* is composed of gamesters, both in war and out. As the boys Bayard and Ringo control their anxiety about the war through play so do Uncle Buck and Uncle Buddy McCaslin enact a charade every night whereby they lock their freed slaves in the big house only to have them sneak out the open back door: "And folks said that Uncle Buck and Uncle Buddy knew this and that the niggers knew they knew it, only it was like a game with rules . . ." (53). Uncle Buck and Uncle Buddy then retire to a slave cabin in which they live and play head-to-head poker: "in the game as they played it between themselves, betting niggers and wagon-loads of cotton with one another on the turn of a single card" (53–54), betting on people and goods they did not possess. Faulkner depicts the old South miming its decline from slave-holding plantation days through games and fantasies with agreed-upon rules. The brothers play three hands of draw poker to see which of them will march with John Sartoris' Jefferson regiment. The whole troop watched Uncle Buddy win and become a sergeant in the ranks.[18]

John Sartoris himself is a rigid, stern figure of real heroic stature. He is not drawn to an outsized scale but is one of Faulkner's soldiers "doing the best he can." As his son Bayard states about his father's heroism, "he was not big, it was just the things he did, that we knew he was doing in Virginia and Tennessee that made him seem big to us" (10), a simple statement that confirms his role in *The Unvanquished* "doing bigger things than he was" (11). A responsible leader of men during the war, John Sartoris carries this role into the reconstruction era when he steers the rebuilding of Jefferson after the Union occupation,[19] and with his soldier/bride, Drusilla Hawk, brutally saves the town from a carpetbagger's administration.

Yet another side to John Sartoris is his flashing, reckless play at war, "scouring all up and down the country, finding Yankees to dodge" (59–60), more reminiscent of his brother, Bayard, in *Sartoris* whose pointless hijinks in the Yankee camp caused his death. John Sartoris is a nimbler, more creative player. In the novel's most complex play interlude, John Sartoris, passing through Jefferson on patrol, engages his son, Bayard, and Ringo in an impromptu horse race. Soaring over the crest of a hill, he confronts a Yankee regiment at rest. In mid-flight, he improvises a "full-scale attack," ordering Ringo to veer off to the side to begin the artifice of ambush while he charges down toward the soldiers shouting "Surround them, boys! Don't let a man escape!" (75). Faulkner has magically transformed the improvised horse race into the extemporaneous attack as John Sartoris creates the illusion. In an instantaneous shift, Faulkner changes the contest into representation (through *agon* transformed into *ilinx*) thus linking both of Huizinga's fundamental play categories. The free play of the horse race becomes the projected drama of the attack fused in one fixed image by Faulkner. Bayard sees the laws of motion and time stop "at the moment when Father's and my horses came over the hill and seemed to cease galloping and to float, hang suspended rather in a dimension without time in it . . ." (75–76).[20]

"Boys, I'm John Sartoris and I reckon I've got you" (76) he announces, proceeding to sustain the fiction of the attack. The Northern officer says, officially challenging John Sartoris' invoked vertigo of being surrounded, "Colonel, I believe you have fooled us. I don't believe there's another man of you but what I see" (78), thus repeating the scepticism of the Union colonel at the verbal play of Rosa Millard. John Sartoris' attack with two boys is a spirited recreation of Bayard's and Ringo's game in the dust at the outset of the novel. Finally, John Sartoris borrows a sporting tactic from the McCaslin brothers and "allows" the Yankees to "slip away at night in their underclothes; Bayard relates, "Father didn't laugh out loud; he just sat there shaking" (70).

The novel progresses through more emblems of play and contest that involve all segments of society. Drusilla Hawk relates a match race between Northern and Southern locomotive engines. Rosa Millard and Ringo oversee a complicated mule swindle in which the Yankees are again out-maneuvered and out-talked by Sartorises. Bayard and Ringo hunting down and murdering the renegade Grumby (who has killed Rosa Millard) and the courtship rituals stipulated by Jefferson matrons for Drusilla are yet two more fine scenes of play that dominate the sections "Vendee" and "Skirmish at Sartoris" respectively.[21]

Drusilla Hawk embodies some of the real dangers inherent in the power of play. Drusilla is one of Faulkner's most heroic and disturbed female characters as she attempts to enter the world of men and soldiers.[22] Renouncing the role of southern "widow-bride," she explicitly becomes a heroic figure as Faulkner initially describes her in the same language he used for Colonel John: "she was not tall; it was the way she stood and walked. She had on pants, like a man. She was the best woman rider in the country" (101). Her crisis is that while her mother and the Jefferson matrons scorn her for becoming a man, or, alternately, a fallen woman, Drusilla wants only to kill Yankees "in the garments not alone of a man but of a common private soldier" (220), to gain the anonymity and acceptance she craves. John Sartoris finds her hiding in the dress reimposed on her: "What's a dress? It don't matter. Come. Get up, soldier'' (231). Yet "she had let Aunt Louisa and Mrs. Habersham choose the game and she had beat them both until that night when Aunt Louisa went behind her back and chose a game she couldn't beat'' (232–33). That "game" is to demand that John Sartoris do the honorable thing and marry her. Drusilla's freedom is finally compromised, for to satisfy Colonel John's code, Drusilla must marry *him*. Faulkner makes a fine distinction as to what defeats her: "They have beat you, Drusilla,'' says Colonel John, but "they" have, in effect, convinced *him* to beat her.

Drusilla is at her mercurial best as voting commissioner on her wedding day, bravely riding with John to defeat the carpetbaggers. Yet even this scene is truncated by Aunt Louisa, purveyor of codes, as Bayard watches her "snatch the polling box from Drusilla and fling it across the yard'' (240), an action corresponding to the one early in the novel when Loosh, the freed slave most committed to the uncertain new order, sweeps away Bayard and Ringo's wood chips of war play, exclaiming, "There's your Vicksburg'' (5). The fragility of play as well as the tenacity of unacceptable reality is brought home to Drusilla, who in her protests "sounded like a little girl that had been caught playing in the mud'' (240). She can only whine, "John said that I—'' (240). After John's death, Drusilla becomes an avenging fury, both obsessed romantic heroine and deranged widow, crooning to the phallic dueling pistols and calling on Bayard to preserve his father's brutal code. Drusilla is the novel's casualty in play. Like John Sartoris, she is claimed by the violent extremes of roles she can only hurl herself into, donning them with a tenacity in which there can be no moderation. As a southern woman caught in the narrow choices given her, her play is even more desperate. If there can be no place for Civil War heroes in postwar society, as the Sartoris chronicles make clear, then Faulkner's Sartoris heroine has an even more impossible choice of roles and they break her.

John Sartoris casts a huge shadow that envelops Drusilla, Bayard, and Ringo. They play to match his play but always come up against the force of his intransigence. Drusilla, in effect, is to John Sartoris what Ringo is to Bayard. She must define herself against him. When Ringo says after emancipation that he "ain't a nigger anymore. [He] done been abolished'' (228), it is also apparent that the war has abolished Drusilla; her role as antebellum flower of southern womanhood has vanished as has Ringo's role of sagacious black squire. Both Ringo and Drusilla belong to a dead past, as does the flashing Colonel John, and they both desire Bayard to take the ultimate vengeance in his father's name, in effect, to validate their deeds and suffering as well.

The Unvanquished is idyllic at moments when play gives respite to the killing but Faulkner never lets the exuberant spirit of the war games become unreal or overly sentimental as the brutal deaths of Grumby, Rosa Millard, and John Sartoris, as well as the paralysis and stasis of Ringo and Drusilla, make clear. To make a game "at war" is not to make a game "of war." John Sartoris strives to uphold his duties and responsibilities while never forgetting that life lived as play is a brave challenge to fate, but he cannot break the cycles of violence. It is his son Bayard's final action, the renunciation of violence, that satisfies the rules of the duel and redeems an ethical dimension. Bayard moves out from under the massive weight of the war's roles and emerges from the thrall of the society that had instituted the roles. Bayard finally breaks faith with the novel's opening play images in the boys' game: to "hold intact the pattern of recapitulant mimic furious victory like a cloth, a shield between ourselves and reality, between us and fact and doom" (4). He moves past the "shield" that his father had been for all the Sartorises and constructs his own rite to transcend "recapitulant mimic furious victory" in a war long since lost to mediate "between us and fact and doom."

THE HAMLET: PERFORMING THEIR NATURE

Characters in *The Hamlet* strive mightily to achieve any sort of "mimic furious victory." Although their "shields" against the reality of Snopesian domination are insubstantial, their continual striving on many levels makes the novel Faulkner's richest statement concerning competition and play. In *Sartoris* and *The Unvanquished,* heroes are mounted men, from dashing would-be cavaliers to Civil War colonels, but in *The Hamlet* the yeomen chase their animals and can never get in the saddle, either literally or figuratively. John Sartoris and Bayard II may "float" over the hilltop and capture the Yankee patrol but such mastery and power are beyond the ken of the men of Frenchman's Bend. What the horse-chasers seek in *The Hamlet* is a unity, an ultimate reality that approaches the sacred.[23] They find themselves in a fanciful and profane illusion where they have become the played or playthings rather than the players, victims of not only Flem Snopes but of Faulkner's Olympian laughing providence in *The Hamlet,* "the prime maniacal Risibility" (191).[24]

The Hamlet is clearly a desacralized environment in which Faulkner is as disengaged and removed from the players and his pawns as he was in *Sartoris.* Although removed, Faulkner endows his characters with tremendous inventive energy and exhibits a pervasive sympathy for the dreamers and the driven. The men in *The Hamlet* are indirectly chasing the dreams of beauty and spirit even as they directly pursue possessions and sexual fulfillment. There is no fixed arena for games and play in *The Hamlet.* The competitions and swindles are played out by Flem Snopes and his less adept victims. Alternately, the men and animals pursue each other over the day and night landscape. A temporarily recognized arena such as the horse lot explodes into a dream in the countryside. Yet the desacralized existence still preserves traces of a "religious valorization" that places "relativity of space" under measurement.[25] If the sacred is preeminently the "real,"[26] the source of life in fecundity, the feminine characters of *The Hamlet* who are major symbols of sensuality—Eula Varner, Houston's cow, the spotted ponies—are heroines in an antimasque of desire and mute longing. They are inscrutable and powerful temptresses tormenting the Attic crew of Yoknapatawpha County. The yeomen desire "to take up [an] abode in objective reality,"[27] but in *The Hamlet* power and freedom are illusions and orientation is impossible.

Huizinga's formal definition of play was that of a "free activity standing quite consciously outside 'ordinary' life as being 'not serious,' but at the same time absorbing the player intensely and utterly."[28] Faulkner in *The Hamlet* plays subtle changes on "ordinary life" and "free activity." In the tale of Labove, the football hero is a dogged worker and achiever yet also a possessed romantic swain. The men of Frenchman's Bend are yoked to their meagre farms and wives yet they are "absorbed intensely and utterly" by the horse auction and the horse chase. Ike Snopes' "free activity" is the pursuit of a cow while Henry Armstid's desperate sense of honor is at stake at the auction and in the digging for gold in Flem Snopes' salted mine. Huizinga wrote that "coupled with this play-sense is a spirit that strives for honour, dignity, superiority and beauty,"[29] and even the lowliest Bend citizens such as Mink Snopes, Ike Snopes, and Armstid yearn instinctively toward such a state although in their cases it is continually undercut.

Since *The Hamlet* has no sacred dimension, no transcendental reference point, the novel remains in a profane realm, its seekers playing out in parody the search for authenticity which is countered by brute Snopesian automatism or Faulkner's mirthful abstention. It is a novel without a hero but with a number of characters seeking the trappings of heroism. Their mode is consistently that of games and play and is dominated by images of pursuit and bartering. The true subjects of *The Hamlet* are competition and play.

Hemingway in *The Sun Also Rises* showed heroism and witnessing in balance through Romero's rites and the momentary sustenance it provided for the spectators: a vital sport, a vital spectatorial form, and a realized heroism. In *The Hamlet,* with a similar large cast, many suitors, a number of games, animals as central sporting adversaries, a climactic festive ceremony, there is a cosmic *imbalance* where heroes go mad, witnesses are outraged and/or impotent, sensuality is made grotesque, and all play forms move out of the control of ritual and take on a desperate caste within the great scenes of physical and verbal comedy. All the while Flem Snopes is subtly defeating Frenchman's Bend by slowly acquiring the roots of commercial empire. Men as pawns are played first by Flem Snopes and ultimately by their own compulsive needs.

Flem Snopes dominates the competition of *The Hamlet* but what is most ominous about the dominance is his relative absence from the narrative. As a player, he has no physical skills, indeed hardly any corporeal existence, and he leaves nothing to chance. He is a compulsive manipulating architect who does not play in any freedom or uncertainty while he is the very antithesis of play's unproductiveness. Flem's victories are triumphs of meticulous strategy in which, soulless and inert, he orchestrates his economic takeover of the Bend before moving on to Jefferson in the last lines of the novel. Deficient though he may be in all human attributes of the games player, his strategy is impeccable and always within the law, which Faulkner shows to be a rigid unyielding force imprisoned by its precedents. The lawsuits of Tull and Eck Snopes are thrown out of court, not even coming near Flem's center of power. Lump Snopes, his less adept kinsman and lieutenant, chortles, "You might as well to quit. You cant beat him" (317) as the men chase their horses all over the county. After Mrs. Armstid is pathetically unable to redeem her five dollars in perhaps Flem's most brutal act, Lump again exclaims in admiration, "By God. You cant beat him" (322). As Flem tries to claim his soul in hell, the Devil can find nothing that will placate him as payment: Flem demands his rights to Paradise (earth) under the law and topples the prince of darkness from his throne.

Faulkner prepares the reader for Flem's demands. As a clerk in Varner's store, he never makes mistakes weighing the farm goods of the yeomen. He is "the still, impenetrable, steadily-chewing face throned behind the scale-beam . . ." (60). Thus, early in the novel, his two roles are prefigured, as the "throned" prince of darkness and in his perversion of the "scales" of justice, the human recourse. Flem's schemes are intricately worked out as he slowly trades paper, goods, animals, and land to great advantage, always one move ahead of the Bend's citizens.

To see Flem as evidence of a life-denying play spirit in Faulkner, however, is to miss the fact that while he is the major adversary to be battled by all the novel's characters, he exists to define the more variegated human yearnings of a score of other characters in *The Hamlet*. Flem brings to Frenchman's Bend the need to win at all costs, the modern capitalist obsession of the competitor, yet those who are partially imprisoned in their submission to Flem nevertheless accomplish a limited rebellion and move competition and playfulness into more vivid and spirited realms.

THE HAMLET: GAMES AND RITUAL

Flem Snopes works his will through his many complicated schemes but his opponents also try their hand at such manipulation and compete badly in tragicomic failure. The pawns in *The Hamlet* do not, as a rule, take Flem's domination or that of a grinning deity without a fight, yet their battles are fruitless. When Houston warns Mink Snopes against letting his yearling graze in Houston's field, he points out the countryside's unspoken rules in the pasturing of stock. When Mink continues to let his yearling trespass, Houston confiscates the calf and gets killed for his trouble. Other characters bend rules and play out schemes. Ratliff attempts a complicated goat swindle in a futile try at entrapping Flem. Lump Snopes hopes to whet the appetites of the Bend's citizens for watching Ike Snopes and Houston's cow so that he may someday charge admission for the spectacle. Finally, Flem snares Ratliff temporarily with the salted gold mine.

The great anger of the competitors in *The Hamlet* is constant and directed at a force which degrades them in their striving. Houston and Mink Snopes, murderer and victim, are equally furious at their lot: Houston at a mocking providence which has claimed his wife, Mink at Flem's good fortune which underscores his own meager bondage. After Mink kills Houston,

Lump Snopes haunts him, demanding that they dig up Houston's body for the fifty dollars Lump believes Houston had carried. They feint and parry, Mink wishing only to be rid of the insistent Lump. Lump bitterly thinks, "The murdering little son of a bitch. . . . I wouldn't have believed it. I wouldn't have believed a man would have to go through all this even for five hundred dollars" (248–49). They play a game of checkers, a nickel a game against fifty dollars: "They began to play—the one with a cold and deadly deliberation and economy of moves, the other with a sort of clumsy speed and dash" (250) until, thirteen games ahead, Lump realizes that Mink is deliberately losing so that when his 25-dollar share has been won, "he'll figure he won't need to risk going where it's at. So now he [Lump] had to completely reverse his entire tactics" (251). The game hilariously rolls on with Lump now losing as fast as he can until at midnight, he tells Mink, "Dont you see how it was tit for tat all the time? You had me and I had you, and couldn't neither—Where we going?" (252). Lump can't control his game and is knocked out two separate times by Mink; Mink becomes only more trapped and desperate, finally assaulting the hollowed-out tree with an axe to remove Houston's body and the money, an effort that is cut short by the sheriff moving in to arrest him as Houston's murderer.

The image of maddened men laboring in the earth for treasure not only ends Mink's game with Lump but foreshadows the concluding game in the novel where Ratliff, Bookwright, and Armstid fall for Flem's elaborate swindle by buying up the Old Frenchman's place to dig for the gold they believe is buried there. The yeomen are farmers who must make the balky earth provide for their families, but that role is perverted here. The gold is yet another grail, couched in the South's past grandeur, the opulence of the old plantation. The men who stealthily dig at night to escape detection must hide from the gold sun, symbol of their hopes, during the day: "they fled the weightless shadow of that, for which awake, they had betrayed themselves" (364). Ratliff and Bookwright wryly admit their defeat and chalk it up to experience, in the end mirthfully seeing who has the most *recently* minted coin planted there by Flem: " '1879' Bookwright said. 'I even got one that was made last year. You beat me.' " Ratliff's flat rejoinder is, " 'You beat me' " (368).[30] Neither of them can convince their partner, the disturbed Armstid, of the truth and he only continues to dig, snarling " 'Get out of my hole. Get outen it' " (368), an image of hopeless possession and greed reminiscent of Boon Hogganbeck's last strangled cry in *The Bear,* Part V, as he sits beneath the tree of gibbering squirrels with his jammed gun.

The poorest dirt farmer in *The Hamlet* ends not by tilling the earth but as Flem's most manic victim. The novel closes with the Bend watching Armstid in his third week of determined excavations, "spading himself into the waxing twilight with the regularity of a mechanical toy and with something monstrous in his unflagging effort, as if the toy were too light for what it had been set to do, or too tightly wound" (372). The image here of a defective toy stamps Armstid as a pawn of Flem's, a carelessly destroyed plaything rather than player. Armstid is played rather than given the dignity of competitor. It is this more hopeless role of plaything, being toyed *with,* that the competitors in *The Hamlet* strive to defeat. Only by asserting themselves in the game do they feel they can overcome being mere objects of the game.

Nowhere in the world of Frenchman's Bend is the need for this assertion more keenly felt than in the harsh and uproarious contests of horse-swapping and horse-buying that dominate "Fool about a Horse" and "Spotted Horses." The imaginative literature about horse-swapping and horse-racing had been an American staple for a century before Faulkner achieved its deft expression in *The Hamlet.* From Southwestern Humor sketches to dime novels and up through the fiction of Charles Van Loan, Sherwood Anderson, Hemingway, and Runyon, the world of the track and of horsemen had been depicted as the arena of dreamers and crooks, of the men who would be kings through the power and speed of swift animals, and of the men who would more coldly manipulate those dreams.[31]

In the fall of 1924 Faulkner was writing of his admiration for Anderson's short fiction, specifically "I'm a Fool," which he later called the best short story in America.[32] By early 1925 Faulkner and Anderson had met and begun a rocky, two-year friendship that was based in part on their childhood experiences. Anderson had worked in his father's harness shop in Ohio, and Faulkner had spent time in his father's livery stable. They even conceived a collaborative literary effort to transcribe a horse dream fantasy of Anderson's, but the project was never completed; however, in April 1925, Faulkner published a 1,500-word story in the New Orleans *Times-Picayune* entitled "Cheest" which read like a short version of "I'm a Fool."[33] Anderson used the racing meet setting for two other stories besides "I'm a Fool": "I Want to Know Why" and "The Man Who Became a Woman." Anderson sensed both the longing for success that gripped track people and the disorder that accompanied overidentification with horses and racing or, by extension, with any force that is swift, powerful, and seductive. His use of themes in these stories was to be refined and made more romantic and grotesque by Faulkner in *The Hamlet*.[34]

Faulkner's brilliant elaboration on the sensuality of the horses will be discussed shortly. First it is necessary to point to more comic and prosaic images of the horse in relation to Frenchman's Bend. The horse has passed from myth to literature and its survival is disproportionate to its displacement in industrial society—which is perhaps why Faulkner returned to the symbol again and again.[35] The horse in agricultural society has always had a welter of uses and associations for transportation and hunting while symbolizing power, strength, and speed. Images of the military hero as the mounted man are vivid in countless cultures and Faulkner creates his yeomen in *The Hamlet* as plebeian inheritors of the grand tales of the historical Jeb Stuart and the Sartorises and thus the ironic inheritors of the central Southern code of chivalry fueled by swift, daring power.

The Pat Stamper–Ab Snopes horse swap in *The Hamlet,* Book I, a revision of "Fool about a Horse" (1936), is a replica of many Southwestern Humor tales that featured a gentleman narrator (in this case, Ratliff) describing a dupe and the playful competition for his money, goods, or animals by a deadpan con man.[36] At the end of a long day of an involved trade of horse, mule, and cream separator, Ab Snopes gets back the very same broken-down horse (inflated into respectable size by a bicycle pump) that he had swapped in the morning. Pat Stamper is a character out of Longstreet or Kirkman or Hooper, only seen from the outside in his commercial role, a genial, part-Snopes, part-Ratliff figure who "played horses against horses as a gambler plays cards against cards, for the pleasure of beating a worthy opponent as much as for gain . . ." (30).

Ab Snopes, Flem's father, is after only a modicum of honor and success in his dealings with Stamper; however, his game is a losing one. He frantically attempts to mount the horse he has swapped for the one he got rid of in the morning but is slammed to the ground repeatedly. As the 8-year-old Ratliff remembers, "It was just exactly like Ab wanted that horse to throw him, hard, like the ability to his bones and meat to stand that ere hard ground was all he had left to pay for something with life enough left to get us home" (42). When he is bested, "Ab wasn't trading now. He was desperate sitting there like he couldn't even see . . ." (41). The seeds of resentment and determination are in Ab and his wife, and in the next Snopes generation, Flem will not be beaten. The inability to end the game, the ability to withstand punishment, and the lack of play spirit are all etched in

Ab through his traumatic and total defeat, first at the hands of Pat Stamper and then through his wife's derision. Twenty-three years later, Ab is still poor, but an accomplished barn-burner and extortionist with no regard for any animal or any person. As Ratliff watches, Ab "turned the team, their heads tossing and yawing, their stride breaking as he sawed them about with absolutely needless violence" (49). Ratliff thinks, "he still handles a horse or a mule like it had done already threatened him with its fist before he even spoke to it" (49), initially identifying the wariness with which all men approach animals in *The Hamlet.*

The violence of Flem Snopes' games is more couched in planning and legalism. In the "Spotted Horses" section of *The Hamlet,* revised from the 1931 story, Ab Snopes' desperation is transferred to the yeomen while Flem Snopes and Buck Hipps split the Pat Stamper figure, Flem never engaging in the literal contest, taking no joy from it but only profit, and Buck Hipps resolutely attempting to maintain a mask of nonchalant shrewdness in the face of potential disaster.

The horse sale in "Spotted Horses" provides fine examples of the formal properties of collective ceremony and secular ritual. Moore and Myerhoff sketch six categories of secular ritual in broad outline: repetition, acting, "special" behavior or stylization, order, evocative presentational style or staging, and the collective dimension.[37] In "Spotted Horses," there is repetition in the time-honored Southwestern horse sale as social occasion in a day-long suspension of drudgery and routine. Roles are acted out by the yeomen as sceptical prodders of Buck Hipps, who strives to be verbally dexterous and masterful, the auctioneer trying to best the men. The horses are severely stylized and symbolized past their prosaic utility, set apart from the mundane into wondrous buys which should not be passed up. The order of the horse sale deceptively masks the "chaos and spontaneity" envisioned by Moore and Myerhoff. That chaos irresistibly breaks out when Buck Hipps attempts to saddle a horse, for the ensuing comic anarchy shatters the "exaggerated precision" of ceremonial order. The ceremony is carefully staged and manipulated to stimulate the interest of the men and to engender a swift commitment from them. Finally, the collective dimension of the ceremony encodes the message of the social meaning: the men *en masse* are in thrall to Flem and his machinations. The ritual is mounted by a negative power that denies the men their freedom.

The horse-lot auction is secular ritual celebrating a Southern tradition with an explicit purpose and implicit relationships, conveyed by a host of symbols and messages that confirm both the reality and the illusion of the scene and hold off disaster, at least until nightfall. As Huizinga stresses, play is voluntary by the quality of freedom alone and marks itself off from the course of natural process. Play is also distinct as to locality and duration,[38] in this case, the corral and then the night-long chase that plays itself out into exhaustion and frustration. But just as surely, these play areas grow out of the prosaic, everyday life of the men. The magic is willed by the participants and the circuit of associations between the real and fanciful is more of a relationship than Huizinga's applied definition would indicate.[39]

Beyond the specific ritual, "Spotted Horses" is always a contest, first between Buck Hipps and the yeomen, but also between the men and the ponies, the men and their women, and finally between the men and their own yearning natures. "Spotted Horses" combines the verbal parries of Southwestern Humor with surreal action writing of great beauty.[40] The scene at the lot is punctuated by sharp verbal rejoinders, a fine example of what Huizinga termed "disputatious play" full of mockery and invective. The commentary centers on the work role of the animals and the playful scepticism of the farmers. Eck Snopes initially says, "Me buy one of them things? When I can go to the river anytime and catch me a snapping turtle or a moccasin for nothing?" (286) and he also opines, "I wouldn't buy nothing I was afraid to walk up and touch" (289) and "What need I got for a horse I would need a bear-trap to catch?" (293). Of course, Eck ultimately owns two horses, the one he buys and the one Buck Hipps gives him to start the bidding, but in reality he has neither horse. He breaks the neck of the gift horse and never catches the one he buys.

Another example of the verbal play of the horse auction is the language of Buck Hipps himself as he tries to stir up commercial interest and suppress the obvious fact of the ponies' wildness. He begins with reference to the work world of the farm and the horses' utility: "Young, sound, good for saddle or work stock, guaranteed to outlast four ordinary horses . . ." (290). When physically threatened by the hooves, his speech breaks into comic fragments of commerce and fearful frustration, "Look him over quick. Them shoulders and—and legs you whoa I'll tear your face right look him over quick boys worth fifteen dollars of let me get a holt of who'll make me a bid whoa you blare-eyed jack rabbit, whoa!" (292–93). The auction is finally completed, all in a difficult day's work for Buck Hipps. In the early evening when he collects his money from Flem Snopes and departs for Jefferson, the narrative shifts from the essentially ritualistic, familiar game between the men of the Bend and the horse trader into a playful pageant of swirling motion and pursuit.

Will Varner and Ratliff both comment on the outcome of Flem's game in "Spotted Horses." As detached and shrewd commentators all during the novel, they attempt to sum up the cost of the sale and the chase. Varner takes his usual whimsical view when he says, "They'll get the money back in exercise and relaxation. You take a man that ain't got no other relaxation all year long except dodging mule-dung up and down a field furrow. . . . If we had just knowed about this in time, we could have trained up a pack of horse dogs. Then we could have held one of these field trials" (313). Varner's detached comic view of the men at play sees the night's frolic as perhaps the occasion for a sporting event; but Ratliff, speaking as always in sympathy for the plight of the men, replies, "That's one way to look at it," meaning to turn the scene into a comic sport spectacle, but he continues, "In fact, it might be a considerable comfort to Bookwright and Quick and Freeman and Eck Snopes and them other new horse owners if that side of it could be brought to their attention, because the chances are ain't none of them thought to look at it in that light yet" (313). Ratliff not only knows that the economic investment of the Bend is of great importance but as a humanist he senses the need of the men to win at something, to chase down their dreams as a matter of pride and honor. What begins as a comic horse deal has real and potentially tragic consequences in the life of an indigent family such as the Armstids. The rural ritual with its familiar motions to both seller and buyers is replaced by a very powerful free play.

THE HAMLET: PLAY AND FREEDOM

The amusement of Will Varner at the men in the chase and Ratliff's concern for real consequences are two responses to the Snopesian game being played at the horse lot. Yet beyond all Flem's swindles, deals, and machinations is a more powerful play spirit projected by Faulkner that leads the characters of *The Hamlet* toward obsessive playing. As Mrs. Littlejohn says in disgust, "You men. . . . See if you cant find something else to play with that will kill some more of you" (310). The men of the Bend "perform their nature," what Faulkner at Virginia called "puerile folly" as well as hope and aspiration.[41] The acting out of their roles is the predominant play in the action as Varner's and Ratliff's visions are absorbed in the great disturbance play creates (its own order), rather than in the consequences perceived from the Snopesian games themselves.

A compellingly dangerous sensual pull on all the men of the Bend drives them beyond Flem Snopes; it is this force which gives them their momentary courage and insight. However, the insight is into a madness reinforced by the power of women and animals that suggests a profound disorder presided over by a mechanical laughing deity, allowing the freedom and uncertainty of play but bringing no lasting result. In play, then, do men in *The Hamlet* approach not the sacred but the ultimate meaning of the profane's greatest mystery, the sensual. The impulse for the men is to lose themselves in another reality, as participants in a sacred ritual desire to be in a self-realizing position; however, they do not find a concrete reality but only ephemeral illusions of beauty and power. Fink has noted that in the power of play, men are "at stake" in an inscrutably threatening sense, that they hide their real selves behind a role and are submerged in it. He states, "We play in the so-called real world, but while playing there emerges an enigmatic realm that is not nothing and yet is nothing real." [42] In *The Hamlet,* such realms are constantly being created wherever characters interact, in horse lots or in chases over the countryside.

The most raucous sensual play in *The Hamlet* is within the mating and courting rituals that are games with strategy but that also have a freedom and unpredictability that place them in the mode of play. Houston contests with Lucy Pate in the courting play that shades closest to a strategic game. As children, Lucy tries to get him through school by doing all his homework and by writing his test papers. On her part, "It was a feud, a gage, wordless, uncapitulating, between that unflagging will not for love or passion but for the married state, and that furious and as unbending one for solitariness and freedom" (211). Houston is wary of her game: "So he won that first point. He failed" (211) but "he believed that he had taken the last point, too, and the game; it was almost two months before he discovered that she too had failed in her last year's examinations" (212); "now it had become a contest between adults" (212) and Houston at sixteen flees his fate "to escape his future" (214). Years later he is inexorably drawn back to marry her. Ike Snopes is a determined suitor, three times apprehending and leading off Houston's cow in a great display of purposeful, instinctive obsession. Labove likewise doggedly waits six years until he can stand no more before accosting Eula. The suitors who contest with Hoake McCarron for Eula's favors are a flighty group of agitated swains who without real strategy hover in the countryside in their buckboards and rigs: "They met at the community parties which would be held in the now empty schoolhouse. . . . They arrived in a group, they chose one another monotonously in the twosing games, the boys clowning and ruthless, loud'' (128). Yet they are working men, ''the eyes filled with the memory of a week of hard labor in fields behind them and knowledge of another week of it ahead . . .'' (132). The pursuit of Eula causes them to become violent and to displace some of the sexual energy. They would ''dismount and hitch the horses and mules and with bare fists fight silently and savagely . . . for the time being freed even of rage and frustration and desire, beneath the cold moon, across the planted land'' (132).

The anger of the suitors in their futility is somewhat alleviated by their scuffles yet the ''moon'' remains ''cold'' to them, a maddening mistress of romance as it capriciously beams down on the reality of their drudgery, the ''planted land.'' In *The Hamlet,* women continually gain the positions of power, either sensual or domestic, while the men battle each other or their own natures. The women of the novel are inscrutable, dominant, Amazon-like, constant in the face of their would-be lovers. When Labove rushes Eula, she is ''big, immobile, almost eye to eye with him in height'' (121); Mink Snopes catches a first glimpse of his future wife and notices ''her height and size and the short hair; he saw not a nympholept but the confident lord of a harem'' (241). The fury of Jody Varner at Eula's voluptuousness is the low comic counterpart to Quentin Compson's incestuous struggle in *The Sound and the Fury.* When Houston apprehends his cow and wrests her back from Ike Snopes, he can only splutter, ''Git on home, you damn whore!'' (178). Not only are some females in *The Hamlet* the purveyors of a dominating sensuality, they are also patient, tireless, and implacable, never believing that the men will behave rationally or achieve any victories. They wait to pick up the shards of the broken dreams. Ab Snopes' wife goes surely about her task of regaining the cream separator. Eula parries her suitors with ease. Lucy Pate picks out Houston and snares him while Mink Snopes suffers a similar fate from his intended.

In ''Spotted Horses,'' Mrs. Littlejohn, Mrs. Tull, and Mrs. Armstid are dogged, earthbound, and concerned with daily survival.[43] They are opposed by the fatally attractive ponies which are distinctly feminized: ''the horses stood in a restive clump, larger than rabbits and gaudy as parrots. . . . Calico-coated, small-bodied, with delicate legs and pink faces in which their mismatched eyes rolled wild and subdued, they huddled, gaudy motionless and alert, wild as deer, deadly as rattlesnakes, quiet as doves'' (275).[44] These dangerous, flighty females are opposed by Mrs. Littlejohn's jingling dinner bell at which sound, "the horses rushed again, the earth of the lot becoming vibrant with the light dry clatter of hooves" (288), as if the horses know the cry of their opponents for the men's attention. All during the day-long auction, Mrs. Littlejohn moves slowly back and forth across her yard, cooking and washing clothes. Henry Armstid plaintively asks at dusk, "who'll help me catch my horse?" (298) and "from Mrs. Littlejohn's kitchen the smell of frying ham came" (298). As the men tentatively move toward the lot to take possession of the ponies, "Mrs. Littlejohn was in her backyard, gathering the garments from the clothesline; they could still smell the ham" (304). Her day is ending while their night chase is about to begin.

The chase of the ponies by the men after they escape from the lot is merely the climax to a recurring subject of men dominated by the women and, by extension, the animals which the men cannot control. They refuse to concede that the animals have more power but are continually defeated and hounded by these agents of a laughing providence. The emblems are many: Ab Snopes is slammed to the ground repeatedly by his horse at Pat Stamper's; I.O. Snopes is "hurled hammer and all into the shrinking-tub" by Houston's stallion at the blacksmith shop. This same stallion stomps Lucy Pate Houston to death, plunging Houston into grief. Houston's dog plagues Mink Snopes as he labors to dig out Houston's body: "Then he heard the swift soft feet behind him and he fell again and on his hands and knees again he watched it soar over him and turn in midair so that it landed facing him, its eyes like two cigar-coals as it sprang at him before he could rise" (259).

It is this vaulting motion of freedom and flight that punctuates all the hallucinatory encounters with powerful animals in *The Hamlet*. Through both the realistic horse sale and the romantic chase of the horses, Faulkner's primary resource is a tremendous grasp of physical motion, now slowed to a taut ballet, now speeded up to a frantic thunder. Such changes in pace are the *sine qua non* of any narrative of physical action. The famous image of Eck Snopes' pony galloping through Mrs. Littlejohn's house and hallway effectively merges the seductive and domestic for a brief suspension of time, but then the horse soars free of the house, "outward, hobgoblin and floating, in the moon" (308).[45] The horse escapes, what none of the married men can ever really do except for the brief interval of the chase. Night has endowed the bodies of the ponies with "almost a brilliance" (304) as "across the dreaming and silver night a faint sound like remote thunder came and ceased" (309).

Even on their first night in the lot the horses had looked seductive and ominous. As dusk gathered, "it˙was merely a translation from the lapidary-dimensional of day to the treacherous and silver receptivity in which the horses huddled . . . in mirage-like clumps from which came high abrupt squeals and the vicious thudding of hooves" (280). Both "squeals" and "vicious thudding" punctuate the night. The dual nature of the animals desired is constant and made eerily vivid "with that other worldly quality of moonlight" (304) (the quality that had seized Eula's suitors, Jack Houston, and Mink Snopes), so that they are "no longer horses, no longer flesh and bone . . ." (304). What starts out to be a horse sale ends with the tinge of madness rampant.

The most vivid images of the horses and men in *The Hamlet* are those of an equilibrated madness, of both animal and pursuer, in which the giddy playfulness of the dangerous creature is matched against the overwhelming desire of the pursuer to finally win something. When Ike Snopes tracks his bovine love over hill and down dale, he is haunted by a furious horse which is almost supernatural in its power and speed: "The sound was everywhere, above and beneath, funneling downward at him, he heard the hooves and as he paused, his breath indrawn, the horse appeared, materialised, furiously out of the smoke, monstrous and distorted, wild-eyed and with tossing mane, bearing down upon him. He screamed too. For an instant they yelled face to face, the wild eyes, the yellow teeth, the long gullet red with ravening gleeful triumph . . ." (174–75). The horse as a force of nonrational, brute speed and strength is matched with the idiot sick with desire. They constitute the twin faces of Faulkner's extreme mirror to be held up to the horse buyers and suitors. In the lot, just before the stampede, the horses overwhelm the men with fear: "for an instant of static horror men and animals faced one another, then the men whirled and ran before a gaudy vomit of long wild faces and splotched chests which overtook and scattered them and flung them sprawling aside . . ." (306). They, men and horses, are a perfectly matched pair since Faulkner stipulates the men are both players and consumed by what they play for. They possess no control over their play but rather have given themselves up to the festive chase. In the end, they are being played, toyed with by that force which renders them helpless.

But what force is it? Not Snopesian in its elemental physical qualities and heightened sensuality, this principle is more fundamental and powerful. Houston, who is involved directly or indirectly in many of the novel's comic and obsessed play interludes, bitterly muses as he chases his cow that "once more he had been victim of a useless and elaborate practical joke at the hands of the prime maniacal Risibility . . .'' (191). This manic laughing god is the first principle in Faulkner's universe in *The Hamlet* and, in yet another comic twist, is responsible for Houston's death. In a black fit of melancholy after his wife's death under the stallion's thumping hooves, Houston says, ''I dont understand it. I dont know why. I wont ever know why. But You cant beat me. I am strong as You are. You cant beat me'' (220).[46]

The novel's next sentence is ''He was still alive when he left the saddle,'' shot down by Mink Snopes. Shaking his fist at the novel's prime mover dispatches him instantly from the novel. One can see this death as the immediate revenge of the laughing god made more absurd by his agent, Mink, who possesses a gun with one bullet, a gun greased with bacon fat. Houston never does know whom or what he is contesting and dies the pawn victim of Player-author Faulkner. Earlier, Houston must have represented Faulkner's own stance toward the novel's unfolding when he labels the ''prime maniacal Risibility'' and thinks afterward that ''he found that the grim icy rage had given way to an even more familiar sardonic humor, a little clumsy and heavyfooted perhaps [as when Houston is murdered], but indomitable and unconquerable above even the ruthless grief'' (191). In a sense, there is no god but a darkly amused omniscient narrator in *The Hamlet* and Flem is the Devil. Play and game, even with a mocking deity or storekeeper devil, are what the characters all put their stake in, with meager result. The horse plaguing Ike Snopes in ''ravening gleeful triumph'' is strongly suggestive of the ''maniacal Risibility'' as sentinel or agent, more tantalizing than Flem Snopes because freer, richly physical, and graceful. Commensurate with man's folly is a god who grins back in mirror-image with power to disrupt and wound: *homo ludens* has been superseded by *deus ludens,* a stand-in for *auctor ludens.* This god's unspoken crime is, of course, to allow a Flem Snopes dominance and do nothing about it, but then Faulkner suggests that is not His sphere.

Faulkner's attitude toward *The Hamlet*'s action personifies what Hayden White describes as Hegel's vision of romantic tragicomedy

which seeks to mediate between the Comic and Tragic visions of the world, but does so only formally—that is, by representing within the same action the representatives of each view, never combining or unifying them, but leaving the world as sundered as it originally found it, with no higher principle of unity being given which consciousness might turn into an object of contemplation for the promotion of wisdom about a world thus severed within itself.[47]

The "consciousness" thus identified in *The Hamlet* has its two main spokes-men in Will Varner and Ratliff, who can put Flem Snopes in perspective but who are ignorant of or unwilling to take on the "maniacal Risibility." Rage is always governed by sardonic humor which controls their reactions in the novel's major sections.

Varner and Ratliff articulate Faulkner's bitter mirth which predomi-nates in *The Hamlet* over the "ruthless grief." Varner is the "shrewd," "merry," and "ruthless" old man who turns the Bend over to Flem Snopes even as the laughing god appears to consign Houston's fate to Mink Snopes. Faulkner explicitly ties Varner to the comic deity when he describes Var-ner's face at the conclusion of "Spotted Horses": "the bushy overhang of the brows which seemed to concentrate downward toward him in writhen immobility, not frowning but with a sort of *fierce risibility* [italics mine]" (313). Varner's heavy brows are reminiscent of Mink Snopes' "fierce in-tractable face with its single eyebrow" (91), further fusing the two men with the Risibility. Furthermore, "writhen immobility" is a deft oxymoron which best describes Faulkner's creative stance in *The Hamlet*—a restless, tormented playfulness that ultimately remains static—as Ratliff's plight makes clear.

Ratliff is, by temperament and intelligence, the real son of Varner, more of a humanitarian, but withal, a detached observer with a "familiar sardonic humor." Ratliff is the primary spectator in a novel filled with spec-tating. Any event in drowsy Frenchman's Bend, no matter how insignifi-cant, is cause for a crowd. Men come to watch Flem clerk at Varner's store; glancing at Eula Varner any time is a popular pastime. Ike Snopes' adven-tures with the cow are promoted by Lump Snopes. Buck Hipps' horse show, of course, draws a crowd. Finally, poor Henry Armstid provides the most bizarre spectacle as he digs continually in his hole. Ratliff pronounces ben-ediction on the generations of human comedy as Eula is carried off by Flem—not Hoake McCarron, the rakeswell, and not Labove, the sporting hero.

Ratliff counters the "doomed and dying summer" with "his eyes darkly impenetrable, quizzical and bemused," as Faulkner bequeathes to him the knowledge of the Risibility's imaginative control over the parade of human engagement and sexuality. Ratliff gazes through the buggy window at Eula's face and muses, "It had not been tragic and now it was not even damned, since from behind it there looked out only another mortal natural enemy of the masculine race" (151).[48] Ratliff ultimately speaks for all the men of the novel as he gauges the power of the women. He can imagine

himself one with Ike in the stall with the cow; he knows the pain of Snopesian pawns, feeling the Player's cold hand in the salted gold mine affair. In
his slightly guilty hysteria, he exclaims, "I never made them Snopeses and
I never made the folks that cant wait to bear their backsides to them. I could
do more but I wont. I wont, I tell you!" (326). Here is Ratliff's cry of
"writhen immobility."

Faulkner has been the maker and shaper of all of them, including
Ratliff whom he crowns, along with Will Varner, as spokesmen for *deus
ludens*. Ratliff's viewpoint is not purchased without cost, a realization of
play at its most foolhardy and inglorious as well as its most necessary, as
the men of the Bend struggle with both Flem Snopes and their own obsessions. Faulkner's great triumph in *The Hamlet* was to clearly limn this viewpoint within "Spotted Horses," a wonderful ritual of horse-buying in daylight and horse-chasing in moonlight where games-playing and enchanted
play illuminate all corners of the play spirit, competitive and sensual alike.

Faulkner's "competitive and sensual" visions of play in *The Hamlet*
exemplify the interaction of what Herbert Marcuse in *Eros and Civilization*
(1966) described as the clash between the performance (reality) principle
and the pleasure principle. Marcuse envisioned a desublimated order of non-
repressive civilization not bound by Freud's reality principle. To explain this
hypothetical civilization's order, Marcuse posited an extension of Friedrich
Schiller's aesthetics of play which Schiller in *Letters on the Aesthetic Education of Man* (1795) had derived from Kant. Schiller's vision was of a
radically aestheticized society in which play as the mediating form of the
sensuous moves sensuality toward a pure form in art that represses its sensual origin.

Faulkner's view in *The Hamlet* may be allied with this idealized concept of play but the concept cannot ultimately contain his play. For Faulkner delivers the men from economic outrage in the horse sale into sensual
bondage to the horse chase. The "freedom from" Snopesian manipulative
secular ritual does not lead to a "freedom to" play; indeed, there *is* no
ultimate dialectically free "freedom to" play in *The Hamlet*. Play is "puerile folly" to a Will Varner but play is also "doing the best [they] can" to
a Ratliff. The yeomen in the chase are still in, to use Marcuse's phrase,
"repressive desublimation" of desire. It is repressive because Faulkner's
sense of the men "performing their nature" is not aestheticized liberation
from reality but a patterning out of reality's conscious and subconscious

currents. The economic desire for acquisition and the sensuous desire for beauty are, once again, the twin faces of desire, mad with "ravening gleeful triumph" (*The Hamlet,* p. 175). The yeomen possess no means of production in the order of play. They are balked at the level of the sensuous impulse and are bereft of creative power as they were of economic leverage at the horse lot. They can only pattern out the circuit of their nature, the sublimation and desire. All pursuit in *The Hamlet* is as unsatisfactory as the horse sale. The end of the horse chase leaves the world of the novel as it found it, or worse, after days and nights of purposeful purposelessness at play.

Faulkner has reified the spotted ponies as desirable objects in the game of economic exploitation at the horse lot and then reified them as desublimated objects of desire in the play of the horse chase. The yeomen receive play's strong current and Ratliff perceives play's urgent necessity, but action and idea remain sundered in a Hegelian riddle. Freedom is finally pursued only as a goal; it can never be an essence in *The Hamlet.* Freedom is what the novel has for a grail instead of the goal of the sacred, for blocking such sacred apprehension is the elusive Risibility. *The Hamlet's* internal dynamic between competition and sensuality finally affirms the romantic tragicomic perspective with the performance of *play's* nature the novel's most completely realized action.

CHAPTER TWELVE

Sport Approaches the Sacred: Hemingway and Faulkner

THE SUN ALSO RISES and *The Hamlet* mimic the ceremonial worlds of the sacred during the major rituals in the novels, the festival of San Fermin and the horse-lot sale of the ponies in "Spotted Horses." At these climactic junctures in each novel, characters are clearly in the profane world, approaching the sensual rather than the sacred. Though solemn in its origin, the festival in *The Sun Also Rises* has lost its primary religious impetus; as Hemingway tersely puts it at the end of a richly descriptive paragraph, "San Fermin is also a religious festival" (153). Hemingway portrays the bullfight as containing all the group ceremonial aspects of ritual reality but, ultimately, the bullfight is a limited mystery because man always endeavors to stay in control of his fate. There is no real giving up of self, rather an assertion of will and the self.

Play, game, and sport vivify the real and aid in temporary illusions of mastering death or pursuing romance but are most clearly seen within a secular realm in which characters ultimately are humbled in their limitations—the suitors of Brett Ashley as well as the suitors of the spotted ponies. Time and space are altered, rules once improvised are fixed, and characters learn briefly who they are in performative ritual before they return to the environments of unrequited love and desire.

In *The Old Man and the Sea* and *Go Down, Moses,* the goal for the hunters, the aged Santiago and Ike McCaslin (age 10 to 72) is to become part of an ordered, natural ritual. They find themselves in an altered universe, approaching mysteries of the sacred where the self moves toward extinction. When play and sport reach toward the sacred, they cease to be free or spontaneous or uncertain but are incorporated into a concrete reality.

Whereas play is often pure form, its activity an end in itself, the sacred is pure content, where man, the player, is defenseless.[1] His inventive rites capture momentarily the sense of the sacred, what he is ultimately held by.[2]

These hunting tales contain an intense wish for a resacralization of time and space. Langer states that the universality of concepts which religion tries to formulate draws all nature into the domain of the sacred.[3] Hemingway disintegrates the terminology of hunter/hunted in *The Old Man and the Sea* to focus on the fierce beauty of the *agon*. Faulkner literally has Ike McCaslin vanish into a sacred wilderness tableau, a choice invested with majesty and troubling consequences in the relentlessly profane arena which demands its sacrifices. Eliade comments, "it is the *sacred* that is preeminently the *real*."[4] He points out that the foundation for rites is "access to sacrality" which reveals "true dimensions to existence."[5]

However, that "access" can be performed in a wide range of forms. Secular ritual may be individual ritualized behavior, as evidenced by Santiago and Ike McCaslin, or collective ceremony such as the annual hunt at Major DeSpain's camp in *Go Down, Moses*. The hunt renews a social grouping through the restatement of its fixed forms. Likewise, a hunting ceremony may attempt to link the immediate with a larger reality, and then ritual moves toward sacred dimensions as in Ike's marking by Sam Fathers after Ike's first kill.[6] The ceremonial kill, the hunter as initiate, and the solitary witnessing in the wilderness are all part of the hunt, a hybrid sport which retains archaic elements of sacrality in dynamic fashion. In modern American society, the wilderness represents a dream of ourselves in our combative virgin youth as the conclusion of *The Old Man and the Sea* and "Delta Autumn" make clear. Santiago is dreaming of the youthful lions on the African beach. Ike McCaslin is remembering Sam Fathers even as he has become a Sam Fathers with no acolyte of his own. The ritual of the hunt in *The Old Man and the Sea* is beyond direct human influence, while in "The Old People," *The Bear*, and "Delta Autumn," the ritual contains a primitive, pagan lament for lost sanctity as well as the truth of present paralysis. The Gulf Stream and the Mississippi wilderness await the imagination and courage of the Ritual Sports Hero; sport is his entré into the sacred environment but in this environment sport falls away before larger questions and realities.

SANTIAGO: THE GULF STREAM
AND HEROIC RESIGNATION

The story of Johnson's charter of Harry Morgan's *Queen Conch* in *To Have and Have Not* was part of a long piece, "One Trip Across," that appeared in *Cosmopolitan* in April 1934; Captain Willie Adams' confrontation with Frederick Harrison was published in the February 1936 *Esquire* as part of "The Tradesman's Return." Before he hurriedly composed two-thirds of *To Have and Have Not* beginning in October 1936, Hemingway had already reinforced the theme of men preying upon men, as well as the great power of the Gulf Stream and its creatures, in his *Esquire* column of April 1936 entitled "On the Blue Water: A Gulf Stream Letter." This article proved not only a conceptualization of the death that awaited Harry Morgan but also announced, almost off-handedly, a tale Hemingway had heard from Carlos Guterriez about an old fisherman whose skiff had been towed out to sea by a giant marlin before he was able to kill it. Some 16 years later, the fisherman, of course, would become Santiago in *The Old Man and the Sea*.

In his brief description of the old fisherman's battle in "On the Blue Water," Hemingway divests him of some of the dignity he would give to Santiago by having him picked up by fishermen: "He was crying in the boat . . . half crazy from his loss and the sharks were still circling the boat" (240). In *To Have and Have Not*, the Coast Guard cutter that comes upon the *Queen Conch* after the gun battle finds Harry mortally wounded amongst the dead Cubans he has hunted on his own decks, the fish lapping at the streams of red blood oozing through the shattered boards of the deck where he lies. Harry is as ravaged as the marlin lashed to the skiff in *The Old Man and the Sea*. Surrounded by death, Harry can only lie there and "take it," a final authenticating of the eerie pride and degradation of the veterans in Freddy's Bar. Harry Morgan as prey for the Cubans, who have "hooked" him, and the blood of all of them as feast for the small fish, underscores the ascendancy of the power of the Gulf Stream and, by the end of *To Have and Have Not*, its dominance.

In "On the Blue Water" and *To Have and Have Not*, the true power of the open sea and its prodigious fish is introduced. In *The Old Man and the Sea*, Santiago courts the Gulf Stream, *la mar*, like a threatening woman subject to fickle moods. He has respect for her as an adversary, yet he also feels at one with her. His other opponents are predators, such as the great marlin, the sharks, or more abstract states such as courage or fear that prey on his mind and spirit. However, he is able to do much more than simply "take it."

Santiago strives to assert his natural liberty as a human being, to know how much of it is his to possess in the face of a great deterministic force. He works to learn ultimately his terms of surrender to a power which encompasses him and his adversaries. Hemingway's battle all along had been waged with a deep mistrust of the loss of control in the *agon*. Santiago is the first Hemingway Ritual Sports Hero to accept, rationally and calmly, the inevitabilities of loss while still defining his own heroism.

Santiago is an heroic laborer in his skiff, going through more tests than schoolboy heroes could ever dream of. His self-sufficiency at his rites begins on a practical level as he manipulates his lines with great care while he draws on all his accumulated experience to deal with the monstrous marlin. The reward for the Ritual Sports Hero is in doing what he is meant to do: Santiago fishes because that is his work. There is no higher utility then correct conduct in the wilderness arena. His professionalism is evidenced in his pragmatic decisions on strategy, the intricate doling out of his energy at certain intervals during the towing of the skiff by the marlin.

Nowhere in Hemingway's fiction is the equation so clear. Sport *is* work for Hemingway, as close an equivalent as he can muster. Work constitutes the great secular deity and confers dignity. The contrast between games and work is made clear when Santiago remembers his youth and hand-wrestling matches that were public spectacles with much wagering. Santiago "played the hand game with the great negro from Cienfuegos,"[7] the very words "play" and "game" once again sounding foreign in Hemingway's work. "They had gone one day and one night with their elbows on a chalkline on the table and their forearms straight up and their hands gripped tight" (67). The battle is one of endurance, resembling Santiago against the marlin. After 24 hours, from Sunday morning to Monday morning, Santiago finally forces his opponent's hand down. The bettors all go off to load sacks of sugar on the Havana dock as the work week begins. Santiago is hailed as "The Champion," but "after that he had a few matches and then no more. He decided that he could beat anyone if he wanted to badly enough and he decided that it was bad for his right hand for fishing" (69). Contests are ultimately not as important as the livelihood of fishing where sporting skill must be preserved. The hand is needed for the work in the boat.

Game and play are not important to Santiago but his fishing prowess is crucial. The ritual of fishing became Hemingway's cleanest and most functional sporting action.[8] The metaphors are always those of the fishing "line," of control of that line, of "hooking it" and holding on, of manipulating the play in the line, of keeping line in reserve. All the motions of the sport are suggestive of emotional and artistic control. The line slowly goes out and Santiago makes "the fish earn each inch of it" for "he was ceding line but more slowly all the time" (82). The ritual of work well done in fishing is the central sports image in the novel.

Exegetes have gleefully pored over *The Sporting News* and baseball record books to analyze Hemingway's use of Joe DiMaggio and baseball in *The Old Man and the Sea*.[9] Beyond DiMaggio's austere, veteran heroism in the face of crippling heel injuries in 1948–49 is Santiago's initial identification of his courage as that shown by a fisherman's son. Santiago "would like to take the great DiMaggio fishing. . . . They say his father was a fisherman. Maybe he was as poor as we are and would understand" (18). Also, the use of DiMaggio as a veteran athlete returning to achieve impressive feats is not the first time Hemingway had reached into the world of popular sport for a real hero. His iconographic use of Juan Belmonte in *The Sun Also Rises* had been a portrait of an aging champion who no longer had passion in his performance. The triumphantly youthful Pedro Romero had garnered all the laurels. Twenty-five years later, drawing DiMaggio as icon, Hemingway very much wanted to believe in a veteran's triumph and he saw DiMaggio in relation not only to Santiago but to himself as a professional, a veteran hero of pride and dignity. Near the end of his active writing career, Hemingway was glad to come home and embrace the figure of an American popular hero who had (in Hemingway's terms) lasted to get his work done,[10] who had survived age and injury to perform with skill.

DiMaggio's reality is assimilated by Santiago on the level of a fellow craftsman in sport. However, Santiago is little interested in human competition. He is more concerned with establishing himself in the natural pantheon as coequal with his adversaries. Santiago comes closer to the center of his life in what Eliade calls in the sacred a "total cleaving to being," a man's participation in a primordial revelation of which he is the guardian.[11] Eliade also states that for *homo religiosus,* the world itself is a living, speaking, meaning thing,[12] and indeed Santiago is constantly addressing the sea, the fish, and the birds as well as his own hands. "How does it go, hand?" (57), Santiago asks as one might ask a friend or teammate in pain. "I'm being towed by a fish and I'm the towing bitt" (42) he thinks. He is being pulled out to sea and must try different ploys to stop the great fish for "he had been pulled down tight into the bow" (81). He says, "Fish. I love you and respect you very much. But I will kill you before this day ends'' (52). Santiago becomes the initiate, ''he who knows,''[13] to whom all parts of the natural world may be called ''brothers,'' the flying fish, the great marlin, even the stars.[14] The equality he feels in the kill is egoless respect for the worthy adversary:[15] ''You are killing me, fish, the old man thought. But you have a right to. Never have I seen a greater, or more beautiful, or a calmer or more noble thing than you, brother'' (92). Harmony exists in the killing world of the Gulf Stream where both Santiago and the marlin have *chosen* to be, an arena out beyond other boats and other fish: ''His choice had been to stay in the deep dark water far out beyond all snares and traps and treacheries. My choice was to go there and find him beyond all people. Beyond all people in the world'' (48).

Beyond all people in the world. The Ritual Sports Hero makes his final discoveries in an arena he does not control but feels privileged to enter. The fish tows Santiago out to sea, the man in no more control than the marlin. They are part of a struggle in which conventional winning and losing are not at issue. Santiago knows about his trade and its techniques; he knows ''how'' and he wants to know ''why.'' As the oldest professional, he is strong and tenacious but as brittle as the skeleton lashed against his skiff.

His maintaining these contradictions of strength and the ultimate tenuous hold on strength defines Santiago's victory. Rather than the *agon* with the marlin and sharks, it is his resignation that constitutes Santiago's heroism. Hemingway at last envisions his enemies of *alea* and *ilinx* in a conception that accounts for both the nobility of the *agon* and its menacing contingencies of fate. Santiago understands what force sent the sharks, he accepts the sharks' degradation, and he is not bitter. Hemingway provides Santiago with a world of sporting forms he can both duel with and live in without being consumed. That world, however, remains truncated in scope when compared to the complexity to which Faulkner drives the hunt in *Go Down, Moses*.

IKE McCASLIN:
ENGAGEMENT AND RENUNCIATION

In chapter 12, ''Devout Observances,'' in *The Theory of the Leisure Class,* Veblen posited the close relationship between sporting temperament and archaic devoutness, stating "sports have some efficacy as a means of grace" and "in the hands of lay organizations, sporting activities come to do duty as a novitiate or a means of induction into that fuller unfolding of the life of spiritual status."[16] Veblen thus formalized what Cooper "unfolded" through the role of Natty Bumppo in *The Pioneers*. Veblen conceived of sport as one activity of the "predatory barbarian" who reappeared in modern society as a gentleman of the leisure class, a war chieftain, or a member of a priestly caste. The career of Ike McCaslin in *Go Down, Moses* encompasses these roles, for Ike is a natural gentleman and master hunter but one who learns to kill with surety and reverence before he ultimately becomes a high priest in abstention from ownership and paternity.[17]

An examination of *Go Down, Moses* will suggest ways in which sporting life is its heart and how it supports Faulkner's larger tale, what Eric Jensen has called, in writing of Ike McCaslin, the portrayal of *homo religiosus* as *homo ludens*.[18] Faulkner alters the focus from *deus ludens* in *The Hamlet* to *homo religiosus* in *Go Down, Moses*. The "prime maniacal Risibility" as dramatic stand-in for *auctor ludens* affected a large number of characters in the driven and spontaneous play of *The Hamlet*. In *Go Down, Moses* the god figure is the "ancient immortal Umpire,"[19] fixed, serious, and acting on a vast historical plane. He is a prime Mover who renders decisions that initiate epochal historical forces such as the institution of slavery in the New World and the Civil War. He is a serious judge of players and is earnestly sought by Cass Edwards and Ike McCaslin. The shift from "Risibility" to "Umpire" moves the deity from a comic to a tragic perspective, and the players do not struggle and strive as much as represent mimetically through large static motions. *The Hamlet* is a swirling, hallucinatory dance of play—agonistic, aleatory, ilinxlike—while *Go Down, Moses* features Ike McCaslin moving toward the assumption of a correct role out of time and space. Yet in *The Hamlet* as well as in the hunting stories of *Go Down, Moses, homo ludens* is primary subject, the deity's pawn, exhibiting both rebellion and awe as he searches for rationales of conduct.

It is Faulkner's control of both the secular ritual of the hunt and its potential for higher ceremony that so consistently sparks "Was," "The Old People," *The Bear,* and "Delta Autumn" into major statement.[20] "Was" is the most elemental of hunting narratives, the tale of pursuit, which occurs in a prelapsarian world that nonetheless contains the evils of possession squarely confronted in the rest of the book.[21] The rituals in *Go Down, Moses'* three central hunting stories are distinctly separated into two groups:

collective ceremonial hunts and individual initiations. Turner differentiates between sequestered and public liminality "which roughly corresponds to the difference between initiation rites and major seasonal feasts." He comments, "in the former, the liminaries are humbled and leveled to make them fit for a higher status or state; in the latter, the liminaries are everybody in the community, and no one is elevated in status at the end of the rites."[22] Faulkner mixes both sequestered and public rites in his hunting tales. The movement from "The Old People" through *The Bear* and "Delta Autumn" is the consistent transformation back and forth of a secular hunt, the festal break for two weeks each November at Major De Spain's camp, Ike's initiation by Sam Fathers in sequestered ritual, and Ike's witnessing in the wilderness, a sacred experience which is his alone at the center beyond the public and sequestered rites. Faulkner's juxtaposition of public ceremony and private revelation is a counterpart of the parallel competition and spontaneous play in *The Hamlet*. Secular ritual for Faulkner from horse lot to hunting camp is always a take-off point to something more deeply personal: the chaos of freedom (the yeomen's chase) in *The Hamlet* or the initiation followed by the *sparagmos* of obliteration (Ike's renunciation of a human role) in *Go Down, Moses*.

"The Old People" begins in sequestered liminality. The *Genesis*-like "At first there was nothing" (163) is broken when Sam Fathers animates the scene simply by touching Ike's shoulder to bring the buck into view, an incarnation miraculous and pure in birth: "he was just there, looking not like a ghost but as if all of light were condensed in him and he were the source of it . . . ." (163). Seeing the buck as he does in beauty and organic relation to the scene frees Ike to shoot at Sam's command. It is Ike's first deer and he runs toward it "with Sam Fathers beside him again" and he, Ike, "standing over it shaking and jerking . . ." (164). Sam tells him to make sure the buck is dead. Ike "drew Sam Fathers' knife across the throat and Sam stooped and dipped his hands in the hot smoking blood and wiped them back and forth across the boy's face" (164). The physical acts of both killing the buck and marking the boy's face with blood validate the true bequest which belongs to the spirit. At this point, sport has achieved its closest relationship to the sacred. When Ike learns to appreciate his relation to nature through his mentor, the woods are never "inimical again" and the flaring gun matches the leaping buck "forever immortal" (178). The novice now belongs in the tableau with the animal in sacred space which is also timeless, hence ultimately real in primordial time which was, is, and will be.

When "Sam's horn rang in the wet gray woods," the expressly sacramental scene opened to the world of secular hunters and animals for "there was a boiling wave of dogs about them" as well as Tennie's Jim and Boon Hogganbeck: "then the men—the true hunters—Walter Ewell whose rifle never missed" and Major De Spain, General Compson, and McCaslin Edmonds. The hunters move in on the boy and "the old dark man . . . who had marked him . . . ." (165). The sacred moment has been severed by the arrival of the sportsmen. The *liminal* initiation rite is broken by the *liminoid* phenomenon of the return of the hunters.

Walter Ewell's role in "The Old People" is an example of Faulkner's differentiation between master hunter and nature's acolyte. Ewell is the best hunter at Major De Spain's camp, yet there is never a moment when he moves out of his role as expert hunter toward a higher definition of his skill. When Ike and Sam Fathers watch the great buck with reverence, Walter Ewell's horn calls them in on the kill of a "little spike buck," but Ewell says, "I would swear there was another buck here that I never even saw" (185). Ewell is an adept hunter but no initiate into deeper mysteries; he cannot "see," which is the great accomplishment of the true initiate in both Hemingway and Faulkner's concept of true witnessing. Later, in *The Bear,* Ewell shoots a buck from the caboose of the train that snakes its way through what is left of the wilderness and, along with General Compson, invents a plan to make the hunting camp into a club and lease the hunting privileges of the woods for money, a clear violation of the contract between nature and man. While technically proficient, Ewell is spiritually deficient; his rifle will never kill an animal of the stature of Old Ben; he inhabits only secular space and is endowed with utilitarian skills.

In the opening of *The Bear,* Faulkner presented vivid homely images of the hunters and the countryside. Old Ben is tauntingly curious, playful in the spirit of the hunt as a worldly old bear, but his nature is transcended by his place in the "yearly pageant-rite of the old bear's immortality" (194). Each autumn the hunters resume the search for Old Ben, not so much for the kill as to play out the secular rite, according to "the ancient and immitigable rules" (192).

As festal sporting event, everyone knows of the coming struggle with Old Ben: "Then in the warm caboose the boy [Ike] slept again while Boon and the conductor and brakeman talked about Lion and Old Ben as people later would talk about Sullivan and Kilrain, and later still, about Dempsey and Tunney" (230). Faulkner emphasizes that such legends of ritual hunts may last for generations. After Old Ben's death, the swamp dwellers, farmers, loggers, sawmill men and town men arrived "mounted and on foot and in wagons . . . filling the little yard and overflowing it until there were almost a hundred of them . . . talking quietly of hunting, of the game and the dogs . . . ."(248). The secular ritual fulfills its role for the community at large.

Parts II and III of *The Bear,* which depict the training of Lion and the death of Ben, Lion, and Sam Fathers, have been ranked with the finest hunting narratives in the language, as majestic and violent as Melville's epic account of Ahab's preparations and final battle with Moby Dick. The last hunt for Old Ben is not our main issue here: what is of importance to the discussion of sport approaching the sacred is Ike's witnessing rather than hunting, his achieving wisdom beyond the kill at the cost of influencing the kill.

While Sam Fathers reminisces in "The Old People," ten-year-old Ike thinks, "And as he talked about those old times and those dead and vanished men of another race from either that the boy knew, gradually to the boy those old times would cease to be old times and would become part of the boy's present, not only as if they had happened yesterday but as if they were still happening . . . ." ("The Old People," 171). Ike's knowledge is held in timeless possession that finally drives him toward correct witnessing. He is an engaged witness since sight and comprehension are so much a part of the initiate's rite. Once initiated, Ike may handle the sacred objects of his fraternity, the tools of a hunter, like the sacraments of bread and wine. Like Jake Barnes watching Romero, reading Turgenev, or fishing in the mountains, Ike will "have it always." As Ike matures, he thinks of Old Ben, the indomitable bear, *"So I will have to see him. . . . I will have to look at him* [italics Faulkner]" (*The Bear,* 204). The hunter, the human witness, is the only one who can truly give testament to natural beauty through "that thin clear quenchless lucidity which alone differed him from this bear and from all the other bears and bucks . . . ." (207).[23] Spectating becomes a most solemn act of the Ritual Sports Hero as the hunting ritual shifts to a sacred witnessing.

Within the religious ritual ceremony, something sacred reveals itself to participants and spectators in an altered form. Eliade writes, "For religious man, space is not homogeneous; he experiences interruptions, breaks in it, some parts of space are qualitatively different from others." All other space is "the formless expanse surrounding it" where the sacred "ontologically" founds the world. Any object that manifests the sacred may become something else but continue to remain itself[24] as the forest wilderness does in *The Bear* when Ike enters it alone and Faulkner writes, "the wilderness coalesced. It rushed, soundless, and solidified . . ." (*The Bear*, 209). Ike's responsibilities are not moral, social, or historical but what Eliade calls *"responsibility on the cosmic plane"* [italics Eliade] where man's "participation in being is assured him by the primordial revelation of which he is the guardian."[25] The repeated cadence of Part IV of *The Bear* is "repudiate" rather than "beget." "Humility" and "pride" continue to battle; now "by possessing one thing other, he would possess them both" (296).

But is Ike McCaslin in such sure possession of humility and pride?[26] How does sport in the form of the hunt relate to his renunciation of ownership and paternity in *The Bear*, Part IV? To take Ike's place in the ordered scene is to become part of the frieze. Ike bears witness and becomes part of the sacred without gun, watch, or compass: "He had left the gun; by his own will and relinquishment he had accepted not a gambit, not a choice, but a condition in which not only the bear's heretofore inviolable anonymity but all the ancient rules and balances of hunter and hunted had been abrogated" (207). The emphasis on rules and competition is voided. At this point, sport terminates in a realm out of time and space. Competition ends, play ends, and freedom ends as well. The "conditions" have been accepted but at a great cost. Ike's decision to renounce his birthright has affected no one positively, not himself nor the Edmonds nor Beauchamp lines of McCaslins. If he has given up stewardship over the land and its people, he has in a fundamental sense vastly reduced his claims to stewardship in the wilderness and Faulkner has difficulty making the hunt resonate after the renunciation.

Ike possesses *his* truth which is not Faulkner's whole truth. Faulkner himself cast doubt on Ike's decision, stating his preference for people who will do something about what they feel is rotten, not "go off into a cave or climb a pillar to sit on."[27] It is important to note that McCaslin Edmonds, Ike's cousin and the man who must assume the burdens Ike puts down, also has been initiated in the hunt by Sam Fathers. He effectively counters Ike's arguments in *The Bear*, Part IV, with a more pragmatic view of responsibility to the land and to people. Cass is qualified because he proves that Ike's perception of wilderness sanctity is not unique. At the end of "The Old People," after sighting the great buck, young Ike bursts out to Cass "But I saw it! I saw him!," and Cass responds, "Steady. I know you did. So did I. Sam took me in there once after I killed my first deer" (187).

Cass shares the initiate's experience but draws different conclusions as man-in-society with, as General Compson says, "one foot straddled into a farm and the other foot straddled into a bank . . ." (250).

The Edmonds line is not always dutiful or humane but shoulders the imperative to act from Cass through Zack Edmonds in "The Fire and the Hearth" in his confrontation with Lucas Beauchamp, to Roth Edmonds. The white Edmonds line descended from female McCaslins and the black Beauchamp line descended from male McCaslins clash frankly and emotionally with each other over rights and heritage. Cass solidly believes, "I am what I am; I will be always what I was born and have always been" (300), and he acts decisively during Reconstruction so that McCaslin holdings "enlarged and increased and would continue so, solvent and efficient and intact . . ." (298). Cass and Ike's extended debate is a less-dramatized but philosophically more resonant counterpart of the argument between Judge Temple and Natty Bumppo in *The Pioneers* and centers on the same issues: public goals, communal conduct, and their relation to personal responsibility.

The powerful dialogue-interview between Cass and Ike is an intensely dialectical application of thought. Both men attempt to expand the range of their thinking about their heritage as they recapitulate the arguments behind the slavery system. They alternately draw back from and violently confront a widening apprehension of the drama they live in.[28] Cass asks pointedly why Ike did not shoot at Old Ben; when Ike does not immediately answer, "McCaslin didn't wait, rising and crossing the room, across the pelt of the bear he had killed two years ago and the bigger one McCaslin had killed before he was born to the bookcase beneath the mounted head of his first buck and returned with the book and sat down again and opened it" (296). Cass has chosen Keats' "Ode on a Grecian Urn"[29] to read to Ike, specifically stanza two with its mighty reflections on stasis and immortality set against the ravages of time. The fact that Cass sees timelessness coexisting with a temporal world of hunting and dead prey, his organic connection between the pelts, mounted heads, and Keats' crafted urn advances a different thesis in which, as Cass says, Keats was "talking about truth. Truth is one. It doesn't change. It covers all things which touch the heart—honor and pride and pity and justice and courage and love" (297). Cass's categories comprise a wider (if shallower) spectrum than Ike's, including pity, justice, and love, areas from which Ike is in flight as a consequence of his choice. But Cass goes even further, stating that his categories "all touch the heart, and what the heart holds to becomes truth, as far as we know truth"

(297). Cass acknowledges, then, Ike's right to interpret truth according to his own lights: what is *is* for him. "What the heart holds" dictates Ike's action. Cass simply wants to establish that the urn (and the heart) may contain more than that solemn decision and that the responses of individuals may be more variegated than Ike's interpretation.

Ike abolishes himself in ritual as he takes a theological-philosophical position, desiring to move closer to the design of what Hegel calls the "Absolute Spirit." Yet, as Hegel warned, no one is ever given to know the total dimensions of this spirit, and Ike's ambition is thus Promethean and overreaching in a spiritual sense, the counterstance to his humility in time and space. Hegel wrote that "art ultimately tends to transcend itself by becoming theology and philosophy, and abolishes itself as sensuous play as it grows increasingly nearer to that full self-consciousness which is Absolute Spirit."[30] Such full self-consciousness is what we have labeled "the sacred" and "playing the sacred" is extended to "playing" the forms of thought in *The Bear*'s major debate.[31]

Ike McCaslin has, according to his lights, "performed his nature," has done what he had to do, but the complex ramifications of his choice reverberate until the end of "Delta Autumn." In *The Bear,* Part V, the ominous signs for Ike at age seventeen are all around him. The hunt club plan of Major De Spain and Walter Ewell has changed to something even worse, the selling of timber rights in the bottom land to a Memphis lumber company. Comic bears are treed in terror and trivialized by chugging trains. Ike himself rides the snake-train to camp, salutes the rattlesnake of dark night with "Chief. Grandfather," and goes to his final witnessing of the manic Boon Hogganbeck beneath the tree with the gibbering squirrels. "Delta Autumn" completes the hunting narrative more than a half-century later in 1940 when the hunters must travel 90 miles by car to reach virgin land.

In "Delta Autumn," no one remains who can apply what Ike may teach. He has taught younger men tracking and technique but they are sexual adults, not worshipful boys. In 1940, Ike has become Sam Fathers but he is querulous and preachy and no one listens to his rhetoric. Ike suffers the derision of both Roth Edmonds and Edmonds' mistress, his own mixed blood relative, who pronounces him loveless, as bereft of *Agapé* as of *Eros*.[32] He lies as in death, hands crossed on his chest, knowing that Roth's deer kill is a doe, a telling ritual sacrifice symbolic of the continuing violence of his own line toward women and the earth.[33]

Ike envisions "the two of them—himself and the wilderness—as coevals . . . the two spans running out together, not toward oblivion, nothingness, but into a dimension free of both time and space" where the "immortal game ran forever before the tireless belling immortal hounds, falling and rising phoenixlike to the soundless guns" (354). Ritual for Ike then has been stripped of its performative aspect and ceases to flow, but the hunt continues. Indeed, the aged Ike "still shot almost as well as he ever had, still killed almost as much of the game he saw as he ever killed; he no longer even knew how many deer had fallen before his gun" (336). The recitation of hunting skill is flat and obligatory, and one suspects that Faulkner was balked at showing the enduring power of the hunt at the end of Ike's lifespan given over to renouncing the violence which the hunt ritualizes. Secular hunters still claim their victims in the wilderness, for the passion of the hunt is relentless. Choosing not to kill Ben as Ike and Sam Fathers had done is finally not applicable to choosing not to own land or people. The sacred always lies beyond the chaos of time and space, but Faulkner suggests a profound abyss between the realms and no replenishment of one by the other.

Sport leads Ike into areas beyond itself and beyond himself which consume his prowess in a calm that reflects a timeless victory as well as a temporal defeat; neither the victory nor the defeat is in the play arena or in game time. To be etched on the urn is to be absolved of mortality but paradoxically to be impotent and locked away from the profane. Ike continues to hunt but he does not baptize or nurture. This sportsman vanishes into the wilderness like Old Ben as he closes the family ledgers in *The Bear*, Part IV, despite living on in body as Nazarene carpenter and chaste husband.

The "buck sprang, forever immortal"; the wilderness "rushed, soundless and solidified" as Old Ben "was just there," "fixed in the green," "bigger, dimensionless," "without motion." Sport, however, remains grounded in physical striving and heroic action. It has above all a commitment to motion and engagement so vividly acted out by Boon and Lion as they fall with Old Ben in the bear's death struggle: "the clinging dog, the bear, the man stride its back, working and probing the buried blade" (*The Bear*, 241). Lion, Boon, and Old Ben are the sporting heroes of *The Bear*. Lion and Boon as the plebeian, mixed-blood killers of Ben are the truly fitting huntsmen who momentarily neutralize the evils of ownership and racial prejudice in *The Bear* through the kill.[34] Their instinctive courage stamps them as performative champions, limited but compelling for the duration of the secular rite.

Ike belies their motion and engagement since his first kill is, in effect, his only and immortal kill. Furthermore, the ritual, whether secular or sacred, displays the will of the celebrants to participate or witness voluntarily in coherent, formal action that has personal and collective resonance. Ike renounces all this; instead he voluntarily dismembers himself, an act of *sparagmos* as ultimately violent in its consequences as any in the sporting ritual. He gains the sacred center by becoming the sacrificial victim. The "dimension free of both time and space" is squarely in the domain of the sacred where the ritual motions of sport dissolve as do human pain and responsibility.

SANTIAGO AND IKE McCASLIN: THE LAST HUNTERS

The last visions of Santiago the fisherman-killer and Ike the hunter-priest are similar and yet different. Both aged sportsmen lie immobile and exhausted.[35] But Santiago has performed with great courage in the contest of his life, and the boy, an unrealized Ike to Santiago's Sam Fathers, sees Santiago as heroic while the old man lies dreaming of the lions of his youth. Ike is in reverie, too, but his dreams are not of strength or victory or even of endurance and he is not at peace.

The cycle of stories in *Go Down, Moses* covers Ike McCaslin from age 10 to 21 and at age 72. Faulkner telescopes the career of the Hemingway sporting hero from the youth of Nick Adams to the last fight of Santiago into a single story sequence. However, Faulkner's last hunter is a more radical figure than Hemingway's fisherman. He is more radical because he embodies all the contradictions inherent in engagement and renunciation and also because of Faulkner's concept of "seeing," of bearing witness, as that fundamental perceptive act that takes spectating to its highest plane.

In *The Sun Also Rises*, crucial passages of spectatorial comprehension involve Brett Ashley. Brett sees "how" Romero makes his passes with the muleta, sees "how" he increases his danger, and then knows "why" the act gives her such pleasure. Her appreciation of technique and the lines of the sporting action transfer her perception of work well done to an aesthetic knowledge which enriches her emotional response. When the bulls are being unloaded in the corral outside Pamplona, Brett watches them drive their horns into the steers: "I saw it," she said. "I saw him shift from his left to his right horn" (140). Her comprehension of the bull's instinctive technique elicits an admiring "Damn good!" from her mentor, Jake Barnes.

Ike McCaslin also cries out "But I saw it! I saw him!" ("The Old People," 187), but in a very different context that clearly points to the divergence between Hemingway's and Faulkner's concept of witnessing. Ike's exclamation occurs at the conclusion of "The Old People" when he tells McCaslin Edmonds of his sighting of the great buck with Sam Fathers. The "it" for Ike is nothing less than the majestic wilderness itself which is the sum of all the lives that had passed away while it remained inviolate; the "him" is cast as the buck himself, personification of the spirit of that timeless freedom. Simply to imagine himself in such a setting is ennobling for young Ike. In *The Bear,* "he would be humble and proud that he had been found worthy to be a part of it too or even just to see it too" (226).

"Seeing" involves different appreciation for Hemingway and Faulkner. It is at the heart of the difference between their views of sport. For Hemingway, what the witness to sport sees is form and technique, the ways in which the hero performs. Through the quality of the hero's work will come the estimates of his character formed by witnesses. Physical motions are achieved graces from Romero through Santiago. For Faulkner, the witness's role is to become part of the ordered scene by a giving up of self, a merging into a reality that is festive and bewildering as in *The Hamlet* or, in essence, into a reality that is timeless and whole, the reality of the sacred in *Go Down, Moses.* Hemingway's witnesses begin as classic empiricists, discriminating through observed experience, and only grudgingly become metaphysicians. Ike McCaslin attempts to obliterate any distance between himself and the sacred. Faulkner then perceives the ritual hunt as containing the roots of its own disolution; sport moves the hunter into a state where the performative act diminishes before a timeless unity. Rules are techniques for Hemingway but cosmic, "ancient and immitigable," for Faulkner.

In *The Old Man and the Sea,* Santiago believes, "You killed him for pride and because you are a fisherman" (105) whereas in *The Bear,* Ike "wished to learn humility and pride in order to become skillful and worthy in the woods" (295) and finally must learn the courage to renounce it all. One cannot deny Santiago's humility. However the humility is in achieving equality in the Great Kill and in accomplishing it with reverence. A sacrifice, a kill, is a must at the center of the sacred for Hemingway.[36] Nothing less than total commitment to the struggle is required. Nothing is bigger than Santiago. He and the marlin are equals in their deadly and sacred relationship; as Santiago says, "Come on and kill me. I do not care who kills who" (92). In *The Bear,* the buck is "Chief . Grandfather," not "brother." Hemingway's respect and engagement in the killer's world of *The Old Man and the Sea* is an absolute: he is a fisherman and the *agon* cannot be renounced. Yet it must be reemphasized that Ike's renouncing the agon does not make him a more exalted figure in Faulkner's eyes, nor does it end the violence Ike deplores in Roth Edmonds in "Delta Autumn." Roth was never Ike's Ike for Ike had no worshipful grandson, no idolatrous boy as does Santiago at the conclusion of *The Old Man and the Sea.*

When Faulkner reviewed *The Old Man and the Sea* in 1952, he spoke of Hemingway coming to a new realization: "this time, he wrote about pity: about something somewhere that made them all: the old man who had to catch the fish and then lose it, the fish that had to be caught and then lost, the sharks which had to rob the old man of his fish; made them all and loved them all and pitied them all. It's all right."[37] It is precisely this inevitability that defines the impact of *The Old Man and the Sea* as Faulkner correctly gauged the novel's thrust. Hemingway accepted and acknowledged rules and order beyond the ones set by the hunter in *ludic* response to danger and fate. Santiago is the first Hemingway Ritual Sports Hero to coexist under the net of fate with the forces which would destroy him. Yet Hemingway, for all the critical interest in the parallels of Santiago to Christ, does sustain a man-centered picture of Santiago under a massive providence. All things are possible before the skill of the experienced and prudent hunter. For the final time, Hemingway constructed intricate defenses for his character. Santiago confronts no other human beings; the Gulf Stream is conveniently voided of all but marlins and sharks. Faulkner's own fiction always matched the determinism of events with enormous human contingency, the "had to" defined through stubborn, often tragic choice by characters not at all convinced of the relative power or exact nature of the deity.

Faulkner's intimation of "something somewhere" took on more wide-ranging speculation in *The Bear* than Faulkner himself found in Hemingway's novel. The deity sensed by Cass Edmonds is "He—this Arbiter, this Architect, this Umpire—condoned—or did He? Or at least did nothing: saw and could not, or did not see; saw, and would not, or perhaps He would not see—perverse, impotent or blind; which?" (258). The halting tentativeness, the attempt to create the outline of an hypothesis, constitutes Cass' uncertainty in describing the role of a God in the heritage of slavery and possessiveness that curses the South. The deity of *The Bear* must be dealt with by all the descendants of Carothers McCaslin. Ike's counterview to that of Cass is that the New World was the last chance for man, their violence and possession "permitted" in Ike's terms but not "condoned," ordered and watched by the deity in the land that "He had vouchsafed them out of pity and sufferance on condition of pity and humility and sufferance and endurance . . . ." (259). As God rained down the Civil War as a last gamble to purify the New World, Ike's resolve is, too, to take a last drastic step to end his line and lift a curse of slavery and possession by one human action, the highest one available to him. His action is Godlike and not human at all. He has become the "Umpire" even as Ratliff and Will Varner spoke for the "Risibility" in *The Hamlet*.

A final irony is that despite each central character's disquisition on a god-figure, Ike, like Santiago, is finally adept only in a world without people. When Ike leaves his gun, compass, and watch, "all the ancient rules and balances of hunter and hunted had been abrogated." The hunt terminates and Faulkner can never really reclaim its significance for *The Bear*, Parts IV and V, or for "Delta Autumn," for Ike's transformation has been achieved. Hemingway has no such philosophical problem because for Santiago, the *agon* is never eclipsed. The harder one struggles in Hemingway's sport, the more one learns. Only in death is there release from competition.

This is, in effect, what Cass Edmonds tries to tell Ike, that the heart may hold his (Ike's) truth along with the emotions and will to assume responsibility in full face of contradictions. And finally, what accounts for the ambiguous power derived from Faulkner's hunting frame is that it provides an activity from which to clearly understand choices of engagement and renunciation and the frustrating deficiencies of both courses of action. Hemingway provides no options. The all-encompassing virtue of Santiago as hunter and witness is, in Faulkner, more tellingly split between heroic figures such as Lion, Boon, and Walter Ewell who are nonhuman, inhumane, and mechanically proficient hunters, respectively, and Ike and Sam Fathers whose skill is dominated by their role as exalted witnesses. For example, Lion, Faulkner's adept killer, has "the will and desire to endure beyond all imaginable limits of flesh in order to overtake and slay" (237). Lion is just one actor in a complex moral and historical drama but unfortunately he sums up much of Santiago's virtue except for the epigrammatic analogues between a hunter's deity and the brotherhood of fisherman and fish. There is no sense of fluid possibility in Santiago's tale, for Hemingway provided a veteran with a victory in performance.

Santiago's struggle is Hemingway's final sporting lesson done in rote fashion with no temptation and little error. In the hero-witness fusion, there is stasis. The only sin, miniscule in relation to Faulkner's disquisition on divine and human culpability, is the "bad kill." But heroic existence in society is not the well-enacted hunt or the "good kill." The problems that knit before the eyes of Ike and Cass can't be solved by the hunt: either by its violence or by its apotheosis in the sacred. Hemingway limited the potential of *The Old Man and the Sea* from the beginning with a "performance not so much emotional as correct,"[38] while Faulkner has seriously questioned what mastery of the wilderness has to do with affecting errant civilization. Ike McCaslin becomes another Faulknerian hero etched in tragedy, for he has possessed the freedom to drive himself out of the world.[39]

The hunt, which is the mode of sport that Hemingway and Faulkner both sense as fullest in its possibilities, is an extremely purposeful act which demands intimate blood sacrifices.[40] In each case, it is the quality of the kill, the spirit thus released into larger experience, that dictates knowledge. For Hemingway, the experience is unrelenting combat in a killer's world where he clears his natural arena of all human influence to strip the *agon* to its sparest state. What Hemingway chooses to excise—a recognized social world with interaction—through the narrowly rendered hunt, Faulkner magnifies through Ike's paralysis as well as Ike's and Cass' viewpoints. Both stances toward the *agon,* total commitment and total abstention, have their weaknesses. Santiago's heroism is unassailable but limited because of the artificiality of the realistic frame. Ike McCaslin's renunciation is highly questionable since it is always portrayed in a world of consequences, the sacred as a goal demanding the sacrifice of the hunter. Faulkner illuminates the context in which the sacred is chosen over the profane, and its cost. We ultimately learn more about people than about marlins or bears. Ike becomes a brittle, dry sage through dramatic and moving events whereas Santiago is presented as the single-minded veteran from the outset. Ultimately, Hemingway willed a last impressive if rigid sporting victory while Faulkner included sport in the most complex of statements about contest and disengagement.

Hemingway was trapped at one fierce pitch of competition whereas Faulkner evidenced tremendous modulations of competition in both spontaneous play and cosmic questioning. Faulkner's commitment to a wider world of play forms as opposed to Hemingway's wary mistrust of most manifestations of the play spirit is finally a dichotomy which allows us to judge the breadth of human spirit in the works of both authors and to finally champion the drive toward freedom over the well-constructed defense.

Conclusion

THE PLAY THEORY that has guided this volume has been one, following Fink, Sutton-Smith, and Ehrmann, which has suggested that play is capable of producing spatial and temporal illusions that become the content of the real and enhance mastery and creativity. To the extent that an author has trusted in the reality of play, in the creation of it in all its consequences for characters, the play spirit has been a guiding force in his narrative, either in spontaneous moments of freedom or in codified games and organized sport. To conclude, a brief last look at sport and the play spirit in four major authors—Hawthorne, Fitzgerald, Hemingway, Faulkner—is in order, to summarize the play to which they committed themselves. Finally, I want to sketch some metamorphoses of the Ritual, School, and Popular Sports Heroes in contemporary fiction and suggest where the subject may be leading at present.

There are two separate but related ways in which the power of play traditionally has been drawn off by the forces of American society. The early Puritan objection to play was that play was frivolous and not serious, that it denied the sobriety that was necessary to live with eyes fixed on sin and death. By the late nineteenth century, the player had become a disciplined laborer whose freedom was lost in the larger competitive society. Hawthorne approached play with the Puritan fear of ahistorical, secular, creative freedom. Fitzgerald welcomed the freedom of play's creative potential. His heroes were dreamer-artists shrinking from the terms of prosaic American success but caught nonetheless in its thrall to achieve their goals. Fitzgerald saw the tragedy of the disciplined American player who must labor toward his vision. Hemingway subscribed to both negative propositions: that play was "not serious" and that the competitor must willingly renounce his freedom to rule-dominated striving. In this sense, he is most typically American in his resentments toward play and he stayed well within his self-assigned strictures. Faulkner understood the horror of American Puritans who confronted the freedom of play (witness the pathetic and terrifying attempts at sex play by Joanna Burden in *Light in August*); he also knew the tragedy of ambitious American illusionists such as Thomas Sutpen in *Absalom, Absalom!*. America traditionally denied play in the name of seriousness or absorbed play in the name of seriousness. The ingrained moral objection to play in the seventeenth century became the material seduction of play into collective forms after the Civil War. In each case, the pressures of society were matched against play's freedom as the theological proscription against play shifted to a secular imperative to play in concert with others for external reward.

Hawthorne and Fitzgerald's use of play developed according to their preference for romance. Whether attempting to recover the magic of a maypole dance or an heroic football game, the imagery was of a frozen moment of past innocence pure and whole that might withstand present evil and dismay. They had little commitment to action and engagement but rather to the vivid idea of the past, historically rooted, romantically charged, imaginatively perceived. The heart of their play was to project and simulate a life-enhancing role and hold fast to it. But for both Hawthorne and Fitzgerald, the world of the "present," be it Puritan-grim or modern-decadent, defeats their golden children who believe, "Dance! dance!. . . . we shall be as we were yesterday" (*MF*, 86), or who "wed unutterable visions to . . perishable breath" (*GG*, 112). Hawthorne's characters do not extend their play to the limits of play because the author-illusionist snaps their reveries, while Fitzgerald breaks his characters on the rack of their heroic illusions.

In contrast, Hemingway and Faulkner allow their characters to play to the limit of their endurance and spirit. By doing so, they add deep understanding of sporting competition with human adversaries, with the natural world, and with a creator. They know games, contests, and sports are proper labor, rooted in the earth, played out in sweat and blood with pain and exhaustion. Whereas Hawthorne and Fitzgerald simulate new realities to deny or to flee the present, Hemingway and Faulkner know competition to *be* the reality in the present; life is the *agon* here and now, with no anterior reference point of victory and innocence. Although Hawthorne did not write of competition and almost never allowed his characters ritual mastery, a cornerstone of any Hemingway victory, Hawthorne resembled Hemingway in that they both held fate to be ever-present, pervading all characters and relationships. For them, the dilemma was to avoid fate or struggle against it and its absolutism. Hawthorne wearily gave in as his characters again and again compromised back under a prior dispensation of sin and grief. Hemingway fought until his classicially tensed hero-victim gained bitter knowledge of man's impotence in the present.

Hawthorne could not write of exaltation in nature or in contest, Fitzgerald could only idealize it, while Hemingway denied any joy in free play but warily defended his territory. Faulkner had none of these defects and most of their strengths in describing states from the magic of illusion to the obsession of competition. Faulkner's work with play images is the most complete for he could create in all the play modes (*agon, alea, mimicry, ilinx*). He could convey a sense of great contest while retaining the low humor of the grotesque or an exalted sense of play's majesty before ultimate realities. His disquisitions on the play of a creator—"Player," "Risibility," "Umpire"—are no less moving for their being jesting, ironic, or philosophically presumptuous. He knew we are always dancing on sarcophagi but that we must transcend "acute, limited excellence," that life lived in the multiverse of play is a strong testament against "taking it." Faulkner's profound commitment to freedom for his characters dictated his receptivity to play. For in play, the ultimate issue is always freedom: how to live through play toward freedom, how to allow play the dominion that grants freedom. This quest lies at the core of the desire to play.

What happens to the Ritual, School, and Popular Sports Heroes as they move into the contemporary era? In general, the Ritual Sports Hero is no longer viable in a society in which solitary confrontation with nature is now only a kind of national ur-dream in vestigial legacy. The School Sports Hero is on the one hand refined and intellectualized into a new sort of Ritual Sports Hero and on the other subsumed and coarsened into an extended version of the Popular Sports Hero. The Popular Sports Hero of contemporary sports spectacle holds center stage.

Santiago and Ike McCaslin appear to have effectively closed down a great fictional tradition of solitary American individualist heroes in the natural world. Their acolytes will not rise to be caretakers of the wilderness which no longer can be preserved in reality or in the imagination. The ritual goals of pride and humility, perception and mastery, are more fragmented and subverted in violent tales that describe the clash of an urban technological present with a more primitive and powerful sporting world. Hemingway suggested ritual was its own reason for being, a secular calming of the emotions. More often in Hemingway, we knew what the Ritual Sports Hero did, not who he was. Sports heroes and their witnesses remained in proportionate balance; however, in contemporary sports fiction, there is chaotic interaction between heroes and witnesses. The best commentary on the surviving Ritual Sports Hero is found in James Dickey's *Deliverance,* Norman Mailer's *Why Are We in Vietnam?,* and Thomas McGuane's *The Sporting Club* and *Ninety-Two in the Shade.*

The School Sports Hero, a figure of irony and satire when altered by Fitzgerald, Hemingway, and Faulkner, has continued as a bewildered, genteel survivor in an uncertain environment. The figure, however, no longer exists *per se* except in the most simple formula tales. The School Sports Hero has, in effect, split in two, becoming a Ritual Sports Hero or a Popular Sports Hero. As a Ritual Sports Hero, he is fragile, impermanent, doomed, not a representative leader, but almost a mutant in his special skill and individual vision. He performs almost completely for his own revelation and is an inscrutable figure to his witnesses whom he frustrates and who effectively destroy him and damage themselves. He achieves no uncomplicated moments of excellence and public acclaim but rather a physical perfection that cannot be allowed to live. Examples include Wright Morris's *The Huge Season,* John Knowles's *A Separate Peace,* John Updike's *Rabbit, Run,* and Frederick Exley's *A Fan's Notes.*

Alternately, the School Sports Hero has now assumed the role of a Popular Sports Hero. The School Sports Hero's public role of self-discipline, which prepared him for leadership, is no longer possible in a sports culture where high school sports stars have advisors and agents, where college stars are already miniconglomerates, and where the term "student-athlete" is ridiculed and abused in the excesses of the college athletic system. The School Sports Hero becomes another arm of general sports spectacle and is indistinguishable from the Popular Sports Hero. The school had been the repository of values for adolescents since the Civil War, but in the contemporary era, the hero is most likely to be a young professional, regardless of the level of competition. The sport then teaches the priorities and values (or lack of values) in the commercial culture that sanctions and sponsors the sport. Henry Wiggen, the puckish pitcher/narrator/"author" of Mark Harris's *The Southpaw* and *Bang the Drum Slowly,* is 21 years old and baseball has been and will be his schooling. He matures in the major leagues whereas in 1900, he would have been a high-spirited undergraduate at Princeton or Yale, albeit with a more genteel pedigree. Philip Roth's Ron Patimkin in

Goodbye, Columbus is a reverse portrait of the School Sports Hero, a genial boob of a basketball star with lines to both Tom Buchanan and to Lardnerian rubes.

The Popular Sports Hero is now triumphant in the genre of sports fiction. There is really no other character. The only living form bequeathed to contemporary sports fiction is that of Lardner: both his shrewd narrators and his exuberant bumpkins (a character such as Henry Wiggen deftly combines both strains). Contemporary sportsworld[1] is reported from the inside by its heroes; they may be cocky, bemused, dismayed, or desperate. Sportsworld has become the single most recognizable American environment with its own styles, organizational bureaucracy, managerial class, and language. American popular sport which began as a record of leisure-time preferences is now an enormous industry, a thriving giant of monopoly capitalism. The Popular Sports Hero now rests uneasily in the maw of this beast. Despite his wealth and fame, he is as alienated as the society that lionizes him.

Since World War II, the modern comic physical innocents of American lore such as Babe Ruth have been replaced with inward antiheroes, riddled with angst and subversive impulses, and sports fiction has faithfully recorded the shift. Contemporary sports heroes in fiction battle a witnessing multitude lost in mass confusion about individual identity. Heroes become victims of a deep resentment against the overachiever in America. "Will you be the best?" asks Harriett Bird, Bernard Malamud's dark lady in *The Natural.* When young pitcher Roy Hobbs brashly answers, "That's right," she shoots him, for which of us, earth-bound and untalented as we are, can truthfully bear such divine arrogance? Heroism of the athlete and his striving for individual achievement become the last quixotic gestures toward success in an antiheroic age. Perplexed heroes play before disturbed witnesses in a bad time. Contemporary American fiction has treated the sports spectacle with a full range of imaginative responses that illuminate cultural dilemmas within the arena that also transcend the arena: the decline of heroism, the submission to authority, the loss of idealism, and the lack of personal validity to experience. The list of works in both comic and serious veins may merely be suggested here.[2]

The future of the sports subject in American fiction lies in three related directions. Play will remain both an individual and a collective paradigm. First, the sports subject will still be the vehicle for intense inward experience. It will chronicle the exalted or exuberant or desperate play of individual heroes who battle to know their physical natures and integrate that knowledge with spirit and sensibility. Second, it will still be the vehicle for intense examination of the organization of society, all the more so as sportsworld more centrally defines our popular culture and its group activities, telling us what and how we play the way we do. However perverted and dismaying the vision, we still want to gain responsible knowledge of our society, and sporting heroes provide models as well as cautionary tales. Finally, the play *of* fiction rises to meet the sport *in* fiction. The author himself is exposed as a player in much of the recent fiction about sport, making aesthetic capital of the boundaries and limitations of his form.

The play, games, and sports of characters in a novel become interior duplicates of the game of the novel,[3] a concomitant exercise in risk and potential satisfaction for the author as player. Basketball, football, and baseball and three novels about them—Updike's *Rabbit, Run,* Don DeLillo's *End Zone,* Robert Coover's *The Universal Baseball Association*—show how fruitful a wedding of sport as American subject and sport as novelistic game can be. The intersection of the novelist's strong sense of fabulation, self-consciousness, and play with the American sports world is kinetic in its possibility. Updike, DeLillo, and Coover transform a subject rooted in American folklore, popular culture, and education—the social world of American sport—into a mirror world of the writer's struggle to create fictional worlds. It is here that the subject of sport in American fiction currently resides, with potential for creative advances in the novel.

In an enormous land where Americans found isolation to be a continuing condition, sport has provided a testing place for the player, a bond of ceremony for the spectator, and a fertile ground for the birth of popular heroes. The current complexity of the presentation of play and sport underscores their importance to writers who may have studied the tenets of Huizinga and of literary modernism in the academy but who have also spent their childhoods, perhaps only metaphorically, at Ebbets Field, the Golden Dome, and Madison Square Garden. Our writers have always created characters at play with the sure knowledge that, in America, to play and to be active in sport is to be in touch with its people, their traditions, and their fantasy lives. In America, few fictional subjects have claimed as much representative power or continue to flourish in as many suggestive and vital forms.

As it becomes more difficult to believe in anything other than our play, we are challenged to discover if there is any actual difference between a belief in play and in playing our beliefs. A belief in play is a commitment to our most spontaneous and joyful selves; playing our beliefs yields secular ritual we can care about and learn from. *Paidia* and *Ludus* may not save us, suggest our authors, but they provide us at one pole with our freedom and at the other pole with our discipline. They define the shape of the creative arena in which we all dwell and invoke the play spirit that is magically ours within that realm.

Notes

PREFACE

1. Constance Rourke, "A Note on Folklore," *The Roots of American Culture and Other Essays* (New York: Harcourt, Brace, 1942), p. 285.

2. The last decade has witnessed an initial flowering of critical methodologies to deal with popular literature and its patterns. The most cogent so far include John G. Cawelti, "Myth, Symbol, and Formula," *Journal of Popular Culture* 8, no. 1 (Summer 1974); Cawelti, *Adventure, Mystery, and Romance* (Chicago: University of Chicago Press, 1976); David Feldman, "Formalism and Popular Culture," *Journal of Popular Culture* 9, no. 2 (Fall 1975); Bruce Kuklick, "Myth and Symbol in American Studies," *American Quarterly* 24, no. 4 (Fall 1972); Donald Dunlop, "Popular Culture and Methodology," *Journal of Popular Culture* 9, no. 2 (Fall 1975); and Hayden White, "Structuralism and Popular Culture," *Journal of Popular Culture* 7, no. 4 (Spring 1974).

3. Two exceptions to this record in contemporary American fiction are Brenda Patimkin in Philip Roth's *Goodbye, Columbus* (1959) and Willa in Jay Neugeboren's *Big Man* (1966).

INTRODUCTION

1. Christopher Lasch comments on the irony that "the appearance of an escapist conception of 'leisure' coincides with the organization of leisure as an extension of commodity production." Lasch, "The Corruption of Sports," *The New York Review of Books,* 28 April 1977, p. 30.

2. Reuel Denney, *The Astonished Muse* (Chicago: University of Chicago Press, 1957), p. 118.

3. Gregory Stone, "American Sports: Play and Display," in John H. Talamini, Charles H. Page, eds., *Sport and Society: An Anthology* (Boston: Little, Brown, 1973), p. 74.

4. Johan Huizinga, *Homo Ludens* (Boston: Beacon Press, 1955), p. 13.

5. Roger Caillois, *Man, Play, and Games,* trans. Meyer Barash (New York: Free Press of Glencoe, Macmillan, 1961), pp. 8–26.

6. Ibid., p. 160.

7. Emil Benveniste quoted in Jacques Ehrmann, "Homo Ludens Revisited," Ehrmann, ed., *Game, Play, Literature. Yale French Studies* 41, pp. 35–36.

8. Eugen Fink, "The Oasis of Happiness: Toward an Ontology of Play," Ehrmann, ed., *Game, Play, Literature*, p. 19.

9. Ibid., p. 22.

10. Ehrmann, "Homo Ludens Revisited," p. 34.

11. Ibid., p. 44.

12. Ibid., p. 55.

13. Caillois, *Man, Play, and Games*, pp. 11, 83.

14. John Loy, "The Nature of Sport: A Definitional Effort," M. Marie Hart, ed., *Sport in the Socio-Cultural Process* (Dubuque, Iowa: Wm. C. Brown, 1972), p. 50 (hereafter referred to as "Hart"). Loy expands on definitions initially formulated by John M. Roberts, Brian Sutton-Smith, "Child Training and Game Involvement," *Ethnology* 1 (1962), p. 166.

15. Loy, "The Nature of Sport," p. 55.

16. Huizinga, *Homo Ludens*, pp. 39, 50–51.

17. Caillois, *Man and the Sacred*, trans. Barash (Glencoe, Ill.: Free Press of Glencoe, 1960), pp. 158–61.

18. Gunther Lüschen, "The Interdependence of Sport and Culture," Hart, p. 33; Allen Guttmann, *From Ritual To Record* (New York: Columbia University Press, 1978), p. 23.

19. Huizinga, *Homo Ludens*, p. 197.

20. Ibid.

21. Caillois, *Man and the Sacred;* Mircea Eliade, *The Sacred and the Profane*, trans. Willard R. Trask (New York: Harcourt, Brace, 1959); Rene Girard, *Violence and the Sacred*, trans. Patrick Gregory (Baltimore: The Johns Hopkins University Press, 1977).

22. Guttmann, *From Ritual to Record*, p. 23.

23. "Sport as system. . . ," Loy, "The Nature of Sport," p. 57; "sport as institutionalized game. . . ," Marshall McLuhan, "Games: The Extension of Man," *Understanding Media: The Extensions of Man* (1964), Hart, p. 147; "games as dramatic models. . . ," McLuhan, "Games: The Extension of Man," p. 150; "sport as popular art. . . ," Edgar Z. Friedenberg, Foreword to Howard Slusher, *Man, Sport, and Existence*," Hart, p. 181; "sport as regulated social interaction. . . ," Nicholas Petryszak, "The Cultural Evolution of Barbarism in Spectator Sports: A Comparative Analysis," *Sport Sociology Bulletin* 6, no. 1 (Spring 1977), p. 26. Petryszak quotes P.E. Frolich, "Sports and Community," Ph.D. Diss. University of Wisconsin, 1952, p. 274; "sport weds man to technical civilization. . . ," Lewis Mumford, "Sport and the Bitch Goddess," *Technics and Civilization* (New York: Harcourt, Brace, and World, 1934), p. 305; "sport acts as transitional institution. . . ," Arnold Beisser, *The Madness in Sports* (New York: Appleton-Century-Crofts, 1967), p. 41; "sport as social imagery. . . ," Denney, *The Astonished Muse*, p. 98; "sport as currency of communication. . . ," Robert Lipsyte, *Sportsworld* (New York: Quadrangle, *New York Times* Book Co., 1975), p. 51; "sport as success story. . . ," John R. Tunis, *The American Way in Sport* (New York: Duell, Sloan, and Pearce, 1958), p. 18; "sport as rationalization of the Romantic. . . ," Guttmann, *From Ritual to Record*, p. 89; "sport is natural religion. . . ," Michael Novak, *The Joy of Sports* (New York: Basic Books, 1976), p. 19.

24. Daniel Hoffman, *Form and Fable in American Fiction* (New York: Oxford University Press, 1965), p. 4.

25. Huizinga, *Homo Ludens*, p. 197.

26. Huizinga, *America, a Dutch Historian's View from Afar and Near* (New York: Harper & Row, 1972), pp. 115–16.

27. Brian Sutton-Smith, "Introduction," Sutton-Smith, ed., *Play and Learning* (New York: Gardner Press, 1979), p. 1.

28. Ibid.

29. Rourke, *American Humor* (New York: Harcourt, Brace, Jovanovich, 1931), pp. 159, 279–80, 283–84, 287.

1. HAWTHORNE: THE PLAY SPIRIT

1. Guttmann, *From Ritual to Record*, pp. 16, 81.

2. Nathaniel Hawthorne, *The Scarlet Letter. The Centenary Edition of the Works of Nathaniel Hawthorne* (Columbus: Ohio State University Press, 1962) I, 231. Subsequent page references to this edition appear in parentheses in the text.

3. Hawthorne, *The Blithedale Romance. The Centenary Edition*, III, 170. Subsequent page references to this edition appear in parentheses in the text.

4. Hawthorne, *The Marble Faun. The Centenary Edition*, IV, 145. Subsequent page references to this edition appear in parentheses in the text.

5. Washington Irving, "Dolph Heyliger," *Bracebridge Hall, or the Humorists, the Writings of Washington Irving* (New York: G.P. Putnam's Sons, 1931) VIII, 214. Subsequent page references to this edition appear in parentheses in the text.

6. James Fenimore Cooper, *The Pioneers* (New York: A.L. Burt, 1899), p. 231. Subsequent page references to this edition appear in parentheses in the text.

7. Henry David Thoreau, "Higher Laws," *Walden* (Cambridge, Mass.: Houghton-Mifflin, Riverside, 1957), p. 145.

8. Nina Baym states that the Roman carnival scene in *The Marble Faun* "recalls moments in Hawthorne's fiction all the way back to " 'My Kinsman, Major Molineux.' " Baym, *The Shape of Hawthorne's Career* (Ithaca: Cornell University Press, 1976), p. 246.

9. Eugen Fink comments that in play, the player hides his real self behind his role and is submerged in it. Fink, "The Oasis of Happiness," p. 23. *Mimicry-ilinx* are states which are pushed to the periphery of public life in advanced cultures as a means of escape. Caillois, *Man, Play, and Games*, p. 97. The above are apt descriptions of the May frolic in "The Maypole."

10. The May ceremonies were the monarchy's attempt to sacramentalize the life of English communal celebration. Robert Herrick's rites of May in *Hesperides* point to this "fusion of the holy and the holiday." Leah Sinanoglou Marcus, "Herrick's *Hesperides* and the 'Proclamation made for May.' " *Studies in Philology* 76, no. 1 (January 1979), pp. 69–70.

11. Richard Harter Fogle, *Hawthorne's Fiction: The Light and the Dark* (Norman, Okla.: University of Oklahoma Press, 1952), pp. 59–69; Hoffman, *Form and Fable*, chap. 7, "The Maypole of Merry Mount and the Folklore of Love," pp. 126–48; Norris Yates, "Ritual and Reality: Mask and Dance Motifs in Hawthorne's Fiction," *Philological Quarterly* 35 (January 1955), pp. 56–70.

12. Baym writes of Hawthorne's "eight moralized fictions" written between 1834 and 1837: "As a group the fictions celebrate the common highway of life and delpore all attempts to step aside from it. . . . The moral truth in these fictions is normative. . . ." Baym, *The Shape of Hawthorne's Career*, p. 55.

13. The Sylvan Dance scene is examined at length in relation to the subsequent Roman Carnival scene by Edgar Dryden, *Nathaniel Hawthorne: The Poetics of Enchantment* (Ithaca: Cornell University Press, 1977), pp. 115–19.

14. "Arcadia" and "the Golden Age" are familiar rhetorical terms in Hawthorne's fiction about play, occurring in "The Maypole" and *The Blithedale Romance* as well.

Two famous paintings that Hawthorne would have known, Francesco Traini (?), *The Triumph of Death*, c.1350, and Nicolas Poussin, *Et in Arcadia Ego*, c.1630, summarize the intrusion of the sudden perception of death into a sylvan world. *The Triumph of Death* fresco depicts an ornate party of lords and ladies on horseback who come upon the open coffins of plague victims. *Et in Arcadia Ego* shows a tomb and its inscription ("I, too, in Arcadia"), being examined by shepherds and a shepherdess. The fourteenth century fresco well describes the mood of the art that created the *Danse Macabre* while Poussin's classical painting is more reminiscent of the tone of Hawthorne's Roman sarcophagus image in *The Marble Faun*.

15. "In the sylvan dance and carnival episodes Hawthorne dramatizes the basic problem of romance, which arises from man's attempt to use his powers of enchantment to solve an important intersubjective conflict through the creation of a 'neutral territory.' " Dryden, *Nathaniel Hawthorne,* p. 119.

16. Kenyon is psychically tarred and feathered by the raucous procession, as was Major Molineux in actuality, but Kenyon is not *of* the procession. In another vein, he is Robin Molineux, scrutinized from the balcony by the "old citizen" whose "haw-haw's" of laughter define Robin's naiveté. In *The Marble Faun* during the carnival, Kenyon is peered at from a balcony by an abbate, by an old Englishman and his daughters, and, finally, by Hilda herself.

17. Baym, *The Shape of Hawthorne's Career,* p. 233.

18. J. Gary Williams, "History in Hawthorne's 'The Maypole of Merry Mount.' " *Essex Institute Historical Collections* 108 (April 1972), pp. 173–89; John P. McWilliams, Jr., "Fictions of Merry Mount," *American Quarterly* 29, no. 1 (Spring 1977), pp. 3–30; Michael Zuckerman, "Pilgrims in the Wilderness: Community, Modernity, and the Maypole of Merry Mount," *The New England Quarterly* 50, no. 2 (June 1977).

19. Foster Rhea Dulles, *America Learns To Play* (New York: D. Appleton-Century, 1940), p. 13.

20. Hoffman, *Form and Fable,* p. 136. The Long Parliament in 1643 had called in all copies of *The King James Book of Sport* and had them burned.

21. Marcus, " 'Present Occasions' and the Shaping of Ben Jonson's Masques," *ELH* 45 (1978), p. 214. The annual inauguration of the Lord Mayor of London was celebrated by a procession from London to Westminster and back on November 9.

22. Charles Feidelson, *Symbolism and American Literature* (Chicago: University of Chicago Press, 1953), pp. 14–15. "The symbolistic and the allegorical patterns in Hawthorne's books reach quite different conclusions; or, rather, the symbolism leads to an inconclusive luxuriance of meaning, while allegory imposes the pat moral and simplified character" (15).

23. Feidelson noted Hawthorne's "sense of the combined power and danger in art" and the "awareness that art claims to be a new and real creation in status and in form and, as such, is not subject to any external discipline." Ibid., p. 234.

24. Dryden, *Nathaniel Hawthorne,* pp. 171–72.

25. Marcus, "Present Occasions," 217.

26. A complementary line of imagery suggests "the deep ruffs, painfully wrought bands, and gorgeously embroidered gloves" (82) of Puritan divines and magistrates. Here is the official embroidery of Boston which Bellingham's decorated mansion represents as well.

2. SPORT AND SOCIETY

1. *The Sketch Book* contains repeated references to seventeenth-century English commentary on holiday play and ritual. In "The Christmas Dinner," Irving writes, "I strongly suspect Master Simon [Bracebridge] to have taken the idea of his [maskings and mummeries] from Ben Jonson's 'Masque of Christmas,' " Irving, *The Sketch Book of Geoffrey Crayon,*

Gent. The Writings of Washington Irving (New York: G.P. Putnam's Sons, 1931), 28, pp. 74–75.

Irving also quotes from Herrick's *Twelfth Night* as well as from "A Christmas Carol Sung to the King in the Presence at Whitehall'": "Dark and dull night, flie hence away/And give the honor to this day/That sees December turn'd to May." Irving, "Christmas Day," *The Sketch Book,* p. 32.

2. William L. Hedges, *Washington Irving* (Baltimore: Johns Hopkins University Press, 1965), p. 168.

3. Irving, *The Sketch Book,* p. 18. Subsequent page references to this edition appear in parentheses in the text. References to "Rip Van Winkle" and "The Legend of Sleepy Hollow" are not paginated due to their multiple printings in countless editions.

4. "Sir Anthony Fitzherbert's *Book of Husbandry;* Markham's *Country Contentments;* the *Tretus of Hunting,* by Sir Thomas Cockayne, Knight; Izzac Walton's *Angler,* and two or three more such ancient worthies of the pen, were his standard authorities" ("Christmas Day," p. 283).

5. Terence Martin, "Rip, Ichabod, and the American Imagination," *American Literature* 31 (May 1959), p. 138.

6. Henry A. Pochmann, "Irving's German Sources in *The Sketch Book,*" *Studies in Philology* 27 (July 1930), pp. 494, 498.

7. Ibid., p. 500.

8. Philip Young, "Fallen From Time: The Mythic Rip," *Kenyon Review* 22 (Autumn 1960), p. 569. Young gives comprehensive accounts of the symbols surrounding the figures of Thor and Odin that are germane to "Rip Van Winkle" and states that "Rip" "is our version of a myth that survives as a description of a nearly forgotten ceremony in the worship of Thor for the production of rain" (564).

9. Fink, "The Oasis of Happiness," pp. 22, 28.

10. "The Legend of Sleepy Hollow" was first placed in the context of sport and society by Wiley T. Umphlett, *The Sporting Myth and the American Experience* (Lewisburg, Pa.: Bucknell University Press, 1975), pp. 40–41. Umphlett echoes the suggestion of Hoffman, *Form and Fable,* p. 240, that Brom Bones points toward the anarchic energy and genial bullying of the frontier backwoodsman.

11. Dolph Heyliger, the young hero of "Dolph Heyliger" in *Bracebridge Hall,* is a Brom Bones figure who has even more associations with games and sports. Like Brom Bones, Dolph was "full of fun and frolic, and had that daring, gamesome spirit" ("Dolph Heyliger," p. 200). A true all-around athlete, Dolph's proficiency earns him acceptance by Squire Antony Vander Heyden and his jocular mates, marriage to the Squire's daughter Marie, and inheritance of the Vander Heyden estate. Dolph's feats include echoes of those of Brom Bones, Ichabod Crane, and Rip Van Winkle: "He was a bold rider; he was famous for leaping and wrestling; he played tolerably on the fiddle; could swim like a fish; and was the best hand in the whole place at fives and nine-pins" (216).

12. Henry Nash Smith, *Virgin Land* (1950), chapter 6, "Leatherstocking and the Problem of Social Order"; Richard Chase, *The American Novel and its Tradition* (1957), chapter 3, "The Significance of Cooper"; and Leslie Fiedler, *Love and Death in the American Novel* (1962), chapter 6, "James Fenimore Cooper and the Historical Romance."

13. Hector St. John de Crevecoeur, Letter III, "What is an American?", *Letters From an American Farmer* (London: J.M. Dent & Sons, 1962), pp. 47, 51–52.

14. The first narrative about Boone that purportedly quoted him directly was that of John Filson, *The Discovery, Settlement and Present State of Kentucke* (1784). Along with Filson, Timothy Flint's most popular biography, *The Life and Adventures of Daniel Boone, the First Settler of Kentucky* (1833) were the source books for the spate of biographies that fol-

lowed: W.H. Bogart, *Daniel Boone and the Hunters of Kentucky* (Boston: Lee & Shepard, 1870); Cecil B. Hartley, *Life and Times of Colonel Daniel Boone* (Philadelphia: G.G. Evans, 1859); and John Bakeless, *Daniel Boone, Master of the Wilderness* (New York: William Morrow, 1939). See also Smith, *Virgin Land,* chapter 5, "Daniel Boone: Empire Builder or Philosopher of Primitivism?"

15. Bogart, *Daniel Boone,* p. 39. Subsequent page references to this edition appear in parentheses in the text.

16. R.W.B. Lewis, *The American Adam* (Chicago: University of Chicago Press, 1955), p. 99.

17. Cooper, *The Deerslayer* (New York: G.P. Putnam's Sons, Mohawk Edition, n.d.), p. 7. Subsequent page references to this edition appear in parentheses in the text.

18. Lewis, *The American Adam,* pp. 100–1.

19. See H. Daniel Peck, *A World By Itself: The Pastoral Moment in Cooper's Fiction* (New Haven: Yale University Press, 1977). Peck is concerned with middle-ground natural or man-made arenas as essential to Cooper's fictional drama. Peck comments on the Glimmerglass ordering everything around it, "a valued centerpoint bound by concentric circles" (83). Likewise, "Cooper's timeless woods hold human action in the stasis of the classical drama" (88). Peck speaks of the formless, curved space of parklike forests (152); "islands of space" (177). Peck feels that as an artist, Cooper's deepest wish was to see American landscape as organized, structured space (189).

20. Fink comments that "the play world is not suspended in a purely ideal world. It always has a real setting and yet is never a real thing among other real things, although it has an absolute need of real things as a point of departure." Fink, "The Oasis of Happiness," p. 24.

21. Ishmael Bush in Cooper's *The Prairie* (1827) is a migratory squatter, a realization of Crevecoeur's dubious model, who has renounced farming and whose "exertions seldom exceeded his wants." Indeed, Bush has a large family of axe-wielding Billy Kirbys, consistently refers to his life in Kentucky and his failure to retain land, and plays a coarsened, sceptical version of Boone to Natty's dignified 80-year-old woods spokesman.

22. Hawthorne's Miles Coverdale in *The Blithedale Romance* cannot translate the daily round in nature into poetry *or* education: "Our labor symbolized nothing, and left us mentally sluggish in the dusk of evening. Intellectual activity is incompatible with any large amount of bodily exercise. The yeoman and the scholar . . .are two distinct individuals, and can never be melted or welded into one substance" (*BR,* 66).

3. SPORT AND THE FRONTIER

1. Hoffman, *Form and Fable,* pp. 78, 81.

2. Dorson, ed., *Davy Crockett: American Comic Legend* (New York: Spiral Press, 1939), p. 115. Subsequent page references to this edition appear in parentheses in the text.

3. Thomas Kirkman, "Jones' Fight," *Spirit of the Times* (1840), rpt. William T. Porter, ed., *The Big Bear of Arkansas and Other Tales* (1845), rpt. Hennig Cohen, William B. Dillingham, eds., *Humor of the Old Southwest* (Cambridge: Houghton-Mifflin, Riverside, 1964), p. 63.

4. Mark Twain, "The Notorious Jumping Frog of Calaveras County," *The Portable Mark Twain* (New York: Viking, 1968), p. 37.

5. See T.H. Breen, "Horses and Gentlemen: The Cutural Significance of Gambling

Among the Gentry of Virginia," *William and Mary Quarterly* 34, No. 2 (April 1977), pp. 239–57.

6. Cantwell, "America is Formed," p. 57.

7. Ibid., p. 59.

8. Breen, "Horses and Gentlemen," p. 250.

9. Betts, "Organized Sport in Industrial America," Ph.D. Dissertation, Columbia University, 1951, p. 14. Some of the great match races included Eclipse–Sir Henry (1823), Grey Eagle–Wagner (1840), Boston–Fashion (1842), and Peytona–Fashion (1845).

10. Ibid., pp. 11–12, 15, 42.

11. John James Audubon, *Audubon and his Journals* (New York: Charles Scribner's Son, 1960), I, pp. 459–62.

12. The best studies on the backwoodsman in fiction remain: Rourke, *American Humor;* Walter Blair, *Native American Humor* (1937); and Kenneth Lynn, *Mark Twain and Southwestern Humor* (1959).

13. These remarks are suggested by Rourke, "A Note on Folklore," *The Roots of American Culture and Other Essays,* pp. 238–50.

14. Lynn, *Mark Twain and Southwestern Humor* (Boston: Little, Brown, 1959), p. 41.

15. The Crockett autobiography was really three volumes put together in a 1923 edition with an introduction by Hamlin Garland: *A Narrative of the Life of David Crockett of the State of Tennessee* (1834), written for the 1835 election campaign; *Colonel Crockett's Tour of the North and Down East* (1835); and *Colonel Crockett's Exploits and Adventures in Texas* (1836).

16. *Davy Crockett's Almanack of Wild Sports in the West* 1, No. 3 (1837), cover rpt. in Dorson, *America in Legend* (New York: Random House, 1973). The 1939 limited Spiral Press edition is a valuable reproduction of the more comic Crockett almanac sketches along with illustrations of the original woodcuts.

17. Ibid., p. 119. Subsequent page references to this edition appear in parentheses in the text. See also Franklin J. Meine, ed., *The Crockett Almanacks. Nashville Series 1835-38* (Chicago: Caxton Club, 1955).

18. For an overview of the transformation of folk hero into popular hero, see Dorson, *American Folklore* (Chicago: University of Chicago Press, 1959), pp. 48, 199, 207.

19. Blair, Meine, eds., *Half-Horse, Half-Alligator: The Growth of the Mike Fink Legend* (Chicago: University of Chicago Press, 1956), pp. 9–13.

20. Dorson, ed., *Davy Crockett,* p. 42.

21. As Crockett relates, "That made Mike kinder sorter wrothy, and he sends a ball after his wife as she was going to the spring after a gourd full of water, and nocked half her coom out of her head, without stirring a hair, and calls out to her to stop for me to take a blizzard at what was left on it." "Col. Crockett Beat at a Shooting Match," *Nashville Crockett Almanac* (1839) in Blair, Meine. eds., *Half-Horse,* p. 66.

Mike decides to teach wife Peg a lesson by making her crawl into a leaf pile, swearing to shoot her if she moves. He then sets the pile on fire and old Peg stands it as long as she can before running for the river, clothes and hair ablaze. Mike's satisfied summation is "There, that'll larn you to be winkin' at them fellers on the other boat." "K," "A Letter to the Western General Advertiser" (11 February 1845), Blair, Meine, eds., *Half-Horse,* pp. 85–86.

22. "Death of Mike Fink," *St. Louis Reveille,* 21 October 1844. Irving's brief portrait of backwoodsman Dirk Sciuler in Diedrich Knickerbocker's *History of New York* (1809) is a model for the whiskey-smelling backwoodsman, part Indian and all idler. Dirk is drunk and disreputable and continually beleaguers the fort. Dirk's links to backwoodsmen of later tales is suggested by Lewis Leary, "Washington Irving," Louis D. Rubin, ed., *The Comic Imagination in American Literature* (New Brunswick, N.J.: Rutgers University Press, 1973), p. 70.

23. Thorpe, "The Disgraced Scalp Lock," *Spirit,* 16 July 1842, rpt. Thorpe, *Mysteries*

of the Backwoods (1846), rpt. Cohen, Dillingham, eds., *Humor of the Old Southwest,* pp. 284-95.

24. See Francis Brinley, *Life of William T. Porter* (New York: D. Appleton & Co., 1860); Norris Yates, *William T. Porter and the "Spirit of the Times"* (Baton Rouge: Louisiana State University Press, 1957), is the definitive study of Southwestern Humor in the newspaper.

25. "We have all derived our tastes for Field sports and racing from our English ancestry." Porter, *Spirit of the Times,* 9 March 1839, p. 1. Porter makes his bid for readers to subscribe to the *American Turf Register,* saying that it had been languishing, but that he viewed "its success as intimately connected with the best interests of the Turf." Porter, *Spirit,* 13 April 1839, p. 62.

26. Porter covered the great sectional match races of Wagner and Grey Eagle and of Boston and Fashion, the latter on 10 May 1842 for $20,000 at the Union Course on Long Island. Boston, the Virginia horse, lost to Fashion from New Jersey.

In reality, Porter never missed an opportunity to print copy on a major prize fight on either side of the Atlantic. In 1842, Porter covered a "Fatal Prize Fight Between Lilly and McCoy for $200 a side at Hastings, N.Y." The report is a grisly round-by-round description of a 120-round, two-hour-and-forty-three-minute slaughter which ends with McCoy's death. From Round 70: "McCoy was now indeed a most unseemly object; both his eyes were black— the left one nearly closed. . . . His very forehead was black and blue; his lips were swollen to an incredible size, and the blood streamed down his chest." Porter, *Spirit,* 17 September 1842, p. 339.

27. By the end of 1848, Thorpe, Hooper, Joseph M. Field, Sol Smith, John S. Robb, Frances A. Durivage, George P. Burnham, and Henry Clay Lewis had all brought out volumes. Yates, *William T. Porter,* p. 53.

28. *Spirit,* 30 July 1845, p. 270.

29. *Spirit,* 1 March 1845, p. 18.

30. Porter (signed), *Spirit,* 15 March 1845, p. 27.

31. A survey of the *Spirit's* index to Volume 16 (Feb. 1846 to Feb. 1847) shows roughly 200 "original contributions" and 87 "literary articles," about half of which had been taken from foreign periodicals. There are 57 items on cricket as opposed to 25 articles on the English turf, 11 boxing reports, 32 articles on pedestrianism (track), 100 accounts of Army or Navy life (both British and American) 53 farming or breeding essays, 27 articles on aquatic sports, mostly yachting regattas, 35 items on fishing, 33 on shooting, 25 on chess, 33 American Racing Calendar Meeting results, 7 tables on the sale of blood stock, and approximately 150 "miscellaneous items" in addition to regular columns.

32. Kirkman owned a plantation in Mississippi and iron works in Tennessee as well as his riding stable. His horse Peytona reputedly won a $100,000 purse on Long Island in 1844. Cohen, Dillingham, eds., *Humor of the Old Southwest,* p. 60.

33. Yates, *William T. Porter,* pp. 115-17. Yates gives the date of publication as 1843. However, in Porter's anthology of the same title, Porter states that the story had appeared in the *Spirit* in 1836.

34. Thomas Kirkman, "A Quarter Race in Kentucky," Porter, ed., *A Quarter Race in Kentucky and Other Sketches* (Philadelphia: Carey and Hart, 1846), p. 24. Subsequent page references to this edition appear in parentheses in the text.

35. Kirkman, "Jones' Fight," Cohen, Dillingham, eds., *Humor of the Old Southwest,* pp. 60-65.

36. Kirkman's reference is perhaps an allusion to the ineffectual Richard Jones in Cooper's *The Pioneers.*

37. Noland published the first of his 45 Pete Whetstone letters in the *Spirit* in 1836; Lewis' "The Indefatigable Bear Hunter" evidences nostalgia for the anachronistic veteran hunter who has outlived his usefulness, a softening of the Mike Fink persona.

38. Kenneth Lynn has linked the problem of Southwestern narrative to the gentlemen

humorists' dismay at the decline of the big planters' political dominance in the Age of Jackson, for "as the Southwestern humorists were less and less able to control ugly realities by means of myth, the vernacular material of their humor ineluctably mastered the gentlemanly style." Lynn, *Mark Twain and Southwestern Humor*, p. 18.

39. Echoing the prejudice against the popular conception of the backwoodsman, Herbert wrote Porter to state that he had adopted the name of "Frank Forester" "to popularize sportsmanship, and to divest it . . . from the prestige of brutality and rudeness." *Spirit*, 9 June 1849, p. 186.

40. See Lewis Pinckney Jones, "William Elliott, South Carolina Nonconformist," *The Journal of Southern History* 17 (August 1951), pp. 361–81.

41. William Elliott, *Carolina Sports By Land and Water* (Charleston, S.C., 1846), p. 100. Elliott paid for an illustrated edition published in 1856.

42. Milton Rickels, *Thomas Bangs Thorpe: Humorist of the Old Southwest* (Baton Rouge: Louisiana State University Press, 1962), pp. 196–201. Thorpe became part owner of the *Spirit* during 1850–51. After squabbles with his co-owners over editorial policy, he sold his interests in the *Spirit* in March 1861, just in time to escape liability in the paper's collapse during the early days of the Civil War.

43. Lynn, *Mark Twain and Southwestern Humor*, p. 52.

44. See the excellent article by J.A. Leo LeMay, "The Text, Tradition and Themes of 'The Big Bear of Arkansas,' " *American Literature* 47, no. 3 (November 1975), 321–42.

45. Thomas Bangs Thorpe, "Tom Owen the Bee Hunter," *The Hive of the Bee Hunter: A Repository of Sketches* (New York: D. Appleton, 1854), p. 47.

46. Peck, *A World By Itself*, p. 49.

47. Longstreet had spent a year at Yale in 1811; he was admitted to the bar in 1815 and became a judge in 1822. In later years he was president of the University of Mississippi (1848–56) and the University of South Carolina (1858–61).

48. Augustus Baldwin Longstreet, "The Turf," *Georgia Scenes* (New York: Harper & Bros., 1859), p. 152. Subsequent page references to this edition appear with story title in parentheses in the text.

49. Lynn, *Mark Twain and Southwestern Humor*, pp. 44–45.

50. W. Stanley Hoole, *Alias Simon Suggs: The Life and Times of Johnson Jones Hooper* (University, Ala.: University of Alabama Press, 1952), pp. 49, 54–57. Porter first noted Hooper in the *Spirit*, 9 September 1843, likening him to Longstreet. Porter began to copy the first Simon Suggs stories from Hooper's *East Alabamian* in early 1845, and the 11 March 1845 *Spirit* carried Hooper's first story written expressly for Porter, "Daddy Biggs's Scrape at Cockrell's Bend." Two further Suggs stories appeared on 17 May and 19 July 1845 in the *Spirit*.

51. Johnson Jones Hooper, *Adventures of Captain Simon Suggs* (Chapel Hill: University of North Carolina Press, 1969), pp. 9–10. Subsequent page references to this edition appear in parentheses in the text.

52. Joseph G. Baldwin, "Simon Suggs, Jr., Esq. of Rackinack Arkansaw," *The Flush Times of Alabama and Mississippi* (New York: D. Appleton, 1854), p. 127.

53. George Washington Harris, "Sporting Epistle from East Tennessee," M. Thomas Inge, ed., *High Times and Hard Times* (Kingsport, Tenn.: Vanderbilt University Press, 1967), pp. 15–16.

54. Harris, "Mrs. Yardley's Quilting," Meine, ed., *Tall Tales of the Southwest* (New York: A.A. Knopf, 1930), p. 160.

55. Harris, "Bill Ainsworth's Quarter Race," Ben Harris McClary, ed., *The Lovingood Papers* (Athens, Tenn.: Tennessee Wesleyan College, 1965), p. 22. "Settled men stood facin' in pairs, with their hats down over thar eyes, whittlin' sticks as they talked, thinkin' more than they sed, an' wonderin' if they'd bet on the right hoss. Or sot, or lay roun in the shades talkin of other races an' other days."

"A Snake-Bit Irishman" originally appeared in the 17 January 1846 *Spirit*. Harris later adapted it to Sut's vernacular and included it in his 1867 collection. Meine, ed., *Tall Tales of the Southwest*, p. 315.

56. Harris, "Sicily Burns's Wedding," Meine, ed., *Tall Tales of the Southwest*, p. 345.

4. ORGANIZED SPORT AND ITS REPORTERS

1. Leo Marx, *The Machine in the Garden* (New York: Oxford University Press, 1964), pp. 343, 354.

2. Hooper died in 1862, Harris in 1869, and Longstreet in 1870. Hooper and Longstreet had ceased to write sketches as early as 1850 in favor of political polemics championing the South's cause. Thorpe died in New York in 1878. For a look at the post-Civil War south's most vital sporting city, see Dale Somers, *The Rise of Sport in New Orleans: 1850—1900* (Baton Rouge: Louisiana State University Press, 1972).

3. The *Spirit* of 30 September 1854 contained the score, Knickerbockers 24, Gothams 13; on 23 December 1854, the *Spirit* reported that three clubs (Knickerbockers, Gothams, and Eagles) had met semiweekly during an eight month season.

4. Walt Whitman, "Song of Myself," *Walt Whitman: Complete Poetry and Selected Prose and Letters* (London: Nonesuch Press, 1971), Song 33, p. 59.

5. See Benjamin G. Rader, "The Quest for Sub-Communities and the Rise of American Sport," *American Quarterly* 29, no. 4 (Fall 1977), pp. 355–69.

6. Dulles, *America Learns to Play*, p. 183; see Lewis Mumford, *The Brown Decades: A Study of the Arts in America, 1865—1915* (New York: Dover Publications, 1955), pp. 82–96, for an introduction to Frederick Law Olmsted, the master builder of urban parks in New York, San Francisco, and other cities; see also Robert Lewis, "Frontier and Civilization in the Thought of Frederick Olmsted," *American Quarterly* 29, no. 4 (Fall 1977), pp. 385–403. Lewis states that Olmsted's proposals for better recreation facilities provided the clearest example of the broad program of genteel civilization. It was inevitable that the urban public would clamor for green space for individual and team sport, and Olmsted's gardens and groves were doomed from the outset to coexist with playing fields and ball diamonds.

7. Betts, "Organized Sport in Industrial America," pp. 138, 140, 157–58. A look at the financial structure of early baseball is contained in economist Ralph Andreano's *No Joy in Mudville: The Dilemma of Major League Baseball* (Cambridge, Mass.: Schenkman, 1965).

8. "Hurrah! this is the way to sail now. Every keel a sunbeam. Hurrah!—Here we go like three tin kettles at the tail of a mad cougar! This puts me in a mind of fastening to an elephant in a tilbury on a plain—makes the wheel-spokes fly, boys, when you fasten to him that way; and there's danger of being pitched out too, when you strike a hill. Hurrah! this is the way a fellow feels when he's going to Davy Jones—all a rush down an endless inclined plane! Hurrah! this whale carries the everlasting mail!" Herman Melville, *Moby-Dick* (Cambridge, Mass.: Houghton-Mifflin, Riverside, 1956), pp. 278–79. Subsequent page references to this edition appear in parentheses in the text.

9. Marx, *The Machine in the Garden*, p. 315.

10. Twain, *Life on the Mississippi. The Writings of Mark Twain: Author's National Edition* (New York: Harper & Bros., 1911), 9, p. 35. Subsequent page references to this edition appear in parentheses in the text.

11. See Betts, "Organized Sport in Industrial America," pp. 34–38 for a factual account of a steamboat racing as sport. Betts reports steamboat races on the Hudson River, the Great Lakes, and lesser rivers as well.

12. Kenneth Lynn and James Cox have attempted to account for the cut-off of idyllic memory by saying that as Twain faced the end of his coming-of-age period as fictional material, he saw technology and industry looming ahead of him as national preoccupations and balked at the prospect. They contend that his resistence pushed him further into what Lynn calls the "Happy Valley" of his childhood in search of the material which became *Tom Sawyer*. Lynn suggests "Old Times" unlocked *Tom Sawyer* much as Twain's trip down the Mississippi in the new South in 1882 opened his eyes for the realistic portrayal of a permanently damaged river society that he used to complete *Huckleberry Finn*. Lynn, *Mark Twain and Southwestern Humor*, pp. 170–71, 227. Cox sees the shift at the end of "Old Times" as the passing to boyhood from apprenticeship, from Tall Tale to fiction; in 1875, Twain was actually reaching the end of his own biography for fiction in writing of Sam Clemens' apprenticeship in 1857. James M. Cox, *Mark Twain: The Fate of Humor* (Princeton: Princeton University Press, 1966), pp. 120–28.

13. Harold Seymour, *Baseball: The Early Years* (New York: Oxford University Press, 1960), pp. 8–10.

14. Twain, "Welcome Home," *Mark Twain's Speeches* (New York: Harper & Bros., 1923), p. 145.

15. See Charles H. Gold, "Mark Twain and 'the damn machine,' " *Book Production Industry & Magazine Production* 53, no. 5 (September 1977).

16. Twain, *A Connecticut Yankee in King Arthur's Court* (New York: Harper & Bros., 1899), p. 367. Subsequent page references to this edition appear in parentheses in the text.

Lynn suggests that Hank Morgan is a Sut Lovingood, a backwoods prankster with technology at his disposal. Lynn, *Mark Twain and Southwestern Humor*, p. 252.

17. The summary of Spalding's career is gleaned from Arthur Bartlett, *Baseball and Mr. Spalding* (New York: Farrar, Straus, & Young, 1950).

18. *New York Clipper*, 30 April 1887. Mack, later to become baseball's most famous owner-manager in the twentieth century with the Philadelphia Athletics, was then 25 and in his second season as catcher for Washington.

19. Albert Johannsen, *The House of Beadle and Adams and its Dime and Nickel Novels* (Norman, Okla.: University of Oklahoma Press, 1950), 2, pp. 50–51. Chadwick (1824–1906) not only edited baseball guides for Beadle and Spalding but was also on the staff of the *Clipper* for thirty years as well as baseball columnist for *Outing* in the 1880s. He remained a staunch defender of the amateur spirit until his death.

20. Another index to baseball's growth is the number of clubs represented at each annual National Baseball Convention. Chadwick noted the rise: 1857, 16 teams; 1858, 25; 1859, 49; 1860, 62; 1861, 34; 1862, 32; 1863, 28; 1864, 30; and 1865, 91. *Beadle's Dime Baseball Player*, 1866 (hereafter referred to as *DBBP*), p. 38. Although Chadwick does not comment, the chart would clearly indicate how the Civil War hurt the development of organized ball.

21. At Burlington, N.J., in August 1874, the White Stockings defeated the Haymakers 1-0, "a score previously unequalled in the annals of the game." *DBBP* (1876), p. 94; Chadwick wrote, "Avoid having ex-captains or ex-managers in your team; or if this cannot be avoided, see to it that no loophole be left for the ambitious hopes of preferment by the ex-captain or manager in the team who has been obliged to accept a subordinate position." *DBBP* (1880), pp. 44–45; in 1874, Harry Wright's Cincinnati Red Stockings and the Philadelphia Athletics went to England where they played ball against each other as well as cricket against English teams. *DBBP* (1880), pp. 46–48.

22. Rex Lardner, *The Legendary Champions* (New York: American Heritage Press, 1972), p. 34.

23. Frank Luther Mott, *A History of American Magazines* (New York: Macmillan, 1941), 4, p. 334.

Among the absurd contests encouraged by Fox in the '80s and '90s were bridge-jumping, a twelve hour walking match, horseback wrestling, female boxing, weight lifting, and wrestling (all scandals at the time), a "going without sleep" contest, rat baiting, teeth lifting, a twelve-hour opium smoking match, and a one-legged clog-dancing competition.

24. Lardner, *The Legendary Champions,* p. 50.

25. In 1920, the romantic, evangelical bard of the vanished frontier, Vachel Lindsay, looked back on his boyhood in an overtly sentimental poem, "John L. Sullivan, The Strong Boy of Boston." The poem was filled with references to many heroes of American popular culture, of which Lindsay found the perfect muscular representative in Sullivan.

26. For boxing in the dime novel, see "Billy Plimmer in and out of the Ring," Street & Smith's *New York Five Cent Library,* 67, 16 December 1893; "Jack Dempsey, the World Beater," Street & Smith's *NYFCL,* 78, 17 March 1894; "Jack Skelly, the Great Featherweight," *NYFCL,* 85.

27. Eugene Field (1850–1895), the *Chicago News'* morning editorial writer and children's rhymester, had crowned Kelly the "King" in 1883 in his "Sharps and Flats" column. Slason Thompson, *Life of Eugene Field* (New York: D. Appleton, 1927), p. 118. Kelly led the National League in batting in 1884 with .354 and in 1886, the year before he was traded to Boston, with .388. He also led the league in runs scored in 1884–86, averaging 133 runs per season. Kelly was elected to the Hall of Fame in 1945.

28. Kelly nearly always slid, "not always falling away and hooking, but sometimes diving head-first away from the base and then reaching a vagrant hand out to catch the bag as he passed, or kicking both his feet rapidly so the baseman could not lay the ball on either, sometimes booting the ball out of the player's hand, once . . . sliding between the spread legs of a previous base runner who had stopped dead just short of home plate. . . ." Robert Smith, *Baseball in America* (New York: Holt, Rinehart and Winston, 1961), p. 70.

29. "Slide, Kelly, slide!/ Your running's a disgrace!/ Slide, Kelly, slide!/ Stay there, hold your base!/ If someone doesn't steal you,/ And your batting doesn't fail you,/ They'll take you to Australia!/ Slide, Kelly, slide!"
From Seymour, *Baseball: The Early Years,* p. 357. The Australia reference is to Spalding's world tour.

30. David Voigt, *American Baseball* (Norman, Okla.: University of Oklahoma Press, 1966), I, pp. 17, 193–195; Betts, "Sporting Journalism in the Nineteenth Century," *American Quarterly* 5 (Spring 1953), pp. 39–56; Seymour, *Baseball: The Early Years,* chap. 27, "The American National Game."

31. An excellent synthesis of Chicago historical context and personal detail is contained in Barbara C. Schaff's *Mr. Dooley's Chicago* (New York: Anchor Press, 1977); see also Elmer Ellis, *Mr. Dooley's America: A Life of Finley Peter Dunne* (New York: Alfred A. Knopf, 1941), pp. 24–25; Betts, "Sporting Journalism"; Hugh Fullerton, "The Fellows Who Made the Game," *Saturday Evening Post,* 21 April 1928, pp. 18–19, 184–88.

32. *Chicago Evening News,* 30 April 1887. Subsequent Dunne citations are all from the *News* and will show date of report in parentheses in the text.

33. In 1887, batters were still allowed four strikes and pitchers were allowed five balls. Billy Sunday, later the famous evangelist, was a light-hitting White Stockings outfielder with a .248 lifetime batting average; however, he was a demon runner with 71 stolen bases during 1888 and 84 steals for Pittsburgh in 1890. In his own field, Sunday became a master of baseball language, sometimes pretending to "slide into heaven" and intoning, "O Lord, give us some coachers out at this tabernacle so that people can be brought home to you. Some of them are dying on second and third base, Lord, and we don't want that."

34. Ade reported the 1892 Sullivan-Corbett fight for the *Chicago Record.* He wrote three dime novel parodies for the *Record:* "Handsome Cyril; or, the Messenger Boy With the Warm Heart"; "Clarence Allen, the Hypnotic Boy Journalist"; and "Rollo Johnson, the Boy

Inventor; or, the Demon Bicycle and its Daring Rider.'' Meine, ed., George Ade, *Stories of the Streets and of the Town from the Chicago Record,* 1893–1900 (Chicago: The Caxton Club, 1941).

35. Ade, "The Fable of the Base Ball Fan Who Took the Only Known Cure," Jean Shepherd, ed., *The America of George Ade* (New York: G.P. Putnam, 1961), p. 56.

36. Mott, *American Journalism* (New York: Macmillan, 1941), p. 443; Betts, "Organized Sport in Industrial America," p. 151; Fullerton, "The Fellows Who Made the Game," p. 188.

An authoritative history of sportswriting in America is badly needed. The encyclopedic histories of Betts, Mott, and Seymour furnish the best leads for future research on this subject.

37. Larzer Ziff, *The American 1890's* (New York: Viking Press, 1966), p. 152. For an overview of the problems of American writers beginning as journalists, see Ziff, "The School in the Cemetary," *The American 1890's,* pp. 146–55.

38. An introductory popular account of baseball and American speech is found in Tristram Coffin's *The Old Ball Game* (New York: Herder & Herder, 1971), pp. 51–75; on "Casey at the Bat," see Coffin, *The Old Ball Game,* p. 158; Martin Gardner, *The Annotated Casey at the Bat* (New York: C.N. Potter, 1956).

39. Betts, "Organized Sport in Industrial America," pp. 197–98, 409; Seymour, *Baseball: The Early Years,* pp. 303, 357.

40. Lee Allen, *100 Years of Baseball* (New York: Bartholomew House, 1950), pp. 34–37.

41. Voigt, *American Baseball,* I, pp. 108–9.

42. Henry Nash Smith, ed., *Popular Culture and Industrialism* (New York: New York University Press, 1967), p. 403; Merle Curti, "Dime Novels and the American Tradition," *Yale Review* 26 (1937), pp. 761–68, rpt. Curti, *Probing Our Past* (New Haven: Yale University Press, 1955).

43. See Mary Noel, *Villains Galore: The Heyday of the Popular Story Weekly* (New York: Macmillan, 1954), chapters 4–6.

44. Beadle's charge to prospective authors:

"Authors who write for our consideration will bear in mind that

We prohibit all things offensive to good taste, in expression or incident—

We prohibit subjects or characters that carry an immoral *taint*—

We prohibit the repetition of any occurrence, which, though true, is yet better untold—"

From Johannsen, *House of Beadle and Adams,* I, p. 4.

45. See Johannsen, *House of Beadle and Adams,* I, xv–xvi, for a complete list of successful Beadle publications.

Some of the more prominent long-run story papers with dates of inception were Street & Smith's *New York Weekly* (1859); Frank Leslie's *Boys' and Girls' Weekly* (1867); Norman Munro's *New York Family Story Paper* (1873); George Munro's *Fireside Companion;* and Frank Tousey's *New York Boys' Weekly* (1876).

46. In the early 1890s, the St. Louis Browns offered a Buffalo Bill show featuring Sitting Bull, plus a regular ball game, all for 50¢. Seymour, *Baseball: The Early Years,* p. 199.

47. George Jenks, "Double Curve Dan the Pitcher Detective; or, Against Heavy Odds," *Beadle's Half Dime Library,* 581, 11 Sept. 1888, p. 1.

48. Ibid., p. 15.

Jenks (1850–1929) was an English journalist who came to America in 1872 and began writing full-time for Beadle in 1886. He knew very little about the actual mechanics of baseball. He believed that he vindicated himself and Dan's miracle pitch in a 1904 article when he blithely stated, "It was a dime novelist who first conceived the possibility of a baseball being made to change its direction at least twice after leaving the hand of the pitcher." Jenks, *The Bookman* 2 (October 1904), p. 114.

49. Jenks, "The Pitcher Detective's Foil; or Double Curve Dan's Double Play," *Beadle's Half Dime Library*, 608, 19 March 1889, p. 15.

50. Jackson Knox, "Shortstop Maje the Diamond Field Detective; or, Old Falcon's Master Game," *Beadle's Dime New York Library*, 515, 5 September 1888, p. 2.

51. Edward Wheeler, "High Hat Harry the Baseball Detective; or, the Sunken Treasure," *Beadle's Half Dime Library*, 416, 14 July 1885, p. 4.

52. "King Kelly, the Famous Catcher; or, the Life and Adventures of the $10,000 Ball-Player," Street & Smith's *New York Five Cent Library*, 85, 16 June 1894.

53. Robert Smith, *Baseball*, (New York: Simon & Schuster, 1947), p. 36.

54. Jenks, "The Pitcher Detective's Foil," p. 2; Jenks, "The Pitcher Detective's Toughest Tussle," *Beadle's Half Dime Library*, 681, 12 August 1890, p. 5.

55. Wheeler, "High Hat Harry," p. 16.

56. See Cantwell, "A Sneering Laugh With the Bases Loaded," *Sports Illustrated*, 23 April 1962, pp. 67–76. Cantwell criticizes early baseball novels for adolescents and concludes that the genre declined when the element of magic or the unexpected bizarre happening was scrapped in favor of realism.

57. This simple tale is not without its attempt at involution. Desperadoes at one point are described as characters "who looked as if they had just stepped out of a dime novel."

58. A representative group of titles would include Frederick Whittaker, "Colonel Plunger," *Beadle's Dime New York Library*, 211, 8 November 1882; Joseph Badger, "The Boy Jockey," *Beadle's Dime New York Library*, 67, 7 May 1879; Jo Pierce, "Jaunty Joe, the Young Horse King," *Beadle's Half Dime Library*, 472, 10 August 1886; "Kent Kasson, the Preacher Sport," *Beadle's Dime New York Library*, 833, 10 October 1894; Jenks, "The Race Course Detective," *Beadle's Dime New York Library*, 868, 12 June 1885; Manning, "Trapping the Race Track Judge," *Beadle's Half Dime New York Library*, 875, 31 July 1895.

59. There are over thirty titles with "sport" in *Beadle's Dime New York Library* between 1886–96. The earlier tales in the sample are usually westerns. The urban "sport" increases in popularity commensurate with the rise of the urban subject in the dime novel.

60. Rourke, *American Humor*, pp. 139–40; Dorson, "Mose the Far-Famed and World Renowned," *American Literature* 15 (1943), pp. 288–300; Edward Vose, "The B'Hoy's of Yale," *Beadle's Dime New York Library*, 32 (1878).

5. LARDNER: THE POPULAR SPORTS HERO

1. On taking over the "In the Wake of the News" column in the *Tribune*, Lardner wrote of ballplayers that "some of them are very nice fellows and others not as nice. They're just like any other set of men." Donald Elder, *Ring Lardner* (Garden City, New York: Doubleday, 1956), p. 72. Cub pitcher Ed Reulbach stated, "If he had any faults, we liked him too much to notice them—he was one of us." Elder, *Ring Lardner*, p. 72.

2. The most famous attack on Lardner for these sentiments was by Clifton Fadiman, "Ring Lardner and the Triangle of Hate," *Nation*, 22 March 1933, pp. 15–17.

3. Ring Lardner, Jr., *The Lardners: My Family Remembered* (New York: Harper & Row, 1976), pp. 85–86; Jonathan Yardley, *Ring: A Biography of Ring Lardner* (New York: Random House, 1977), p. 154.

4. Elder, *Ring Lardner*, p. 109.

5. Ring Lardner, *You Know Me Al* (New York: Scribner's, 1960), pp. 98–99. Subsequent page references to this edition appear in parentheses in the text.

6. Another early series character of Lardner's resembled Jack Keefe in his economic circumstances and opinions. He was Chicago police detective Fred Goss, hero of *Own Your Own Home*, a series of four stories begun in 1915 and collected into a novel in 1919. A series character speaking in witty vernacular was the bright narrator, "Gullible," of *Gullible's Travels*, begun in 1916. This narrator is closest to Lardner's "in-character" mask in numerous stories in later years. Walton Patrick, *Ring Lardner* (New York: Twayne, 1963), p. 27.

7. Broun travelled with the Giants for the *New York Tribune* from 1911 to 1914 and was a close friend of Mathewson. Lardner wrote an admiring portrait entitled "Matty," *American Magazine*, August 1915.

8. Lardner, "My Roomy," *The Ring Lardner Reader* (New York: Scribner's, 1963), p. 515.

9. See Lardner, "Tyrus: The Greatest of Them All," *American Magazine*, June 1915. For an account of the last sad years of Cobb's life as a disease-ravaged, paranoid millionaire, see Al Stump, "The Fight to Live," Edward Ehre, Irving T. Marsh, eds., *Best Sports Stories 1962* (New York: E.P. Dutton, 1962), pp. 35–55.

10. Other early baseball stories include "Sick 'Em," *Saturday Evening Post*, 25 July 1914; "The Poor Simp," *SEP*, 11 September 1915; "The Crook," *SEP*, 24 June 1916; "The Hold Out," *SEP*, 24 March 1917; and "The Yellow Kid," *SEP*, 23 June 1917.

11. Elder, *Ring Lardner*, p. 170, from a Lardner 17 July 1921 syndicated column.

12. See Lardner, "Sport and Play," Harold Stearns, ed., *Civilization in the United States* (New York: Harcourt, Brace, 1922), p. 461.

13. Patrick, *Ring Lardner*, pp. 125–26.

14. Elder, *Ring Lardner*, p. 160.

15. Ibid., p. 162.
In the 1915 *American Magazine* series, Lardner had put Cicotte on his personal major league All-Star team.

16. Lardner's only real competitors of any stature in popular sports fiction during the early modern period were Charles Van Loan and Zane Grey. Van Loan had been a sportswriter in both San Francisco and New York. He wrote more than forty stories collected in 1919 in three volumes: *Score by Innings*, containing baseball stories; *Taking the Count*, about boxing; and *Old Man Curry*, comprised of horse-racing tales. Van Loan created a more populous sporting world than Lardner; however, his host of humorous ballplayers, managers, trainers, and hangers-on included few true villains and fewer neurotics. Although Van Loan did not experiment with narration nor satirize his sports subjects, it was he who perceived Lardner's talent and mentioned him in 1914 to George Horace Lorimer, whose *Saturday Evening Post* initially published the six Jack Keefe episodes that became *You Know Me Al*. Zane Grey's enormous successes came in other popular forms but he dabbled in stories of semipro and professional baseball as well as stories with a college hero. For his baseball stories, he drew on his experience as an outfielder for Newark, N.J. in the Atlantic League in 1896. *The Red Headed Outfield and Other Stories* (1915) included plots derived from Van Loan's and Lardner's tales of "rubes," fans, and team life, but his narration was an unsuccessful mix: half-stilted, half-colloquial.

A popular writer on the periphery of early modern sports fiction was Heywood Broun (1888–1939), best known in the 1920s and 1930s as a tireless liberal columnist married to feminist Ruth Hale. Broun began as a New York City sportswriter, joining the 1911 freshman class of Damon Runyon and Grantland Rice, but Broun soon moved from the sports scene to become a star columnist on Herbert Swope's *New York World*. Broun wrote only two novels, *The Boy Grew Older* (1923) and *The Sun Field* (1923). They were the earliest book-length adult fiction about popular sport and sportswriting which Broun viewed with a refined, puckish perspective.

17. Lardner, "Champion," *The Ring Lardner Reader*, p. 239. Subsequent page references to this story appear in parentheses in the text.

18. At the conclusion of "The Fight," Longstreet broke from his narrator's role to comment, "Thanks to the Christian religion, to schools, colleges, and benevolent associations, such scenes of barbarism and cruelty as that which I have been just describing are now of rare occurrence, though they may still be occasionally met with in some of the new counties. . . . The peace officers who countenance them deserve a place in the Penitentiary." Longstreet, "The Fight," *Georgia Scenes*, p. 53.

19. Lardner, "Hurry Kane," *The Ring Lardner Reader*, p. 517.

20. This theory has been applied explicity to Lardner's views on baseball with evidence largely from his nonfiction in Leverett Smith, "The Diameter of Frank Chance's Diamond: Ring Lardner and Professional Sports," *Journal of Popular Culture* 6, no. 1 (Summer 1972), pp. 139–44, and incorporated into Smith, *The American Dream and the National Game* (Bowling Green: Bowling Green University Popular Press, 1975), pp. 110–16.

21. Lardner's vision of the new American suburban life was first identified by Rourke, *American Humor*, pp. 291–94.

22. Virginia Woolf, "American Fiction," *Collected Essays* (London: Harcourt, Brace and World, 1966), 2, p. 118.

23. Lardner, "Contract," *The Ring Lardner Reader*, p. 389.

24. Early film comedians filled the screen with their physical skill and grace as well as with their use of sport in their scenarios. Comedians and classic films include Charlie Chaplin, *The Champion* (1916), *Modern Times* (1936); Buster Keaton, *Battling Butler* (1926), *College* (1927); Harold Lloyd, *The Freshman* (1925); The Marx Brothers, *Horsefeathers* (1932); and W. C. Fields, *Never Give a Sucker an Even Break* (1937).

For a look at sport in early cinema, see Cantwell, "Sport Was Box Office Poison," *Sports Illustrated*, 15 September 1969, rpt. Talamini, Page, eds., *Sport and Society*, pp. 441–54.

25. A writer with a penchant for comic dialogue and the depiction of the Broadway scene was Damon Runyon (1880–1946) whose short fiction was as popular in the 1930s, as Lardner's work had been in the 1920s. Runyon was another refugee from the sport beat. He first came to New York City from Denver to write sports for Hearst's *American*. By 1914, like Broun and Lardner, Runyon had his own column, "This Mornin's Mornin'," and he wrote on every topic of sporting interest. He made up for his late start in fiction by publishing 55 stories between 1931 and 1939.

Runyon explored a world of high-rollers, bookmakers, gangsters, their molls and hangers-on. His laconic style attempted to combine a quaint formal diction with understated sarcasm and underworld argot. The peculiar style that resulted, however, was often strained, dull, and flat, in every way inferior to Lardner's narration. Runyon took a number of two-dimensional eccentrics through a series of comic misadventures that most often took place in the sporting world. His Broadway characters were companions to the 1890s "sports," members of the fringe society that lived off wagering and the entertainment business. He was at his best in creating horseplayers, bookies, and hoods, quixotic philosophers of the school of bad tips and the rub-out, heavy losers who kept coming back for more action.

26. Heywood Broun, "Nature the Copycat," *It Seems To Me* (New York: Harcourt, Brace, 1935), p. 298.

6. THE INCARNATION OF THE COLLEGE ATHLETIC HERO

1. Ralph Waldo Emerson, "The American Scholar," *Nature, Addresses and Lectures: The Complete Works of Ralph Waldo Emerson* (Cambridge: Houghton Mifflin, Riverside Press, 1903), I, 81.

2. Francis A. Walker, "College Athletics," *The Harvard Graduates' Magazine* 2 (September 1893) pp. 3–5; rpt. Walker, *Discussions in Education* (New York: Henry Holt, 1899), pp. 262–63.

3. See James Phinney Munroe, *A Life of Frances Amasa Walker* (New York: Henry Holt, 1923). Walker had risen to the rank of Brevet Brigadier General during the Civil War. He was Chief of the United States Bureau of Statistics in 1870, superintendent of the 1880 National Census, and from 1873 to 1881 Professor of Economics at Yale's Sheffield School before becoming president of MIT. He consistently stood fast against MIT's absorption by Harvard in the early 1890s.

4. Emerson, "The American Scholar," p. 114; Walker, "College Athletics," pp. 6–7.

5. Samuel Eliot Morison, ed., Francis Parkman, *The Parkman Reader* (Boston: Little Brown, 1955), p. 10.

6. Henry Adams, *The Education of Henry Adams* (Boston: Houghton Mifflin, 1918), p. 38.

7. Thomas Wentworth Higginson, "Saints and Their Bodies," *Atlantic Monthly* (March 1858), p. 583. Subsequent page references to this article appear in parentheses in the text.

8. Tilden G. Edelstein, *Strange Enthusiasm: A Life of Thomas Wentworth Higginson* (New Haven: Yale University Press, 1968), p. 21. Higginson looked back to his Harvard years (1837–41) where he loved "the old-time football,—the very thud of the ball, the scent of bruised grass, the mighty rush of a hundred men" now changed for "there is something insufficient in the presence of a whole university sitting and shivering in the chill wind around an arena where a few picked gladiators push and wrestle." Higginson, *Cheerful Yesterdays* (Boston: Houghton Mifflin, 1896), pp. 59–60. He remembered an era when "my friends were as careful to point out the men who were 'great swells' in chemistry or in Greek as to call my attention to the 'celebrated stroke, Goldie' " (60).

9. Higginson, ed. *Harvard Memorial Biographies*, 2 vols., (Cambridge, Mass.: Severn and Francis, 1866). Page references to this edition appear in parentheses in the text.

10. The sports most frequently mentioned in the *Memorial Biographies* with times noted were boating (10), football (7), gymnastics (6), and boxing (5). Other activities cited were skating, swimming, fencing, riding, climbing, walking, "throwing a ball," and the ubiquitous "muscular exercises."

11. The two remaining Harvard heroes, the brothers Charles Russell Lowell '54 and James Jackson Lowell '58 seem included more for their having been Lowells, Higginson's close friends, and intellectual heroes (both were class valedictorians). No real mention of sport is contained in their biographies.

12. Emerson, *The Journals of Ralph Waldo Emerson*, ed. Edward W. Emerson, Waldo E. Forbes (Boston, New York, 1909–1914), 9, p. 577 (entry of November 1863). Cited in George Frederickson, *The Inner Civil War* (New York: Harper and Row, 1965), p. 178.

13. Bliss Perry, *The Amateur Spirit* (Cambridge: Houghton-Mifflin, 1904), p. 34.

14. Henry Adams (Harvard '58) remembered Higginson the adolescent as "Bully Hig," one of his "trustiest leaders" in a "game of war on Boston Common" with snowballs.

Adams saw Higginson "struck by a stone over the eye and led off the field bleeding in rather a ghastly manner." Adams, *The Education of Henry Adams,* p. 41.

Higginson had attended Harvard briefly during 1851. He became Captain of the Ist Massachusetts Regiment in 1861 and was invalided out of the war in 1863. After the war he settled into a 50-year career as a Boston banker and was a founding patron of the Boston Symphony Orchestra.

The sixth man to whom the Soldier's Field was dedicated was Edward Dalton, an heroic Civil War surgeon.

15. "It is well for us all, for you and for the boys of future days, to remember such deeds and such lives and to ponder on them. These men loved study and work, and loved play, too. They delighted in athletic games and would have used this field which is now given to the College and to you for your health and recreation. But my chief hope in regard to it is . . . that it will remind you of the reason for living, and your duties as men and citizens of the Republic." Henry Lee Higginson, "The Soldier's Field," (address of June 10, 1890, at Harvard), Bliss Perry, ed., *Life and Letters of Henry Lee Higginson* (Boston: Atlantic Monthly Press, 1921), p. 535.

16. Higginson, "Address of Welcome to the Harvard and Yale Football Teams," (address of December 9, 1892, University Club, Boston) *Harvard Graduates' Magazine,* I, 1892–93, 361.

Henry Adams also mentions Savage as a staunch champion in an 1850 Beacon Street snowball fight against "a swarm of blackguards from the slums." Adams, *The Education of Henry Adams,* pp. 41–42.

17. Walker, "College Athletics," p. 14.

18. "Football had a tremendous burden to carry; it would have to be a miniature Civil War, without, it was hoped, the carnage, in which young men of coming generations could learn the lessons which . . . Higginson and Walker had learned in a harder school." Frederickson, *The Inner Civil War,* p. 224.

19. "Sport and Study," *Harper's Weekly,* 18 October 1873, p. 926.

20. The *Harper's Weekly* editorial commented, "We are disposed to think that the popular taste was veering around in that direction [towards the muscular Christian] before gentlemen of the Guy Livingstone order roused the envious admiration of the young novel-reader." *Guy Livingstone* (1857), written by English author George Lawrence, became an American best-seller. It combined unequal amounts of Rugby, horsemanship, duelling, and decadent romance in the tale of a young muscular English squire, half-Heathcliff and half-Tom Brown who destroys himself through inhuman loves and hates.

Wilkie Collins in *Man and Wife* (1870) created a similar cad of a sportsman in Geoffrey Delamayn, a hero at stroke-oar for Oxford, but a cruel man who plots his wife's murder. In an angry preface, Collins went out of his way to criticize England's "average young athlete," stating flatly, "He and his muscles and his slang are, in my opinion, alike unworthy of literary illustration. They are beneath literary notice." Collins, *Man and Wife* (London: Chatto and Windus, 1870), vii.

21. Henry James, *The Portrait of a Lady* (Cambridge, Mass.: Houghton Mifflin, Riverside, 1956), p. 105. Subsequent references to this edition appear in parentheses in the text.

22. Nathaniel S. Shaler, "The Athletic Problem in Education," *Atlantic Monthly* 63 (January 1889), pp. 79–88. Shaler was a pioneering geologist who studied under Louis Agassiz. He had been captain of the 5th Kentucky Battery in 1862 and, like Walker, was an example of the new, pragmatic, innovative educator. In 1891 he became Dean of Lawrence Scientific School at Harvard. See Shaler, *The Autobiography of Nathaniel Southgate Shaler* (Boston: Houghton-Mifflin, 1909).

23. Walt Whitman's life-long advocacy of physical culture was underscored in an 1888 interview when he stated, "Sports take people out of doors, get them filled with oxygen—

generate some of the brutal customs (so-called brutal customs) which, after all, tend to habituate people to a necessary physical stoicism." Quoted by Horace Traubel, "Talks with Walt Whitman," 16 September 1888, *American Magazine* (July 1907), pp. 101–2.

24. Thorstein Veblen, *The Theory of the Leisure Class* [1899] (New York: Modern Library, 1934), pp. 3, 17, 301.

25. Santayana's Harvard undergraduate hero, Oliver Alden, in *The Last Puritan* (1936), a novel he worked on for more than three decades, is a football hero with a cold heart. The America of concentrated group action is not for him.

26. George Santayana, "Philosophy on the Bleachers," *The Harvard Monthly*, (July 1894), rpt. *George Santayana's America: Essays on Literature and Culture* (Urbana: University of Illinois Press, 1967), pp. 123–24.

27. Richard Harding Davis, "A Day with the Yale Team," *Harper's Weekly*, 18 November 1893, p. 1110.

28. See Alison Danzig, *Oh, How They Played the Game* (New York: Macmillan, 1971) and *The History of American Football* (Englewood Cliffs, N.J.: Prentice Hall, 1966) for the fullest records of Camp's contributions to modern football.

29. Harford Powel, Jr., *Walter Camp: The Father of American Football* (Boston: Little, Brown, 1926), p. 101.

30. Theodore Roosevelt, "The American Boy," *The Roosevelt Book* (New York: Scribner's, 1914), p. 6.

31. Roosevelt, "Value of an Athletic Training," *Harper's Weekly*, 23 December 1893, p. 1236.

32. William Henry Harbaugh, *Power and Responsibility: The Life and Times of Theodore Roosevelt* (New York: Farrar, Straus, and Cudahy, 1961), pp. 103–4. Dean scored a touchdown to beat Yale 12–6 on November 22, 1890, for Harvard's first victory over Walter Camp and Yale in fifteen years. Morris A. Bealle, *The History of Football at Harvard 1874–1948* (Washington, D.C.: Columbia, 1948), pp. 69–72.

33. Stephen Crane, "Harvard University against the Carlisle Indians," *New York Journal*, 1 November 1896, rpt. in Fredson Bowers, ed., The University of Virginia Edition of the Works of Stephen Crane, *Stephen Crane: Tales, Sketches, and Reports* (Charlottesville: University of Virginia Press, 1973), 8, pp. 669–72; Crane, "How Princeton Met Harvard at Cambridge," *New York Sun*, 8 November 1896, Bowers, ed., *Stephen Crane*, 8, pp. 673–76.

34. Crane, Norris, and Davis attended seven colleges among them but none of the three writers ever graduated: Crane (Lafayette, Syracuse); Davis (Swarthmore, Lehigh, Johns Hopkins); and Norris (California-Berkeley, Harvard).

35. John Berryman, *Stephen Crane* (New York: Meridian, 1950), p. 19; Fairfax Downey, *Richard Harding Davis and His Day* (New York: Scribner's, 1933), p. 22; Warren French, *Frank Norris* (New York: Twayne, 1962), p. 19; R.W. Stallman, *Stephen Crane: A Biography* (New York: George Braziller, 1968), p. 32.

36. See Edwin Cady, *Stephen Crane* (New York: Twayne, 1962), pp. 101–2 for the best remarks about Crane and the game trope.

37. Stallman, *Stephen Crane*, p. 181. This statement was also attributed to Crane by Hamlin Garland. Berryman, *Stephen Crane*, p. 28.

38. Berryman, *Stephen Crane*, p. 73.

39. Danzig, *Oh, How They Played the Game*, p. 10.

40. Davis, *The Cuban and Porto Rican Campaigns* (New York: Scribner's, 1898), pp. 152–53.

41. Crane, *The Red Badge of Courage*, ed. Scully Bradley, Richard Croom Beatty, and E. Hudson Long (New York: W.W. Norton, 1962), p. 11. Subsequent page references to this edition appear in parentheses in the text.

42. Quoted in Stallman, *Stephen Crane*, p. 183.

43. Cady envisions Crane struggling against "the most contagious forms of neo-romanticism" so exemplified by Roosevelt. Cady, "Stephen Crane and 'The Strenuous Life,' " *ELH* 28, no. 4 (December 1961), p. 379.

44. Frank Norris, "Ethics of the Freshman Rush," *Wave*, 4 September 1897, p. 2.

45. Norris, "The Week's Football," *Wave*, 21 November 1896, p. 13.

46. Norris [Marmaduke Masters], "Types of Western Men: The College Man," *Wave*, 25 April 1896, p. 6.

47. Norris, "The College Man as a Feature of San Francisco Society," *Wave*, 2 January 1897, p. 3.

48. Norris, "The Week's Football," *Wave*, 17 October 1896, p. 11; *Wave*, 24 October 1896, p. 13; *Wave*, 21 November 1896, p. 13.

49. Norris, "Travis Hallett's Halfback," *The Overland Monthly* (January 1894), rpt. in *Collected Writings of Frank Norris* (New York: Doran, 1928), 10, p. 153. Subsequent page references to this edition appear in parentheses in the text.

50. This improbable metamorphosis is freely accomplished in greater detail through the outlandish changes in personality and temper that come over Yale hero Ross Wilbur and his Viking mate Moran in Norris's *Moran of the Lady Letty* (1898). While Wilbur coarsens and toughens his spirit on the high seas, Moran is Norris's female fantasy of a primitive "daughter of the Norman" who unfortunately lives the beast-gentle[woman] metamorphosis in reverse and dies a helpless female.

The last word on the gentleman/beast hero may be heard in the bark of Buck, the great dog in Jack London's *Call of the Wild* (1903), who is torn from his easy life in the "Southlands" of California to become a sled-dog team leader in the Yukon where his primitive instincts emerge. Buck is a fine athlete, a spirited leader of team members, as successful as a School Sports Hero before he answers London's final "call."

51. Donald Pizer, *The Novels of Frank Norris* (Bloomington, Ind): Indiana University Press, 1966), p. 43.

52. Norris wrote a one-act romance, "In the Heat of the Battle," *Wave*, 19 December 1896, where a Yale halfback's status as suitor for the hand of Miss Tressie Tremont rises and falls on his performance in the Harvard-Yale game. He wins both the game and the girl.

53. Norris, *Vandover and the Brute* (New York: Grove Press), p. 143.

54. Vandover observes, "Among the crowd in the barroom, three members of the winning team—heroes, with bandages about their heads—were breaking training for the first time in many long weeks." Norris, *Vandover*, p. 295. With the insertion of the bandaged gridiron soldiers, Norris invokes the stereotyped Civil War/football image, as did Crane.

55. Norris is most certainly drawing on the first Stanford-California game played on March 19, 1892, in San Francisco's Haight Park with Stanford, then in its first year of existence, winning 14–10 before 8,000 spectators. Norris and some fraternity brothers watched the contest from atop a rented stagecoach. Kevin Starr, *Americans and the California Dream 1765–1915* (New York: Oxford University Press, 1973), p. 336.

56. Norris, "Novelists of the Future," *Boston Evening Transcript*, 27 November 1901, rpt. Donald Pizer, ed., *The Literary Criticism of Frank Norris* (Austin: University of Texas Press, 1964), pp. 13–14.

57. Norris, "This Animal of a Buldy Jones," Norris, *Collected Writings* (New York: Doran, 1928), 4, p. 108. "Buldy Jones" originally appeared in the *Wave*, 17 July 1897, rpt. *McClure's Magazine* 12 (March 1899).

58. Gerald Langford, *The Richard Harding Davis Years* (New York: Harper & Row, 1961), p. 105; Downey, *Richard Harding Davis*, p. 79, quoted from H.W. Boynton, *New York Evening Post*, 25 April 1916, at Davis' death.

59. Downey, *Richard Harding Davis*, p. 63.

60. Davis, "The Thanksgiving Day Game," *Harper's Weekly*, 9 December 1893, rpt. James High Moffat, Frank Presbrey, eds., *Athletics at Princeton: A History* (New York: Frank Presbrey, 1901), p. 359. Davis covered the November 24, 1895 Yale-Princeton game for William Randolph Hearst's *New York Journal*. His fee was $500, the highest price ever paid for a single piece of reporting until that time.

61. Davis, *Stories for Boys* (New York: Scribner's, 1891).

62. Joseph R. McElrath, Jr., "Frank Norris: A Biographical Essay," *American Literary Realism* 11, no. 2 (Autumn 1978), p. 225.

63. Norris, *Moran of the Lady Letty* [1898], *The Complete Edition of Frank Norris*, 3, p. 202.

Norris took Van Bibber over the brink to outright parody in "Van Bubble's Story": "That night he went to dinner at the house of the Girl He Knew . . . young Charding-Davis put on a Yale sweater and football knickerbockers and the headdress of feathers he had captured from a Soudanese Arab while acting as a war correspondent for an English syndicate. . . . During the dinner young Charding-Davis was illustrating a new football trick he had just patented with the aid of ten champagne bottles and the Girl's pet Skye terrier." Norris, "Van Bubble's Story," *Wave*, 14 December 1897, rpt. *Frank Norris of the "Wave,"* (San Francisco: The Westgate Press, 1931), pp. 90–91.

64. Emerson, "The American Scholar," p. 93.

65. Walker, "College Athletics," p. 13.

7. THE BOYS' SCHOOL SPORTS STORY

1. Edwin Cady, *The Light of Common Day* (Bloomington: Indiana University Press, 1971), pp. 100–1.

2. Monica Kiefer, "Mental Pabulum of Godly Children," William Targ, ed., *Bibliophile in the Nursery* (Cleveland: World Publishing Co., 1957), p. 321.

3. John Cawelti, *Apostles of the Self-Made Man* (Chicago: University of Chicago Press, 1965), pp. 106, 111.

4. Early contributors included Joel Chandler Harris, Frank Stockton, Bret Harte, Theodore Roosevelt, and Rudyard Kipling. Twain's *Tom Sawyer Abroad* appeared in the 1890s. Walter Camp had a football column on occasion until 1910. Three of Davis' early boys' stories, "The Great Tri-Club Tennis Tournament," "Richard Carr's Baby," and "The Midsummer Pirates," first appeared in *St. Nicholas*. Crane sent a sketch about a dog named Jack to the magazine in 1891 but was rejected in a note informing him that the editors had a backlog of dog stories. Stallman, *Stephen Crane*, p. 31.

5. Noah Brooks (1830–1903), the author, was a journalist in New England and California for decades. He was about to assume duties as Abraham Lincoln's private secretary when the President was assassinated in 1865. His early baseball novel, *Our Baseball Club and How It Won the Championship*, was published in 1884.

6. Seven years after the serial appeared, Brooks wrote a short article for *St. Nicholas* (March 1887) in which he fondly traced the genesis of the military episodes in "The Fairport Nine" all the way back to a patriotic speech he had heard as a boy on behalf of presidential candidate William Henry Harrison. He relates the brave Civil War deeds of the boys who heard that speech ("The lesson in patriotism was not in vain"), a small-town echo of Henry Higginson's comrades at Harvard brought up to date on the diamond in 1880.

A recent study corroborates the view that baseball as well as football could be a martial metaphor in post-Civil War America. See David Lamoreaux, "Baseball in the Late Nineteenth

Century: The Source of Its Appeal," *Journal of Popular Culture* 11, no. 3 (Winter 1977) pp. 597–613.

7. Rupert Hughes, "The Lakerim Athletic Club," *St. Nicholas* 25 (November 1897–October 1898).

Two major exceptions to the lack of fanciful imagination in the village sport stories are Albert Stearns, "Chris and the Wonderful Lamp," *St. Nicholas* (December 1894–June 1895) and Ralph Henry Barbour, "Billy Mayes' Great Discovery," the story of a boy whose bat is made of magic hoki-moki wood, a prototype of Roy Hobbs' bat "Wonderboy" in Bernard Malamud's *The Natural*.

8. Mott, *Golden Multitudes* (New York: Macmillan, 1947), pp. 308, 320.

9. Another Rugby boy from 1846 to 1849 was Lewis Carroll, whose fantasy and fiction contributed to a parallel Victorian obsession with logic games and board games along with strenuous sport. Carroll intensely disliked aggressive sport. Of Rugby School, he stated, "I cannot say that I look back upon my life at a Public school with any sensations of pleasure, or that any earthly considerations would induce me to go through my three years again." Derek Hudson, *Lewis Carroll* (London: Constable, 1954). p. 46.

10. W.H.G. Armytage, Edward C. Mack, *Thomas Hughes* (London: Ernest Benn, 1952), p. 100.

11. Ibid., p. 28.

12. Thomas Hughes, *Tom Brown's Schooldays* (New York: Belford, Clarke, 1884), p. 71. Subsequent page references to this edition appear in parentheses in the text.

13. "Muscular Christianity" was a term first applied by English reviewers to the philosophy in the novels of Hughes' friend and fellow Christian Socialist, Charles Kingsley, especially his *Yeast* (1848) and *Alton Locke* (1850). Kingsley vehemently protested the categorization.

14. Hughes, *Tom Brown at Oxford* (New York: F.M. Lupton, 1862), p. 112. Subsequent page references to this edition appear in parentheses in the text.

15. Santayana, "A Glimpse of Yale," *The Harvard Monthly* (December 1892), rpt. *George Santayana's America*, p. 54.

16. Van Wyck Brooks grumpily concluded, "In schools like Groton and Saint Paul's, the tendency to revert to England in educational methods, in sports and in manners denoted the secession of the fashionable classes from the democratic forms of the old republic." Brooks, *New England Indian Summer* (New York: E.P. Dutton, 1940), p. 331.

17. Armytage, Mack, *Thomas Hughes,* p.41.

18. Ibid., pp. 133, 139, 174–84, 227–50.

19. Lytton Strachey, *Eminent Victorians* (Middlesex, England: Penguin, 1971), p. 187.

20. Armytage, Mack, *Thomas Hughes,* p. 193.

21. Bracebridge Hemyng, "Jack Harkaway in New York," *Beadle's Half Dime Library,* 101, 1 July 1879. Representative titles in the series included shameless pilfering from Hughes: *Jack Harkaway's Schooldays* and *Jack Harkaway at Oxford,* but also the Americanized *Jack Harkway out West among the Indians.*

Early representatative dime titles that touched on the schoolboy hero included Albert Aiken, "The Winning Oar," *Beadle's Dime New York Library,* 91, 7 April 1880; George Jenks, "Git Thar Owney," *Beadle's Half Dime Library,* 485, 9 November 1886; R.T. Emmet, "Dashing Dick, The Young Cadet," *The Boys of New York,* 690, 3 November 1888; and, in the spirit of cultural exchange, Cornelius Shea, "The Yankee Prince; or, Greg Graham at Rugby," *Golden Hours,* 509–510, 30 Oct. and 6 Nov. 1887.

22. See John O. Lyons, *The College Novel in America* (Carbondale: Southern Illinois University Press, 1962). The majority of pre-1900 college novels take place at Harvard and are "uniformly episodic accounts of pranks, athletic events, and tavern bouts." Lyons, *The College Novel,* pp. 8, 181, 191–92. Flandreau had a diminished view of sport's importance: "At Harvard, athletics are occasionally a means to a man's becoming identified with the sort of

people he wishes to be one of; but I have never known them to be an end." Charles Flandreau, *Harvard Episodes* (Boston: Copland & Day, 1897), pp. 17–18.

23. Major league baseball players with a story to themselves included King Kelly, Boston third baseman Billy Nash, and New York Giant shortstop "Yale" Murphy (Yale '93), whose nickname stemmed from his college years. Norman Munro featured a serial, "Amos Rusie, Prince of Pitchers," *Golden Hours*, 6 August 1898, which placed the Giant pitcher, reputedly the hardest thrower of the decade, in early adolescence pitching for a boys' team and saving his girlfriend, Fanny, from abduction by evil tramps.

24. Frank Earll, "Brave Colonel Teddy; or Ranchero, Rough Rider, Governor," *Golden Hours*, 565, 26 November 1898. Roosevelt was aged considerably to star in Street & Smith's *Young Rough Riders Weekly* (1899).

Roosevelt's son, Quentin, brought his school baseball team to practice on the White House grounds in 1908, and T.R. remarked in a letter to another son, Archie, that Quentin's play gave him hope "that one of my boys will not take after his father in this respect, and will prove able to play the national game." Roosevelt, *Theodore Roosevelt's Letters to His Children* (New York: Scribner's, 1919), p. 222.

25. Quentin Reynolds, *The Fiction Factory* (New York: Random House, 1955), p. 89.

26. Patten managed the Camden, Maine baseball team in the summer Knox County League in 1890–91. See Gilbert Patten, "Sand on the Diamond: Reminiscences of a Bush League Manager," *Outlook*, 13 June 1923, pp. 176–80.

27. There were 27 Patten stories published under his name by Beadle and Adams between 1883 and 1895, the bulk of them after January 1889. However, his aliases were several: "Wyoming Will," "William Patten," and "William West Wilder." John Levi Cutler, *Gilbert Patten and His Frank Merriwell Saga* (University of Maine, 1934), pp. 111–12.

28. "I'm very shallow and that's no surprise to me. I've long more than half-suspected it—in fact I've been quite sure of it." Cutler, *Gilbert Patten*, p. 81; "of course my style was verbose and sloppy. Writing under pressure, how could I have done otherwise? Anyhow, Street & Smith were not paying for style, they were buying stories that young readers would enjoy and buy. And of course such composition, indulged in for years, formed writing habits I've never been able to correct." Gilbert Patten, *Frank Merriwell's Father* (Norman, Okla.: University of Oklahoma Press, 1964), p. 180.

29. See J.P. Guinon, "Reprints of the Merriwell Series," *Dime Novel Round Up*, 271, 15 April 1955, pp. 26–33.

30. Numbering of references to Merriwell novels will first cite the *Tip Top* issues in parentheses followed by the Merriwell Library novel number. Page references are exclusively from the novels.

31. The first Dick Merriwell novel was *Dick Merriwell at Fardale* (285–288), 76. Frank had been something of a ventriloquist so Patten gave Dick the power to talk to wild animals and birds, but to Patten's chagrin, the idea "just didn't click" with readers. James M. Cain, "The Man Merriwell," *Saturday Evening Post* 11 June 1927, p. 132.

Frank Merriwell, Jr. was introduced in 1913. The series was written primarily by John Whitson who had produced Jack Lightfoot for Street & Smith in 1905 and had briefly filled in for Patten in 1900.

32. Patten, *Frank Merriwell's Sports Afield* (42–46), 58, p. 104.

33. Ibid., p. 223.

34. Cooper, too, knew something of mischief at Yale, allegedly having been expelled for roping a donkey in the chair of his tutor. Van Wyck Brooks, *The World of Washington Irving* (Kingsport, Tenn.: E.P. Dutton, 1944), p. 222.

35. Patten, *Frank Merriwell's Fun* (281–284), 51, p. 254.

36. Patten, *Frank Merriwell on the Road* (213–216), 34, pp. 15–16.

37. Patten, *Frank Merriwell in Wall Street* (9–12 in *New Tip Top Weekly*), 159, p. 117.

38. Patten, *Frank Merriwell's Fun,* p. 209.

39. O.G. Smith said that static scenes of, for example, Merriwell feeding a horse, could only bore the boys. In a burst of aesthetic theory, Patten replied, "Those two pages are just as interesting to them as though I had Frank ride the horse in front of the express train and grab the girl off the cow-catcher. Get your mind off action. Action is what killed the old dime novel." Cain, "The Man Merriwell," p. 129.

40. Norris, "The College Man as a Feature of San Francisco Society," *Wave,* 2 January 1897, p. 3.

41. Merriwell was the boyhood hero of Jordan Olivar, the Yale football coach from 1952 to 1962. In 1962 Olivar said, "If I had him today, he'd be quarterback." Robert H. Boyle, *Sport: Mirror of American Life* (New York: Little, Brown, 1963), p. 246. Albie Booth, the eight-letter man for Yale in the early 1930s, was consistently referred to as Frank Merriwell. In his last appearance for Yale in 1932, he hit a grand slam home run in the ninth inning to beat Harvard, 4–3. *Ibid.,* p. 246.

42. Series begun by Tousey to compete with *Tip Top Weekly* included *Work and Win, Pluck and Luck, The Young Athlete's Weekly,* and *Wide Awake Weekly.*

43. Barbour's early boys' sports fiction included *For the Honor of the School* (1900), *On Your Mark* (1904), *Behind the Line* (1905), *The Spirit of the School* (1907), *Double Play* (1909), and *Teammates* (1911).

44. A useful anatomy of the school and series sports story is Walter Evans' "The All-American Boys: A Study of Boys' Sports Fiction," *Journal of Popular Culture* 6, no. 1 (Summer 1972) pp. 104–21.

45. *Ibid.,* p. 110.

46. Not all school sports narratives were serious tales of maturation and earnest toil. Feeding a democratic reaction to college privilege were burlesques of the new convention. In his drama *The College Widow* (1904), George Ade used his ear for popular dialect to embellish the first successful satire of college football, its coaches, pious educators, and romantic coeds. George Fitch also portrayed a comic series of bumpkin misadventures in his Siwash series that was serialized in the *Saturday Evening Post* and collected in *At Good Old Siwash* (1911).

Zane Grey wrote a college baseball novel, *The Young Pitcher* (1911), which closely resembles a Barbour novel about a freshman in college slowly gaining acceptance by his teammates as he proves his skill and tolerance; Lester Chadwick's Baseball Joe Library included a volume in which heroic pitcher Joe Matson attended Yale. Gilbert Patten wrote a series about a major league baseball player named Lefty Locke and a "College Life" series about one Hal Boltwood.

Barbour's two most noteworthy descendants were William Heyliger (1884–1955) and John R. Tunis (1889–1974). Heyliger was less prolific than Barbour but more candid in portraying the problems of big-time college sport in the 1920s and 1930s. Tunis (Harvard '11) wrote school sports fiction including *The Iron Duke* (1938) and *All-American* (1942), as well as two of the earliest sports novels about girls, *American Girl* (1930) and *Champion's Choice* (1940). Tunis wrote a whole series about a fictional Brooklyn Dodger team whose players were as familiar a group to American boys in the 1940s and 1950s as were Pete Reiser, Pee Wee Reese, and Duke Snider. Tunis's work was the very best of his era.

47. Contemporary with and similar to the elite university tales of Johnson and Williams were the school sports fiction of Ralph Paine (Yale '94) and Arthur Stanwood Pier (Harvard '95). Paine was a member of the Yale crew and football team, a war correspondent in Cuba and China, and a popular naval historian. His Yale novels included *The Stroke Oar* (1908), *College Years* (1909), *The Fugitive Freshman* (1910), *Sandy Sawyer, Sophomore* (1911), *Campus Days* (1912), and *Sons of Eli* (1917). Pier wrote brief histories of Harvard and St. Paul's

School and edited the *Harvard Graduates' Magazine* (1918–30). His fictionalized St. Paul's was "St. Timothy's" at which he set his prep school novels including *Boys of St. Timothy's* (1904), *The New Boy* (1908), and *Grannis of the Fifth* (1914), while other series of his later boys' books solely emphasized sport.

48. *The Prodigious Hickey* was first published as *The Eternal Boy* (1909) and reprinted along with three other Lawrenceville short novels, *The Varmint* (1910), *The Hummingbird* (1910), and *The Tennessee Shad* (1911).

49. Johnson certainly modelled Stover after Yale's All-American end Frank Hinkey '95 who never weighed more than 158 pounds but who was a ferocious hitter for his size and who led Yale to four consecutive victories over Harvard.

50. Owen Johnson, *Stover at Yale* (New York: Frederick A. Stokes, 1912), p. 79.

51. Ibid., p. 385.

52. Richard Hofstadter, *Social Darwinism in American Thought 1860–1915* (Philadelphia: University of Pennsylvania Press, 1945), p. 42.

53. See David Lamoreaux, "*Stover at Yale* and the Gridiron Metaphor," *Journal of Popular Culture* 11, no. 2 (Fall 1977), pp. 330–44. Johnson made an abortive return to the Lawrenceville prep novel with the more frivolous *Skippy Bedelle: His Sentimental Progress from the Urchin to the Complete Man of the World* (New York: Little, Brown, 1922).

54. Fitzgerald's copy of *Princeton Stories* was a 1912 limited Scribner's edition that was not for general sale. It contained the imprint "with the best wishes of the Princeton Alumni" and was a gift book that Fitzgerald most likely picked up in Princeton. He underlined phrases in "When Girls Come To Princeton" that pertain to the color, texture, and background of an 1890s dance weekend but made no marks in the sports material in the stories. Courtesy of Princeton University Library.

55. Jesse Lynch Williams, "College Men," *Princeton Stories* (New York: Scribner's, 1906), p. 269.

56. A less adept look at Princeton life was contained in James Barnes, *A Princetonian* (New York: G.P. Putnam's, 1896), and Fitzgerald owned a copy. Putnam's announced in 1896 a series that included not only *A Princetonian* but W.K. Post's *Harvard Stories* and J.S. Wood's *Yale Yarns,* proof that hard-cover publishers were as eager to pick up on reader interest in schoolboy life as were Street & Smith with the Merriwell series in the pulps.

Augustus Baldwin Longstreet, the much-celebrated Southwestern Humorist (see chapter 3), wrote a novel of young, Southern, card-playing rogues of the early 1800s who wind up at Princeton for a year. They break all gaming prohibitions and are expelled in a full faculty trial for keeping a "disorderly room." In *Master William Mitten; or, A Youth of brilliant talents who was ruined by bad luck* (Macon, Ga.: J.W. Burke, 1889), Mitten is a young cad whose sins break his sainted mother's heart. He then dies "by that disease so common to gamblers, and so fatal to all, consumption" (363). The novel is really a masked tract, preaching temperance and moderation, but Longstreet, who attended Yale in 1811, affords one of the earliest looks at schoolboy life, circa 1800. He validates the Southern influence at Princeton so noticeable in Fitzgerald's School Sports Heroes.

57. Clair Bee's Chip Hilton is the representative high school hero with his cheerful, self-effacing manner and outstanding athletic achievement. Bee wrote 23 Chip Hilton novels in the 1940s and 1950s. It is ironic that Bee, an outstanding baseball coach at Long Island University, found his team's star, Sherman White, implicated with fixers in the 1951 college basketball scandals and LIU subsequently dropped basketball for several years. Chip Hilton would have wept at the whole affair.

8. FITZGERALD: THE SCHOOL SPORTS HERO

1. F. Scott Fitzgerald, "Princeton," *College Humor* (December 1927), rpt. Arthur Mizener, ed., *Afternoon of an Author* (Princeton: Princeton University Library, 1957), p. 72.

2. Fitzgerald, "Reade, Substitute Right Half," John Kuehl, ed., *The Apprenticeship of F. Scott Fitzgerald* (New Brunswick, N.J.: Rutgers University Press, 1965), pp. 28–33.

3. Andrew Turnbull, *Scott Fitzgerald* (New York: Scribner's, 1962), pp. 21, 35, 38.

4. Kuehl, "Scott Fitzgerald's Reading," *Princeton University Library Chronicle* 22, no. 1 (Autumn 1960), p. 87. Kuehl quotes from Fitzgerald's Scrapbook III.

5. Fitzgerald, *This Side of Paradise* (New York: Scribner's, 1920), pp. 4, 17, 33, 106, 209. Subsequent page references to this edition appear in parentheses in the text. For an analysis of Amory's reading lists, see Dorothy Ballweg Good, " 'A Romance and a Reading List': The Literary References in *This Side of Paradise*," *Fitzgerald-Hemingway Annual*, 1976, pp. 35–64.

6. In his sixth-form year at Newman in 1912, Fitzgerald led his team to victory with his "snap and bang" runs. Turnbull, *Scott Fitzgerald*, p. 38.

7. Fitzgerald had a specific Princeton football image in mind as well. In 1927 he wrote, "A year ago in the Champs Elysées I passed a slender dark-haired young man with an indolent characteristic walk. Something stopped inside me; I turned and looked after him. It was the romantic Buzz Law whom I had last seen one cold fall twilight in 1915, kicking from behind his goal line with a bloody bandage round his head." Fitzgerald, "Princeton," pp. 72–73.

8. Fitzgerald, "The Freshest Boy," *Babylon Revisited and Other Stories* (New York: Scribner's, 1960), p. 190. Subsequent page references to this edition appear in parentheses in the text.

9. Fitzgerald, "Basil and Cleopatra," Jackson L. Bryer, John Kuehl, eds., *The Basil and Josephine Stories* (New York: Scribner's, 1973), p. 185. Subsequent page references to this edition appear in parentheses in the text.

10. Turnbull, *Scott Fitzgerald*, p. 36. Fitzgerald injured an ankle in a Princeton practice. He wore his black Newman jersey in his three days on the field. Turnbull, *Scott Fitzgerald*, p. 44.

11. In 1922 Williams sent Fitzgerald a copy of his 1910 novel *The Married Life of the Frederic Carrolls* and inscribed it "For the Married Life of the F. Scott Fitzgeralds," and added, "Hoping that the brilliant author of The Beautiful and the Damned will be indulgent to me, remembering that this book was written in the dark ages—the first decade of this century." Williams to Fitzgerald, 19 March 1922. Courtesy of Princeton University Library.

12. Major Mosby as dashing Southern hero is remembered by Dick Diver in *Tender is the Night* for as a boy "he sat again on his father's knee, riding with Moseby [sic] while the old loyalties and devotions fought on around him." Fitzgerald, *Tender is the Night* (New York: Scribner's, 1934), p. 101. John Mosby's most successful attack with his irregulars came on 14 October 1864 when he destroyed a Union train at Harper's Ferry and made off with the Union payroll of $168,000 in greenbacks.

13. Princeton gave the Confederacy at least eight brigadier generals, fourteen colonels, and many lesser officers. Thomas Jefferson Wertenbaker, *Princeton 1746–1896* (Princeton: Princeton University Press, 1946), p. 270.

14. Fitzgerald, "Princeton," p. 71.

15. Ibid.

16. See John Davies, *The Legend of Hobey Baker* (Boston: Little, Brown, 1966); Matthew J. Bruccoli, "Fitzgerald's Marked Copy of *This Side of Paradise*," *Fitzgerald-Hemingway Annual* (1971), p. 66.

17. It is difficult to track any specific references to Stover in *This Side of Paradise* but a possible source for Dick Humbird could be Fitzgerald's adapting the title of *The Hummingbird* (1910), an Owen Johnson Lawrenceville novel that while not about Stover is about pint-sized Dennis de Brian de Boru Finnegan, whose irrepressible Irish wit and pluck make him a comic version of Amory or Basil at St. Regis'. Other possible associations with Dick Humbird include Dick Merriwell, Dick Diver, Dick "Humbug," and Horatio Alger's "Ragged Dick." Humbird/Hummingbird is well within Fitzgerald's predilection for creative naming.

18. Fitzgerald, *This Side of Paradise,* pp. 113, 116, 129, 253, 259.

19. Although Fitzgerald could write "Don't wake the Tarkington ghosts," in his notes for *The Last Tycoon* in reference to what he felt was Tarkington's oversentimentalized style and lack of candor about adolescence, he certainly used Tarkington's "ghost" in the Allenby scene and in *Tender is the Night* (see chapter 9).

20. Veblen, *The Theory of the Leisure Class,* p. 256, 260.

21. Fitzgerald, *The Great Gatsby* (New York: Scribner's, 1925), p. 7. Subsequent page references to this edition appear in parentheses in the text.

22. Richard Lehan, *F. Scott Fitzgerald and the Craft of Fiction* (Carbondale, Ill.: Southern Illinois University Press, 1966), pp. 91–93; another source for Buchanan is noted in John B. Humms, "Edward Russell Thomas: The Prototype for *Gatsby's* Tom Buchanan?" *Markham Review* 4, pp. 38–39.

23. Turnbull, *Scott Fitzgerald,* p. 42. Fitzgerald had provided only the former image in *This Side of Paradise,* although Amory does tell amusedly of Princeton's "Slim" Languedoc and his battles to stay eligible to "beat Yale this fall" as in "conic sections" class he "lazily shifts his six-foot-three of football material and tries to concentrate" (95).

24. Sumner's most influential book was *Folkways* (1906). See chapter 17, "Popular Sports, Exhibitions, and Drama," which exhibits Sumner's immensely learned juxtapositions of ancient and modern public amusements. Phelps remained on the Yale faculty for 41 years (1891–1932). At Yale as an undergraduate (1883–87), he had been on the second baseball nine, had played varsity tennis, and had won a championship in cross-country. He played baseball until age 45 and tennis doubles until age 70.

25. In 1927, Fitzgerald admitted worrying "up to the middle of sophomore year" whether he should have gone to Yale. He wondered if he were "missing a great American secret." Fitzgerald, "Princeton," p. 70.

26. Turnbull, *Scott Fitzgerald,* p. 265.

27. Fitzgerald and Crisler exchanged several letters in the 1930s with Fitzgerald suggesting backfield formations and strategy. Fitzgerald wrote a brief football fantasy "The Ants At Princeton" (*Esquire,* June 1936), and Crisler replied, "Your little satire was quite interesting and I have a notion that Princeton might meet with more success in the next year or two if we had some good rugged ants as candidates for a football team." Crisler to Fitzgerald, 10 March 1936. Courtesy of Princeton University Library.

28. Turnbull, *Scott Fitzgerald,* pp. 174, 211–12, 249, 321.

29. Lillian Ross, "How Do You Like It Now, Gentlemen?" *New Yorker,* 13 May 1950, rpt. Robert Weeks, ed., *Hemingway: A Collection of Critical Essays* (Englewood Cliffs, N.J.: Prentice Hall, 1962), p. 31.

30. Fitzgerald, "Princeton," pp. 70–71.

31. Fitzgerald, "The Bowl," *Saturday Evening Post,* 21 January 1928, p. 95. Subsequent page references to this story appear in parentheses in the text.

32. The term is borrowed from Erving Goffmann, *Frame Analysis* (Cambridge, Mass.: Harvard-Norton, 1974).

33. Sutton-Smith, "Epilogue: Play as Performance," *Play and Learning,* p. 310.

34. Sutton-Smith, "Introduction," *Play and Learning,* p. 1.

35. Fink, "The Oasis of Happiness," pp. 24–25, 28–29.

36. Huizinga, *Homo Ludens*, p. 13.

37. Robert Sklar, *F. Scott Fitzgerald, The Last Laocoon* (New York: Oxford, 1967), p. 168.

38. Ibid., p. 251.

39. Fitgerald, *Tender is the Night* (New York: Scribner's, 1934), p. 166. Subsequent page references to this edition appear in parentheses in the text.

40. Fitzgerald's romances seem most reminiscent of *The Blithedale Romance*. Gatsby and Dick assume the role of Zenobia in her bravura performance to win Hollingsworth while Hollingsworth stands as the solid, heavily masculine figure of will such as Tom Buchanan or Tommy Barban. Nick Carraway and Rosemary Hoyt are, respectively, both more and less perspicacious narrator figures than Miles Coverdale. Priscilla, Daisy, and Nicole are not capable in the flesh of living up to the roles in which they are projected but they come out as nominal victors in struggles not of their choosing. Tragedy befalls the skilled players, Zenobia and Gatsby. In Dick Diver's case, it is a slow reversal which winds him down and back past earlier stages of his life toward America and his origins.

41. Dick's idealism is challenged by Sklar's forceful thesis that "the true neurotic in *Tender* is not Nicole Diver but her husband" and "where her disintegration stems from one ugly incident, his distintegration stems from the very core of his personal identity." Sklar, *F. Scott Fitzgerald,* p. 285.

42. Fitzgerald, "Ring," *The Crack Up* (New York: J. Laughlin, 1945), p. 36. Subsequent page references to this edition appear in parentheses in the text.

43. Turnbull, *Scott Fitzgerald,* pp. 136–37.

44. The best description of their friendship may be found in Ring Lardner, Jr., *The Lardners: My Family Remembered* (New York: Harper & Row, 1976).

45. Lardner, Jr., *The Lardners,* p. 155.

46. See Sklar, *F. Scott Fitzgerald,* pp. 277–79 for his convincing analysis of Fitzgerald's imaginative links between Abe North and Abraham Lincoln and between Dick Diver and Ulysses S. Grant.

47. Although Hemingway is often described as cruel in turning on his sponsors after career help, it is instructive to remember Fitzgerald's "Ring" as well as Abe North's career and death, especially since Fitzgerald has been portrayed as an innocent victim of Hemingway's literary paranoia in the 1930s.

9. THE SCHOOL SPORTS HERO AS SATIRIC EMBLEM

1. Ernest Hemingway, *The Sun Also Rises* (New York: Scribner's, 1926), pp. 3–4. Subsequent page references to this edition appear in parentheses in the text.

2. William Faulkner, *The Hamlet* (New York: Random House, third edition, 1964), p. 112. Subsequent page references to this edition appear in parentheses in the text.

3. Charles A. Fenton, *The Apprenticeship of Ernest Hemingway* (New York: New American Library, 1961), p. 15.

4. Ibid., p. 17.

5. Otto McFeeley to Malcolm Cowley, 25 July 1948, quoted in Scott Donaldson, *By Force of Will: The Life and Art of Ernest Hemingway* (New York: Viking, 1977), p. 61.

6. Fenton, *The Apprenticeship of Ernest Hemingway,* p. 20.

7. Hemingway, *The Torrents of Spring* (Middlesex, England: Penguin Books, 1961), p. 71.

8. Hemingway, "In Another Country," *Snows of Kilimanjaro and Other Stories* New York: Scribner's, 1936), pp. 65–70.

9. Hemingway, "A Way You'll Never Be," *Snows,* pp. 82–94.

10. Hemingway, "Soldier's Home," *In Our Time* (New York: Scribner's, 1925), pp. 87–102.

11. Hemingway, *Death in the Afternoon* (New York: Scribner's, 1932), p. 183. Subsequent page references to this edition appear in parentheses in the text.

12. Hemingway, "The Short Happy Life of Francis Macomber," *Snows,* pp. 121–54.

13. Hemingway quoted in Lillian Ross, "How Do You Like It Now, Gentlemen," Weeks, ed., *Hemingway: A Collection of Critical Essays,* p. 23.

14. Accounts of Hemingway's unscheduled bouts include his scuffle with Max Eastman in Maxwell Perkins' office in 1933 after Eastman had (in Hemingway's mind) cast doubt on Hemingway's masculinity in Eastman's *New Republic* review of *Death in the Afternoon.* See Donaldson, *By Force of Will,* pp. 186–87; Carlos Baker, *Ernest Hemingway: A Life Story* (New York: Scribner's, 1969), pp. 403–4. See also Morley Callaghan's remembrances of his boxing with Hemingway in Paris in the summer of 1929; Callaghan, *That Summer in Paris* (New York: Dell, 1963), pp. 121–22, 211–14. For a popular summary of Hemingway's public incidents in macho pose, see Donaldson, "Boxing and Brawling," *By Force of Will,* pp. 63–69.

15. Baker reports that Harold Loeb, Hemingway's model for Robert Cohn, had Hudson's *Green Mansions* as his favorite novel. Baker, *Ernest Hemingway,* p. 144.

Fitzgerald commented further on the problems of sentimental romanticism when Dick Diver grimly surveyed a World War I battlefield in France and mused, "There was a century of middle class love spent here." Fitzgerald, *Tender is the Night,* p. 57.

16. Veblen, *The Theory of the Leisure Class,* p. 254.

17. A brief for Cohn as a romantic hero is best presented in Robert W. Lewis, Jr., *Hemingway on Love* (Austin: University of Texas Press, 1965), pp. 21–25. Lewis cites Arthur L. Scott, "In Defense of Robert Cohn," *College English* 18 (March 1957), pp. 309–14; Robert O. Stephens, "Hemingway's Don Quixote in Pamplona," *College English* 23 (December 1961), pp. 216–18.

18. Extended commentary on this scene is found in Mark Spilka, "The Death of Love in *The Sun Also Rises,*" Charles Shapiro, ed., *Twelve Original Essays on Great Novels* (Detroit: Wayne State University Press, 1958), rpt. Weeks, ed., *Hemingway: A Collection of Critical Essays,* pp. 134–35.

19. Joseph Blotner, *Faulkner: A Biography* (New York: Random House, 1974), I, 140, 234, 278–79. Hereafter referred to as "Blotner."

20. Ibid., 165–66.

21. Ibid., 203, 235, 248, 278–81, 287, 318, 327.

22. Ibid., 436.

23. In Irving's "Dolph Heyliger," the young hero is the finest athlete in the Hudson River Valley and is saved from a life of medical study in one dreary room by Squire Antony Van Der Heyden. Dolph marries Van Der Heyden's blooming daughter, Marie, and settles into a life of ease, "cherrily growing merrier as he grew older and wiser," while improving the local breed of race horses and game cocks.

24. Cecil D. Eby, Jr., "Ichabod Crane in Yoknapatawpha," *Georgia Review* 16 (Winter 1962), pp. 465–69.

25. For the name "Labove," Faulkner is undoubtedly drawing on Colonel Felix Labauve (1809–1879), who was born in France, was brought to South Carolina as a child by relatives, settled in Mississippi in the late 1830s, and later became a wealthy landowner, lawyer, and state legislator. His will established the Felix Labauve Scholarships at the University of Mississippi for "orphans, children of worthy parents and citizens of DeSoto County." Paul H. Saunders, "Colonel Felix Labauve," *Publications of the Mississippi Historical Society* 7

(1903), 131–40. The fund was noteworthy in granting opportunities to young men who could not otherwise attend college, and it was still solvent in the 1920s during Faulkner's association with the university. The Alger-like rhetoric of Labauve's bequest is in line with Faulkner's language in describing Labove's hard work.

26. For a detailed comparison of the Labove-Eula tale to Southwestern Humor, see M. Thomas Inge, "William Faulkner and George Washington Harris: In the Tradition of Southwestern Humor," Inge, ed., *The Frontier Humorists* (Hamden, Conn.: Archon Books, 1975), pp. 272–73.

Faulkner combined the Ichabod Crane and Brom Bones figures in Labove as a single conception. Labove's passion resembles that of lonely Sut Lovingood for sensual Sicily Burns whom Harris apotheosized in grotesquely rich description that is a possible source for Faulkner's portrait of Eula. Labove's ultimate frustration was prefigured by Sut's as well when Sicily Burns turned the joke back on the arch-jokester in "Blown Up With Soda."

27. Faulkner did create Labove in the image of Possum Mcdaniel, the misdirected Oxford High School end who broke Faulkner's nose on his game-saving tackle in 1915. Blotner, II, 1016.

28. Faulkner wrote that Book IV of *The Hamlet* "happens in 1890 approximately." Faulkner to Saxe Cummins, Oct. 1939, Blotner, ed., *Selected Letters of William Faulkner* (New York: Random House, 1977), p. 115. He later revised the date to 1906–7. See note 30, chapter 11.

29. Labove graduates with two degrees, a master of arts and a bachelor of laws, just as Ichabod Crane had taught school and studied law at the same time in his years after Sleepy Hollow. Labove even finds time to form and coach a Frenchman's Bend basketball team in the dawn of the Naismith Era (the first intercollegiate game was in 1893). He takes them to St. Louis "where in overalls and barefoot, they won a Mississippi Valley Tournament against all comers" (112).

30. The first coach of the football team was Professor Bondurant of the Latin Department, who had just finished graduate work "in the East" and thought that a combination of Yale Blue and Harvard Crimson would be promising as the Ole Miss colors. James Allen Cabaniss, *A History of the University of Mississippi* (University, Miss.: University of Mississippi Press, 1949), p. 129.

31. Of Labove, Faulkner wrote that "he believed that he must read, compass and absorb and wring dry with something of that same contemptuous intensity with which he chopped firewood, measuring the turned pages against the fleeing seconds of irrevocable time like the implacable inching of a leaf worm" (111).

32. *Coke* is a tome read by other Faulkner law students at the University of Mississippi. Bayard Sartoris II had "just opened [his] Coke" when news of his father's murder reached him in "An Odor of Verbena" in *The Unvanquished*. Charles Bon reads *Coke* in *Absalom, Absalom!*

33. Tarkington (1869–1946) achieved notoriety with his adolescent heroes in *Penrod* (1914) and *Seventeen* (1916). Fitzgerald admired his depiction of young sentimentalists but felt that he was ultimately evasive and insincere with his talent. It may be noted that Tarkington's boys as a group have less to do with athletics than any other roster of schoolboy characters.

10. HEMINGWAY: EXEMPLARY HEROISM AND HEROIC WITNESSING

1. Jackson Benson pointed out that discovering the fundamentals of human behavior in games is very much like discovering them in surviving folk tales or myths, and he added that

hunting, fishing, and bull fighting are sports which have not atrophied through popular treatment. Benson, *Hemingway: The Writer's Art of Self-Defense* (Minneapolis: University of Minnesota Press, 1969), p. 81.

2. Guttmann, *From Ritual to Record*, pp. 80, 89.

3. I am indebted to an unpublished article by Michael Oriard, "The Tragic and Comic Games of William Faulkner." "Faulkner's game vision is thus a combination of the comic and tragic games, complicated by irony. . ." (29).

4. In a wry validation of modern sport as subject matter, Guttmann comments, "When we can no longer distinguish the sacred from the profane or even the good from the bad, we content ourselves with the minute discriminations between the batting average of the .308 hitter and the .307 hitter." Guttmann, *From Ritual to Record*, p. 55.

5. Sally F. Moore, Barbara G. Myerhoff, "Introduction: Secular Ritual: Forms and Meanings," Moore, Myerhoff, eds., *Secular Ritual* (Assen/Amsterdam, the Netherlands: Van Gorcum, 1977), p. 3.

6. Ibid., p. 21.

7. Myerhoff, "We Don't Wrap Herring in a Printed Page: Fusion, Fictions and Continuity in Secular Ritual," Moore, Myerhoff, eds., *Secular Ritual,* p. 200.

8. Huizinga, *Homo Ludens,* p. 14.

9. Suzanne Langer, *Philosophy in a New Key* (Cambridge: Harvard University Press, 1942), pp. 151–54.

10. Ibid., p. 155.

11. Moore, Myerhoff, "Introduction: Secular Ritual," p. 8.

12. Eliade, *The Sacred and the Profane,* p. 23.

13. Ibid., p. 24.

14. As early as 1945, Malcolm Cowley had identified the "ritual hunger" in Hemingway's characters. Cowley, "Nightmare and Ritual in Hemingway," Weeks, ed., *Hemingway: A Collection of Critical Essays,* pp. 47–48.

15. Eliade, *The Sacred and the Profane,* p. 72; Richard Lehan wrote, "Hemingway alone among modern writers based his novels on the architectonic assumption that the process by which life gives way to death can be ritualized." Lehan, "Hemingway Among the Moderns," Richard Astro, Jackson Benson, eds., *Hemingway in Our Time* (Corvallis: Oregon State University Press, 1973), p. 208.

16. Fink, "The Oasis of Happiness," p. 22.

17. Moore and Myerhoff quote Durkheim in his observations about Australian aborigines where he pictures ritual as repetitive, being performed over and over while cyclically celebrating and renewing a social group. Moore, Myerhoff, "Introduction: Secular Ritual," p. 5.

18. Eliade, *The Sacred and the Profane,* p. 71.

19. Caillois, *Man and the Sacred,* p. 157.

20. Moore, Myerhoff, "Introduction: Secular Ritual," p. 11.

21. Sutton-Smith notes that play, game, sports, and ritual "are all part of novel-frame-making behavior; that there can either be a zest to these novelties (called playfulness) or a sobriety (called religious fervor)." Sutton-Smith, "Epilogue: Play as Performance," *Play and Learning,* p. 319.

22. See Smith, *The American Dream and the National Game,* pp. 51–103.

23. Hemingway's abundant sports material appears in a number of formats. In the 1930s, he wrote essays on hunting and fishing in what Philip Young called his *Esquire* decade. His short stories about various sporting experiences include "Fifty Grand," "The Killers," "The Battler," "My Old Man," "Big Two-Hearted River," "A Pursuit Race," "Soldier's Home," "The Three Day Blow," "The Gambler, the Nun, and the Radio," "An Alpine Idyll," "Cross Country Snow," "The Undefeated," and "The Short Happy Life of Frances

Macomber." *The Green Hills of Africa* is a rambling discourse on safari in Kenya while *Death in the Afternoon* and *The Dangerous Summer* are hymns to Spanish culture and the bullfight, with the former being perhaps the finest sporting book ever written by an American. Four of his novels—*The Sun Also Rises, To Have and Have Not, The Old Man and the Sea, Islands in the Stream*—are about sport on varying levels.

24. Anyone writing of Hemingway's relation to sport, heroes, and witnesses, must begin with Benson, *Hemingway: The Writer's Art of Self-Defense.*

25. Victor Turner, "Variations on a Theme of Liminality," Moore, Myerhoff, eds., *Secular Ritual,* p. 39. "Our own term 'liturgy' is from the Greek *leos* or *laos,* 'the people,' and *ergon* 'work' (cognate as our linguists here well know with Old English *weorc,* and German *werk,* and ultimately derived from the Indo-European base *werg-o* 'to do, act')."

26. As shown in an excellent article by John Griffith, "Rectitude in Hemngway's Fiction: How Rite Makes Rite," Astro, Benson, eds., *Hemingway in Our Time,* pp. 159–74.

27. Caillois, *Man and the Sacred,* p. 103; Eliade, *The Sacred and the Profane,* p. 45.

28. See Caillois, "Sacred Time," *Man and the Sacred,* p. 68 and following; "Theory of the Festival," p. 163 and following.

29. Ibid., p. 71.

30. Langer, *Philosophy in a New Key,* pp. 157–58.

31. Caillois, *Man and the Sacred,* pp. 97–98.

32. Langer comments as to how mimesis dwindles to ritual in an activity such as the bullfight. The ritual becomes an act of reference rather than representation. Langer, *Philosophy in a New Key,* p. 156. Bullfighting is known by what it refers to—mastery through the ritual kill. Much of the elemental danger is removed in highly stylized performance. Yet as Moore and Myerhoff point out, by acting in forms of ritual, ideas, values, and social relationships are all objectified and reified. Moore, Myerhoff, "Introduction: Secular Ritual," p. 14.

33. Turner, "Variations on a Theme of Liminality," pp. 43–47.

34. Lehan, "Hemingway Among the Moderns," p. 196.

35. Moore, Myerhoff, "Introduction: Secular Ritual," p. 7; Turner, "Variations on a Theme of Liminality," p. 40.

"It is always possible that deep divisions within the social field from which participants enter into competitive contest may break out into violence that is rooted in relationships outside the contest itself." Max Gluckman, Mary Gluckman, "On Drama, and Games and Athletic Contests," Moore, Myerhoff, eds., *Secular Ritual,* p. 240.

36. Hemingway relates a truly primitive ritual kill of a deadly bull by revenge-obsessed relatives of a dead gypsy boy, *Death in the Afternoon,* p. 25.

37. Girard, *Violence and the Sacred,* p. 102.

38. In Eakins' *Salutat* (1898), the victorious fighter heads for his dressing room, his hand raised acknowledging the cheers from the crowd that flow over and around him in the mezzanine. As in Eakins' *Taking the Count* (1898), the fans are overwhelmingly present. The fighter himself is suffused in a soft white light, his arm extended toward the multitude in a graceful display of rippling muscle.

39. Guttmann, *From Ritual to Record,* p. 42.

40. Griffith, "Rectitude in Hemingway's Fiction," p. 162.

41. Reuel Denney first identified Hemingway's spectatorial forms. Denney, *The Astonished Muse,* pp. 122–23.

42. Philip Young, *Ernest Hemingway: A Reconsideration* (New York: Harcourt, Brace and World, Harbinger, 1966). See chapter 1, "Adventures of Nick Adams," pp. 29–54.

43. Mark Spilka first commented that Jake Barnes' feelings about sport shape the novel. Spilka, "The Death of Love in *The Sun Also Rises,*" p. 131.

44. Jake Barnes cannot find a suitable ritual to control his vertigo after being battered

by Cohn. Instead he recalls a similar dizziness after a high school football game which links him to Cohn and helpless schoolboy heroism. Instead of reading Turgenev in his hotel room, Jake winds up in Cohn's room watching Cohn in his schoolboy polo shirt. They resemble a pair of schoolboy roommates, unlucky in love and unable to change their circumstances.

45. Eliade, *The Sacred and the Profane*, pp. 188–89.

46. Joseph Waldmeir notes that procedure becomes rule for Hemingway's characters. Waldmeir, "Confiteor Hominem," Weeks, ed., *Hemingway: A Collection of Critical Essays*, p. 165.

47. Lawrence R. Broer, *Hemingway's Spanish Tragedy* (University, Ala.: University of Alabama Press, 1973).

48. Ibid., p. 6.

49. Hemingway, *A Farewell to Arms* (New York: Scribner's, 1929), p. 327.

50. In recent years, critics have gone many rounds with Hemingway's boxing stories. See Fenton, "No Money for the Kingbird: Hemingway's Prizefight Stories," *American Quarterly* 4 (Winter 1952), pp. 339–50; Lewis, "Hemingway's Concept of Sport and 'Soldier's Home,' " *Rendezvous* 5 (Winter 1970), pp. 19–27; James J. Martine, "Hemingway's 'Fifty Grand': The Other Fight(s)," *Journal of Modern Literature* 2 (September 1971), pp. 123–27. All of the above articles are collected in Benson, ed., *The Short Stories of Ernest Hemingway: Critical Essays* (Durham, N.C.: Duke University Press, 1975).

51. Jack London, "The Ape and the Tiger," *New York Sun*, 28 June 1910, rpt. Irving Shepard, ed., *Jack London's Tales of Adventure* (Garden City, N.Y.: Hanover House, 1956), p. 140.

London's turbulent youth had little to do with college sport heroism although he spent a semester at Berkeley in 1896. As a teenager he had boxed for money in the back rooms of Oakland bars and he later reported numerous fights, writing his most famous dispatches for the *New York Herald* in 1910 on the Jack Johnson– Jim Jeffries fight in Reno, Nevada. Even after achieving fame as an author, he still covered local matches at the West Oakland Athletic Club for the *Oakland Herald*. Richard O'Connor, *Jack London: A Biography* (Boston: Little Brown, 1964), p. 229.

52. London's excellent portrayals of boxes in action as well as his descriptions of crowds and their reactions were prose versions of the art of Eakins and George Bellows. London could describe a fighter in the dignified realism of some of Eakins' classic portraits; he could also capture the claustrophobic ring and the grotesque fighters and fans of Bellows' dramatically naturalistic lithographs and prints such as *Stag at Sharkey's* (1909), *Between Rounds* (1923), and *Dempsey Through the Ropes* (1924).

53. See my article, "Jack London and Boxing in *The Game*," *Jack London Newsletter* 3, no. 2 (May–August 1976), pp. 67–72.

When boxer Joe Fleming dies, his skull fractured upon hitting the canvas, his young lover, Genevieve, prefigures the tone and mood of Frederick Henry at the death of Catherine: "This, then, was the end of it all . . . the thrilling nights of starshine, the deliciousness of surrender, the loving and being loved. She was stunned by the awful facts of this Game she did not understand." London, *The Game* (New York: Macmillan, 1905), p. 179.

54. Hemingway, "Fifty Grand," *Snows*, pp. 95–120.

55. Hemingway's one extended boxing piece in the 1930s was his savage commentary in *Esquire* on what he felt to be Max Baer's cowardice in the ring against Joe Louis on 24 September 1935. Hemingway, "Million Dollar Fright," *Esquire* 4 (December 1935). His criticism concluded, characteristically enough, that "Max Baer had never bothered to learn his trade."

56. Jim Randolph in *The Web and the Rock* is Wolfe's stereotypical Tom Buchanan figure, no ethnic son, but rather the fair-haired ex-college athlete at thirty, worn-down, disil-

lusioned, and also living in the past. See Wolfe, *The Web and the Rock,* chapter 10, "Olympus in Catawba."

57. The sports hero in the 1930s competed in no heightened dimension and approached no mysteries. Pilot Roger Shumann crashed into Lake Ponchartrain in *Pylon;* Joe Bonaparte ran his car off the road in *Golden Boy;* Robert killed Gloria and meekly stood trial for murder in *They Shoot Horses;* Studs Lonigan wasted away his pugnacious youth and died of heart failure at thirty; and Lefty Bicek was on his way to the electric chair. When Lefty is finally confronted with evidence of his guilt for murder, he says, "Knew I'd never get t'be twenty-one anyhow," his final defeat coming only minutes after winning his first professional fight. His words point to the light years between the boy champions of past decades and the tainted heroes of Hard Times.

58. Pulp fiction about sport in the 1930s featured boys with a new veneer of toughness. More boys were bullying, overwhelmingly strong and violent, or they were dedicated junior careerists. Tough tales of squat offensive guards coexisted along with the stories of glamorous backs. Neighborhood leagues, factory teams, and military service teams provided primary story subjects. Ethnic teams vied with prep and high school boys as the heroes of stories. Some of the best known Boys' Pulp Sports Series of the 1930s included Street & Smith's *Sports Story Magazine, Ace Sports Monthly, Dime Sports Magazine, Sports Novels,* and *All-American Football Magazine.*

The young boy athlete of the 1930s was represented away from the team or school world in serious fiction. He was most often not an All-American boy, nor was he a sensitive, wounded spectator like Nick Adams. Instead, he was an ethnic youth, either Nebraska Crane (part Indian) in Wolfe's *The Web and the Rock* (1939), Italian (Joe Bonaparte), Polish (Lefty Bicek) or Irish (Studs Lonigan).

59. Young, "To Have Not: Tough Luck," David Madden, ed., *Tough Guy Writers of the Thirties* (Carbondale, Ill.: Southern Illinois University Press, 1968), p. 43; Young, *Ernest Hemingway: A Reconsideration,* p. 199.

60. Baker, *Hemingway: A Life Story,* p. 228.

61. Hemingway, "On the Blue Water: A Gulf Stream Letter," *Esquire* (April 1936), rpt. William White, ed., *By-Line: Ernest Hemingway* (New York: Scribner's, 1967), p. 242. Subsequent page references to this edition appear in parentheses in the text.

62. Baker, *Hemingway: A Life Story,* p. 228.

63. Hemingway, *To Have and Have Not* (New York: Scribner's, 1937), p. 80. Subsequent page references to this edition appear in parentheses in the text.

64. Both of the boxers, Ad Francis and Ole Andreson, are defeated examples of inhumanity. Whereas Ad is malformed, punched out of all physical shape, a sharply menacing hulk of aggression and insanity, Ole is a passive victim, having "got in wrong," the physical prowess hero resigned to death. Physical punishment, "taking it," is Hemingway's obsessive symbol for endurance, sometimes heroic as with Romero, Harry Morgan, or Santiago, sometimes combined with a sickly pride in such bruising defeat as in Ad Francis, in the veterans in Key West in *To Have and Have Not,* in Manuel Garcia in "The Undefeated," or in certain manic-heroic matadors in *Death in the Afternoon.* "They all bust their hands on me," says Ad Francis with a smile.

65. Griffith, "Rectitude in Hemingway's Fiction," p. 172.

11. FAULKNER: THE PLAY SPIRIT

1. Huizinga, *Homo Ludens,* p. 129.
2. Nicholas Rinaldi, "Game Imagery and Game Consciousness in Faulkner's Fiction," *Twentieth Century Literature* 10, no. 3 (October 1964), 108–18.

3. On play in *The Unvanquished,* see James Memmott, "Sartoris *Ludens:* The Play Element in *The Unvanquished," Mississippi Quarterly* 29 no. 3 (Summer 1976), pp. 375–87. On play in *The Hamlet,* see Richard K. Cross, "The Humor of *The Hamlet," Twentieth Century Literature* 12, no. 4 (January 1967), pp. 203–15; Donald E. Houghton, "Whores and Horses in Faulkner's 'Spotted Horses,' " *Midwest Quarterly* 11 (1970), pp. 361–69. On play and ritual in *The Bear,* see John Lydenberg, "Nature Myth in Faulkner's *The Bear,"* Francis Lee Utley, Lynn Z. Bloom, Arthur F. Kinney, eds., *Bear, Man, and God* (New York: Random House, second edition, 1971), pp. 160–67; Eric Jensen, "The Play Element in Faulkner's *The Bear," Texas Studies in Language and Literature* 6, no. 2 (Summer 1964), pp. 170–87.

4. Quoted in Jensen, "The Play Element," 176.

5. William Faulkner, 1956 interview, Malcolm Cowley, ed., *Writers At Work: "The Paris Review" Interviews* (New York: Viking Press, Compass Book, 1959), p. 137.

6. M.E. Bradford, "On the Importance of Discovering God: Faulkner and Hemingway's *The Old Man and the Sea," Mississippi Quarterly* 20 (1967), p. 161.

7. Huizinga, *Homo Ludens,* p. 13.

8. Ibid., p. 89; Caillois, *Man and the Sacred,* "War and the Sacred," pp. 163–80.

9. Bayard II speaks of Aunt Jenny Sartoris "and the panes of colored glass which she had salvaged from the Carolina house where she and Father and Uncle Bayard were born," Faulkner, *The Unvanquished* (New York: Alfred E. Knopf, 1938), p. 271. Subsequent page references to this edition appear in parentheses in the text.

10. Faulkner, *Sartoris* (New York: Signet, New American Library, 1964), p. 25. Subsequent page references to this edition appear in parentheses in the text.

11. Pilots and airplanes fascinated Faulkner from his earliest years. In 1909, at age twelve, he had seen a group of air daredevils in Memphis and had carefully filled pages with drawings of goggled pilots and their fragile planes. In 1918 he eagerly sought admission to RAF pilot training and was finally accepted into a Canadian wing in Toronto in July 1918 where he was in training for the final five months of the war. Faulkner's first published prose fiction in the University of Mississippi's *The Mississippian,* entitled "Landing in Luck," was an account of an RAF cadet's first flight. Blotner, I, 139–40, 207, 253.

His three published air stories were "All the Dead Pilots" and "Ad Astra," another World War I Sartoris story, and "Death Drag," a story of barnstorming stunt flyers with similarities in theme to *Pylon* that is a more successfully realized shorter narrative on honor and desperation.

12. A heretofore unpublished Sartoris story, "With Caution and Dispatch" (*Esquire,* September 1979), follows John Sartoris III ("Johnny") as he repeatedly crashes his Sopwith Camel while trying to catch up with his RAF squadron in France. The tale expressly links English schoolboy sport, English war history, the American south, and American popular sport in one extended image of an English general reviewing the RAF squadron: "and behind them, in turn, the line of waiting aeroplanes dull and ungleaming in the intermittent sun across which the general's voice still came, telling again the old stale tale: Waterloo and the playing fields of Eton and here a spot that is forever England. Then the voice was in actual retrograde in a long limbo filled with horses—Fontenoy and Agincourt and Crécy and the Black Prince—and Sartoris whispering to his neighbor from the side of his rigid mouth: 'What nigger is that? He's talking about Jack Johnson' " (51).

13. Bayard is definitely southern kin to other post-World War I sensitive romantics, both lost and loveless, including Jay Gatsby and Jack Barnes, as well as to more insensitive characters such as Tom Buchanan and Robert Cohn.

14. Faulkner, "All the Dead Pilots," (1931). Faulkner, *Collected Stories of William Faulkner* (New York: Random House, 1950), p. 511.

Faulkner, "Ad Astra," *The American Caravan* 4 (1931), rpt. Faulkner, *Collected Stories,* pp. 407–30; "Death Drag," *Scribner's Magazine* (January 1932), rpt. Faulkner, *Collected Stories,* pp. 185–206.

Faulkner began flight instruction in a Waco bi-plane in February 1933 and was flying solo by August. For the next two years he and his brother, Dean, were involved in air fairs and exhibitions in and around Oxford. In February 1934 Faulkner had attended the week-long ceremonies and contests surrounding the opening of Shushan Airport in New Orleans on land reclaimed from Lake Ponchartrain. These air races were not without accidents, narrow escapes, and sensational death crashes. For the best accounts correlating Faulkner's New Orleans air show experience with *Pylon,* see Blotner, I, 834–37; Michael Millgate, *The Achievement of William Faulkner* (London: Constable, 1966), p. 138.

15. A deadly coda to *Pylon* turned out to be the crash and death of Dean Faulkner in a Waco bi-plane on 13 November 1935. In a final irony to the *Pylon* of air show spectacle, the expansion of the Oxford, Mississippi, Dean Faulkner Memorial Airport was approved in 1936 as a $65,000 WPA project, a monument to one last fool of a flying Sartoris. Blotner, I, 909, 936.

16. Millgate, *Achievement of Faulkner,* p. 141.

17. Irving Howe has labeled the reporter as a caricature of the modern hero of sensibility. Howe, *William Faulkner: A Critical Study* (Chicago: University of Chicago Press, 1951), p. 218. There are echoes of *Miss Lonelyhearts* in the tale of the disturbed reporter who is browbeaten by his editor, but the story also contains bows to the popular genre of the newspaper drama such as *Front Page.* The most enthusiastic comment on the structure of *Pylon* is in Hyatt H. Waggoner, *William Faulkner from Jefferson to the World* (Lexington: University of Kentucky Press, 1966), pp. 121–32.

18. Uncle Buddy's victory over Uncle Buck is consistent with the poker prowess he exhibits in "Was" (*Go Down, Moses*), where he outplays Hubert Beauchamp to reclaim his brother Buck from "Warwick" with a minimum of damages.

19. General Ulysses S. Grant had occupied Oxford, Mississippi in November–December 1864.

20. See Richard P. Adams, *Faulkner: Myth and Motion* (Princeton: Princeton University Press, 1966). Adams defines the "frozen moment" in Faulkner as "imagery in which the dynamic quality of life is immediately and sharply opposed to artificial stasis" (12). Adams also speaks of Faulkner "stopping the motion of life in order to make it communicable in terms of esthetic value" (202).

21. For an extended analysis of these play moments in *The Unvanquished,* see Memmott, "Sartoris *Ludens,*" pp. 380–84.

22. For a survey of Drusilla Hawk's mythic analogues, see David Williams, *Faulkner's Women: The Myth and the Muse* (Montreal, London: McGill-Queen's University Press, 1977), pp. 210–13.

23. Benveniste quoted in Ehrmann, "Homo Ludens Revisited," Ehrmann, ed., *Game, Play, Literature,* p. 36.

24. Fink comments, "the perplexing world-formula, according to which Being in its totality functions like play, may perhaps make us aware of the fact that play is no harmless, peripheral or even 'childish' thing . . . we mortal men are 'at stake' in an inscrutably threatening way." Fink, "The Oasis of Happiness," Ehrmann, ed., *Game, Play, Literature,* p. 29.

25. Eliade, *The Sacred and the Profane,* p. 23.

26. Ibid., p. 28.

27. Ibid.

28. Huizinga, *Homo Ludens,* p. 13.

29. Ibid., p. 75.

30. See note 28, chapter 9.

In the Random House-Vintage third edition of *The Hamlet* (1964), part of a trilogy containing *The Town* and *The Mansion,* Faulkner altered several dates in *The Hamlet* in an effort to straighten out the Snopes chronology. He changed "1871" to "1891" and "1879" to "1901," thus moving up *The Hamlet*'s dates by some fifteen to twenty years. In a preface to

The Mansion (1959), he had defended such alteration and at Virginia, he further licensed his liberties, saying that if you invent a "private domain," then you are master of its time. He concluded testily, "I have the right, I think, to shift these things around wherever it sounds best, and I can move them about in time and, if necessary, change their names. This would be 1906 or 07 this happened. That is, the more you write, the more you've got to compromise with such facts as time and place." *Faulkner in the University*, p. 29.

31. William Porter bought the *American Turf Register* in 1839 and began to include fiction in its pages while his *Spirit of the Times* collected and published the diverse sporting sketches of the Southwestern writers whose stories often involved horse trading. From 1870 to 1900, race track fiction was the province of the dime novel and story paper.

32. Blotner, I, 388.

33. Ibid., 402, 412.

34. In "My Old Man" (1922), Hemingway's boy narrator echoes the Anderson-like melting feeling about race horses: "when he went by me I felt all hollow inside he was so beautiful."

35. John T. Flanagan, "The Mythic Background of Faulkner's Horse Imagery," *Folklore Studies in Honor of Arthur Palmer Hudson* (Chapel Hill: The North Carolina Folklore Society, 1965), p. 136.

36. *The Hamlet* was one of Faulkner's most reworked novels. The genesis of the Snopes family dated as far back as 1926–27 when a first fragment entitled "Father Abraham" depicted the coming of the Snopes clan to Frenchman's Bend. For a complete list of the manuscripts of *The Hamlet*, see Jo-Anne V. Creighton, *William Faulkner's Craft of Revision* (Detroit: Wayne State University Press, 1977), p. 161. See also Millgate, *Achievement of Faulkner*, pp. 180–85.

37. Moore and Myerhoff, "Secular Ritual: Forms and Meanings," pp. 7–8.

38. Huizinga, *Homo Ludens*, pp. 7–10.

39. Sutton-Smith's comments on the "structural part of play" fit the dynamic of interaction in *The Hamlet:* "it is a subset of voluntary behaviors . . . involving a selective mechanism which reverses the usual contingencies of power so as to permit the subject (or subjects) to frame a controllable and dialectical simulation of the moderately unmastered arousals and reductions of everyday life in a way which is alternately vivifying and euphoric." Sutton-Smith, "Epilogue: Play as Performance," *Play and Learning*, p. 309.

40. Harry Modean Campbell, Ruel E. Foster, *William Faulkner: A Critical Appraisal* (Norman, Okla.: University of Oklahoma Press, 1951) initially identified the two complementary strains of frontier and surrealist humor in Faulkner (94–114).

41. Flanagan, "The Mythic Background," p. 138; Houghton, "Whores and Horses," pp. 361–62.

42. Fink, "The Oasis of Happiness," pp. 23, 29.

43. Houghton, "Whores and Horses," pp. 361–63.

44. Faulkner's distinctive technique is that of jamming adjectives together to create a variety of oxymoronic effects. See Walter J. Slatoff, *Quest for Failure: A Study of William Faulkner* (Ithaca: Cornell University Press, 1966), pp. 85–86.

45. Consider the close parallel between Faulkner's tremendous description of the horse in Mrs. Littlejohn's hallway and G.W. Harris's Sut Lovingood and his strategically introduced cow disrupting the nuptials in "Sicily Burns's Wedding," Meine, ed., *Tall Tales of the Southwest* (New York: Alfred E. Knopf, 1930), pp. 346–47.

46. Jack Houston expresses the same cosmic grief after the death of his wife as does Frederic Henry in *A Farewell To Arms* at the death of Catherine. Whereas Hemingway doggedly treats the tragedy as given and unfathomable, Faulkner triumphs over the determinism in comedy darkened by Mink's murder of Houston.

47. Hayden White, *Metahistory: The Historical Imagination in Nineteenth Century Europe* (Baltimore: Johns Hopkins, 1973), p. 93.

48. White quotes Hegel's *Philosophy of History* to the effect that the essence of the comic vision is in an " 'infinite geniality and confidence capable of rising superior to its own contradiction and experiencing therein no taint of bitterness or sense of misfortune whatever.' " White, *Metahistory*, p. 96.

12. SPORT APPROACHES THE SACRED: HEMINGWAY AND FAULKNER

1. Huizinga quoted by Caillois, *Man and the Sacred*, p. 157.
2. Such captivity leads the hunter to conceive of his sport in a sacred context. Santiago muses, "If you love him, it is not a sin to kill him. Or is it more?" Hemingway, *The Old Man and the Sea* (New York: Scribner's, 1952), p. 105.
3. Langer, *Philosophy in a New Key*, pp. 151, 158.
4. Eliade, *The Sacred and the Profane*, p. 95.
5. Ibid., pp. 191, 193.
6. For definitions of secular ritual here extended to *The Old Man and the Sea* and *Go Down, Moses*, see Moore, Myerhoff, "Introduction: Secular Ritual," pp. 4–5, 12.
7. Hemingway, *The Old Man and the Sea*, p. 67. Subsequent references to this edition appear in parentheses in the text.
8. Two of the most moving early scenes of self-mastery in Hemingway are Nick's fishing the Big Two-Hearted River and Jake Barnes' lyrical fishing trip to the Spanish mountain country. Jake experiences his own real gratification through the work well done in treading the streams, baiting the lines, pulling in the trout, and wrapping them in ferns. The mock communion service performed by Jake and Bill Gorton in the mountains gives calming testament to their initial uneasiness and grateful knowledge that they are in a temporarily sanctified place. Two of the best-realized scenes in *To Have and Have Not* occur on Harry Morgan's boat during fishing trips. The dramatic opening section of *Islands in the Stream* (of which Santiago's tale was initially to have been a part) with Thomas Hudson, Roger Davis, and Hudson's sons is built on a tense battle for a huge marlin.
9. On Hemingway's use of baseball and Joe Dimaggio in *The Old Man and the Sea*, see George Monteiro, "Santiago, Dimaggio, and Hemingway: The Aging Professionals of *The Old Man and the Sea*," Bruccoli, ed., *Hemingway-Fitzgerald Annual 1975* (Englewood, Col.: Indian Head Press, 1975), pp. 273–80; James Barbour, Robert Sattelmeyer, "Baseball and Baseball Talk," *Hemingway-Fitzgerald Annual 1975*, pp. 281–87; Sam S. Baskett, "The Great Santiago: Opium, Vocation, and Dream in *The Old Man and the Sea*," *Hemingway-Fitzgerald Annual 1976*, pp. 230–42; and Smith, *The American Dream and the National Game*, pp. 86–95.
10. Hemingway wrote in *Death in the Afternoon* that "the great thing is to last and get your work done and see and hear and learn and understand" (278).
11. Eliade, *The Sacred and the Profane*, p. 94.
12. Ibid., p. 165.
13. Ibid., pp. 188–89.
14. Santiago frequently addresses the fish in the spirit of brotherhood (pp. 46, 57, 74, 76, 92, 94).
15. Girard quotes Henri Hubert, Marcel Mauss, *Sacrifice: Its Nature and Function* (Chicago: University of Chicago Press, 1968) to the effect that "because the victim is sacred, it is criminal to kill him—but the victim is sacred only because he is to be killed." Girard, *Violence and the Sacred*, p. 1.

16. Max Lerner, intro., Veblen, *The Theory of the Leisure Class*, p. 46; Veblen, ibid., p. 299.

17. See John Lydenberg, "Nature Myth in Faulkner's *The Bear*," Francis Utley *et al.*, eds., *Bear, Man, and God* (hereafter referred to as *"B.M.G."*), pp. 160–67 for a full introduction to this theme.

Joseph Campbell's four functions of man's mythology apply to Ike McCaslin's roles. Campbell says that myth (1) creates in man a sense of awe in powers and circumstances beyond his control; (2) enables man better to understand the natural world order; (3) gives man a framework in which society may be seen as coherent; and (4) gives man a way to understand intricacies of his own psyche. Campbell quoted in David O. Miller, *Gods and Games* (New York: World, 1970), p. 138.

18. Jensen, "The Play Element in Faulkner's *The Bear*," p. 186.

19. Faulkner, "The Old People," *Go Down, Moses* (New York: Random House, 1942), p. 181. Subsequent references to this edition appear with story title (where relevant) in parentheses in the text.

20. Utley points out that not only is hunting a masculine way of life in the South, but that as one of the most ancient of sports, it has a center of ceremony that must be respected. Utley, "Pride and Humility: The Cultural Roots of Ike McCaslin," *B.M.G.*, pp. 167–68.

Faulkner had been involved in hunting experiences from his earliest years, going to General Stone's hunting camp as a boy and in September 1927 making the first of his annual pilgrimmages to the lodge on the edge of the Delta, thirty miles from Oxford. He had always played stalking games of skill, endurance, and woodcraft with his brothers while participating in the riding to hounds and the pursuit of quarry such as hares. Blotner, I, 9, 280–81, 559.

See Creighton, *Faulkner's Craft of Revision*, pp. 85–148 for the most detailed look at the composition of *Go Down, Moses*.

21. For a study of "Was," not discussed in any detail here, see Karl F. Zender, "A Handful of Poker: Game and Ritual in Faulkner's 'Was,' " *Studies in Short Fiction* 11, No. 1 (Winter 1974), pp. 53–60.

22. Turner, "Variations on a Theme of Liminality," pp. 38–39.

23. Warren Beck has written that Faulkner insists on transmuting "the factual-objective into the descriptive-definitive colored by his imagination and elaborated by his resourcefulness in language." Beck, "William Faulkner's Style," Frederick J. Hoffman, Olga W. Vickery, eds., *William Faulkner: Three Decades of Criticism* (New York: Harcourt, Brace & World, Harbinger, 1963), p. 147.

24. Eliade, *The Sacred and the Profane*, pp. 12, 20.

25. Ibid., p. 93.

26. Lewis Simpson, "Ike McCaslin and the Second Fall of Man," *B.M.G.*, p. 205. Simpson states that Ike can now use his gun prudently for a lifetime of correct hunting.

Dubious looks at Ike's heroism are found in David H. Stewart, "Ike McCaslin, Cop-Out," *B.M.G.*, p. 219; Arthur F. Kinney, "Faulkner and the Possibilities for Heroism," *B.M.G.*, pp. 237, 247; and William Van O'Connor, "The Wilderness Theme in Faulkner's *The Bear*," Hoffman, Vickery, eds., *William Faulkner*, p. 329.

27. Adams, *Myth and Motion*, p. 138, quoting Frederick L. Gwynn, Blotner, eds., *Faulkner in the University* (New York: Random House, Vintage, 1959), pp. 245–46. Faulkner also balanced his criticism of Ike's withdrawal from life by stating that Ike has achieved "serenity . . . what would pass for Wisdom" through his observing what Sam Fathers had taught him at age twelve for the rest of his life. *Faulkner in the University*, p. 54.

28. The dialectical implications of *The Bear*, Part IV are suggested by Frederic Jameson's remarks on a dialectical literary criticism. See Jameson, *Marxism and Form* (Princeton: Princeton University Press, 1971), pp. 306–7, 372.

29. "Ode on a Grecian Urn" is Faulkner's repeated reference point for mediation on "myth and motion," specifically in *Sartoris*, *Light in August*, and *The Bear*.

30. Jameson, quoting Hegel in *Marxism and Form*, p. 331.

31. The "sensuous play" of art is sustained *as* art by Faulkner in the creative collaboration between Quentin Compson and Shreve McCannon in *Absalom, Absalom!*

32. Utley, "Pride and Humility," *B.M.G.*, p. 187.

33. Girard contends that "the objective of ritual is the proper reenactment of the surrogate-victim mechanism; its function is to perpetuate or renew the effects of this mechanism; that is to keep violence outside the community." *Violence and the Sacred*, p. 92.

Bulls, marlins, and bears function effectively as ritual victims in hunts. However, the surrogate victims in *Go Down, Moses* are McCaslin blacks and women and they are never truly replaced by any hunting sacrifice. Violence toward them is done with impunity because they are outside the community and violence is not "radically generative" as Girard explains about the sacrifice of the ritual victim. Sacrificial victims are distinguishable from nonsacrificable beings, for "between these victims and the community a crucial social link is missing, so they can be exposed to violence without fear of reprisal." Girard, *Violence and the Sacred*, p. 13. This missing "crucial social link" separates white McCaslins from black McCaslins: one side enslaves and continues to oppress the other from Lucius Quintus Carothers McCaslin to Roth Edmonds. Thus Faulkner appears to agree with Girard's concept of the sacrificial victim while not believing in the vital substitution of sacrificial for surrogate victim. Surrogates *are* sacrificed in Faulkner, and, ironically, the social chaos described by Girard is the result.

34. The last hunt for Old Ben is totally consistent with the structural principles of ritual defined by Terence S. Turner: "As the medium through which contact between levels is made, ritual embodies the very phenomenon from which it serves to insulate the profane social and conceptual order: the direct and potentially disruptive contact between structural levels of discrepant power and generality." Turner, "Transformation, Hiearchy and Transcendence: A Reformulation of Van Gennep's Model of the Structure of Rites de Passage," Moore, Myerhoff, eds., *Secular Ritual*, p. 66.

35. Neither hunter-priest receives the reverent tributes accorded Natty Bumppo in Cooper's idealized death scene and funeral of Natty at the conclusion of *The Prairie*, a novel in which he hunted less and less while functioning primarily as 80-year-old sage.

36. Hemingway thus makes a correct interpretation of ritual sacrifice, according to the concepts of Girard.

37. Faulkner, review of *The Old Man and the Sea*, *Shenandoah* (Fall 1952), quoted in Bradford, "On the Importance of Discovering God," p. 159.

38. Benson, *Hemingway: The Writer's Art*, p. 181.

39. Like Thomas Sutpen in *Absalom, Absalom!*, Ike is the architect of his own inflexible design, benign in comparison to Sutpen's evil though it may be; like Joe Christmas in *Light in August*, whose plight Faulkner stated was that he had "evicted himself from mankind," Ike has to live with that grave decision. Faulkner, quoted in M. Thomas Inge, ed., *Studies in "Light in August"* (Columbus, Ohio: Charles F. Merrill, 1971), p. 3.

40. Both Faulkner and Hemingway insisted that there was little or no symbolism in *The Bear* and *The Old Man and the Sea*, and although one might account for defensive responses to the host of critics, the fact remains that in the authors' public statements, these were simple and universal stories, the opacity of which accounted for the proliferation of meanings. Faulkner said, "I simply told a story which was a natural, normal part of anyone's life in familiar and to me interesting terms without any intent to put symbolism in it." Gwynn, Blotner, eds., "Faulkner's Commentary on *Go Down, Moses*," *B.M.G.*, p. 115. Hemingway's reaction to the tremendous public reception of *The Old Man and the Sea* was that the book's secret was that there wasn't any symbolism for "sea equaled sea, old man was old man, the boy was a boy, the marlin was itself, and the sharks were no better and no worse than other sharks." Baker, *Ernest Hemingway: A Life Story*, p. 505.

These statements may be accounted for in both cases by the fact that the sporting rite is already so intensely symbolic of primary myths that no real transformation *is* intended at the time of composition. A rite is already a binding reenactment of a deeply-held belief with its own narrative "plot." Thus Hemingway and Faulkner's fiction about the hunt is the novelist's subjective narrative about the rite, in effect, the textual myth about the playing out through the rite of an essential belief.

CONCLUSION

1. "Sportworld" as a total environment is best defined by Lipsyte, *Sportsworld*, ix–xv.

2. Baseball: Mark Harris, *The Southpaw* (1953), *Bang the Drum Slowly* (1956); Bernard Malamud, *The Natural* (1952); Philip Roth, *The Great American Novel* (1973); Robert Coover, *The Universal Baseball Association, Inc., J. Henry Waugh, Prop.* (1969); Jay Neugeboren, *Sam's Legacy* (1977); Jerome Charyn, *The Seventh Babe* (1979); Lomar Herrin, *The Rio Loja Ringmaster* (1977); William Brashler, *The Bingo Long Traveling All-Stars and Motor Kings* (1973); John Sayles, *Pride of the Bimbos* (1975); Barry Beckham, *Runner Mack* (1972).

Football: Gary Cartwright, *The Hundred Yard War* (1968); James Whitehead, *Joiner* (1971); Frederick Exley, *A Fan's Notes* (1968); Peter Gent, *North Dallas Forty* (1973); Dan Jenkins, *Semi-Tough* (1972); Don DeLillo, *End Zone* (1972); Gary K. Wolf, *Killerbowl* (1976); Frank Deford, *Cut'n Run* (1973); Sam Koperwas, *Westchester Bull* (1976).

Basketball: John Updike, *Rabbit, Run* (1960); Jeremy Larner, *Drive, He Said* (1964); Neugeboren, *Big Man* (1966); Lawrence Shainberg, *One on One* (1970); Charles Rosen, *Have Jump Shot, Will Travel* (1974); Bob Levin, *The Best Ride to New York* (1978); Walter Kaylin, *The Power Forward* (1979); Todd Walton, *Inside Moves* (1978).

3. See Robert Detweiler, "Games in Modern American Fiction," *Contemporary Literature* 17, No. 1 (Winter 1976), for a first definitional essay on games of/in fiction.

Index

Adams, Henry, 133, 335-36n14, 336n16; *The Education of Henry Adams*, 133

Adams, William, 157

Ade, George, 98-99, 119, 330-31n34, 342n46; *Fables in Slang*, 98; "The Fable of the Coming Champion who was Delayed," 98; "The Fable of the Caddy Who Hurt His Head While Thinking," 98; "The Fable of the Base Ball Fan Who Took the Only Known Cure," 98; *The College Widow*, 342n46

Agon: Huizinga and Caillois's definition of, 2, 4; in Classic American Literature, 16-17; in frontier sport, 60-61; in Southwestern Humor, 60-63; in Crockett almanacs, 67; in school sports story, 156; in Faulkner, 232, 312-13; in *The Hamlet*, 236, 297; in Hemingway, 239, 254, 261, 294, 296, 312; in *The Sun Also Rises*, 245-47; in *The Old Man and the Sea*, 254, 292; in *Go Down, Moses*, 309

Aldrich, Thomas Bailey, 157; *The Story of a Bad Boy*, 157

Alea: Huizinga and Caillois's definition of, 2; in modern games and sport, 17; in frontier sport, 60-61; in Southwestern Humor, 60-63; in J. J. Hooper, 78; in *The Hamlet*, 236, 297; Hemingway's fear of, 238, 244-45, 254, 296; in Faulkner, 313

Alger, Horatio, 157, 170-71, 209

Algren, Nelson, 255, 257; *Never Come Morning*, 257, 352n57

Almanac Sports Hero, 18, 61, 64-69, 80

American Turf Register, The, 69, 74, 84

Anatomy of Melancholy, 40

Anderson, Sherwood, 278; "I'm a Fool," 278; "The Man Who Became a Woman," 278; "I Want to Know Why," 278

Anson, Cap, 91, 96-97

Arnold, Matthew, 159, 161-62

Arnold, Thomas, 159-61, 163, 189

Audubon, John James, 8, 64

Baker, Hobart Amory Hare, 187-88, 203, 207, 219, 267

Baldwin, Joseph G., 80; *The Flush Times of Alabama and Mississippi*, 80

Barbour, Ralph Henry, 171-74, 176, 178, 182; *The Halfback*, 172; *Left End Edwards*, 172; *Weatherby's Inning*, 172-73; *Fullback Foster*, 172-73; "For the Honor of the School," 182

Barnes, James, 343n56

Baseball: in "Song of Myself," 84; early development of, 84-85; Albert Spalding and, 90-92; Mark Twain and, 90-92; in *A Connecticut Yankee in King Arthur's Court*, 91; and baseball guide books, 92-93; and nineteenth century journalism, 92-93, 96-100; Finley Peter Dunne and, 96-98; George Ade and, 98; in the Dime Novel, 102-6; Lardner and, 110-19, 127-28, 204-5; Norris and, 149-51; in the school sports story, 158; Theodore Roosevelt and, 164, 341n24; Frank Merriwell and, 168; Fitzgerald and, 204-5; in *The Great Gatsby*, 205; in *The Old Man and the Sea*, 295, 356n9; in contemporary American fiction, 314-16, 359n2; nineteenth century growth of, 329n20, 329n21; Billy Sunday and, 330n33; early

Index

Dickey, James, 314; *Deliverance,* 314
Dickinson, Emily, 133
Dimaggio, Joe, 247, 295, 356*n*9
Dryden, Charles, 98, 111
Dryden, Edgar, 34, 321*n*13
Dunne, Finley Peter, 96-99, 111, 119, 330*n*31
Durkheim, Emile, 234; *The Elementary Forms of the Religious Life,* 234

Eakins, Thomas, 95, 246, 350*n*38, 351*n*52; *Salutat,* 246, 350*n*38; *Taking the Count,* 350*n*38
Eby, Cecil, 220
Egan, Pierce, 94
Eggleston, Edward, 158; *The Hoosier Schoolboy,* 158
Ehrmann, Jacques, 3, 4, 311
Election Day: sport and play in *The Scarlet Letter,* 30, 32-34, 39, 61
Eliade, Mircea, 5, 236, 292, 295, 301
Eliot, T. S., 206
Elliott, William, 73-74; *Carolina Sports By Land and Water,* 74
Emerson, Ralph Waldo, 132-33, 136, 153-54, 193; "The American Scholar," 132-33, 154, 193; "Voluntaries," 136-37
Exley, Frederick, 314; *A Fan's Notes,* 314

Falkner, Johncy, 218
Falkner, Murray, 219
Farrell, James, 255, 257
Faulkner, Dean, 219, 354*n*15
Faulkner, William, 2, 10-11, 55, 180, 190, 208-10, 218-228, 231-37, 255, 260-92, 296-309, 311-14, 353*n*12, 354-55*n*30, 357*n*20, 358*n*31, 358*n*33; *Go Down, Moses,* 55, 232, 236, 262-64, 291-92, 296-98, 305-6, 358*n*33; *The Hamlet,* 180, 208, 218-27, 232-33, 235-36, 262-64, 273-90, 297-98, 308, 354-55*n*30; *The Bear,* 235, 263, 277, 292, 297-301, 303-4, 306-8; *Pylon,* 255, 263, 267-68, 354*n*14, 354*n*15; *The Unvanquished,* 262-66, 268-73; *Sartoris,* 262, 264-68, 270, 273-74; *Flags in the Dust,* 265; "An Odor of Verbena," 265, 269; "All the Dead Pilots," 267; "Vendee," 271; "Skirmish at Sartoris," 271; "Cheest," 278; "Fool About a Horse" (section of *The Hamlet*), 279; "Spotted Horses" (section of *The Hamlet*), 280-82, 284, 286-89, 291; *The Sound and the Fury,*

284; "Delta Autumn," 292, 297-98, 303-4; "The Old People," 292, 297-301, 306; "Was," 297; *Light in August,* 312, 358*n*39; *Absalom, Absalom!,* 312, 358*n*31, 358*n*39; "With Caution and Dispatch," 353*n*12
Fay, Sigourney Webster, 196
Feidelson, Charles, 32, 322*n*22, 322*n*23; *Symbolism and American Literature,* 322*n*22, 322*n*23
Fiedler, Leslie, 6
Field, Eugene, 330*n*27
Field, Joseph N., 68, 73; "The Death of Mike Fink," 68
Fink, Eugen, 3, 43, 283, 311
Fink, Mike, 2, 59, 61-62, 64, 67-69, 76, 83, 87, 101, 106, 120
"Finnegan the Umpire," 99
Fishing: in *The Pioneers,* 51-52; in Thoreau, 54-55; William Elliott on, 74; in *To Have and Have Not,* 257-59; in *The Old Man and the Sea,* 293-96, 306-7; as metaphor for Hemingway, 295, 356*n*8
Fitch, George, 342*n*46; *At Good Old Siwash,* 342*n*46
Fitzgerald, F. Scott, 2, 11, 110, 120, 127, 139, 173, 177-78, 180-207, 208-11, 214, 218-19, 224-27, 253, 261, 267, 311-12, 314, 343*n*54, 343*n*56, 344*n*7, 344*n*11, 345*n*17, 345*n*27, 346*n*40, 347*n*15; *The Great Gatsby,* 11, 139, 180-81, 190-96, 198-202, 205-7, 312; *This Side of Paradise,* 173, 177, 181-89, 195-97, 199, 206, 219, 267; "Reade, Substitute Right Half," 181; "The Perfect Life," 184; "Basil and Cleopatra," 184, 196-97; "May Day," 191; "The Freshest Boy," 195; "The Bowl," 196, 198-99; "Princeton," 198, 344*n*7; *Tender is the Night,* 199, 202-3, 205, 207, 225, 347*n*15; 348*n*33; *The Beautiful and the Damned,* 202; "The Ants at Princeton," 345*n*27
Fitzgerald, Zelda, 204
Fitzsimmons, Bob, 95
Flandreau, Charles, 163; *The Diary of a Harvard Freshman,* 163
Football: in pre-Civil War era, 134; on Bloody Monday, 136-37; Walter Camp's innovations in, 140; paintings and sketches by Remington, 141; Crane, Norris, and Davis in, 142; and *The Red Badge of Courage,* 143-46; 1890s roughness in, 143; Norris and differences between eastern and western